Hana-Kimi

For You in Full Blossom

5

story and art by
HISAYA NAKAJO

HANA-KIMI
For You In Full Blossom
VOLUME 5
STORY & ART BY HISAYA NAKAJO

Translation/David Ury
English Adaptation/Gerard Jones
Touch-Up Art & Lettering/Gabe Crate
Design/Izumi Evers
Editor/Jason Thompson

Managing Editor/Megan Bates
Editorial Director/Elizabeth Kawasaki
Editor in Chief/Alvin Lu
Sr. Director of Acquisitions/Rika Inouye
Sr. VP of Marketing/Liza Coppola
Exec. VP of Sales & Marketing/John Easum
Publisher/Hyoe Narita

Hanazakari no Kimitachi he by Hisaya Nakajo ©Hisaya Nakajo 1997
All rights reserved. First published in Japan in 1998 by
HAKUSENSHA, Inc., Tokyo. English language translation rights in
America and Canada arranged with HAKUSENSHA, Inc., Tokyo.
New and adapted artwork and text © 2005 VIZ Media, LLC.
The HANA-KIMI logo is a trademark of VIZ Media, LLC.
The stories, characters and incidents mentioned in this
publication are entirely fictional.

Printed in the U.S.A.

Published by VIZ Media, LLC, P.O. Box 77010, San Francisco, CA 94107

Shôjo Edition
10 9 8 7 6 5 4 3 2

First printing, February 2005
Second printing, August 2006

www.viz.com
store.viz.com

CONTENTS

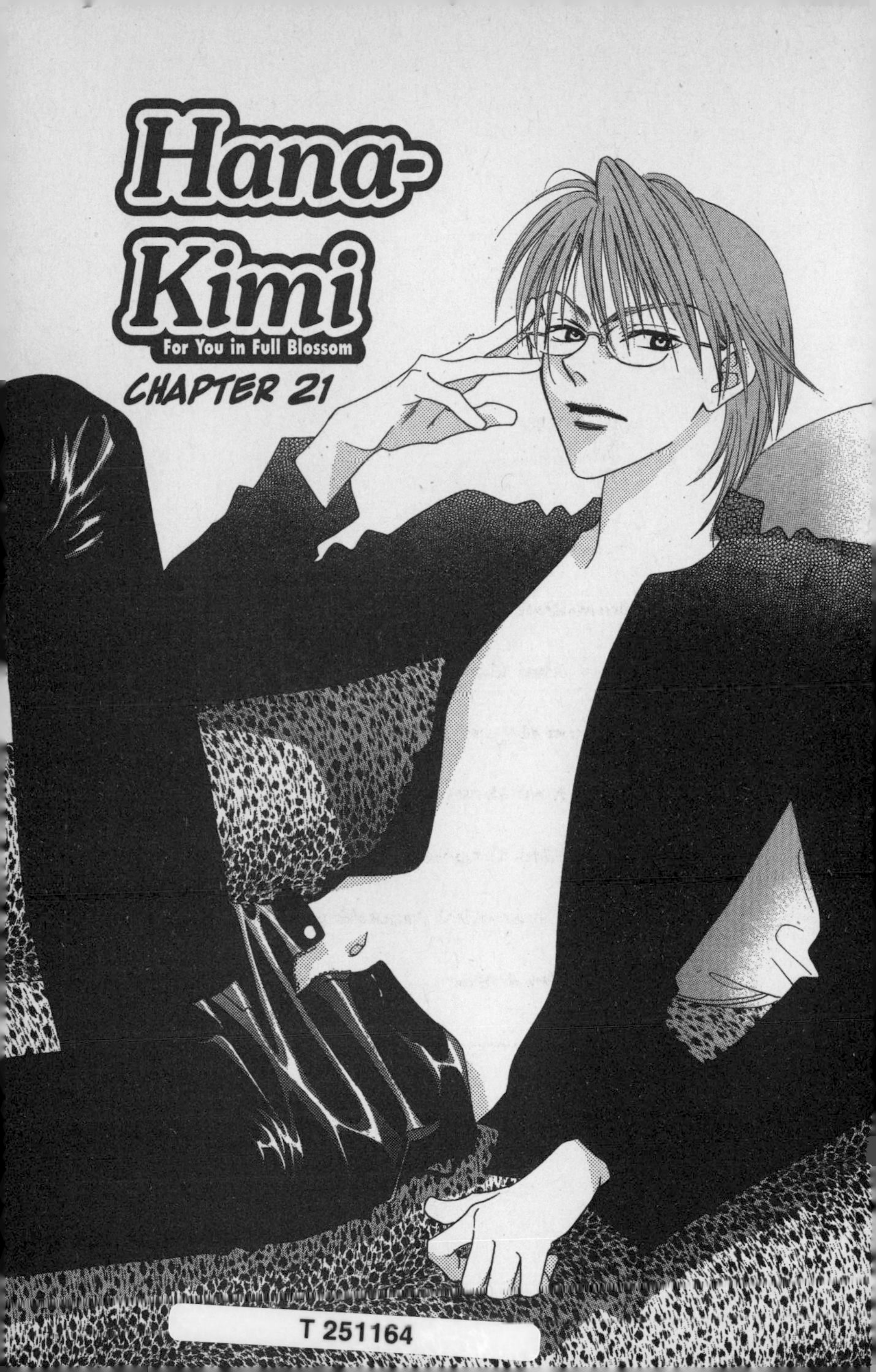
Hana-
Kimi
For You in Full Blossom
CHAPTER 21

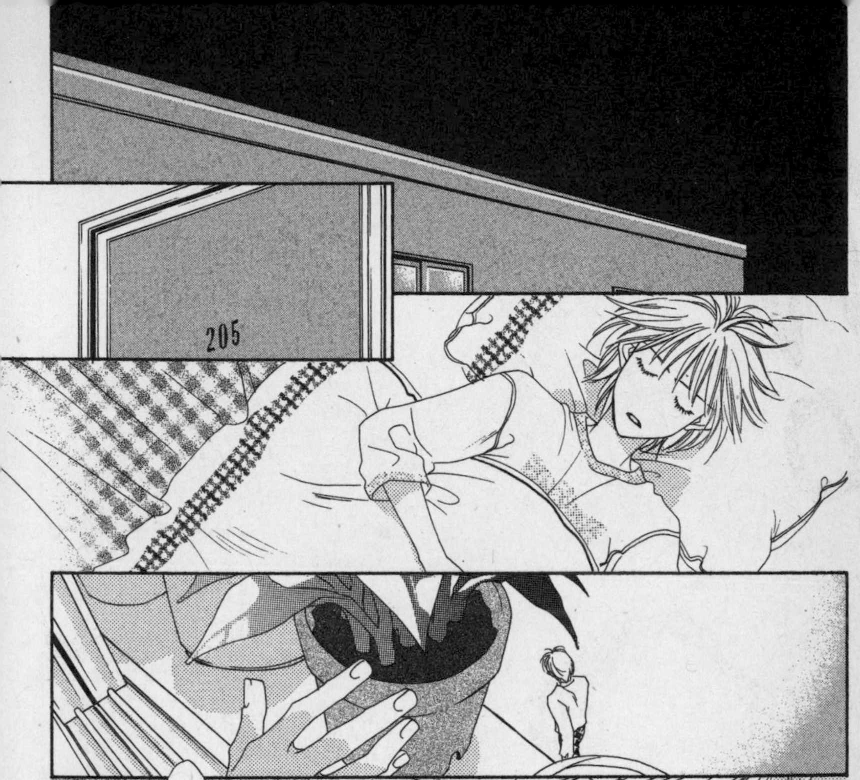
205

Book Signing

ON SUNDAY, MAY 24TH 1998 I DID MY FIRST BOOK SIGNING!! I WAS SO HAPPY WHEN I SAW A LINE OF FANS WAITING IN THE RAIN JUST TO SEE ME! THANK YOU! ♪ NORMALLY I DON'T HAVE THE OPPORTUNITY TO MEET MY FANS, SO IT WAS FUN! ♪ THEY SOLD TICKETS, AND THERE WAS A TIME LIMIT, SO I DIDN'T GET TO SIGN FOR 100% OF THE FANS WHO CAME, BUT I'D LIKE TO DO IT AGAIN SOMETIME.

ALTHOUGH MY HANDS MAY DIE.

My friends Yuki-sensei and M-chan even came to the signing.

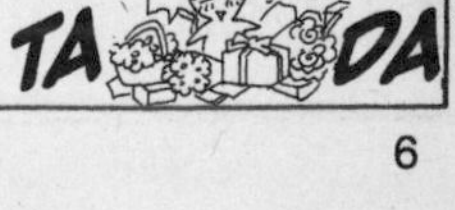
Mountain of Presents
TA DA

M-CHAN CAME DRESSED AS YOO FROM "MINPI." THANK YOU!

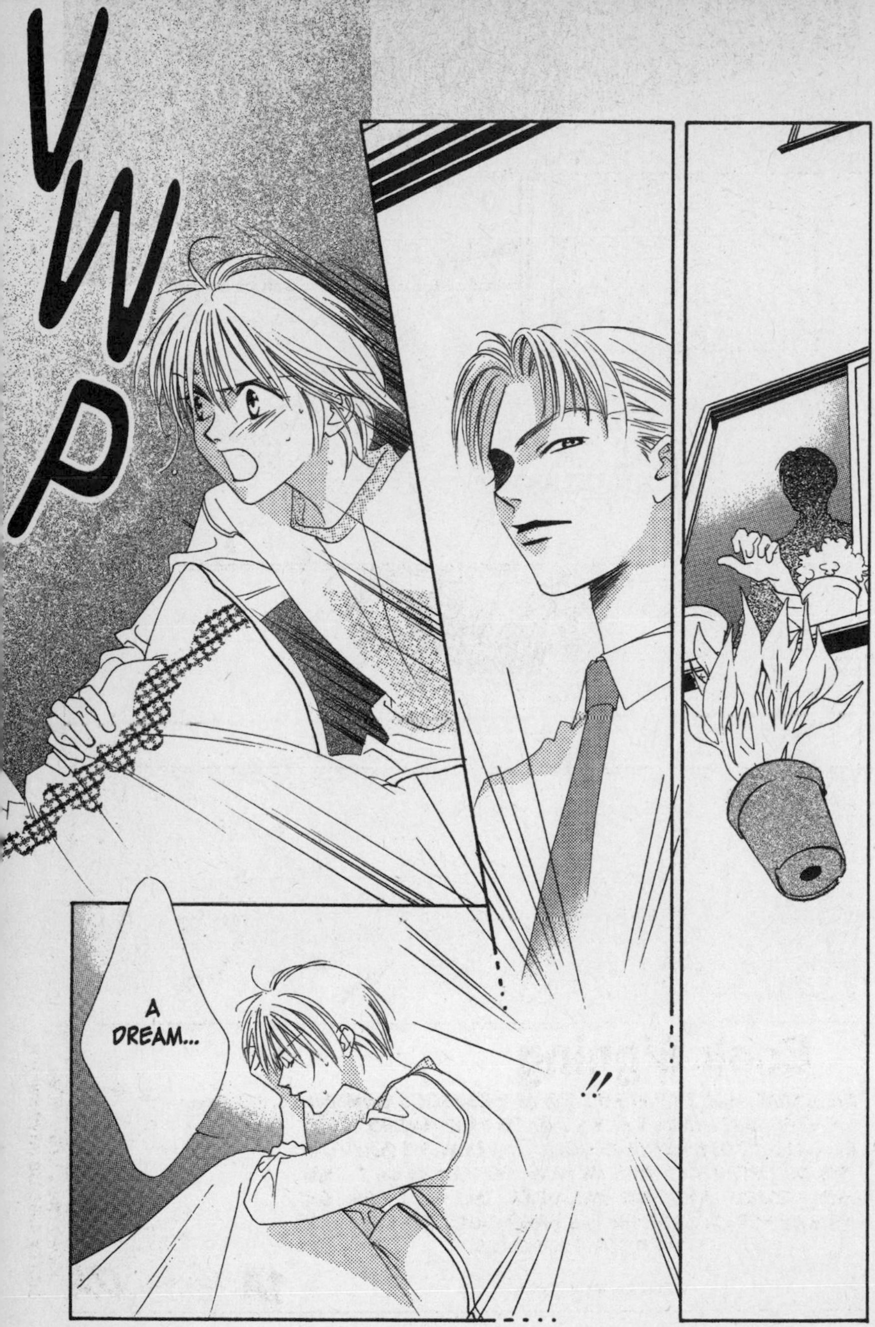
VWP
!!
A DREAM...

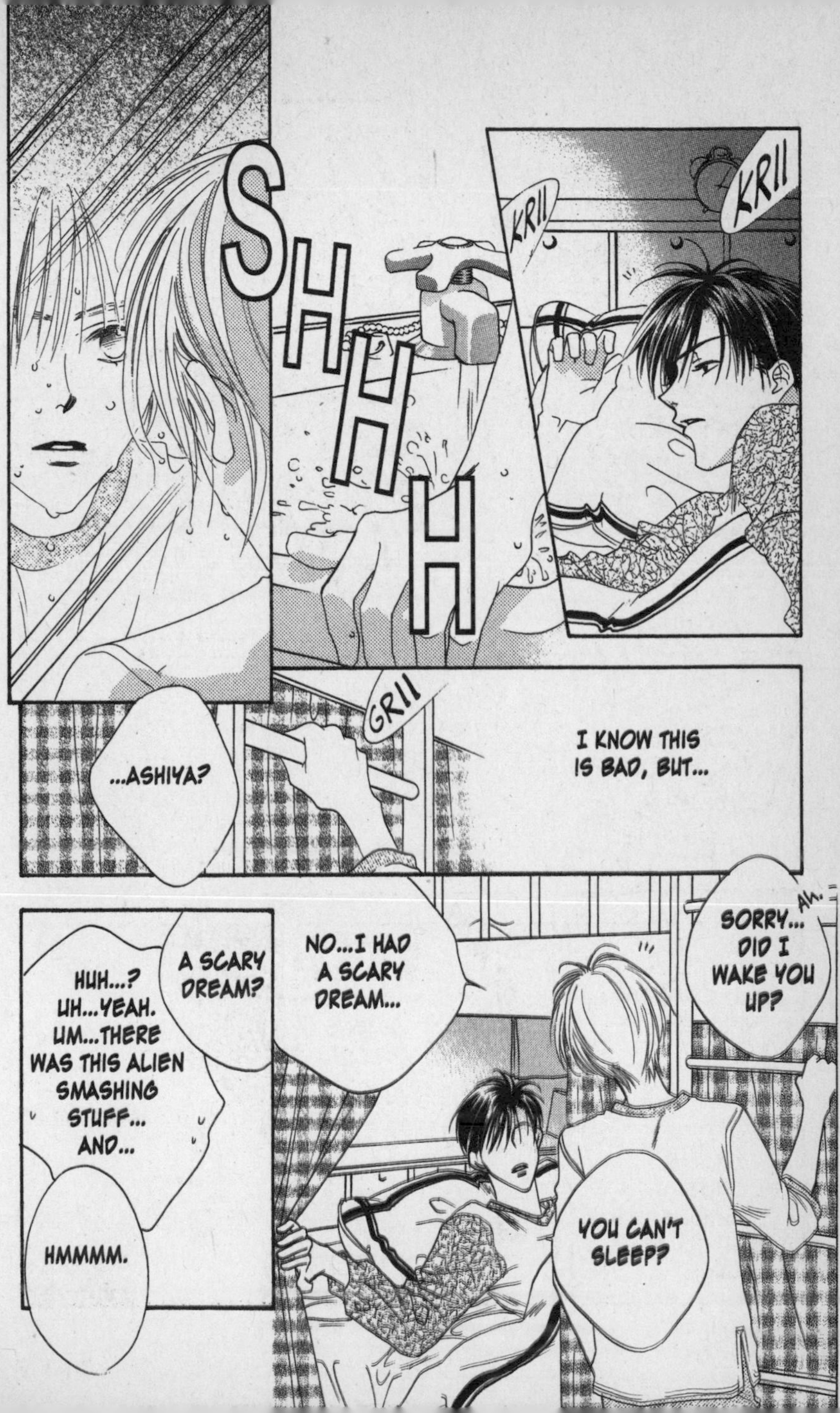
KRII
KRII
SHHHH
I KNOW THIS IS BAD, BUT...
GRII
...ASHIYA?
AH.
SORRY... DID I WAKE YOU UP?
YOU CAN'T SLEEP?
NO...I HAD A SCARY DREAM...
A SCARY DREAM?
HUH...? UH...YEAH. UM...THERE WAS THIS ALIEN SMASHING STUFF... AND...
HMMMM.

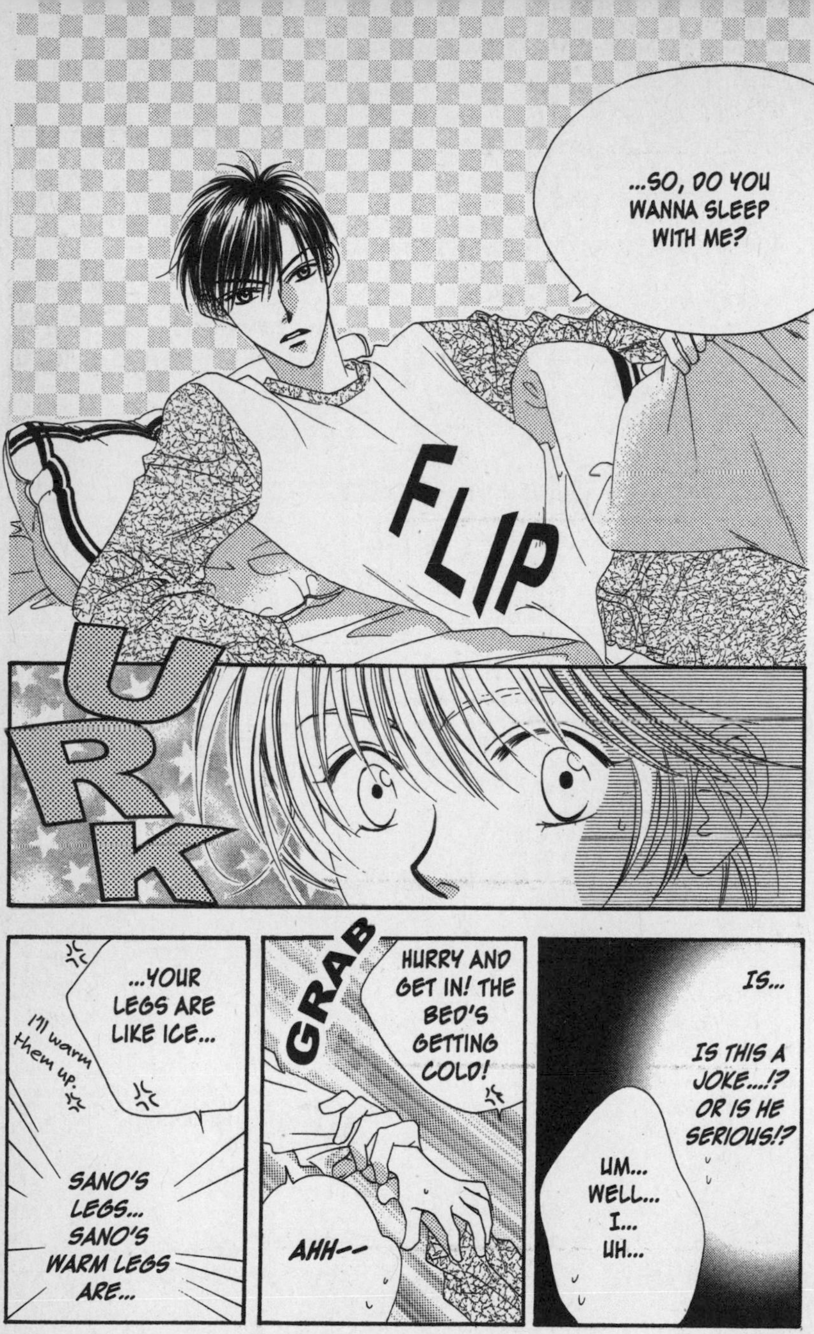
...SO, DO YOU WANNA SLEEP WITH ME?
FLIP
URK
IS...
IS THIS A JOKE...!? OR IS HE SERIOUS!?
UM... WELL... I... UH...
GRAB
HURRY AND GET IN! THE BED'S GETTING COLD!
AHH--
...YOUR LEGS ARE LIKE ICE...
I'll warm them up.
SANO'S LEGS... SANO'S WARM LEGS ARE...

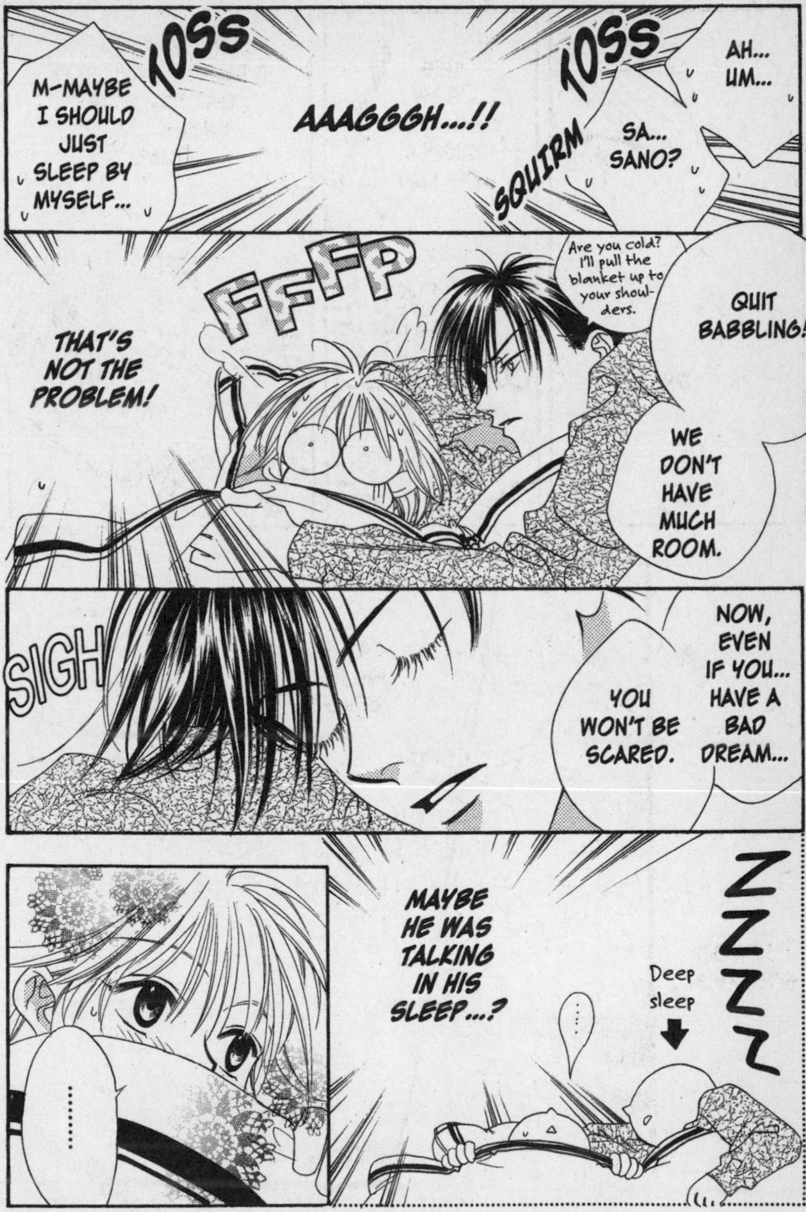
AH... UM...
SA... SANO?
SQUIRM
TOSS
AAAGGGH...!!
TOSS
M-MAYBE I SHOULD JUST SLEEP BY MYSELF...
QUIT BABBLING!
Are you cold? I'll pull the blanket up to your shoul-ders.
WE DON'T HAVE MUCH ROOM.
FFFP
THAT'S NOT THE PROBLEM!
NOW, EVEN IF YOU... HAVE A BAD DREAM...
YOU WON'T BE SCARED.
SIGH
ZZZZ
Deep sleep
......
MAYBE HE WAS TALKING IN HIS SLEEP...?
....

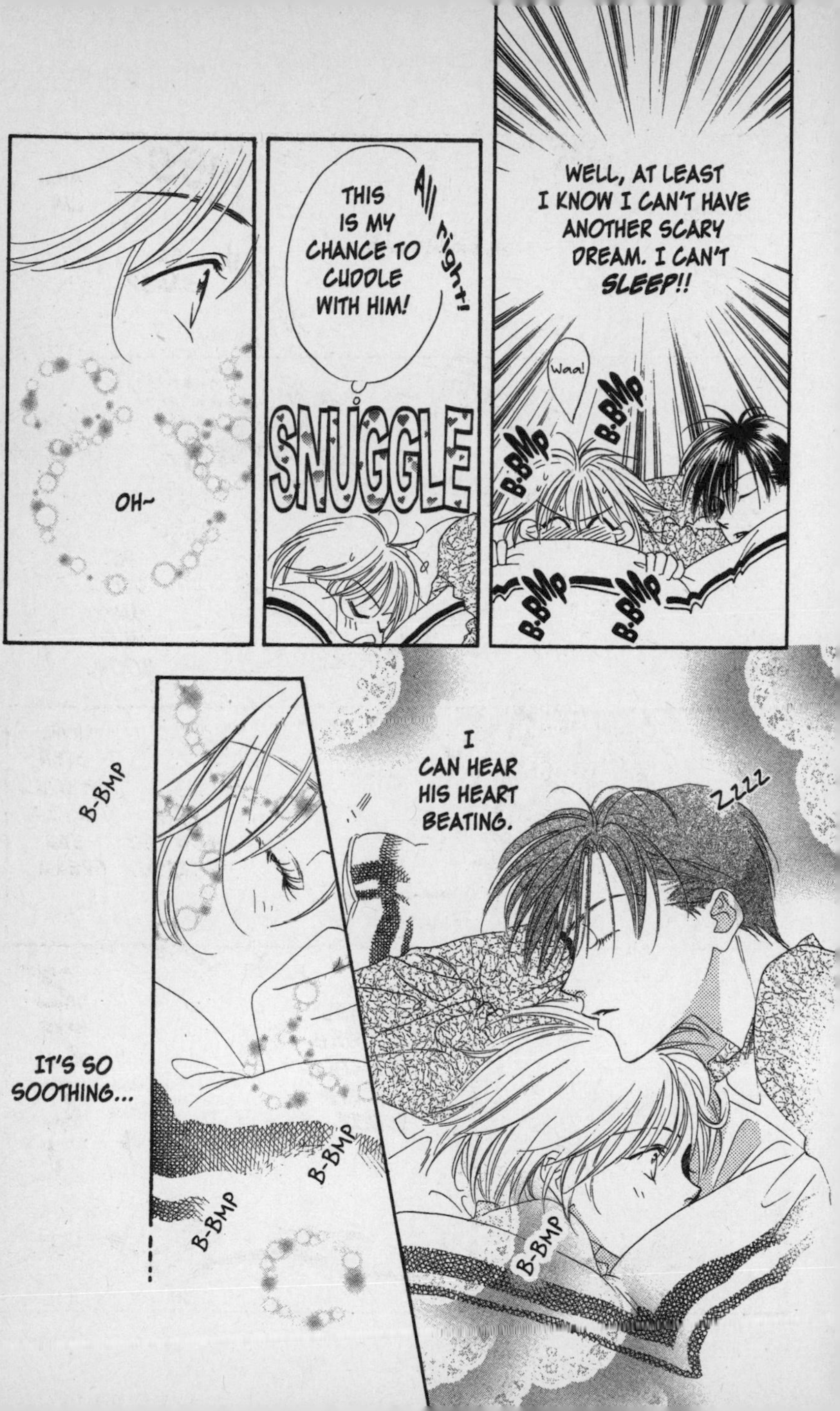
WELL, AT LEAST I KNOW I CAN'T HAVE ANOTHER SCARY DREAM. I CAN'T SLEEP!!
Waa!
B-BMP
B-BMP
B-BMP
B-BMP
All right!
THIS IS MY CHANCE TO CUDDLE WITH HIM!
SNUGGLE
OH~
I CAN HEAR HIS HEART BEATING.
ZZZZ
B-BMP
B-BMP
B-BMP
IT'S SO SOOTHING...
B-BMP

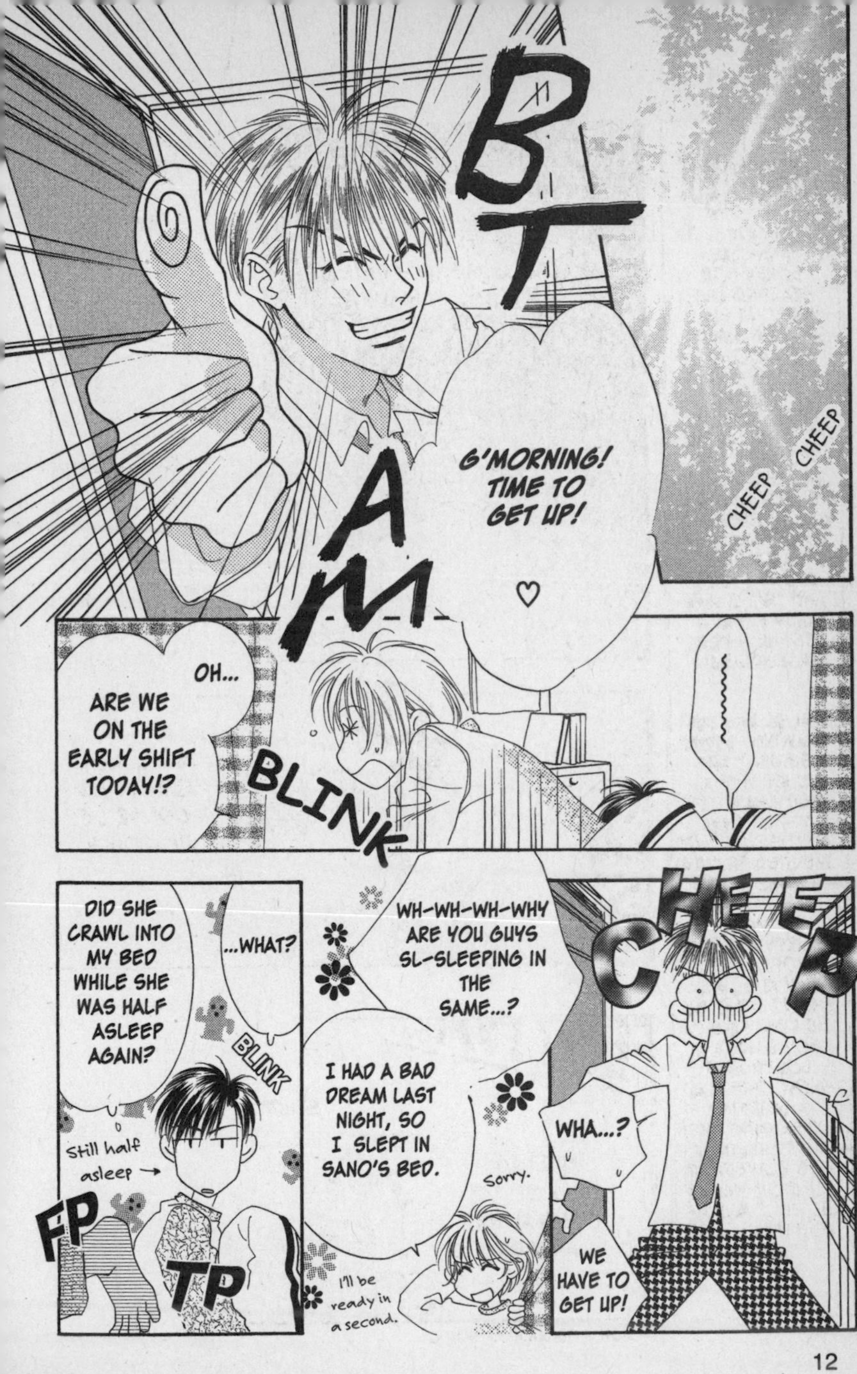
BTAM
G'MORNING! TIME TO GET UP! ♡
CHEEP CHEEP
CHEEP
OH... ARE WE ON THE EARLY SHIFT TODAY!?
BLINK
CHEEP
WH-WH-WH-WHY ARE YOU GUYS SL-SLEEPING IN THE SAME...?
WHA...?
WE HAVE TO GET UP!
I HAD A BAD DREAM LAST NIGHT, SO I SLEPT IN SANO'S BED.
Sorry.
I'll be ready in a second.
...WHAT?
DID SHE CRAWL INTO MY BED WHILE SHE WAS HALF ASLEEP AGAIN?
BLINK
Still half asleep →
FP
TP

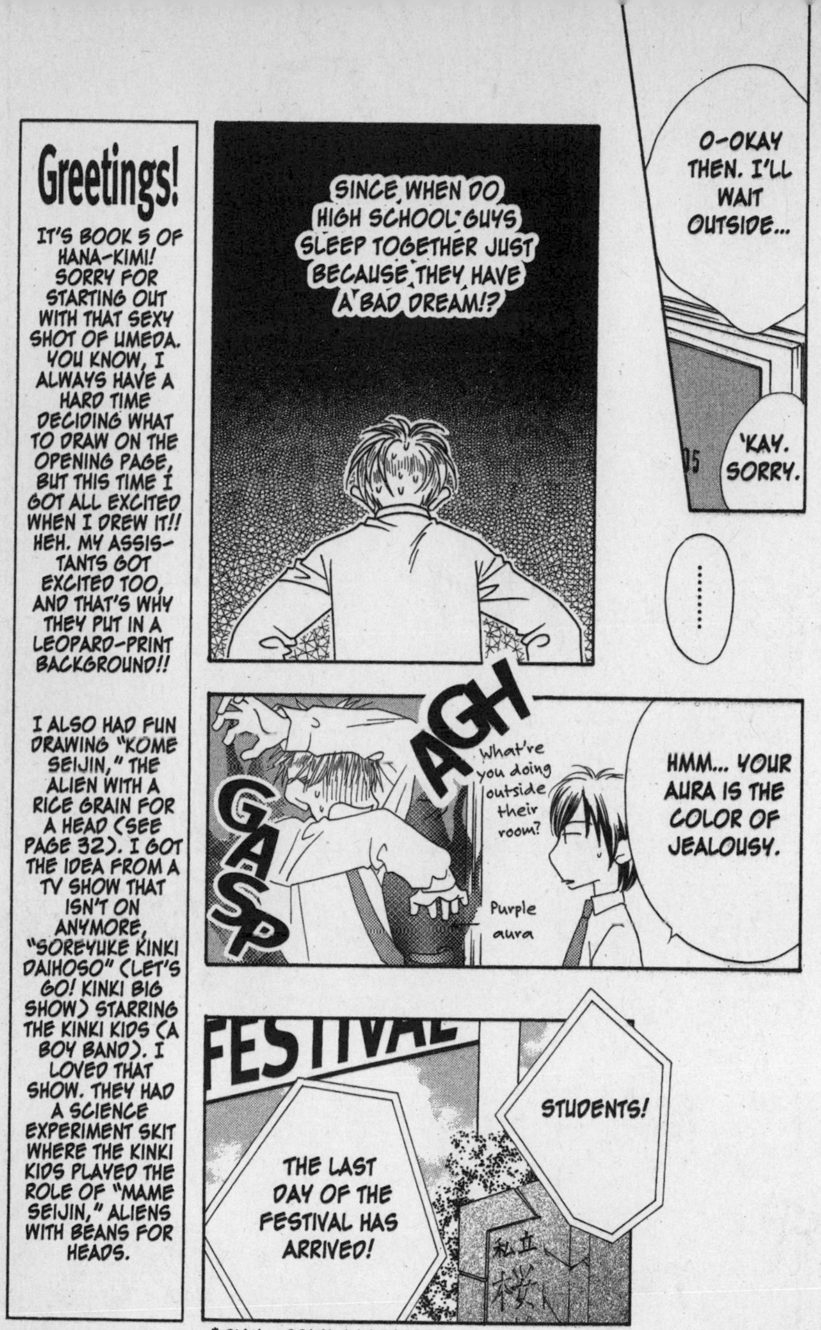
O-OKAY THEN. I'LL WAIT OUTSIDE...
'KAY. SORRY.
SINCE WHEN DO HIGH SCHOOL GUYS SLEEP TOGETHER JUST BECAUSE THEY HAVE A BAD DREAM!?
......
HMM... YOUR AURA IS THE COLOR OF JEALOUSY.
What're you doing outside their room?
AGH
GASP
Purple aura
STUDENTS!
THE LAST DAY OF THE FESTIVAL HAS ARRIVED!
FESTIVAL
* SIGN = OSAKA HIGH SCHOOL

Greetings!

IT'S BOOK 5 OF HANA-KIMI! SORRY FOR STARTING OUT WITH THAT SEXY SHOT OF UMEDA. YOU KNOW, I ALWAYS HAVE A HARD TIME DECIDING WHAT TO DRAW ON THE OPENING PAGE, BUT THIS TIME I GOT ALL EXCITED WHEN I DREW IT!! HEH. MY ASSISTANTS GOT EXCITED TOO, AND THAT'S WHY THEY PUT IN A LEOPARD-PRINT BACKGROUND!!

I ALSO HAD FUN DRAWING "KOME SEIJIN," THE ALIEN WITH A RICE GRAIN FOR A HEAD (SEE PAGE 32). I GOT THE IDEA FROM A TV SHOW THAT ISN'T ON ANYMORE, "SOREYUKE KINKI DAIHOSO" (LET'S GO! KINKI BIG SHOW) STARRING THE KINKI KIDS (A BOY BAND). I LOVED THAT SHOW. THEY HAD A SCIENCE EXPERIMENT SKIT WHERE THE KINKI KIDS PLAYED THE ROLE OF "MAME SEIJIN," ALIENS WITH BEANS FOR HEADS.

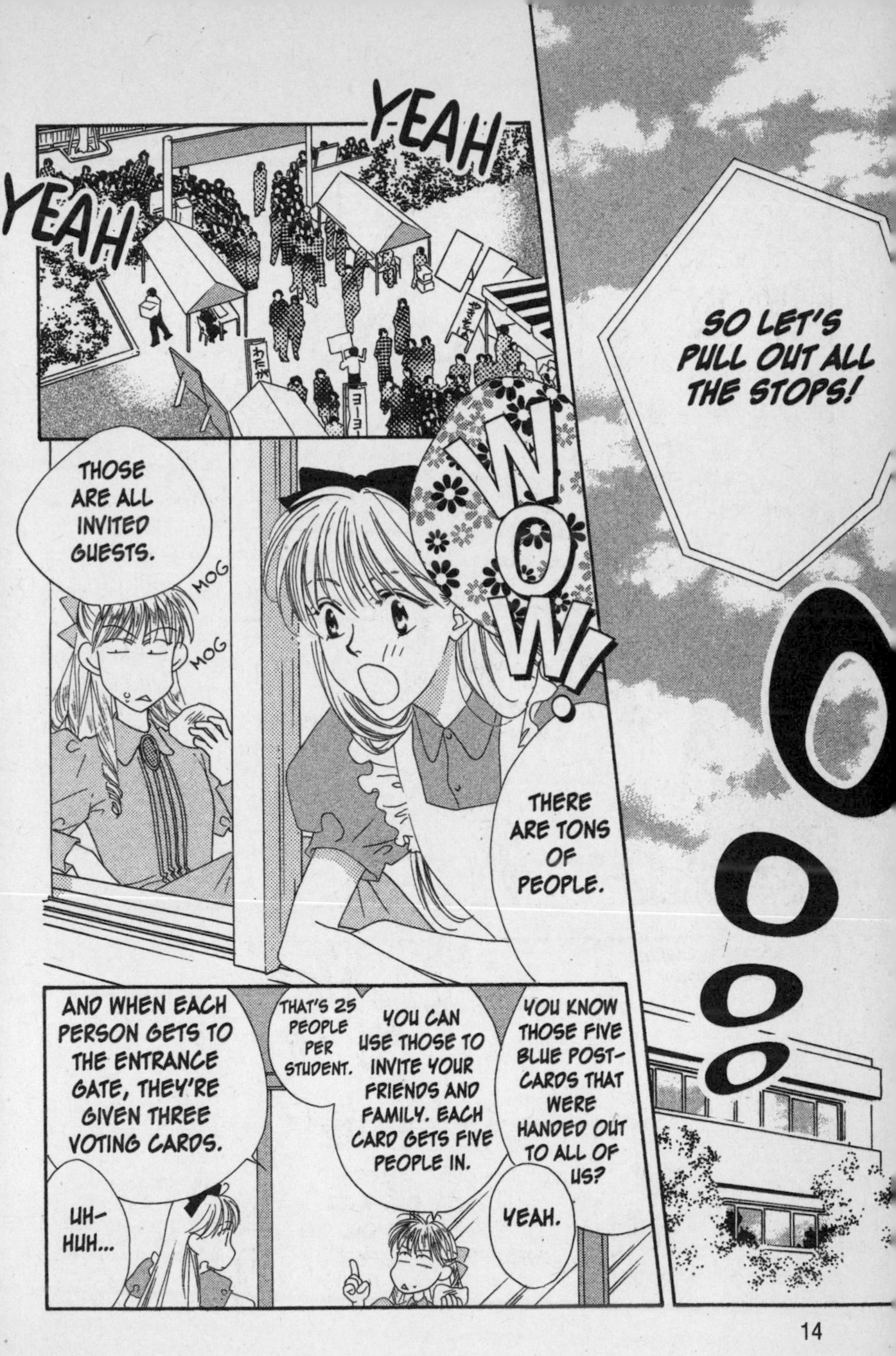
SO LET'S PULL OUT ALL THE STOPS!
Oooo
YEAH
YEAH
WOW!
THERE ARE TONS OF PEOPLE.
THOSE ARE ALL INVITED GUESTS.
MOG MOG
YOU KNOW THOSE FIVE BLUE POST-CARDS THAT WERE HANDED OUT TO ALL OF US?
YEAH.
YOU CAN USE THOSE TO INVITE YOUR FRIENDS AND FAMILY. EACH CARD GETS FIVE PEOPLE IN.
THAT'S 25 PEOPLE PER STUDENT.
AND WHEN EACH PERSON GETS TO THE ENTRANCE GATE, THEY'RE GIVEN THREE VOTING CARDS.
UH-HUH...

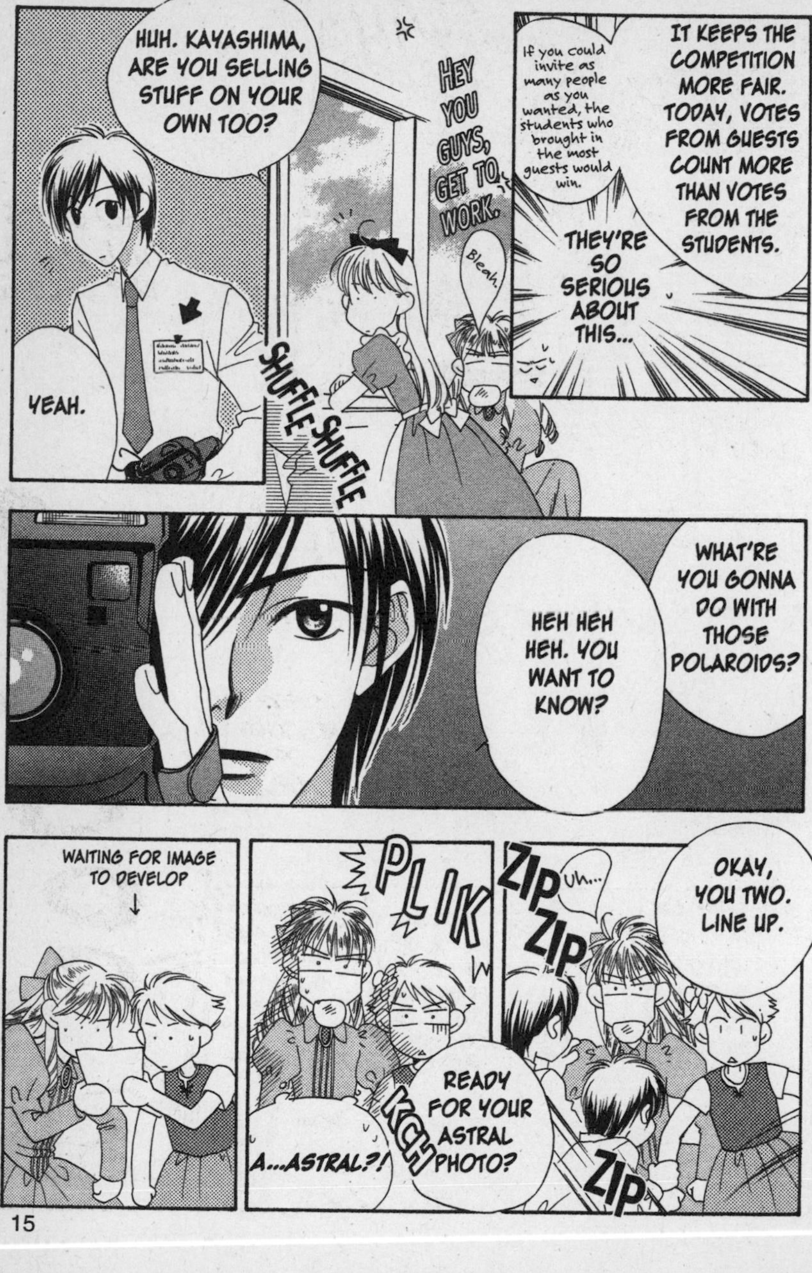
IT KEEPS THE COMPETITION MORE FAIR. TODAY, VOTES FROM GUESTS COUNT MORE THAN VOTES FROM THE STUDENTS.
If you could invite as many people as you wanted, the students who brought in the most guests would win.
THEY'RE SO SERIOUS ABOUT THIS...
HEY YOU GUYS, GET TO WORK.
Bleah.
SHUFFLE SHUFFLE
HUH. KAYASHIMA, ARE YOU SELLING STUFF ON YOUR OWN TOO?
YEAH.
WHAT'RE YOU GONNA DO WITH THOSE POLAROIDS?
HEH HEH HEH. YOU WANT TO KNOW?
OKAY, YOU TWO. LINE UP.
Uh...
ZIP ZIP
ZIP
PLIK
READY FOR YOUR ASTRAL PHOTO?
KCH
A...ASTRAL?!
WAITING FOR IMAGE TO DEVELOP

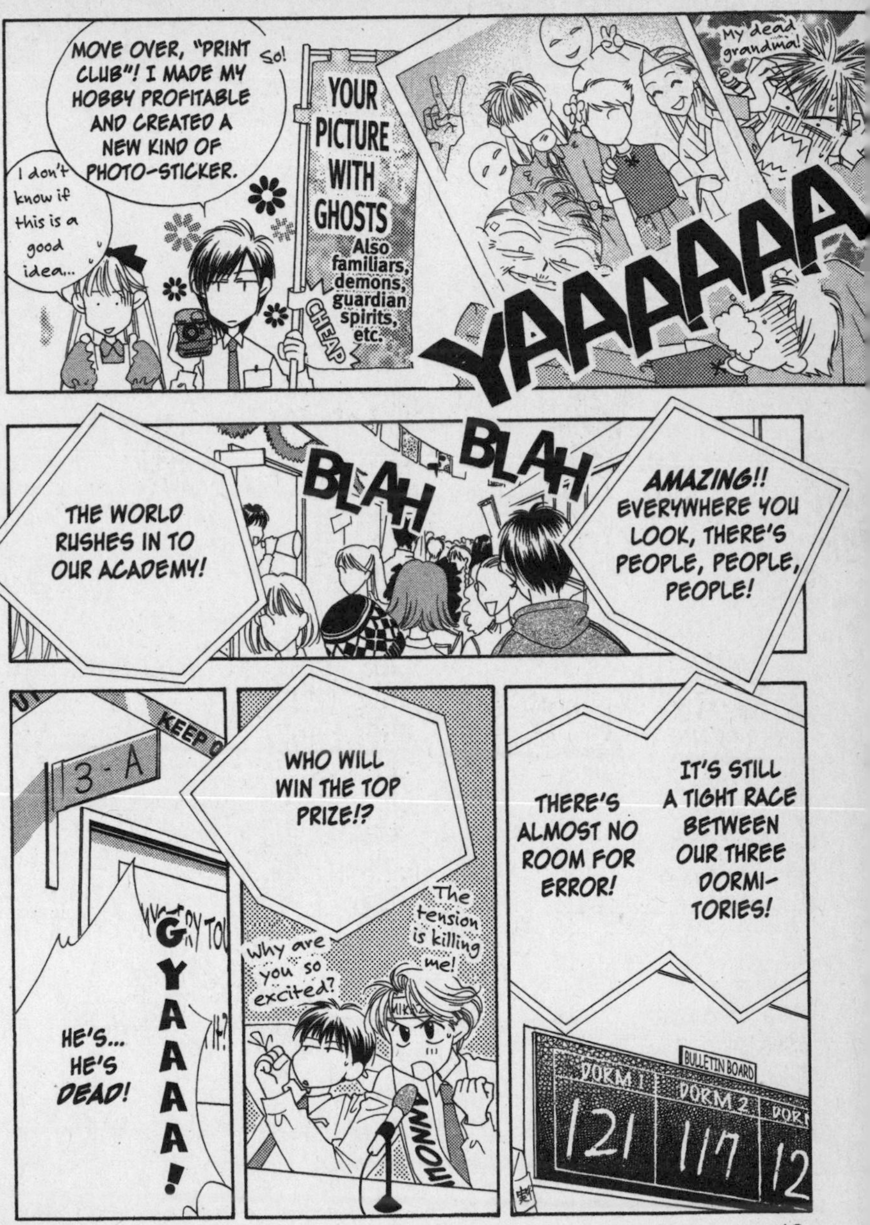
My dead grandma!
YAAAAAA
So!
MOVE OVER, "PRINT CLUB"! I MADE MY HOBBY PROFITABLE AND CREATED A NEW KIND OF PHOTO-STICKER.
YOUR PICTURE WITH GHOSTS
Also familiars, demons, guardian spirits, etc.
CHEAP
I don't know if this is a good idea...
AMAZING!! EVERYWHERE YOU LOOK, THERE'S PEOPLE, PEOPLE, PEOPLE!
BLAH
BLAH
THE WORLD RUSHES IN TO OUR ACADEMY!
IT'S STILL A TIGHT RACE BETWEEN OUR THREE DORMI-TORIES!
THERE'S ALMOST NO ROOM FOR ERROR!
BULLETIN BOARD
DORM 1
121
DORM 2
117
WHO WILL WIN THE TOP PRIZE!?
The tension is killing me!
Why are you so excited?
3-A
GYAAAAA!
HE'S... HE'S DEAD!

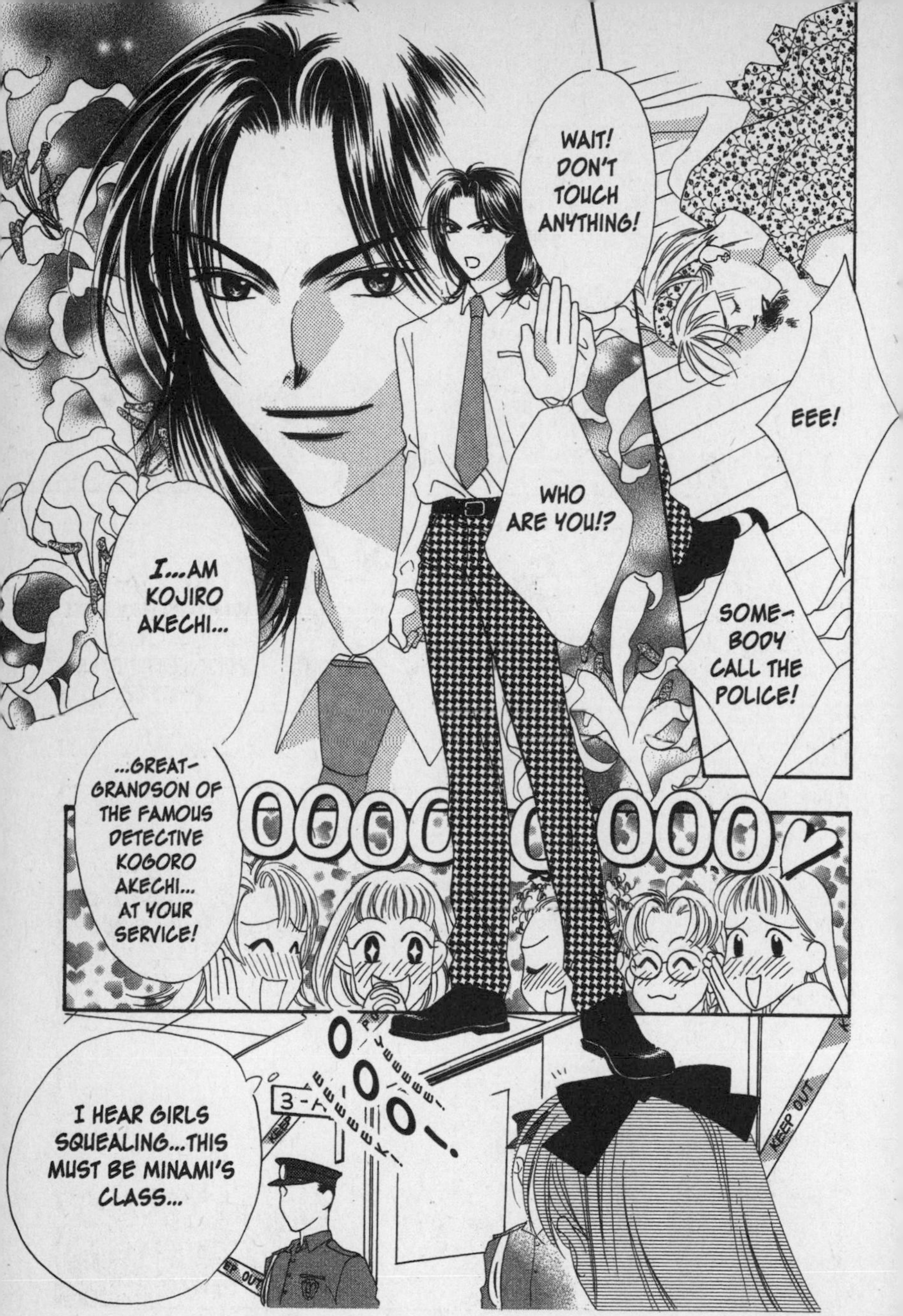
EEE!
SOME-BODY CALL THE POLICE!
WAIT! DON'T TOUCH ANYTHING!
WHO ARE YOU!?
I...AM KOJIRO AKECHI...
...GREAT-GRANDSON OF THE FAMOUS DETECTIVE KOGORO AKECHI... AT YOUR SERVICE!
OOOOOOOOO
OOO!
I HEAR GIRLS SQUEALING...THIS MUST BE MINAMI'S CLASS...
3-A
KEEP OUT

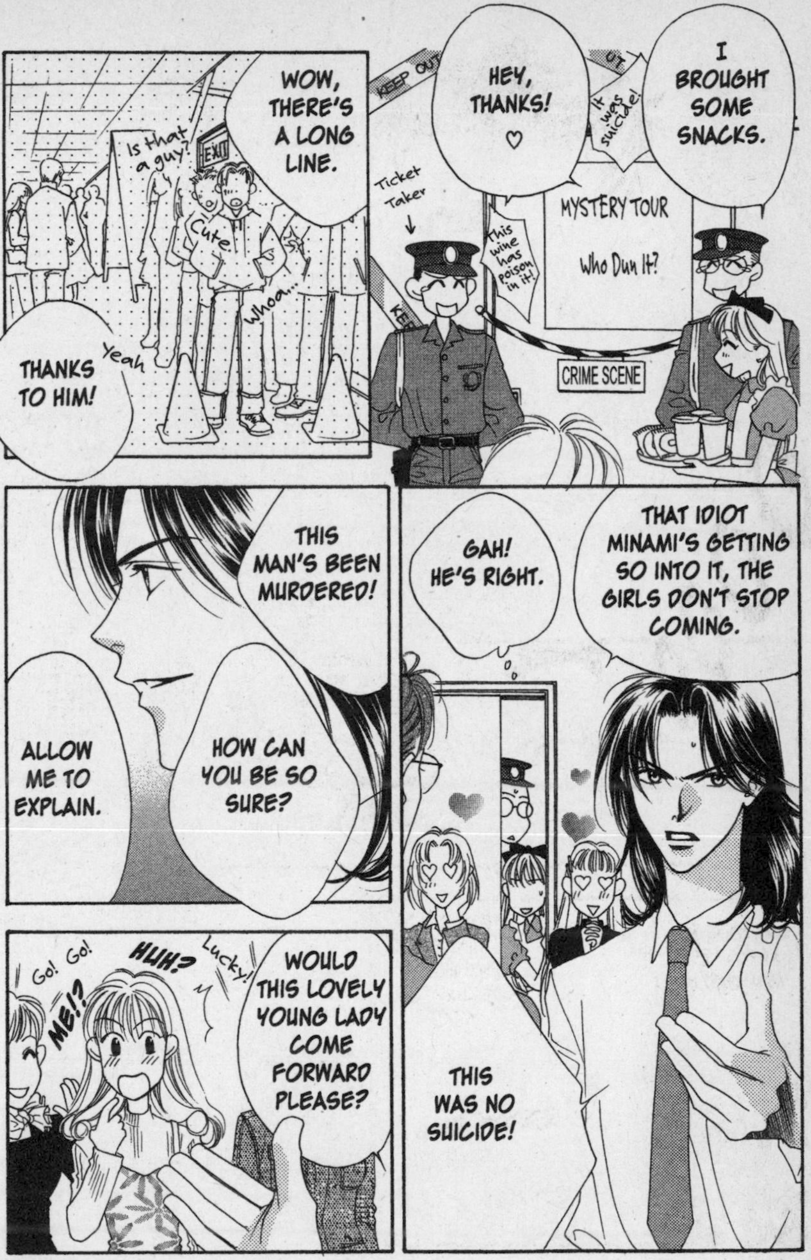
I BROUGHT SOME SNACKS.
HEY, THANKS! ♡
KEEP OUT
It was suicide!
MYSTERY TOUR
Who Dun It?
CRIME SCENE
This wine has poison in it!
Ticket Taker
WOW, THERE'S A LONG LINE.
EXIT
Is that a guy?
Cute.
Whoa...
Yeah
THANKS TO HIM!
THAT IDIOT MINAMI'S GETTING SO INTO IT, THE GIRLS DON'T STOP COMING.
GAH! HE'S RIGHT.
THIS WAS NO SUICIDE!
THIS MAN'S BEEN MURDERED!
HOW CAN YOU BE SO SURE?
ALLOW ME TO EXPLAIN.
WOULD THIS LOVELY YOUNG LADY COME FORWARD PLEASE?
Lucky!
HUH?
ME!?
Go! Go!

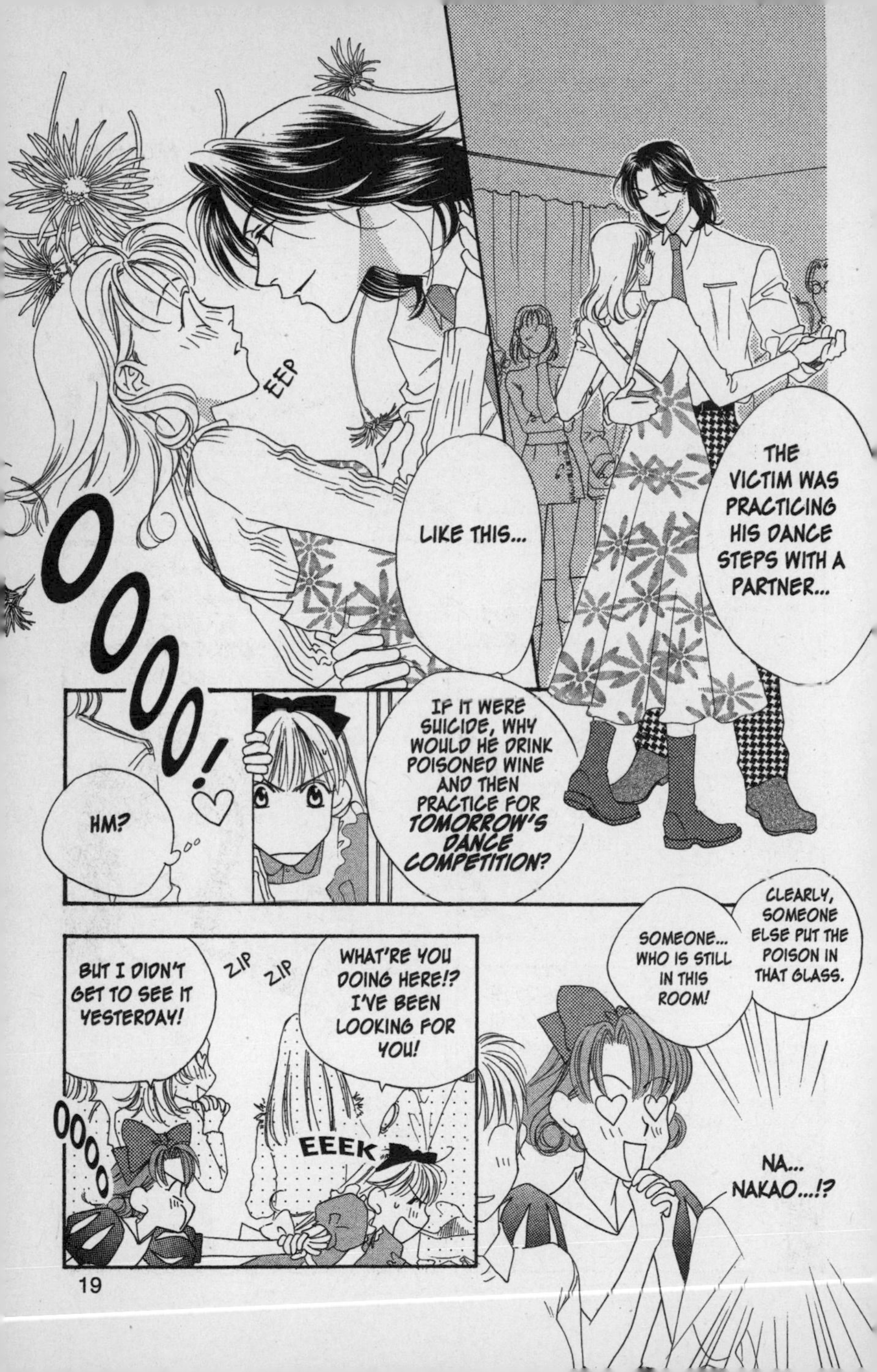
THE VICTIM WAS PRACTICING HIS DANCE STEPS WITH A PARTNER...
LIKE THIS...
EEP
OOOO!
IF IT WERE SUICIDE, WHY WOULD HE DRINK POISONED WINE AND THEN PRACTICE FOR *TOMORROW'S DANCE COMPETITION*?
HM?
CLEARLY, SOMEONE ELSE PUT THE POISON IN THAT GLASS.
SOMEONE... WHO IS STILL IN THIS ROOM!
NA... NAKAO...!?
WHAT'RE YOU DOING HERE!? I'VE BEEN LOOKING FOR YOU!
ZIP
ZIP
BUT I DIDN'T GET TO SEE IT YESTERDAY!
EEEK
OOOO

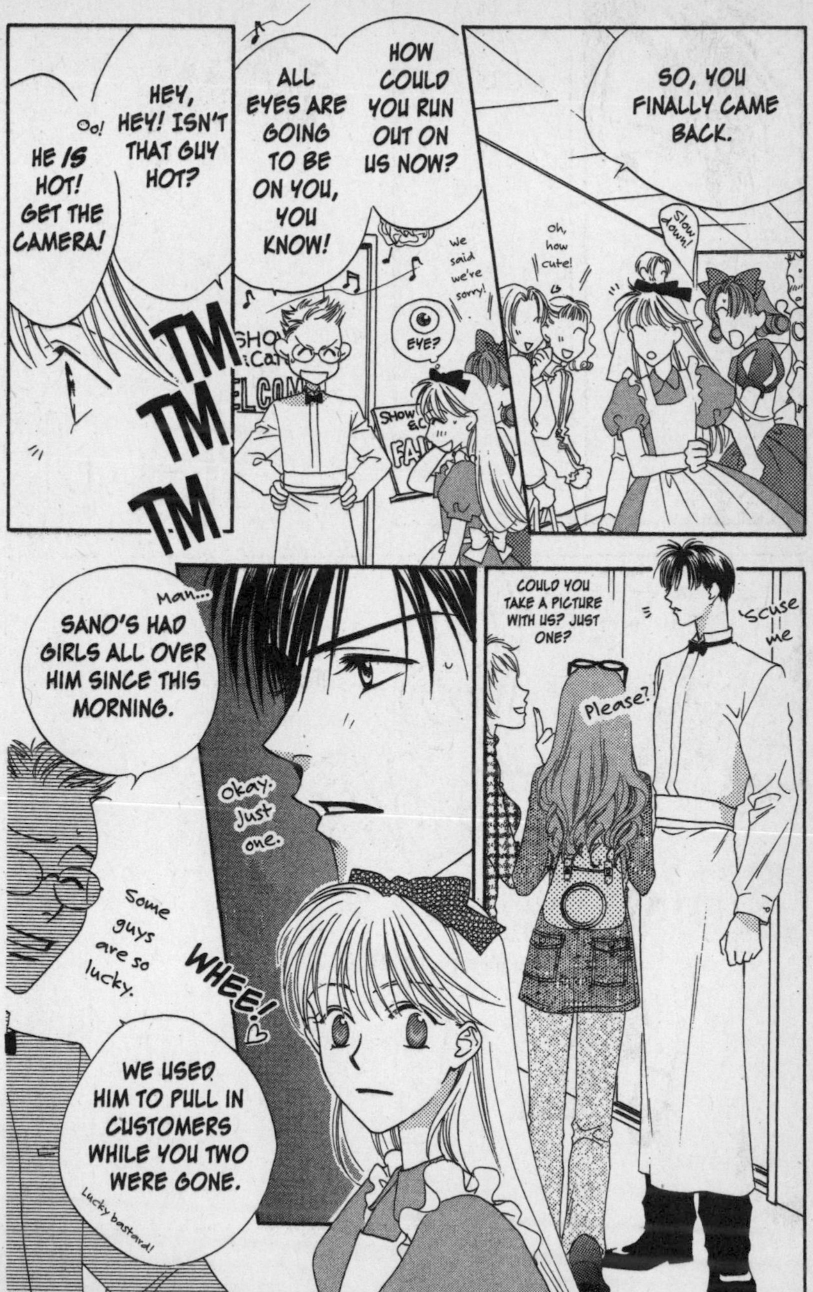
SO, YOU FINALLY CAME BACK.
Slow down!
Oh, how cute!
HOW COULD YOU RUN OUT ON US NOW?
ALL EYES ARE GOING TO BE ON YOU, YOU KNOW!
We said we're sorry!
EYE?
HEY, HEY! ISN'T THAT GUY HOT?
Oo!
HE IS HOT! GET THE CAMERA!
TM TM TM
COULD YOU TAKE A PICTURE WITH US? JUST ONE?
'Scuse me
Please?
Okay. Just one.
Man...
SANO'S HAD GIRLS ALL OVER HIM SINCE THIS MORNING.
Some guys are so lucky.
WHEE!
WE USED HIM TO PULL IN CUSTOMERS WHILE YOU TWO WERE GONE.
Lucky bastard!

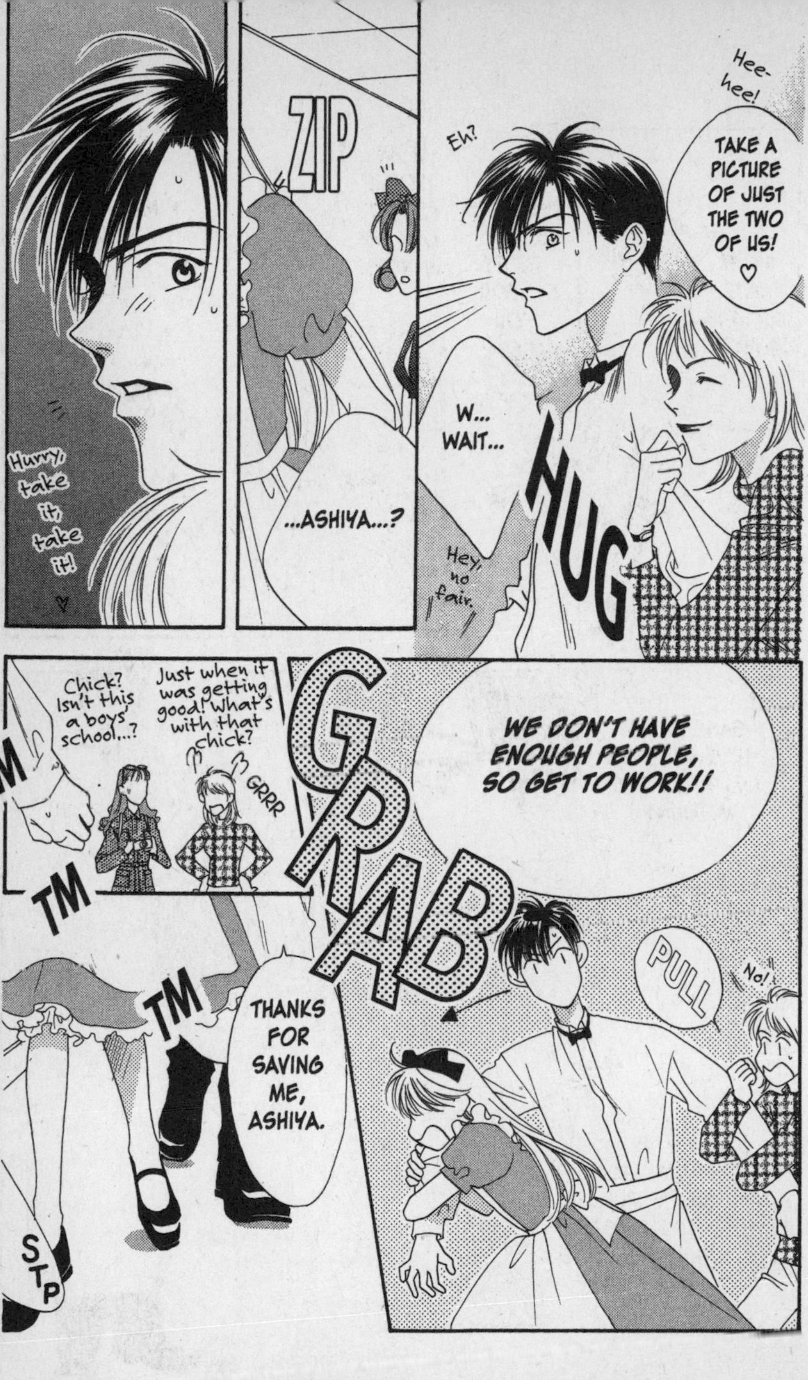
Hee-hee!
TAKE A PICTURE OF JUST THE TWO OF US! ♥
Eh?
W... WAIT...
HUG
Hey, no fair.
ZIP
...ASHIYA...?
Hurry, take it, take it! ♥
GRAB
WE DON'T HAVE ENOUGH PEOPLE, SO GET TO WORK!!
PULL
No!
Just when it was getting good! What's with that chick?
GRRR
Chick? Isn't this a boys' school...?
TM
TM
TM
THANKS FOR SAVING ME, ASHIYA.
STP

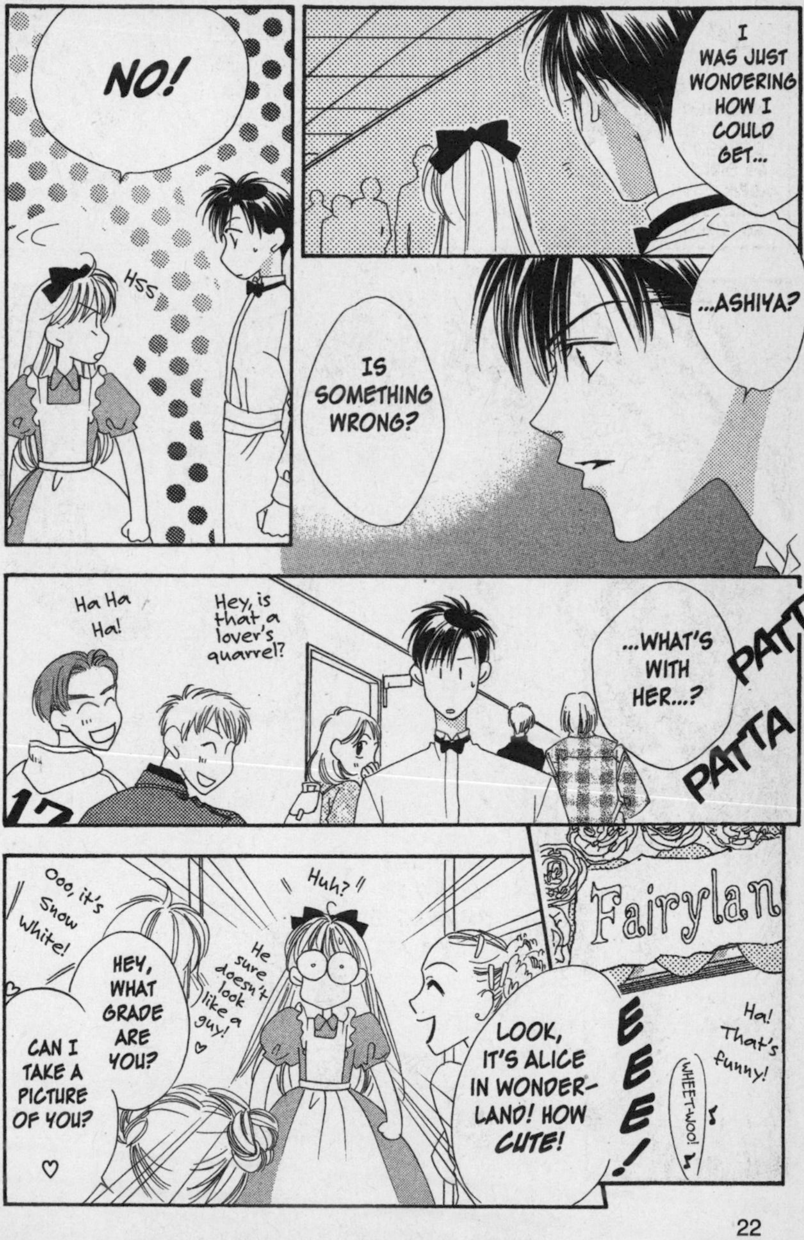
I WAS JUST WONDERING HOW I COULD GET...
...ASHIYA?
IS SOMETHING WRONG?
NO!
HSS
PATTA PATTA
...WHAT'S WITH HER...?
Hey, is that a lover's quarrel?
Ha Ha Ha!
Fairylan
Ha! That's funny!
WHEET-WOO!
EEE!
LOOK, IT'S ALICE IN WONDER-LAND! HOW CUTE!
Huh?!!
He sure doesn't look like a guy!
HEY, WHAT GRADE ARE YOU?
Ooo, it's Snow White!
CAN I TAKE A PICTURE OF YOU?

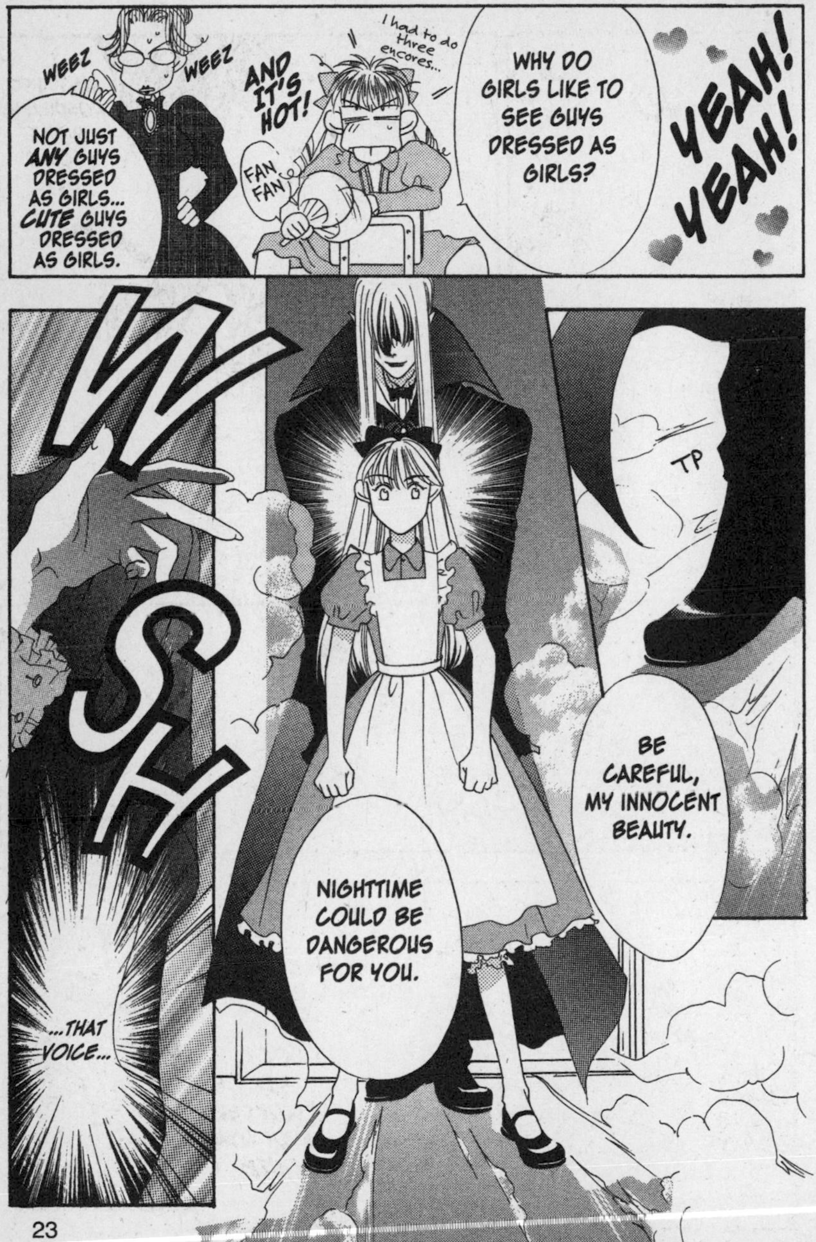
YEAH! YEAH!
WHY DO GIRLS LIKE TO SEE GUYS DRESSED AS GIRLS?
I had to do three encores...
AND IT'S HOT!
FAN FAN
WEEZ WEEZ
NOT JUST ANY GUYS DRESSED AS GIRLS... CUTE GUYS DRESSED AS GIRLS.
TP
BE CAREFUL, MY INNOCENT BEAUTY.
NIGHTTIME COULD BE DANGEROUS FOR YOU.
WSSH
...THAT VOICE...

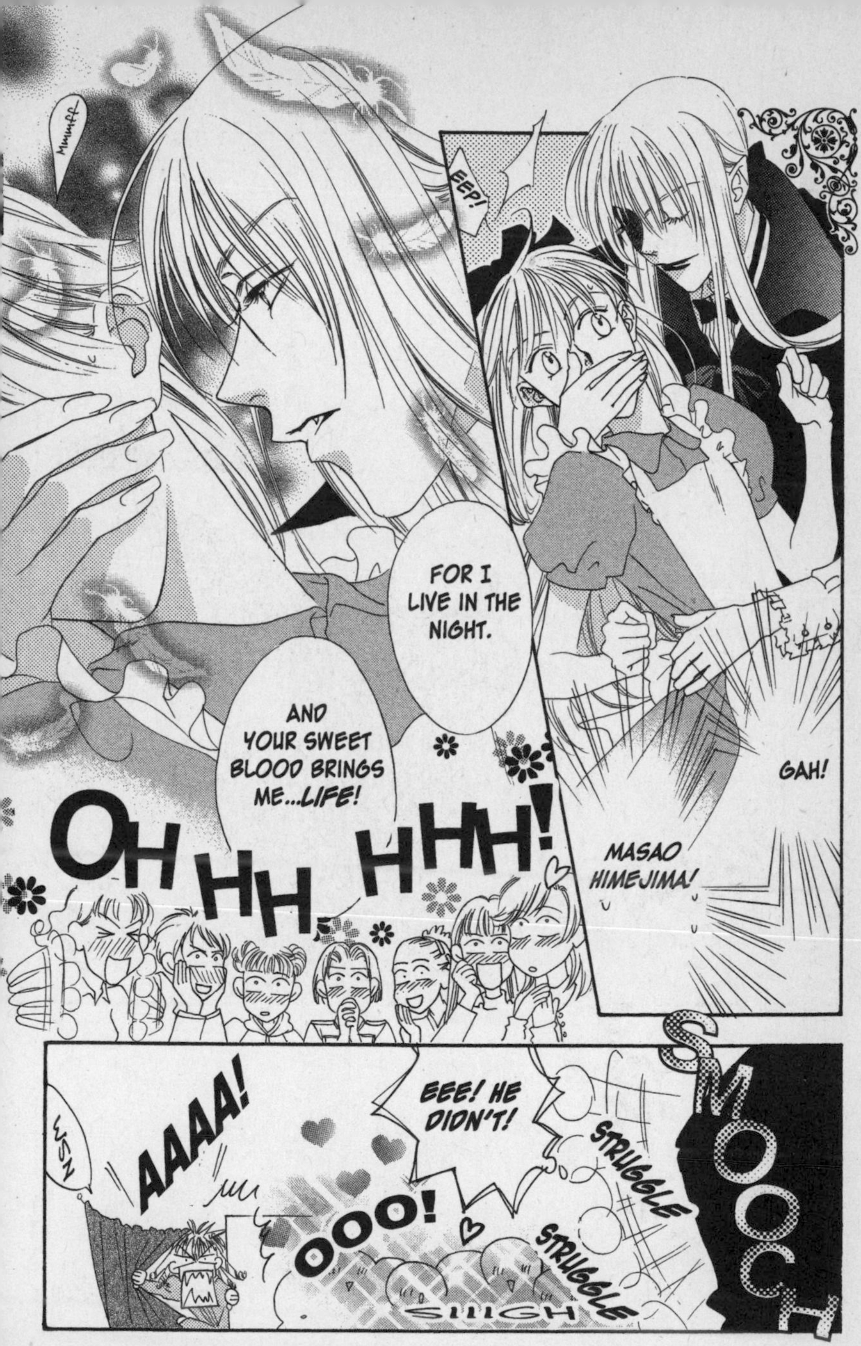
EEP!
GAH!
MASAO HIMEJIMA!
Mmmff
FOR I LIVE IN THE NIGHT.
AND YOUR SWEET BLOOD BRINGS ME...LIFE!
OHHHHHHH!
SMOOCH
STRUGGLE
STRUGGLE
EEE! HE DIDN'T!
OOOO!
SIIIGH
AAAA!
WSN

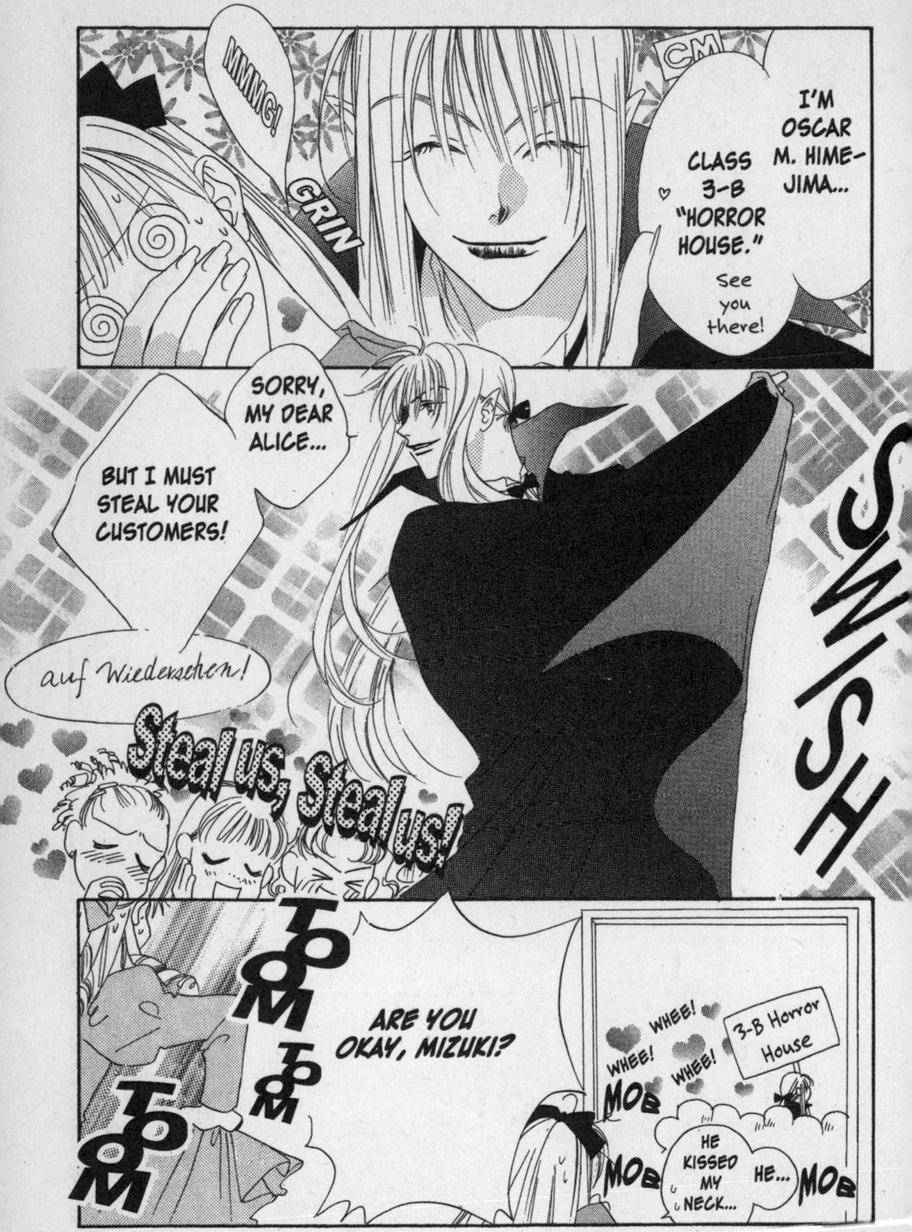
CM
I'M OSCAR M. HIME-JIMA...
CLASS 3-B "HORROR HOUSE."
See you there!
GRIN
MMMG!
SWISH
SORRY, MY DEAR ALICE...
BUT I MUST STEAL YOUR CUSTOMERS!
auf Wiedersehen!
Steal us, Steal us!
3-B Horror House
WHEE!
WHEE!
WHEE!
WHEE!
MOB
MOB
HE...
MOB
HE KISSED MY NECK...
MOB
ARE YOU OKAY, MIZUKI?
TOOM
TOOM
TOOM

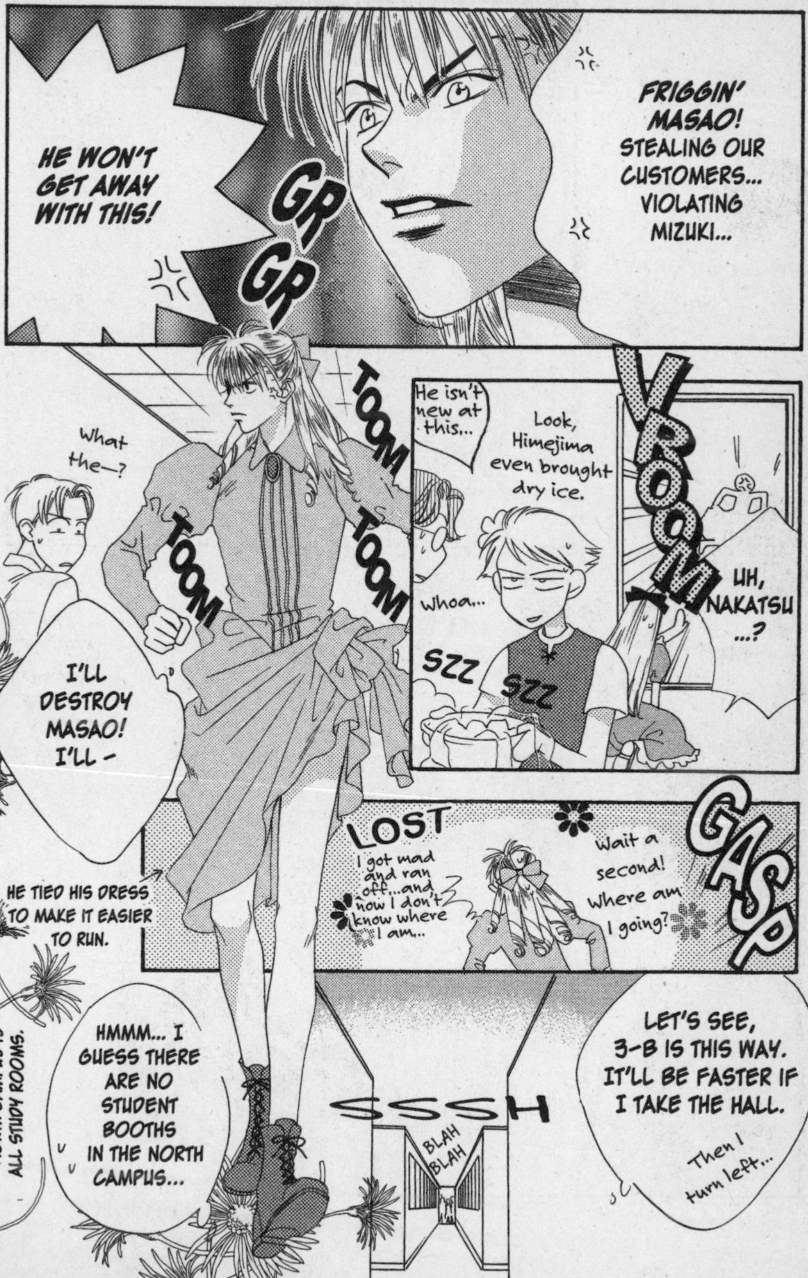
FRIGGIN' MASAO! STEALING OUR CUSTOMERS... VIOLATING MIZUKI...
GR GR
HE WON'T GET AWAY WITH THIS!
VROOM
UH, NAKATSU ...?
He isn't new at this...
Look, Himejima even brought dry ice.
Whoa...
SZZ SZZ
TOOM TOOM TOOM
What the—?
I'LL DESTROY MASAO! I'LL -
HE TIED HIS DRESS TO MAKE IT EASIER TO RUN.
GASP
Wait a second! Where am I going?
LOST
I got mad and ran off...and now I don't know where I am...
LET'S SEE, 3-B IS THIS WAY. IT'LL BE FASTER IF I TAKE THE HALL.
Then I turn left...
SSSH
BLAH BLAH
HMMM... I GUESS THERE ARE NO STUDENT BOOTHS IN THE NORTH CAMPUS...
* NORTH CAMPUS IS ALL STUDY ROOMS.

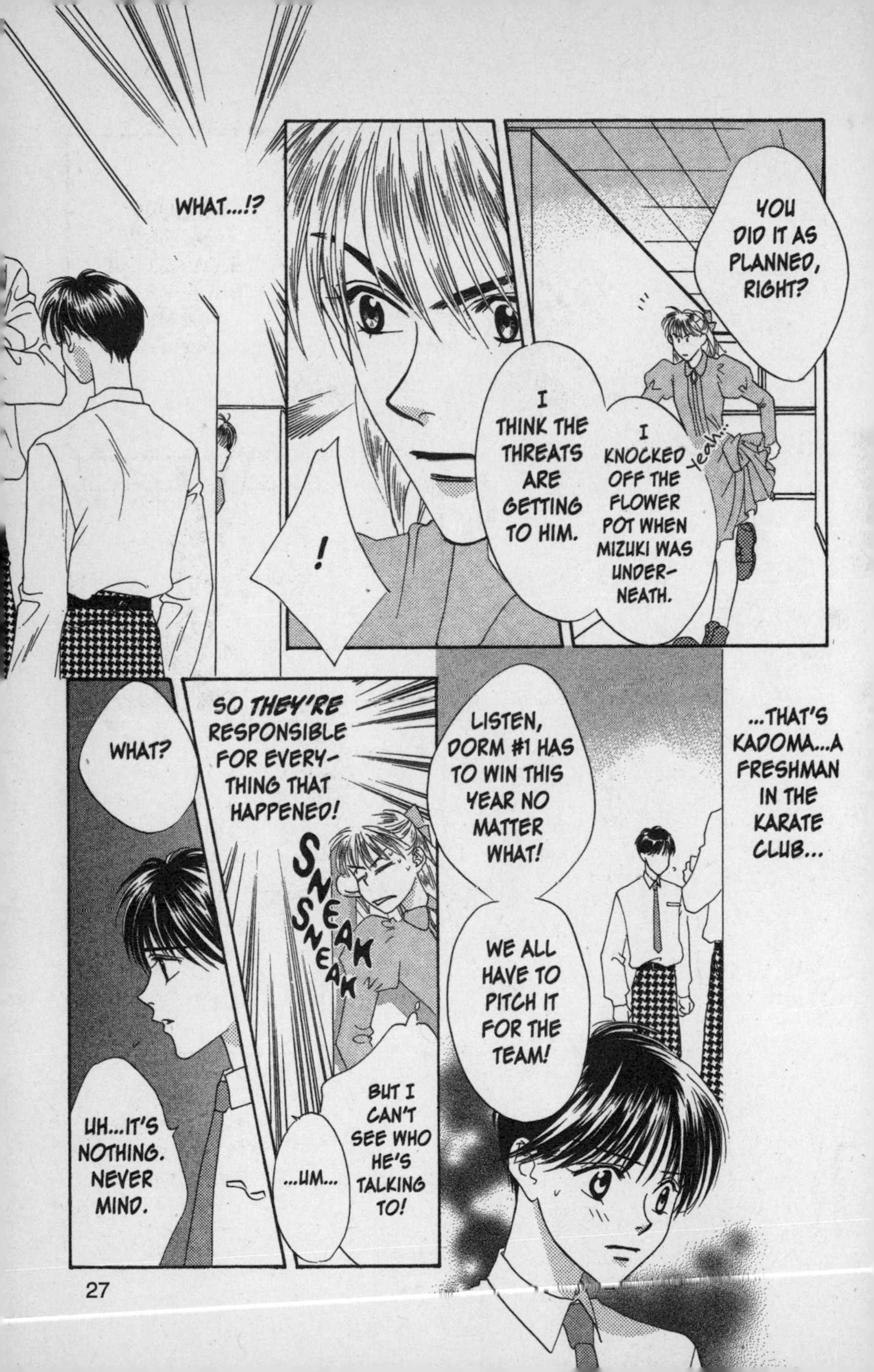
YOU DID IT AS PLANNED, RIGHT?
I KNOCKED OFF THE FLOWER POT WHEN MIZUKI WAS UNDERNEATH.
yeah...
I THINK THE THREATS ARE GETTING TO HIM.
!
WHAT...!?
...THAT'S KADOMA...A FRESHMAN IN THE KARATE CLUB...
LISTEN, DORM #1 HAS TO WIN THIS YEAR NO MATTER WHAT!
WE ALL HAVE TO PITCH IT FOR THE TEAM!
SO THEY'RE RESPONSIBLE FOR EVERYTHING THAT HAPPENED!
SNEAK SNEAK
BUT I CAN'T SEE WHO HE'S TALKING TO!
...UM...
WHAT?
UH...IT'S NOTHING. NEVER MIND.

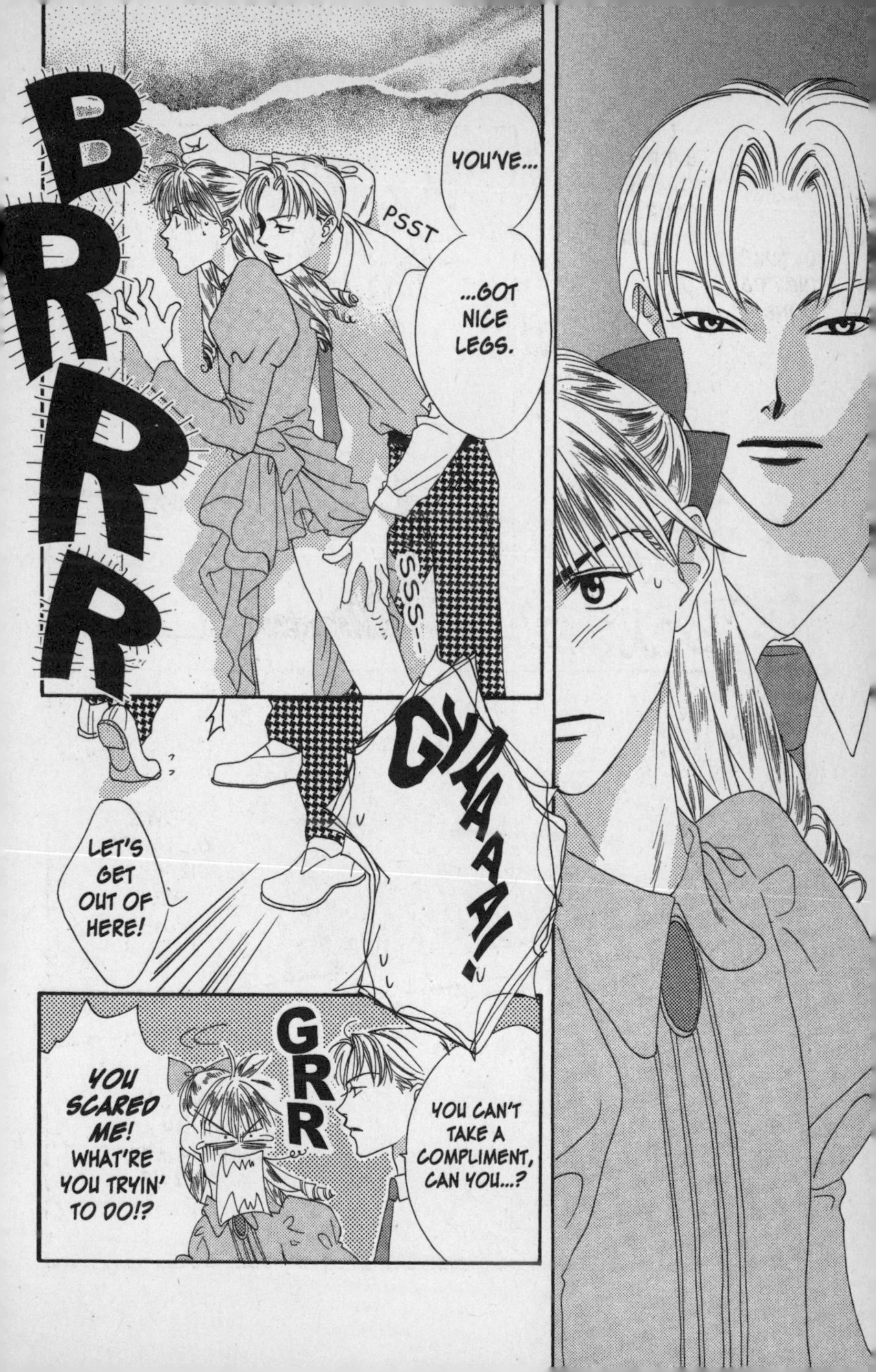
YOU'VE...
PSST
...GOT NICE LEGS.
BRRR
SSS--
GYAAAA!
LET'S GET OUT OF HERE!
YOU CAN'T TAKE A COMPLIMENT, CAN YOU...?
GRR
YOU SCARED ME! WHAT'RE YOU TRYIN' TO DO!?

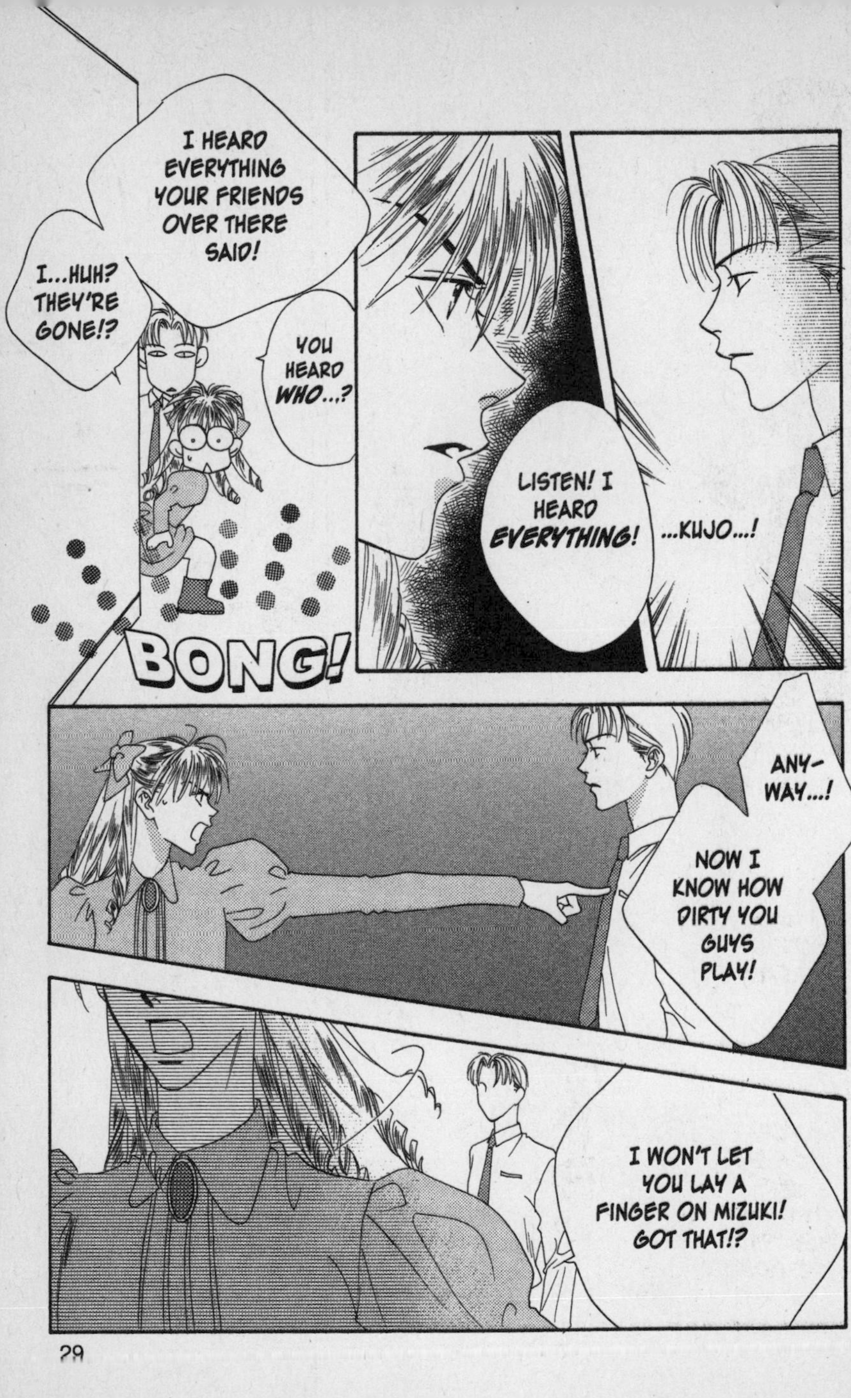
...KUJO...!
LISTEN! I HEARD EVERYTHING!
I HEARD EVERYTHING YOUR FRIENDS OVER THERE SAID!
YOU HEARD WHO...?
I...HUH? THEY'RE GONE!?
BONG!
ANY-WAY...!
NOW I KNOW HOW DIRTY YOU GUYS PLAY!
I WON'T LET YOU LAY A FINGER ON MIZUKI! GOT THAT!?

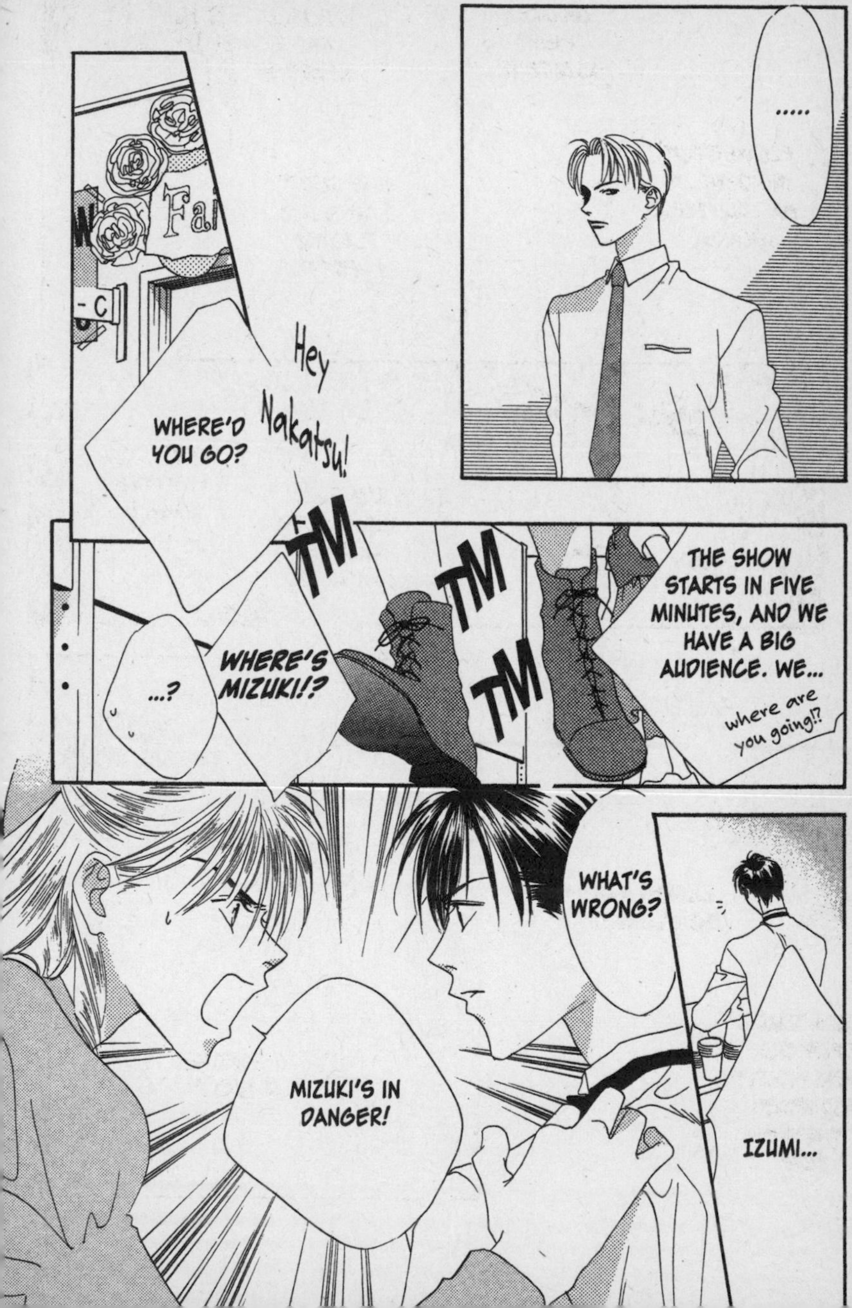
.....
Hey Nakatsu!
WHERE'D YOU GO?
THE SHOW STARTS IN FIVE MINUTES, AND WE HAVE A BIG AUDIENCE. WE...
where are you going!?
TM
TM
TM
WHERE'S MIZUKI!?
...?
IZUMI...
WHAT'S WRONG?
MIZUKI'S IN DANGER!

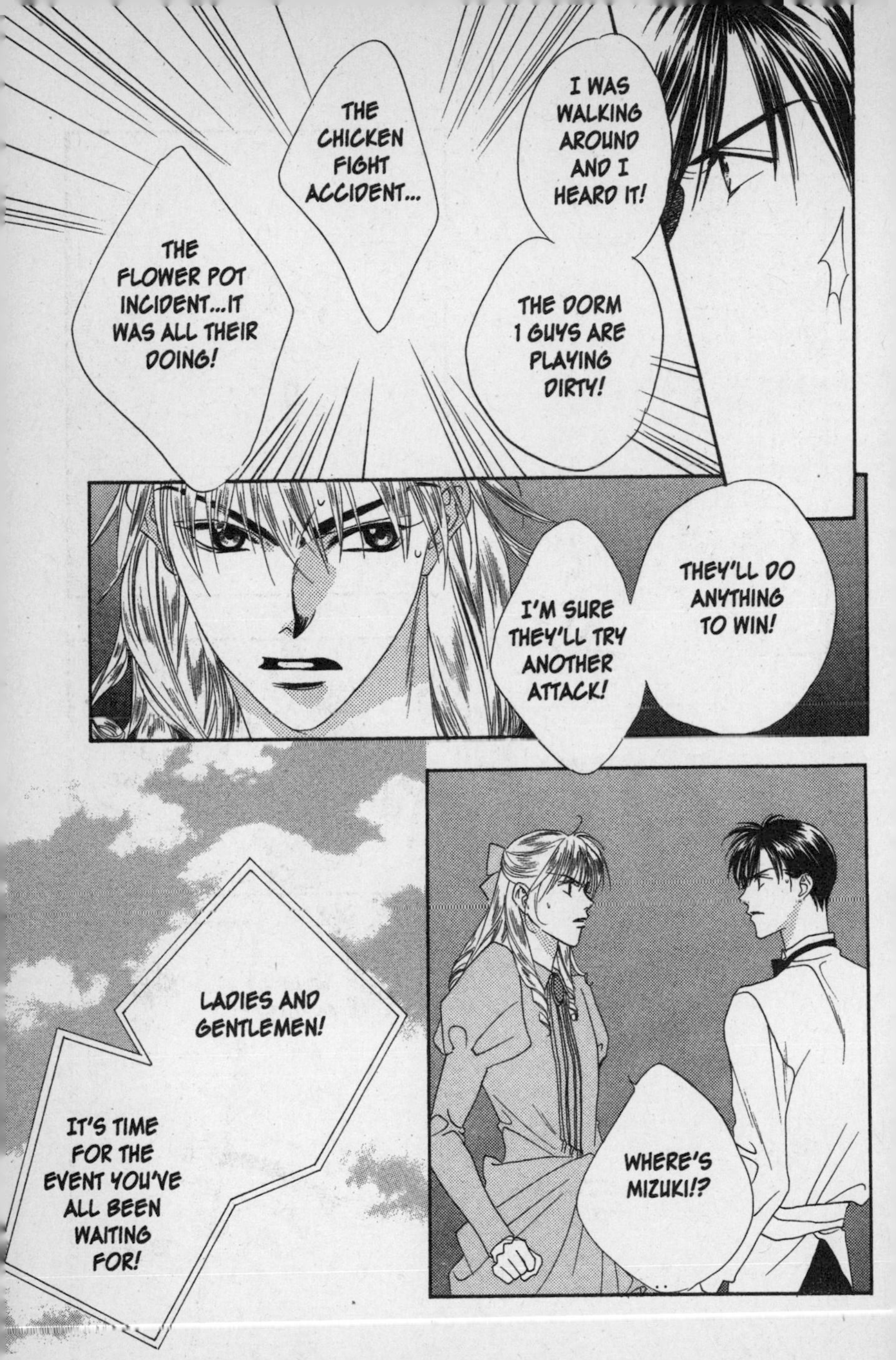
I WAS WALKING AROUND AND I HEARD IT!
THE DORM 1 GUYS ARE PLAYING DIRTY!
THE CHICKEN FIGHT ACCIDENT...
THE FLOWER POT INCIDENT...IT WAS ALL THEIR DOING!
THEY'LL DO ANYTHING TO WIN!
I'M SURE THEY'LL TRY ANOTHER ATTACK!
WHERE'S MIZUKI!?
LADIES AND GENTLEMEN!
IT'S TIME FOR THE EVENT YOU'VE ALL BEEN WAITING FOR!

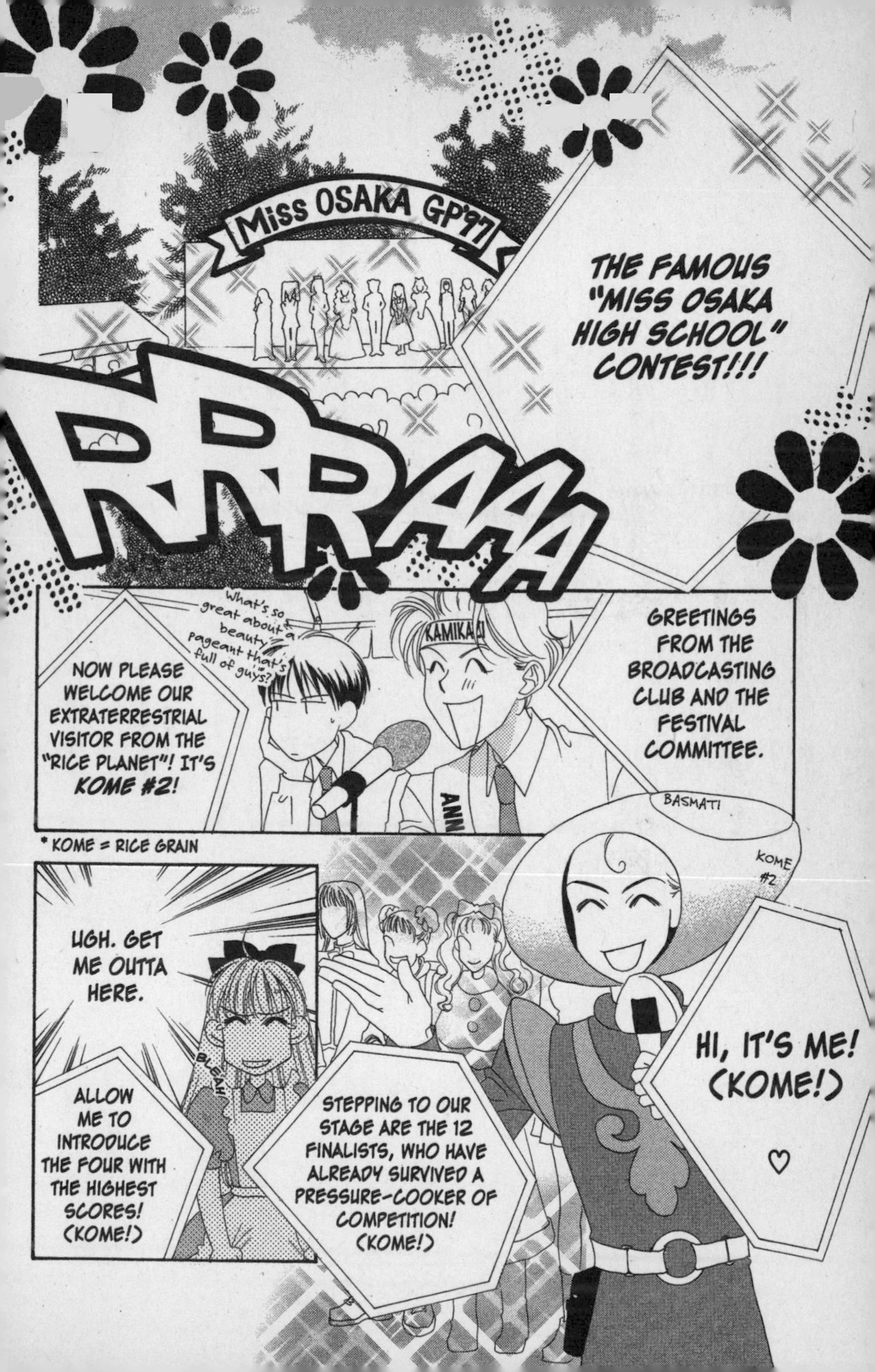
Miss OSAKA GP'97
THE FAMOUS "MISS OSAKA HIGH SCHOOL" CONTEST!!!
RRRAAA
GREETINGS FROM THE BROADCASTING CLUB AND THE FESTIVAL COMMITTEE.
ANN
What's so great about a beauty pageant that's full of guys?
NOW PLEASE WELCOME OUR EXTRATERRESTRIAL VISITOR FROM THE "RICE PLANET"! IT'S KOME #2!
* KOME = RICE GRAIN
BASMATI
KOME #2
HI, IT'S ME! (KOME!) ♡
STEPPING TO OUR STAGE ARE THE 12 FINALISTS, WHO HAVE ALREADY SURVIVED A PRESSURE-COOKER OF COMPETITION! (KOME!)
ALLOW ME TO INTRODUCE THE FOUR WITH THE HIGHEST SCORES! (KOME!)
UGH. GET ME OUTTA HERE.
BLEAH!

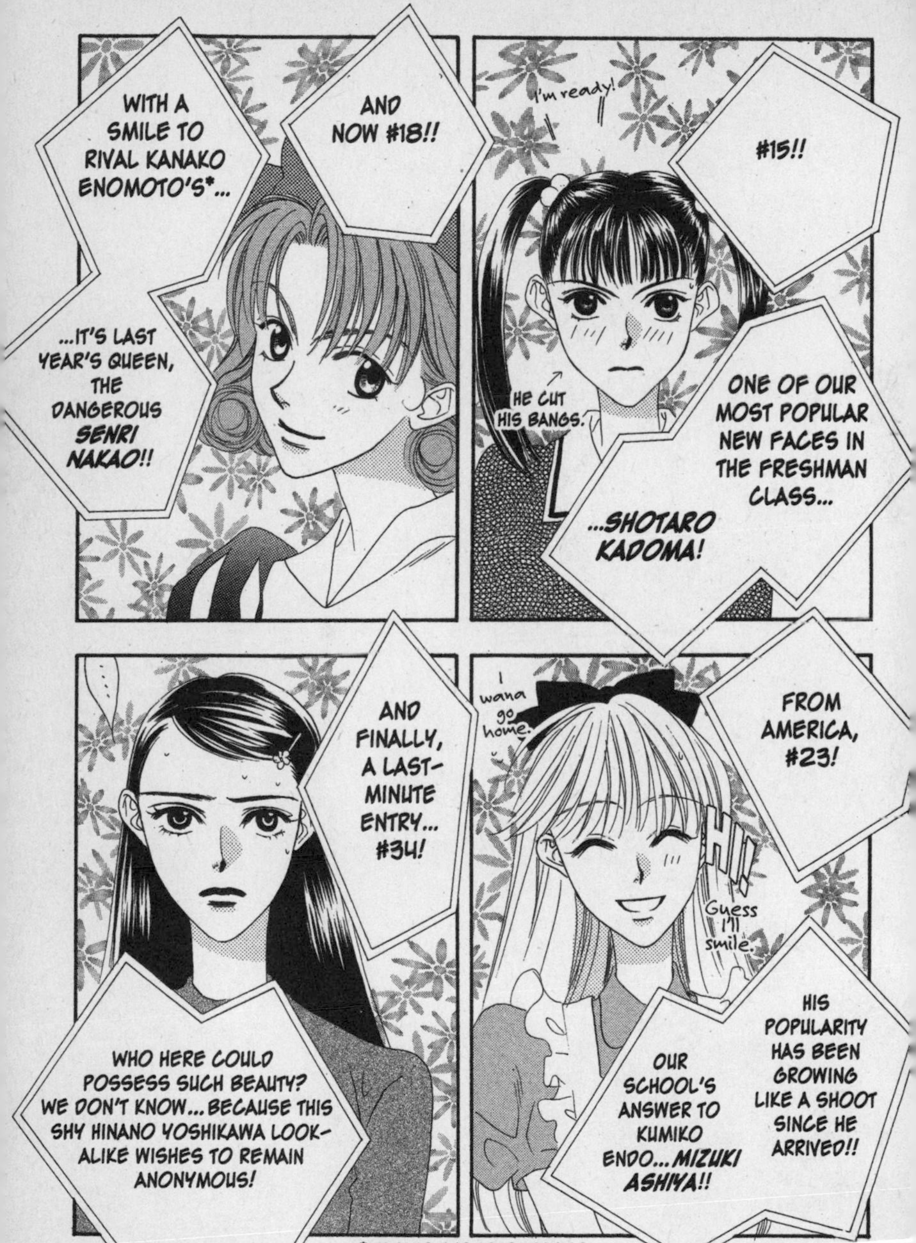
#15!!
I'm ready!
ONE OF OUR MOST POPULAR NEW FACES IN THE FRESHMAN CLASS...
HE CUT HIS BANGS.
...SHOTARO KADOMA!
AND NOW #18!!
WITH A SMILE TO RIVAL KANAKO ENOMOTO'S*...
...IT'S LAST YEAR'S QUEEN, THE DANGEROUS SENRI NAKAO!!
FROM AMERICA, #23!
I wana go home.
HI!
Guess I'll smile.
HIS POPULARITY HAS BEEN GROWING LIKE A SHOOT SINCE HE ARRIVED!!
OUR SCHOOL'S ANSWER TO KUMIKO ENDO... MIZUKI ASHIYA!!
AND FINALLY, A LAST-MINUTE ENTRY... #34!
...
WHO HERE COULD POSSESS SUCH BEAUTY? WE DON'T KNOW... BECAUSE THIS SHY HINANO YOSHIKAWA LOOK-ALIKE WISHES TO REMAIN ANONYMOUS!

* KANAKO ENOMOTO, KUMIKO ENDO AND HINANO YOSHIKAWA ARE JAPANESE ACTRESSES.

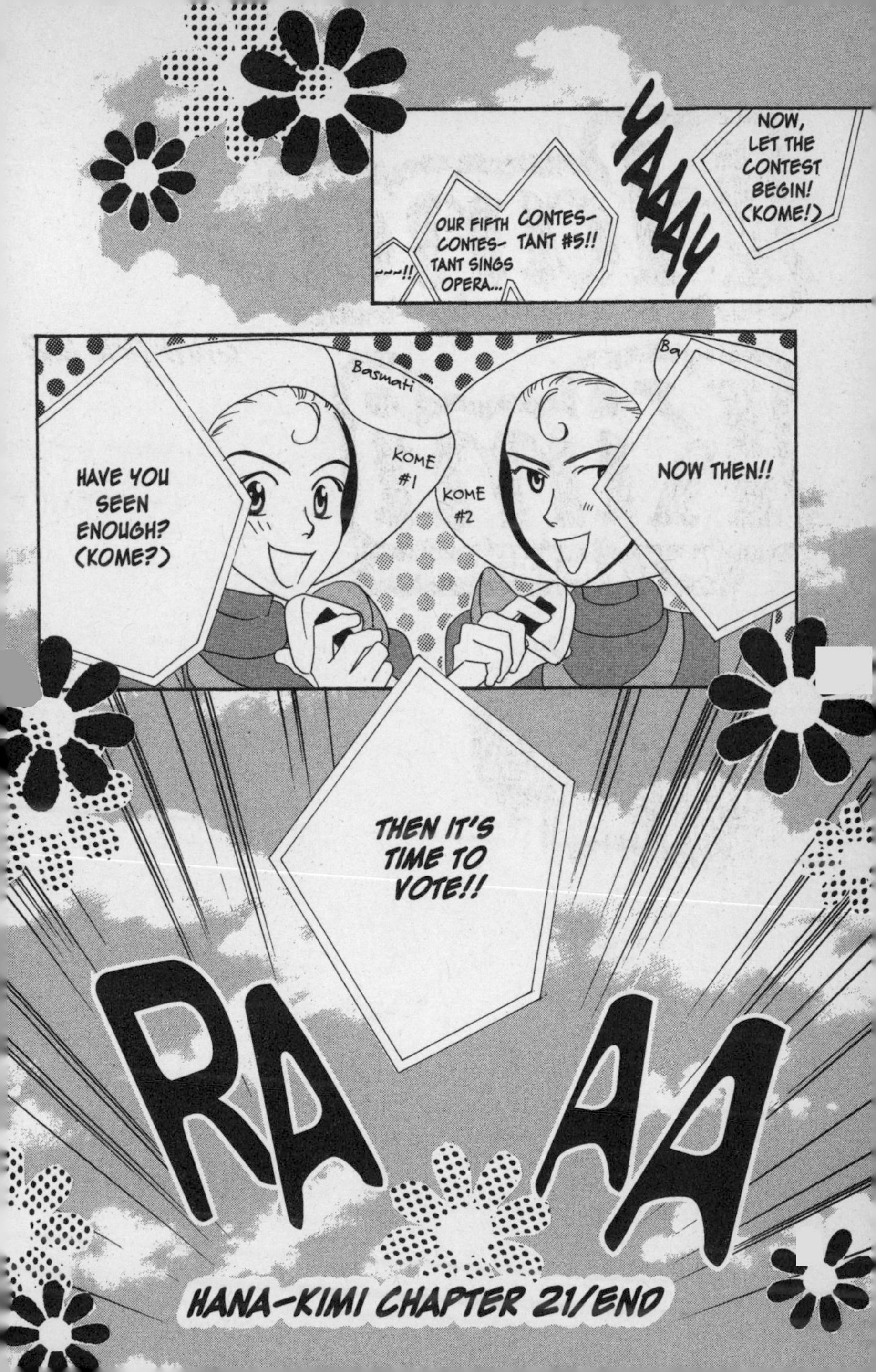
NOW, LET THE CONTEST BEGIN! (KOME!)
YAAAAY
CONTESTANT #5!!
OUR FIFTH CONTESTANT SINGS OPERA...
---!!
NOW THEN!!
Basmati
KOME #1
KOME #2
HAVE YOU SEEN ENOUGH? (KOME?)
THEN IT'S TIME TO VOTE!!
RAAA
HANA-KIMI CHAPTER 21/END

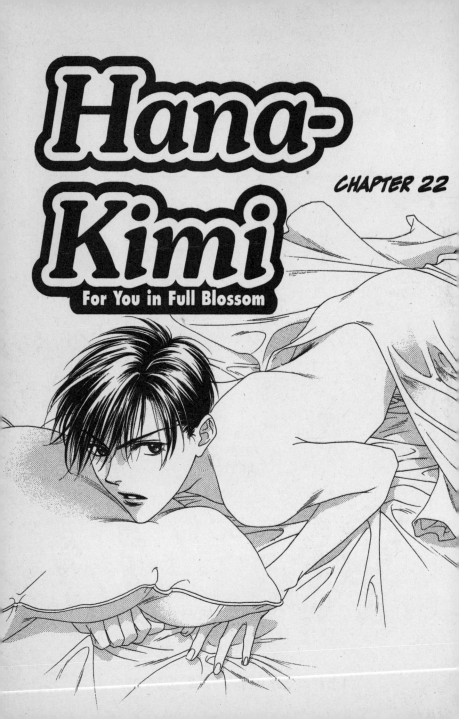

Hana-Kimi

Kimi

For You in Full Blossom

CHAPTER 22

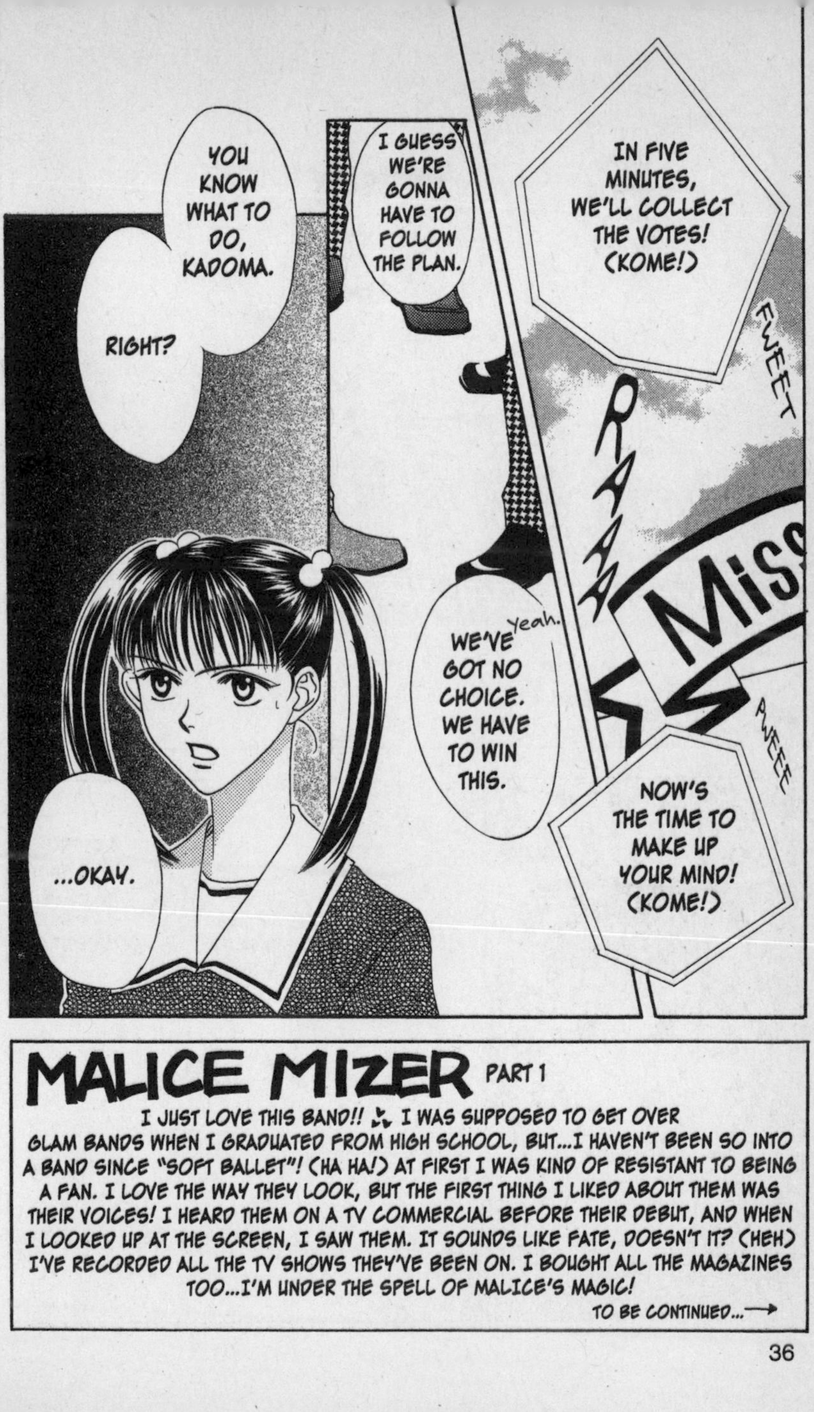
IN FIVE MINUTES, WE'LL COLLECT THE VOTES! (KOME!)
FWEET
RARRA
Miss
PWEEE
NOW'S THE TIME TO MAKE UP YOUR MIND! (KOME!)
I GUESS WE'RE GONNA HAVE TO FOLLOW THE PLAN.
Yeah.
WE'VE GOT NO CHOICE. WE HAVE TO WIN THIS.
YOU KNOW WHAT TO DO, KADOMA.
RIGHT?
...OKAY.

MALICE MIZER PART 1

I JUST LOVE THIS BAND!! I WAS SUPPOSED TO GET OVER GLAM BANDS WHEN I GRADUATED FROM HIGH SCHOOL, BUT...I HAVEN'T BEEN SO INTO A BAND SINCE "SOFT BALLET"! (HA HA!) AT FIRST I WAS KIND OF RESISTANT TO BEING A FAN. I LOVE THE WAY THEY LOOK, BUT THE FIRST THING I LIKED ABOUT THEM WAS THEIR VOICES! I HEARD THEM ON A TV COMMERCIAL BEFORE THEIR DEBUT, AND WHEN I LOOKED UP AT THE SCREEN, I SAW THEM. IT SOUNDS LIKE FATE, DOESN'T IT? (HEH) I'VE RECORDED ALL THE TV SHOWS THEY'VE BEEN ON. I BOUGHT ALL THE MAGAZINES TOO...I'M UNDER THE SPELL OF MALICE'S MAGIC!

TO BE CONTINUED...→

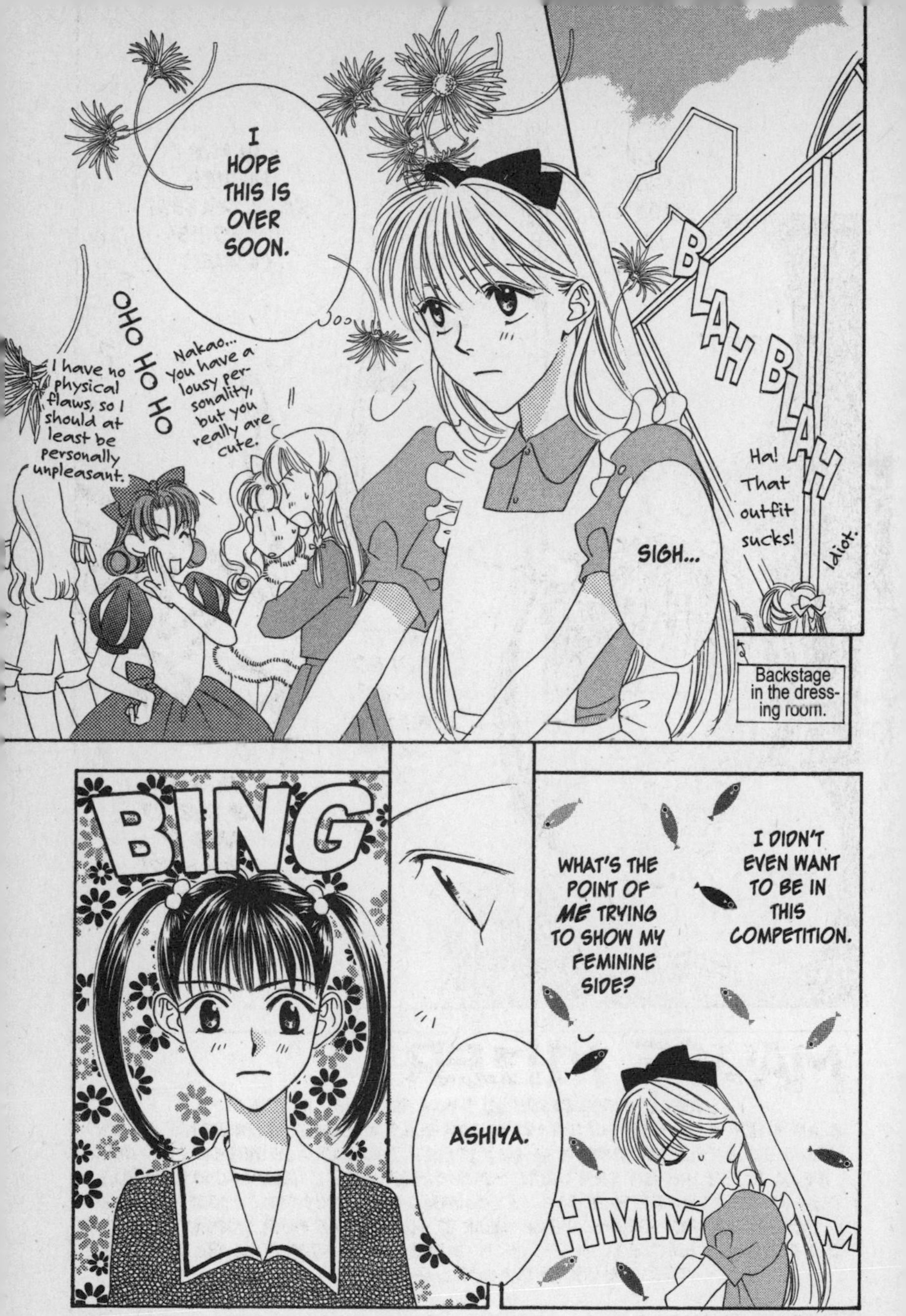
BLAH BLAH BLAH
Ha! That outfit sucks!
Idiot.
Backstage in the dressing room.
SIGH...
I HOPE THIS IS OVER SOON.
Nakao... you have a lousy personality, but you really are cute.
OHO HO HO
I have no physical flaws, so I should at least be personally unpleasant.
I DIDN'T EVEN WANT TO BE IN THIS COMPETITION.
WHAT'S THE POINT OF ME TRYING TO SHOW MY FEMININE SIDE?
HMMMM
ASHIYA.
BING

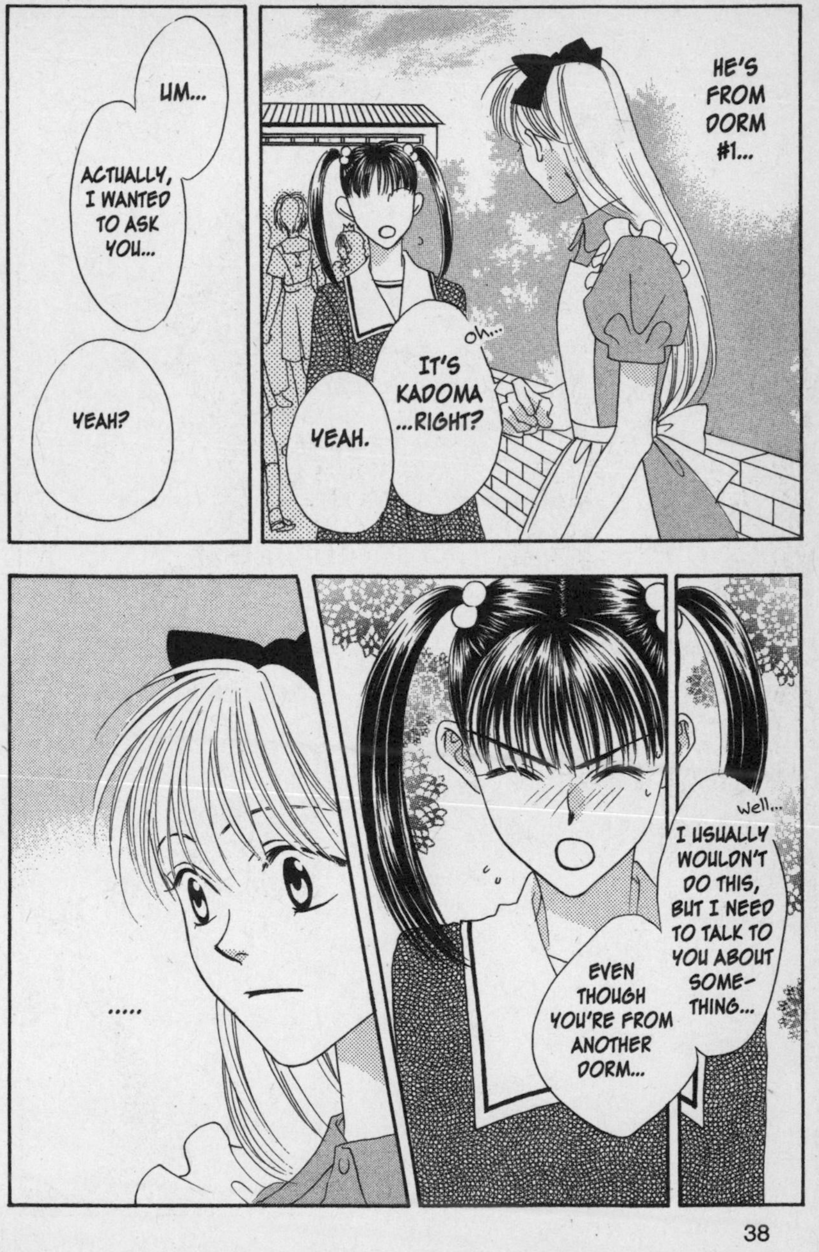
HE'S FROM DORM #1...
oh...
IT'S KADOMA ...RIGHT?
YEAH.
UM...
ACTUALLY, I WANTED TO ASK YOU...
YEAH?
well...
I USUALLY WOULDN'T DO THIS, BUT I NEED TO TALK TO YOU ABOUT SOME-THING...
EVEN THOUGH YOU'RE FROM ANOTHER DORM...
.....

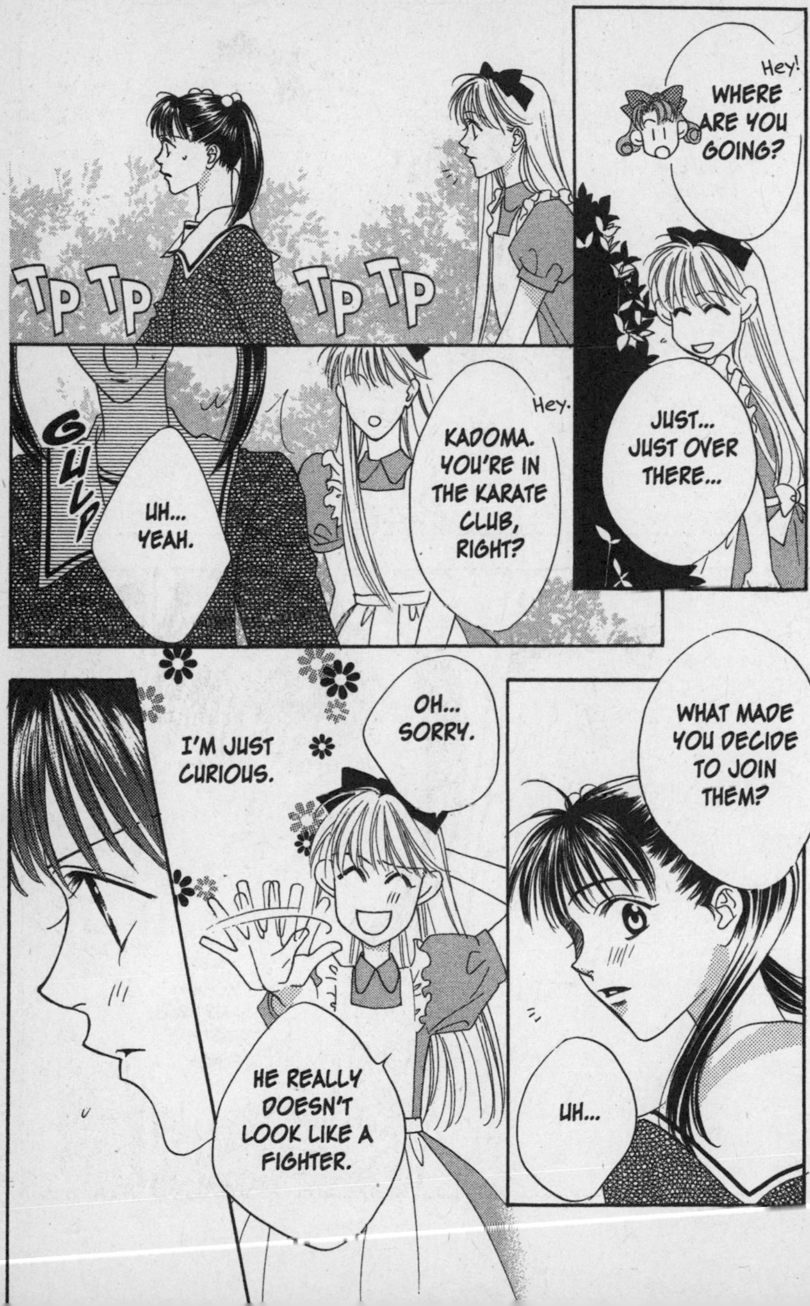
Hey!
WHERE ARE YOU GOING?
JUST... JUST OVER THERE...
TP TP
TP TP
Hey.
KADOMA. YOU'RE IN THE KARATE CLUB, RIGHT?
GULP
UH... YEAH.
WHAT MADE YOU DECIDE TO JOIN THEM?
UH...
OH... SORRY.
I'M JUST CURIOUS.
HE REALLY DOESN'T LOOK LIKE A FIGHTER.

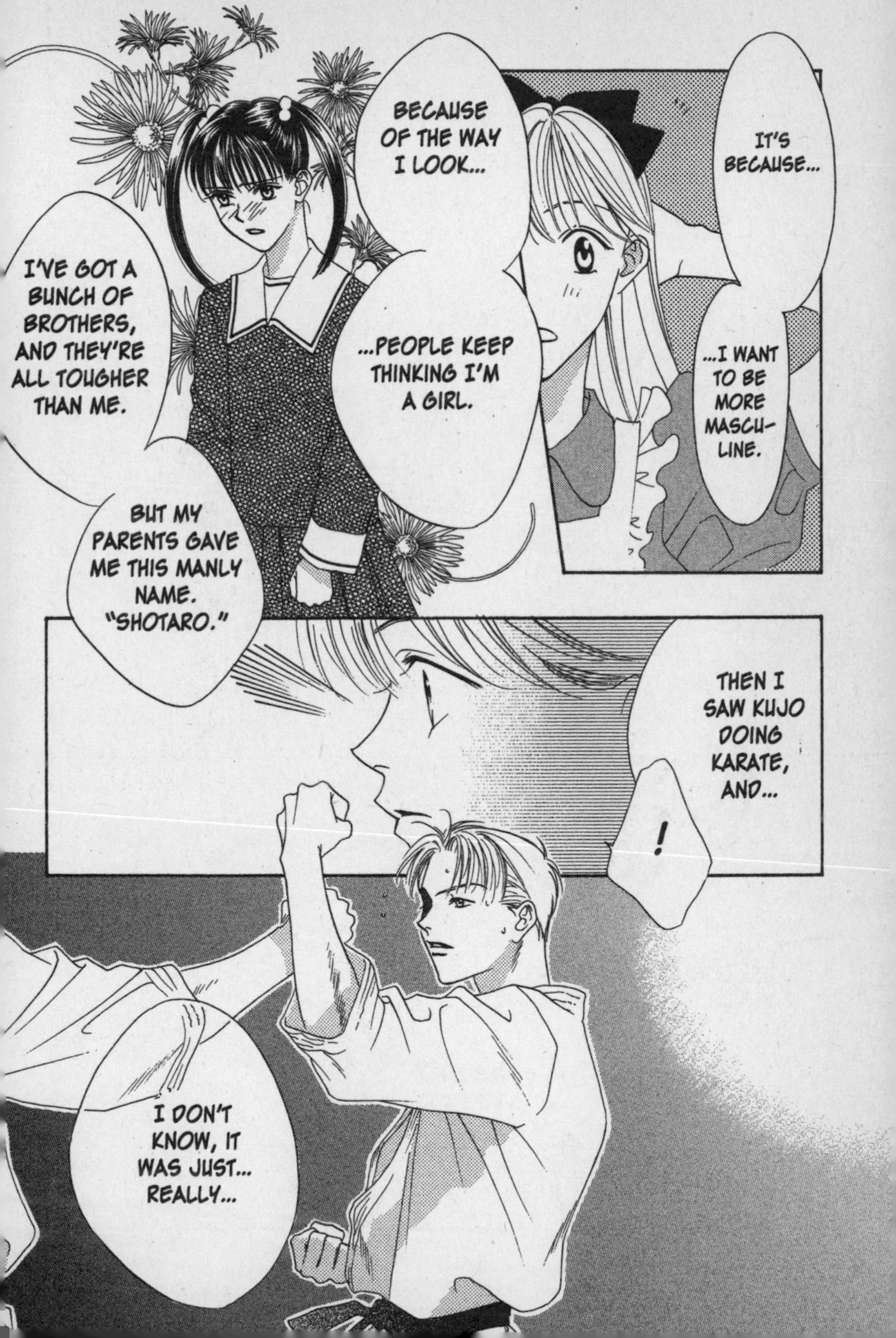
IT'S BECAUSE...
...I WANT TO BE MORE MASCU-LINE.
BECAUSE OF THE WAY I LOOK...
...PEOPLE KEEP THINKING I'M A GIRL.
I'VE GOT A BUNCH OF BROTHERS, AND THEY'RE ALL TOUGHER THAN ME.
BUT MY PARENTS GAVE ME THIS MANLY NAME. "SHOTARO."
THEN I SAW KUJO DOING KARATE, AND...
!
I DON'T KNOW, IT WAS JUST... REALLY...

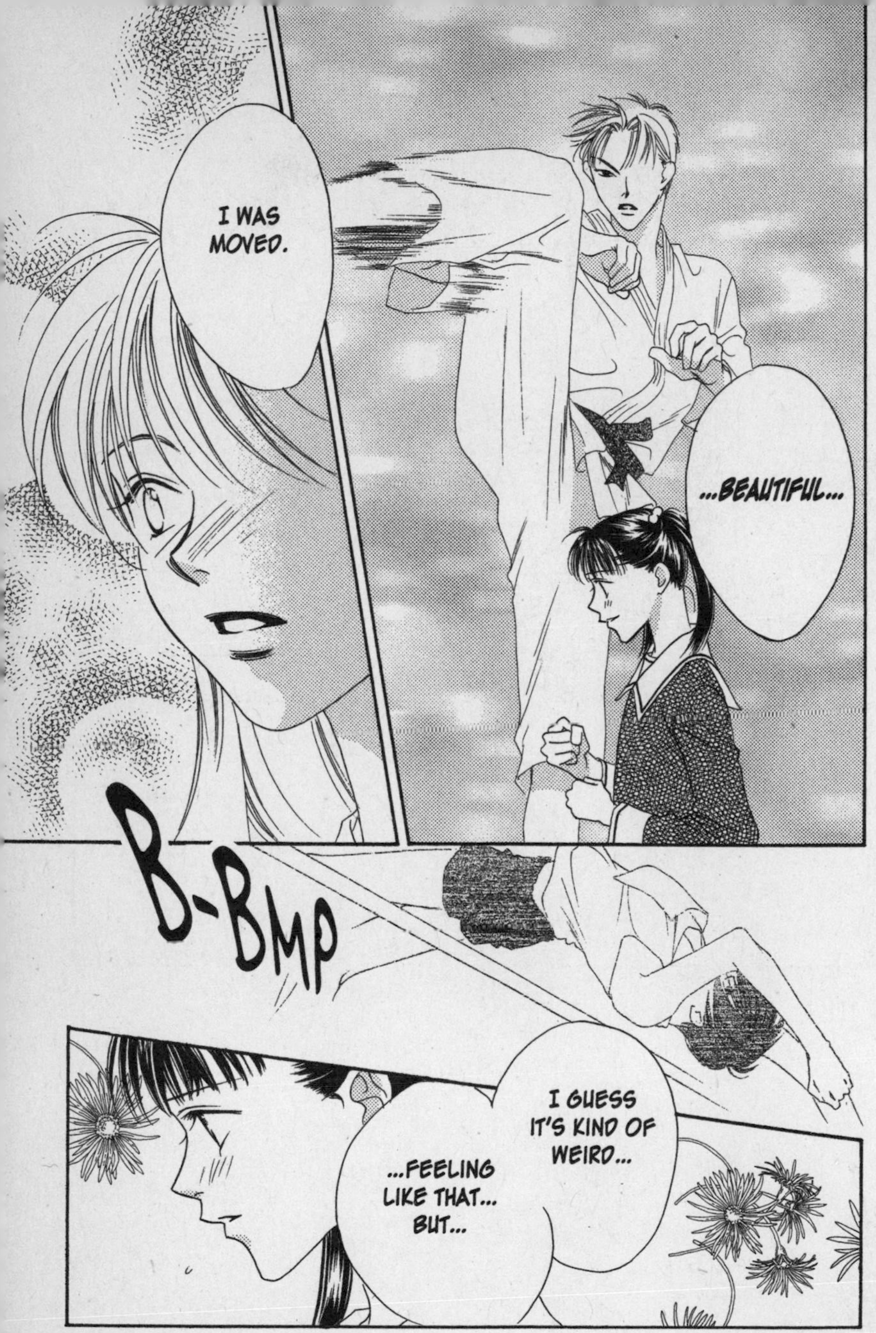
...BEAUTIFUL...
I WAS MOVED.
B-BMP
I GUESS IT'S KIND OF WEIRD...
...FEELING LIKE THAT... BUT...

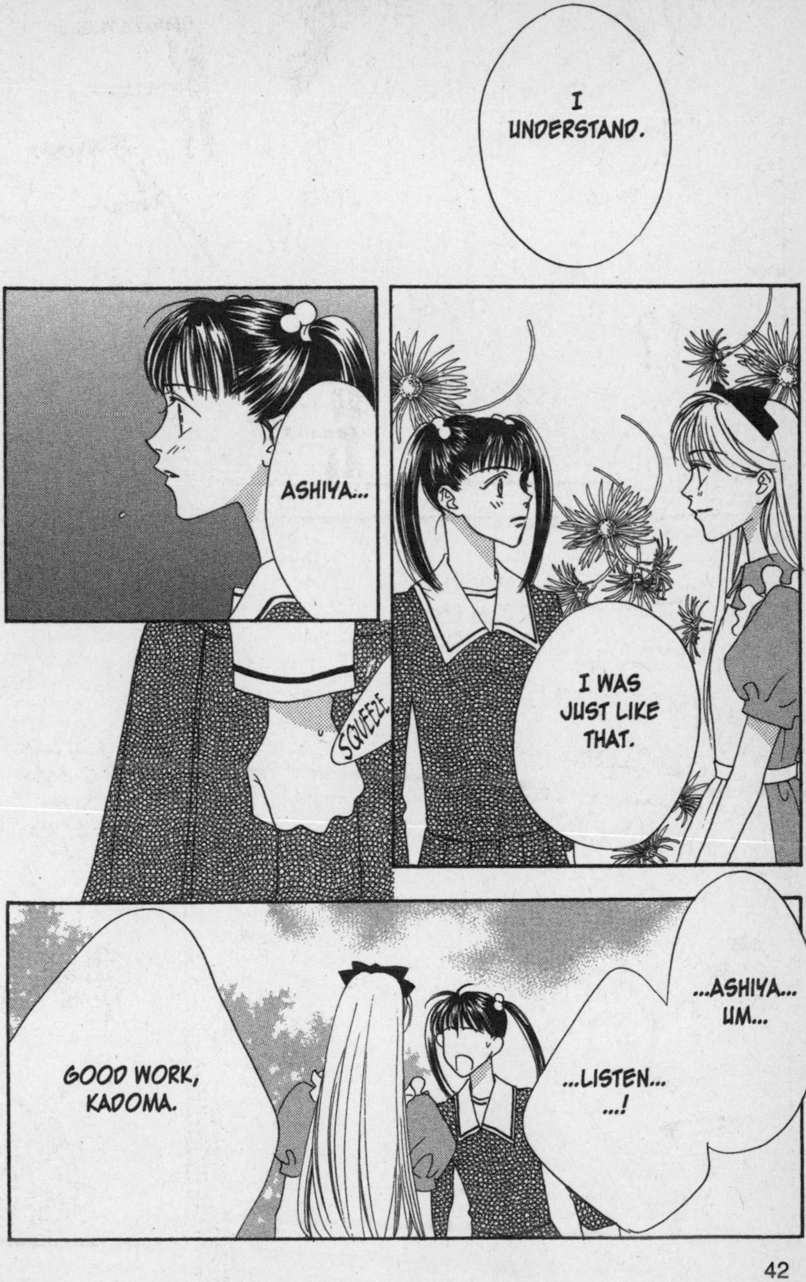
I UNDERSTAND.
I WAS JUST LIKE THAT.
ASHIYA...
SQUEEZE
...ASHIYA... UM...
...LISTEN... ...!
GOOD WORK, KADOMA.

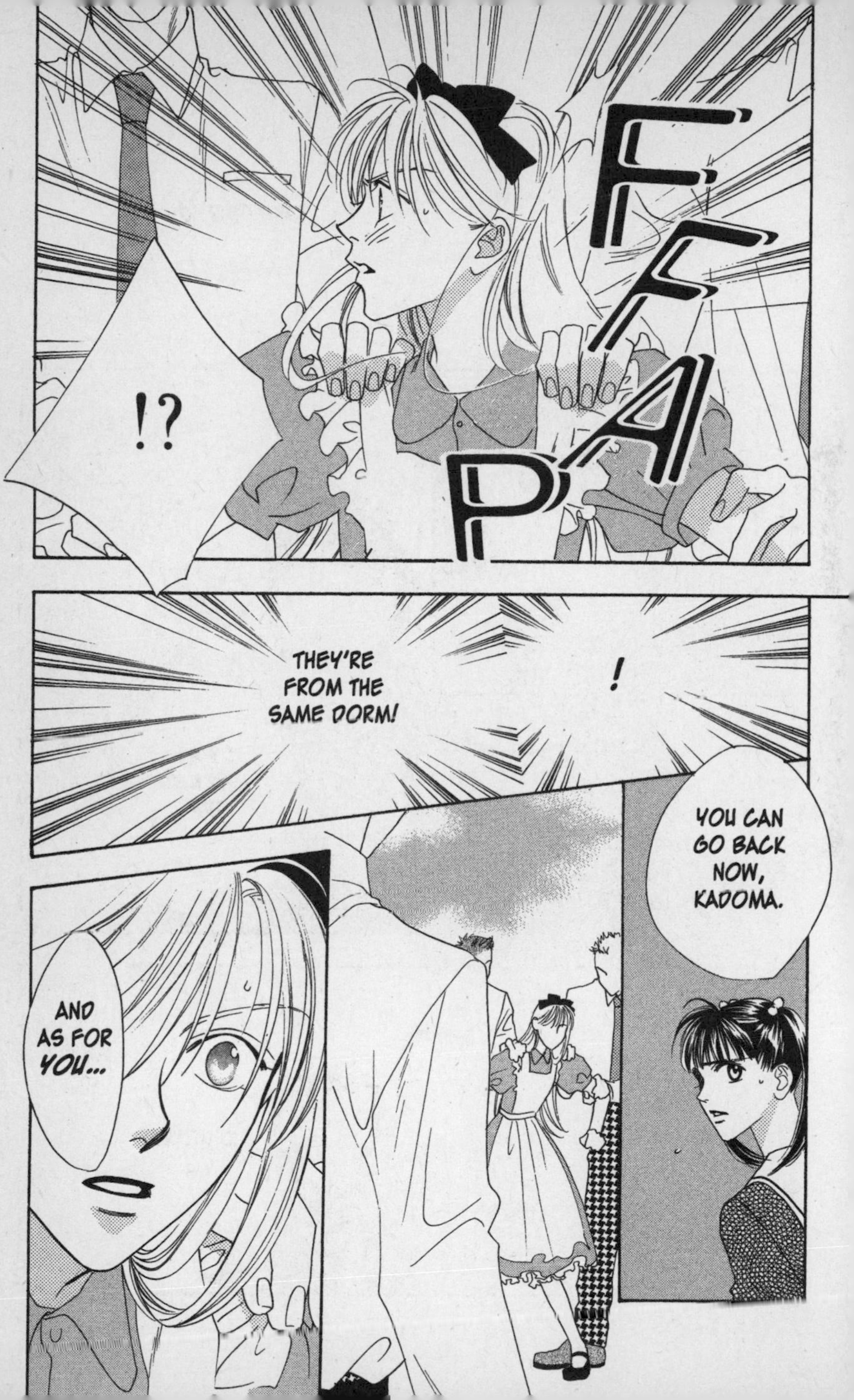
FFAP
!?
!
THEY'RE FROM THE SAME DORM!
YOU CAN GO BACK NOW, KADOMA.
AND AS FOR YOU...

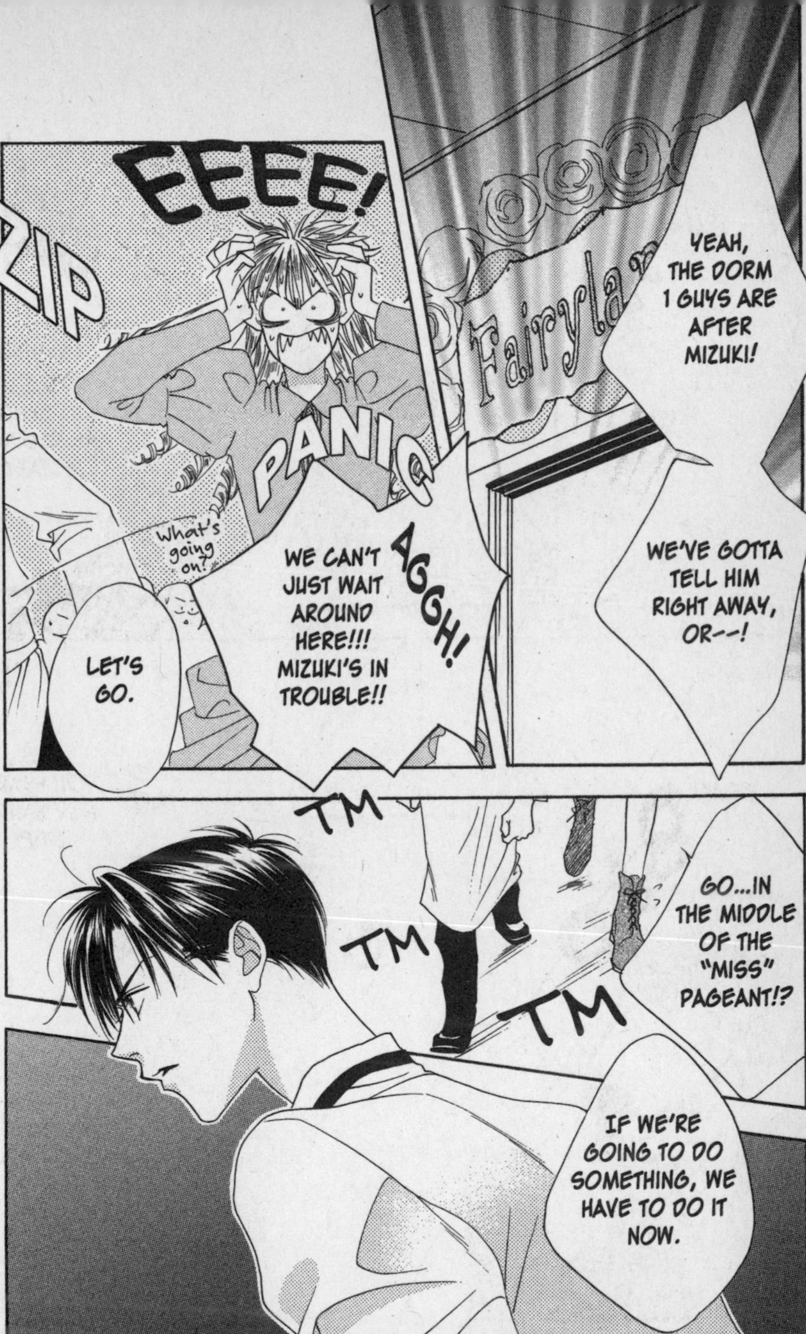
YEAH, THE DORM 1 GUYS ARE AFTER MIZUKI!
WE'VE GOTTA TELL HIM RIGHT AWAY, OR--!
EEEE!
ZIP
PANIC
AGGH!
WE CAN'T JUST WAIT AROUND HERE!!! MIZUKI'S IN TROUBLE!!
What's going on?
LET'S GO.
GO...IN THE MIDDLE OF THE "MISS" PAGEANT!?
TM
TM
TM
IF WE'RE GOING TO DO SOMETHING, WE HAVE TO DO IT NOW.

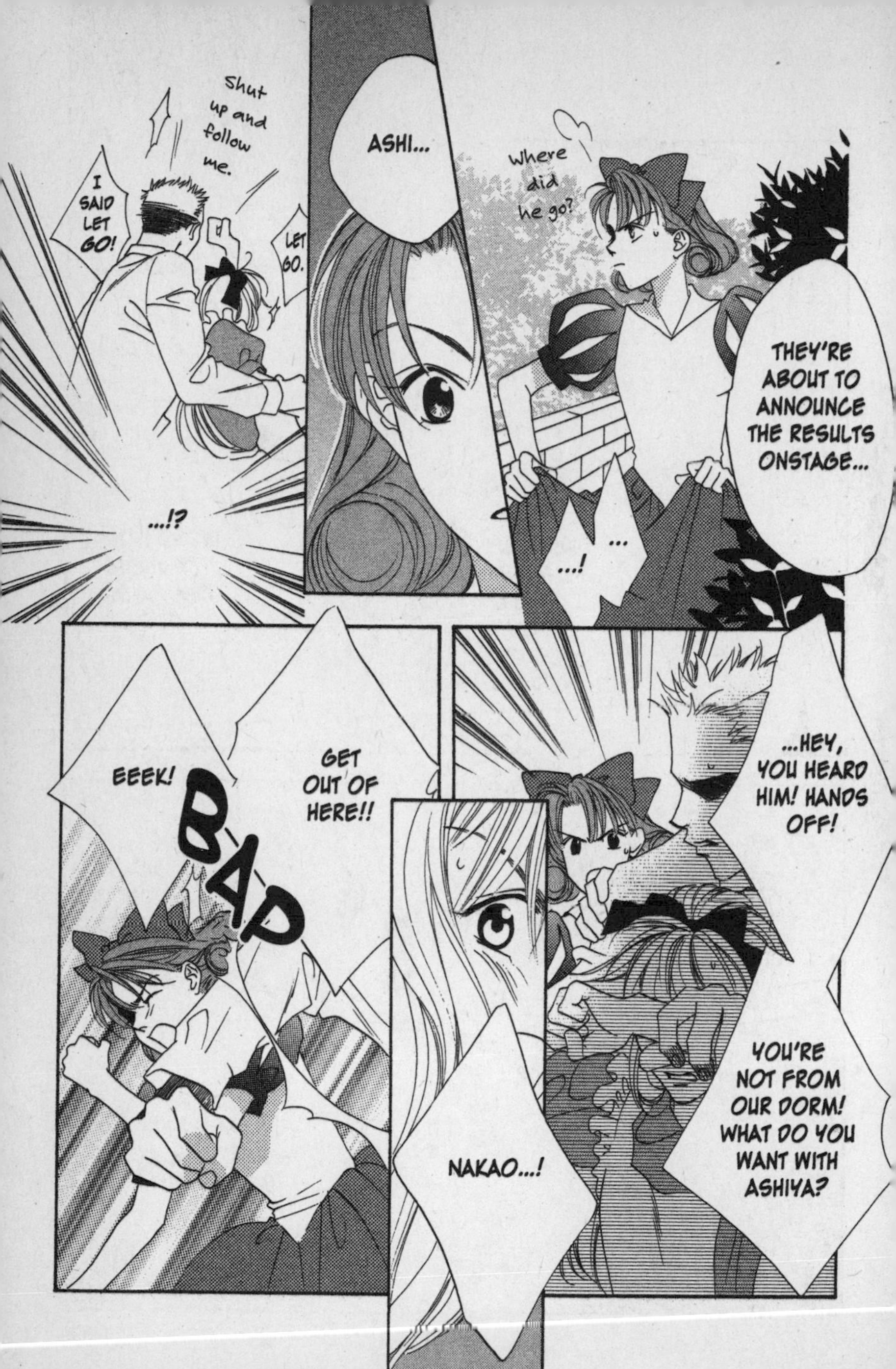
Where did he go?
THEY'RE ABOUT TO ANNOUNCE THE RESULTS ONSTAGE...
...
...!
ASHI...
Shut up and follow me.
LET GO.
I SAID LET GO!
...!?
...HEY, YOU HEARD HIM! HANDS OFF!
YOU'RE NOT FROM OUR DORM! WHAT DO YOU WANT WITH ASHIYA?
NAKAO...!
GET OUT OF HERE!!
EEEK!
BAP

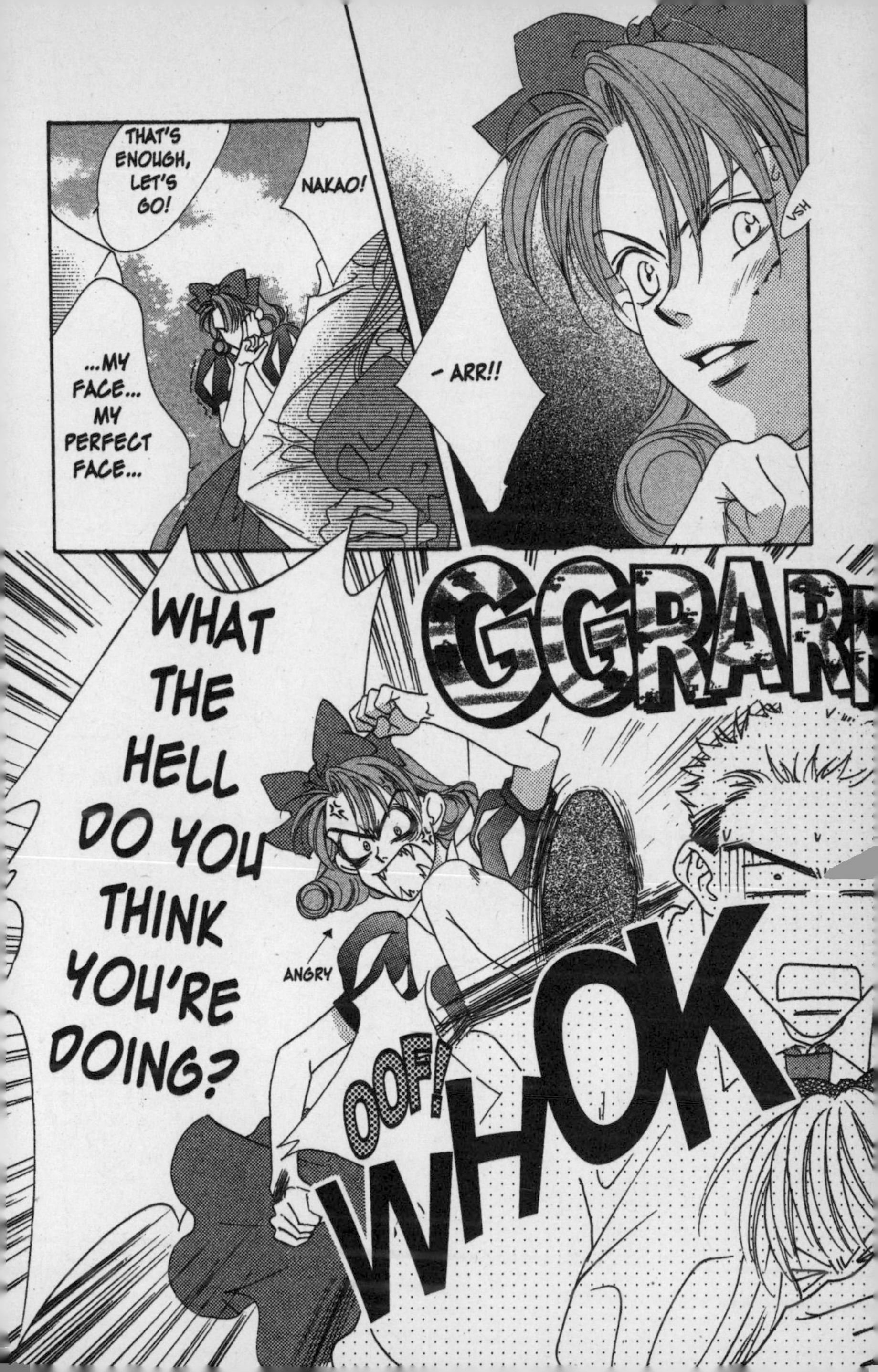
VSH
- ARR!!
NAKAO!
THAT'S ENOUGH, LET'S GO!
...MY FACE... MY PERFECT FACE...
GGRAR
WHAT THE HELL DO YOU THINK YOU'RE DOING?
ANGRY
WHOK
OOF!

WHISPERED SECRETS

SANO THE GIGOLO?

THE SECOND SEXY SHOT IN THIS VOLUME OF HANA-KIMI IS OF SANO (PAGE 35). I DON'T KNOW IF IT WORKS, BUT WHEN I DRAW HIM, I USUALLY TRY TO MAKE HIM LOOK SEXY. WHY? WELL, IZUMI IS KIND OF A SECRET PERVERT, YOU KNOW. (HA HA!) ONE OF MY FRIENDS WHO SAW THAT PAGE LAUGHED, "IT WOULD LOOK REALLY SCARY IF THERE WERE $100 BILLS SCATTERED ALL OVER." WHEN I TOLD ANOTHER FRIEND SHE SAID, "IF THERE WERE A PAIR OF GLASSES SITTING ON THE SHEETS, THEN IT WOULD LOOK LIKE SANO WAS A PROSTITUTE." I SAID, "YOU GUYS ARE EVIL." ...BUT I COULDN'T STOP LAUGHING.

Who would his customer be, Umeda?

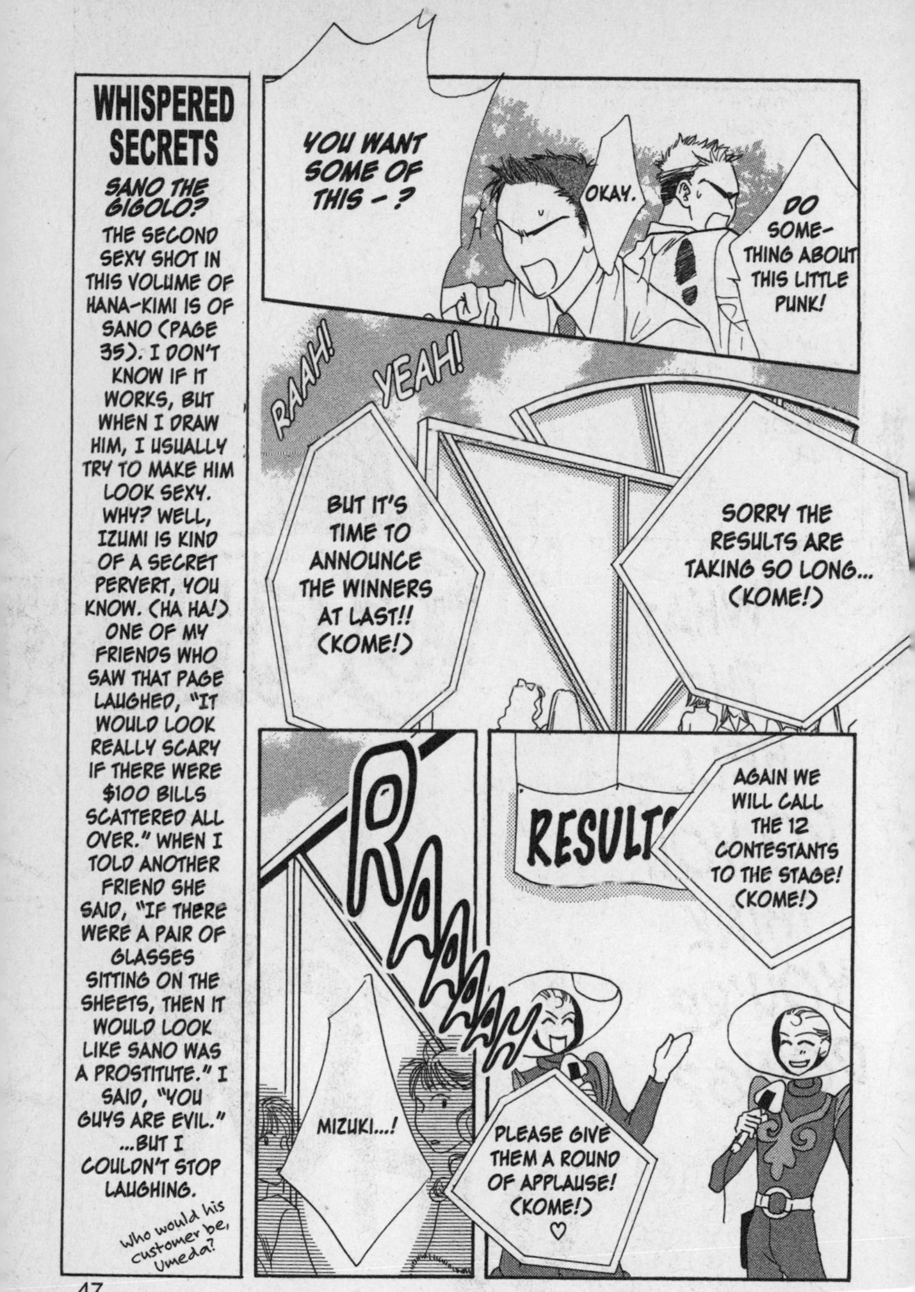
DO SOMETHING ABOUT THIS LITTLE PUNK!
OKAY.
YOU WANT SOME OF THIS - ?
YEAH!
RAAH!
SORRY THE RESULTS ARE TAKING SO LONG... (KOME!)
BUT IT'S TIME TO ANNOUNCE THE WINNERS AT LAST!! (KOME!)
RESULTS
AGAIN WE WILL CALL THE 12 CONTESTANTS TO THE STAGE! (KOME!)
PLEASE GIVE THEM A ROUND OF APPLAUSE! (KOME!) ♡
RAAAAY
MIZUKI...!

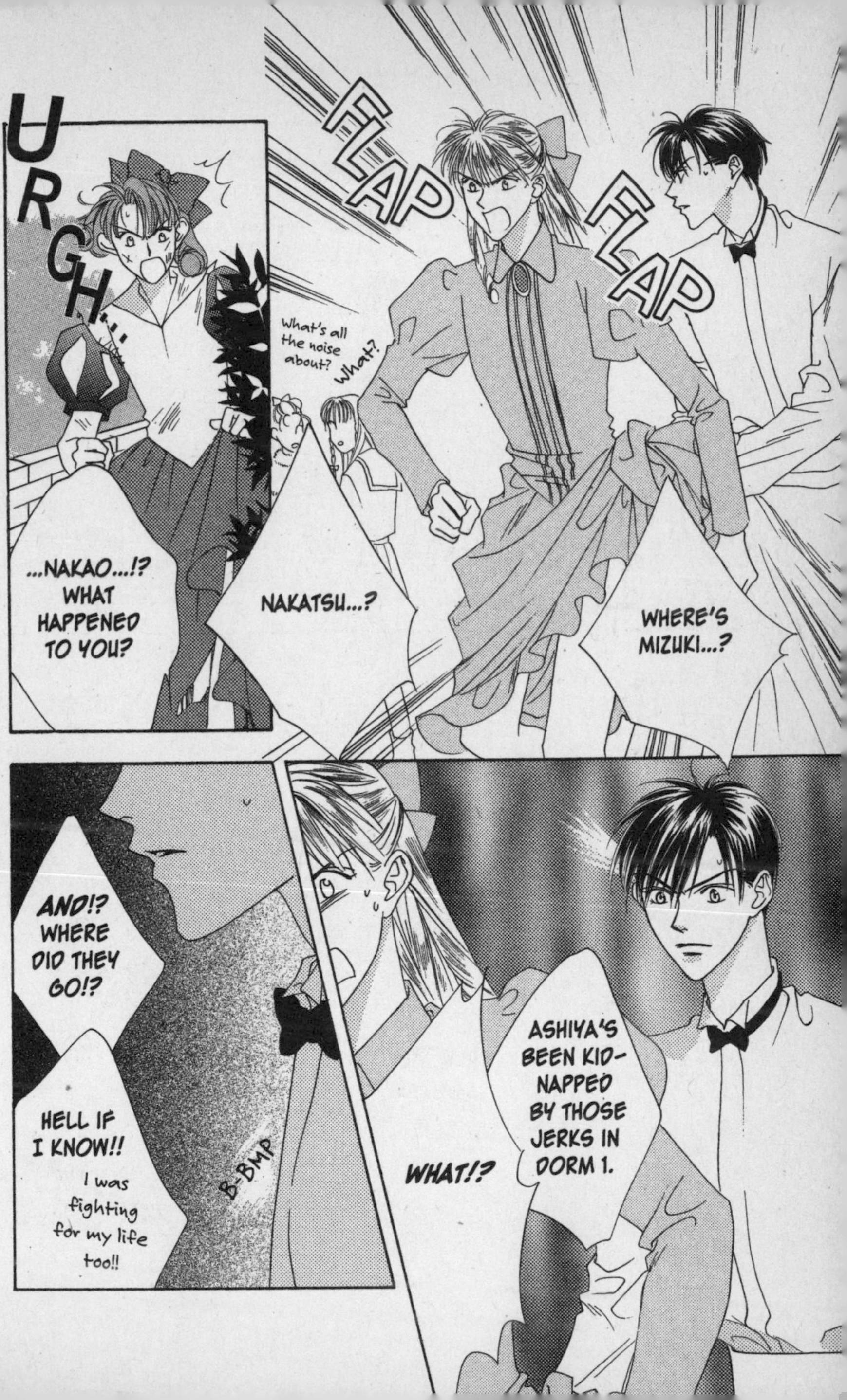
FLAP
FLAP
WHERE'S MIZUKI...?
NAKATSU...?
What?
What's all the noise about?
URGH...
...NAKAO...!? WHAT HAPPENED TO YOU?
ASHIYA'S BEEN KID-NAPPED BY THOSE JERKS IN DORM 1.
WHAT!?
B-BMP
AND!? WHERE DID THEY GO!?
HELL IF I KNOW!!
I was fighting for my life too!!

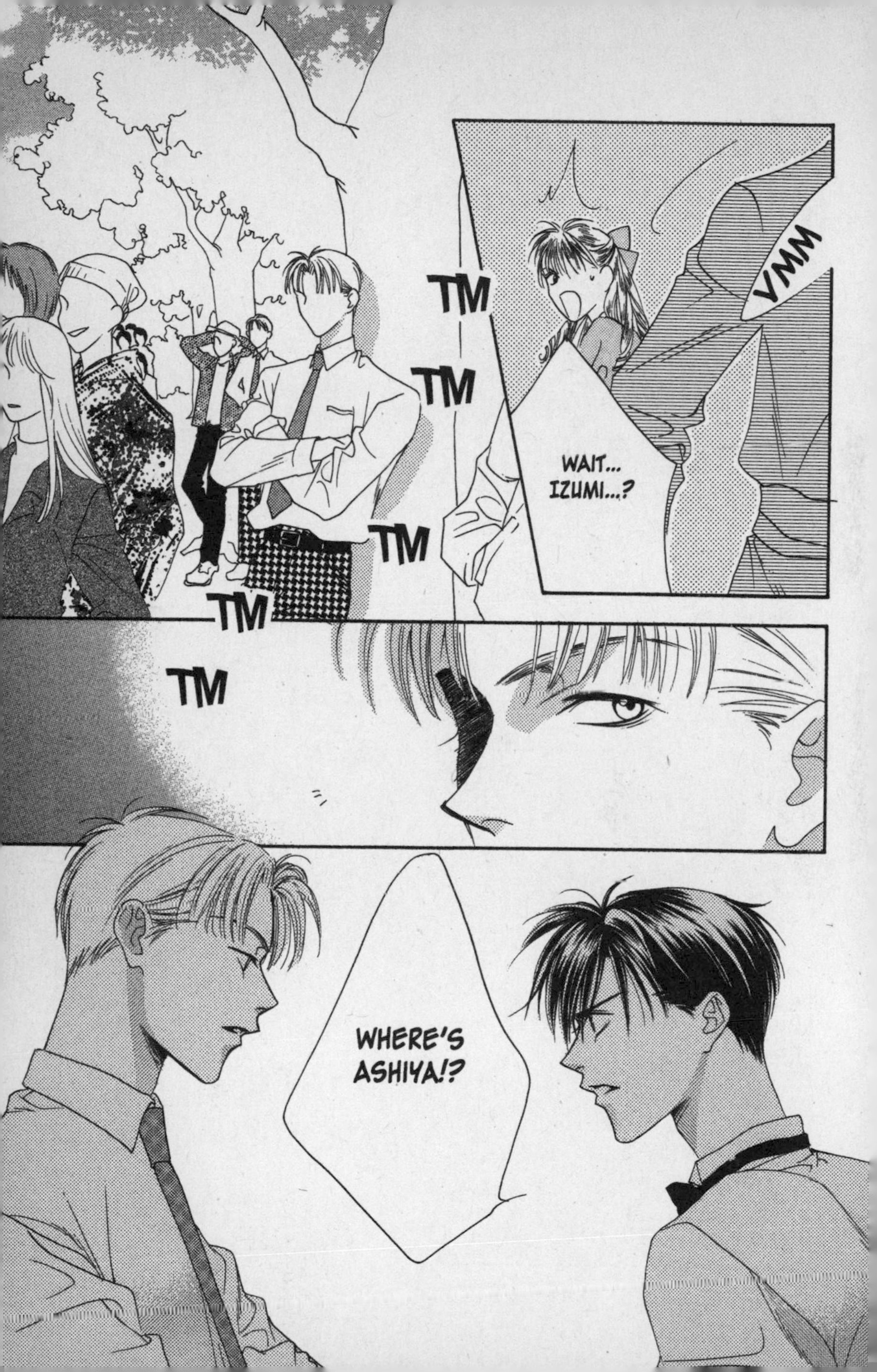
YMM
WAIT... IZUMI...?
TM
TM
TM
TM
TM
WHERE'S ASHIYA!?

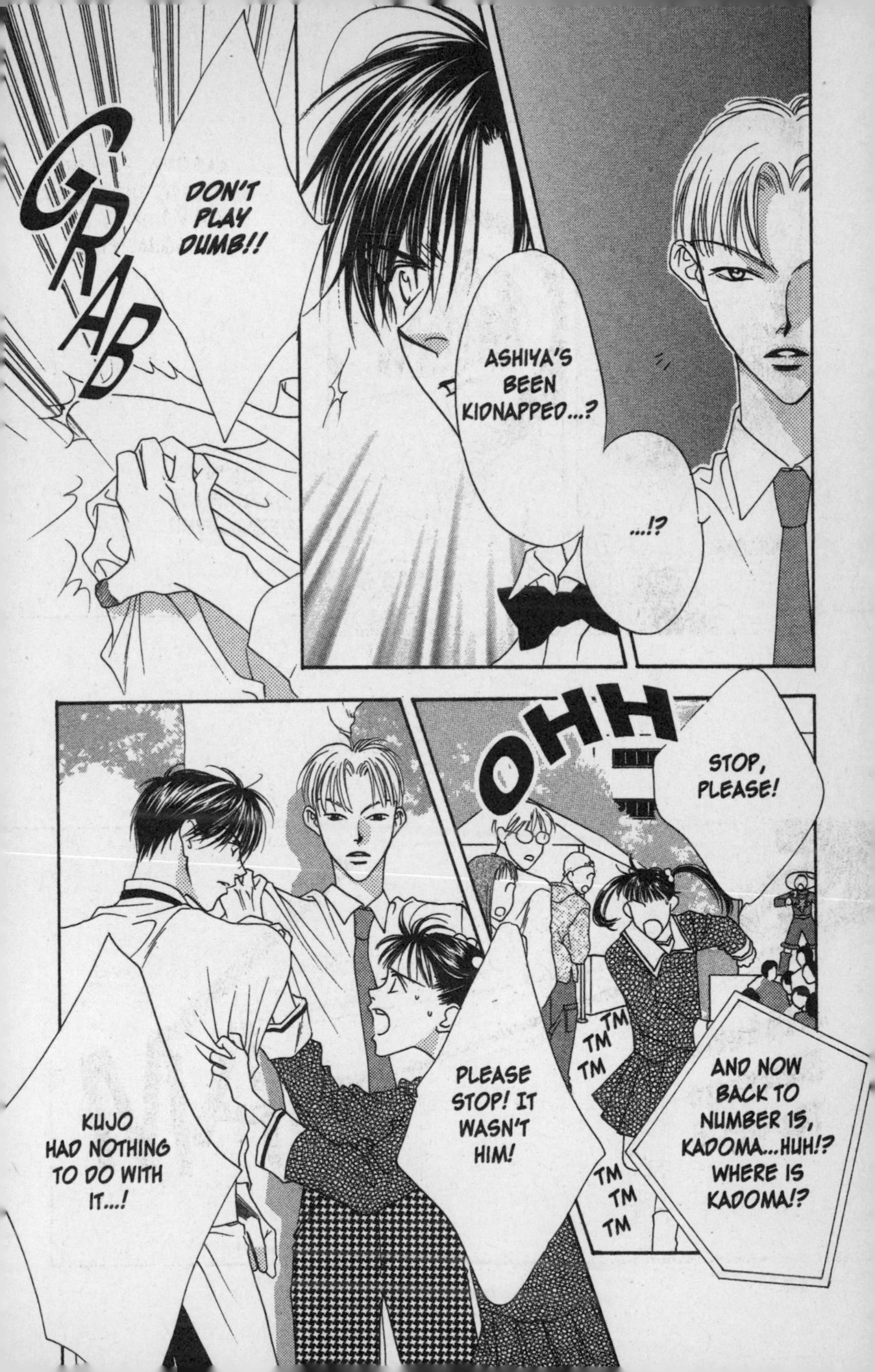
ASHIYA'S BEEN KIDNAPPED...?
...!?
GRAB
DON'T PLAY DUMB!!
OHH
STOP, PLEASE!
AND NOW BACK TO NUMBER 15, KADOMA...HUH!? WHERE IS KADOMA!?
TM TM TM
TM TM TM
PLEASE STOP! IT WASN'T HIM!
KUJO HAD NOTHING TO DO WITH IT...!

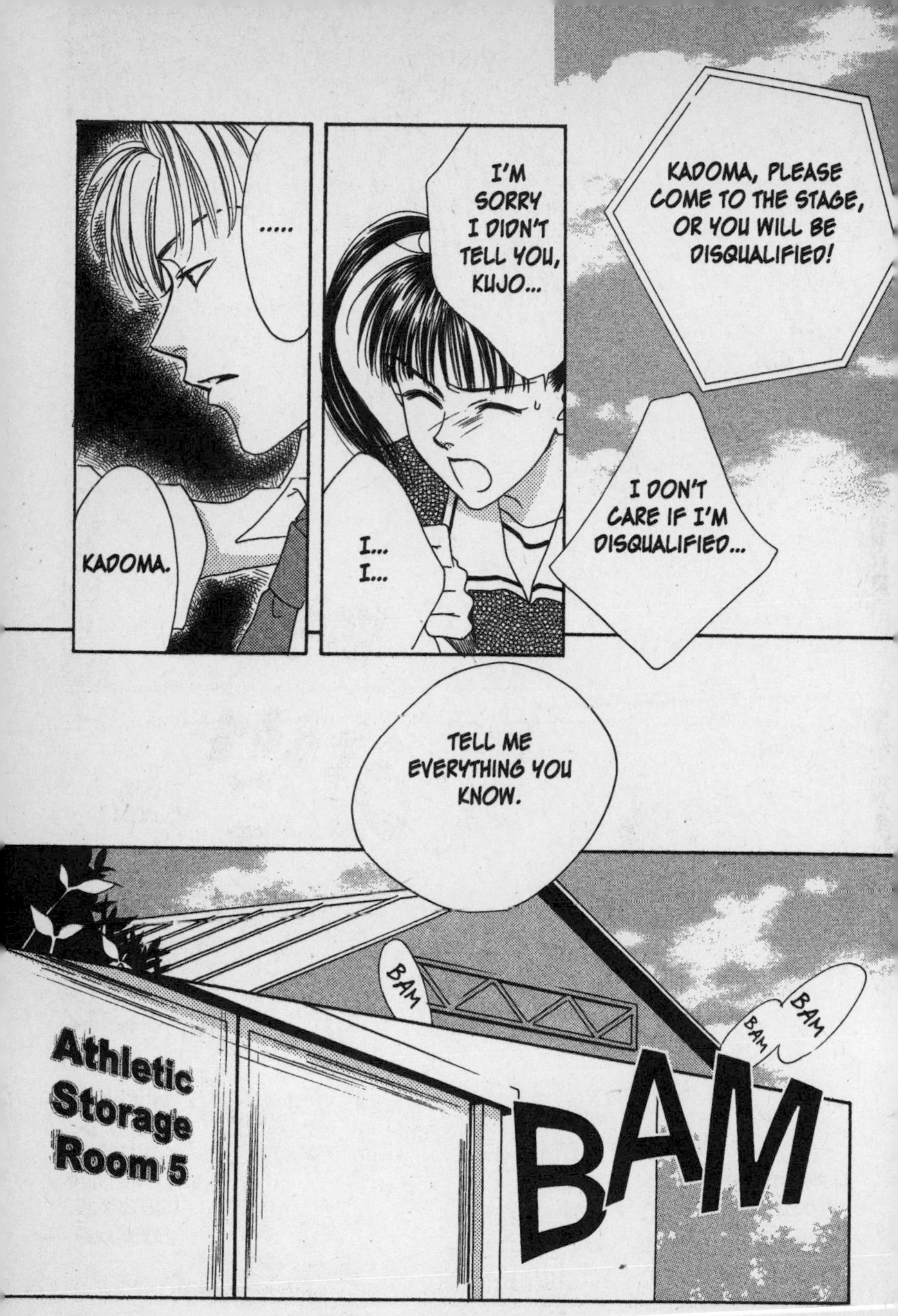
KADOMA, PLEASE COME TO THE STAGE, OR YOU WILL BE DISQUALIFIED!
I'M SORRY I DIDN'T TELL YOU, KUJO...
I... I...
.....
KADOMA.
I DON'T CARE IF I'M DISQUALIFIED...
TELL ME EVERYTHING YOU KNOW.
Athletic Storage Room 5
BAM
BAM
BAM
BAM

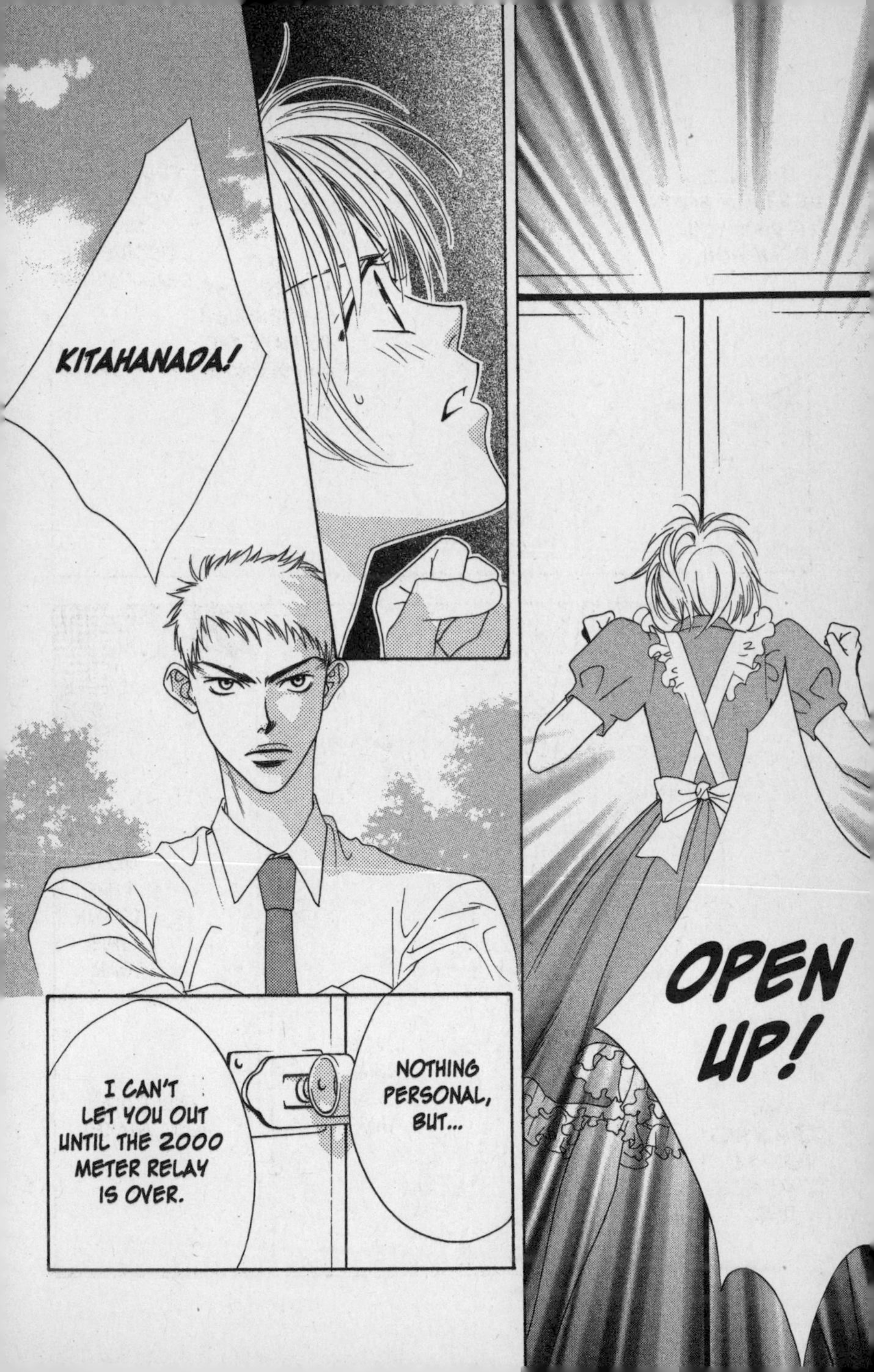
OPEN UP!
KITAHANADA!
NOTHING PERSONAL, BUT...
I CAN'T LET YOU OUT UNTIL THE 2000 METER RELAY IS OVER.

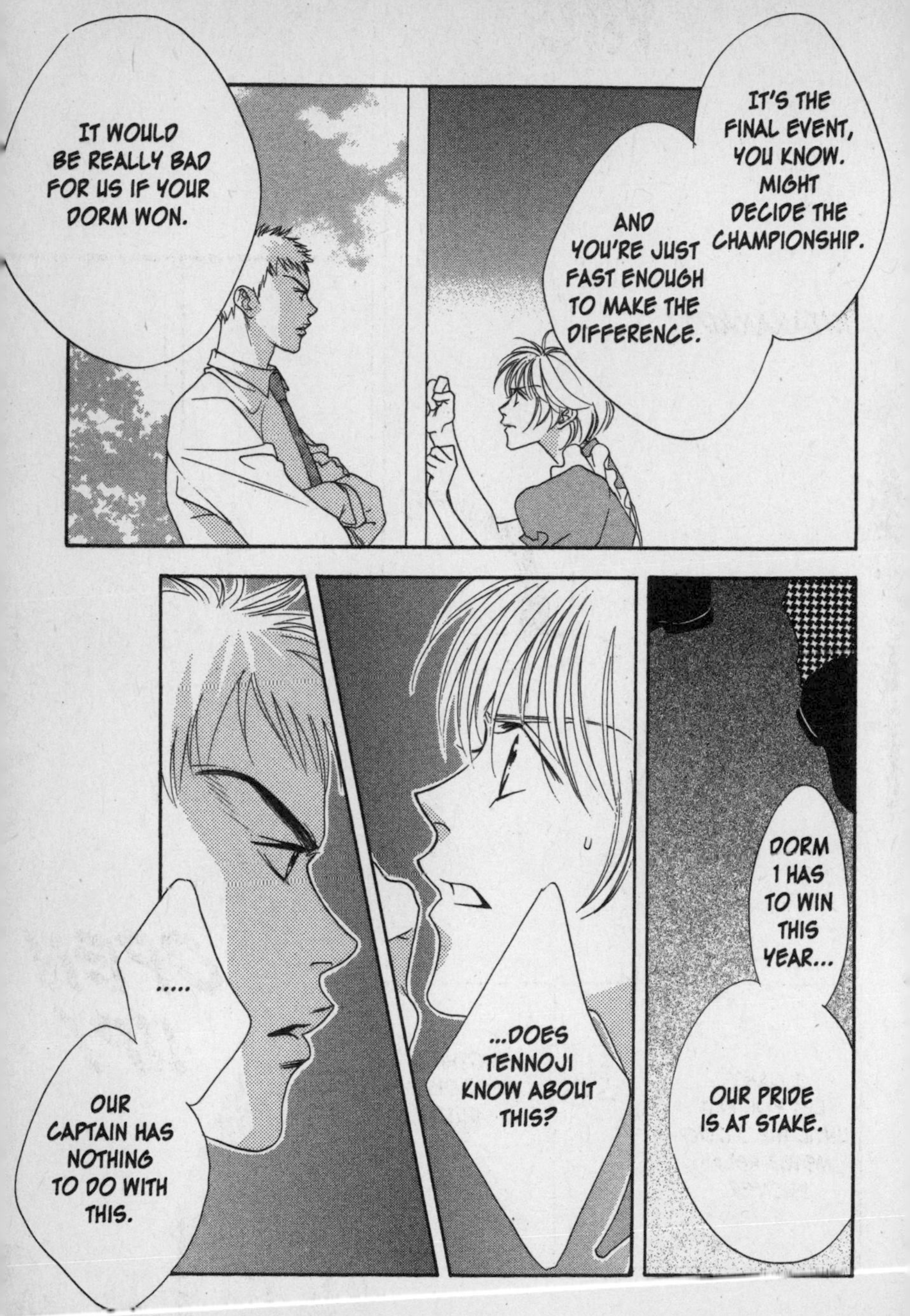
IT'S THE FINAL EVENT, YOU KNOW. MIGHT DECIDE THE CHAMPIONSHIP.
AND YOU'RE JUST FAST ENOUGH TO MAKE THE DIFFERENCE.
IT WOULD BE REALLY BAD FOR US IF YOUR DORM WON.
DORM 1 HAS TO WIN THIS YEAR...
OUR PRIDE IS AT STAKE.
...DOES TENNOJI KNOW ABOUT THIS?
.....
OUR CAPTAIN HAS NOTHING TO DO WITH THIS.

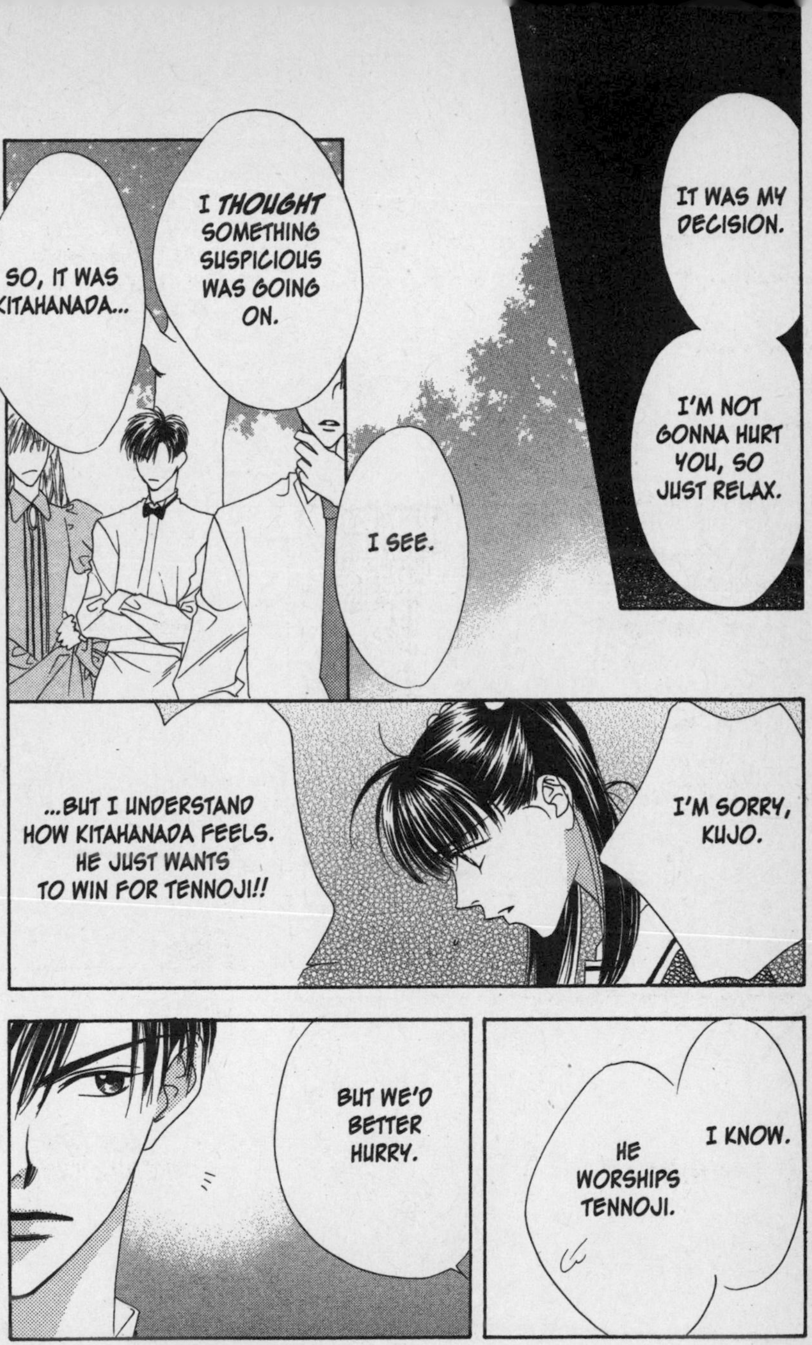
IT WAS MY DECISION.
I'M NOT GONNA HURT YOU, SO JUST RELAX.
I *THOUGHT* SOMETHING SUSPICIOUS WAS GOING ON.
SO, IT WAS KITAHANADA...
I SEE.
I'M SORRY, KUJO.
...BUT I UNDERSTAND HOW KITAHANADA FEELS. HE JUST WANTS TO WIN FOR TENNOJI!!
I KNOW.
HE WORSHIPS TENNOJI.
BUT WE'D BETTER HURRY.

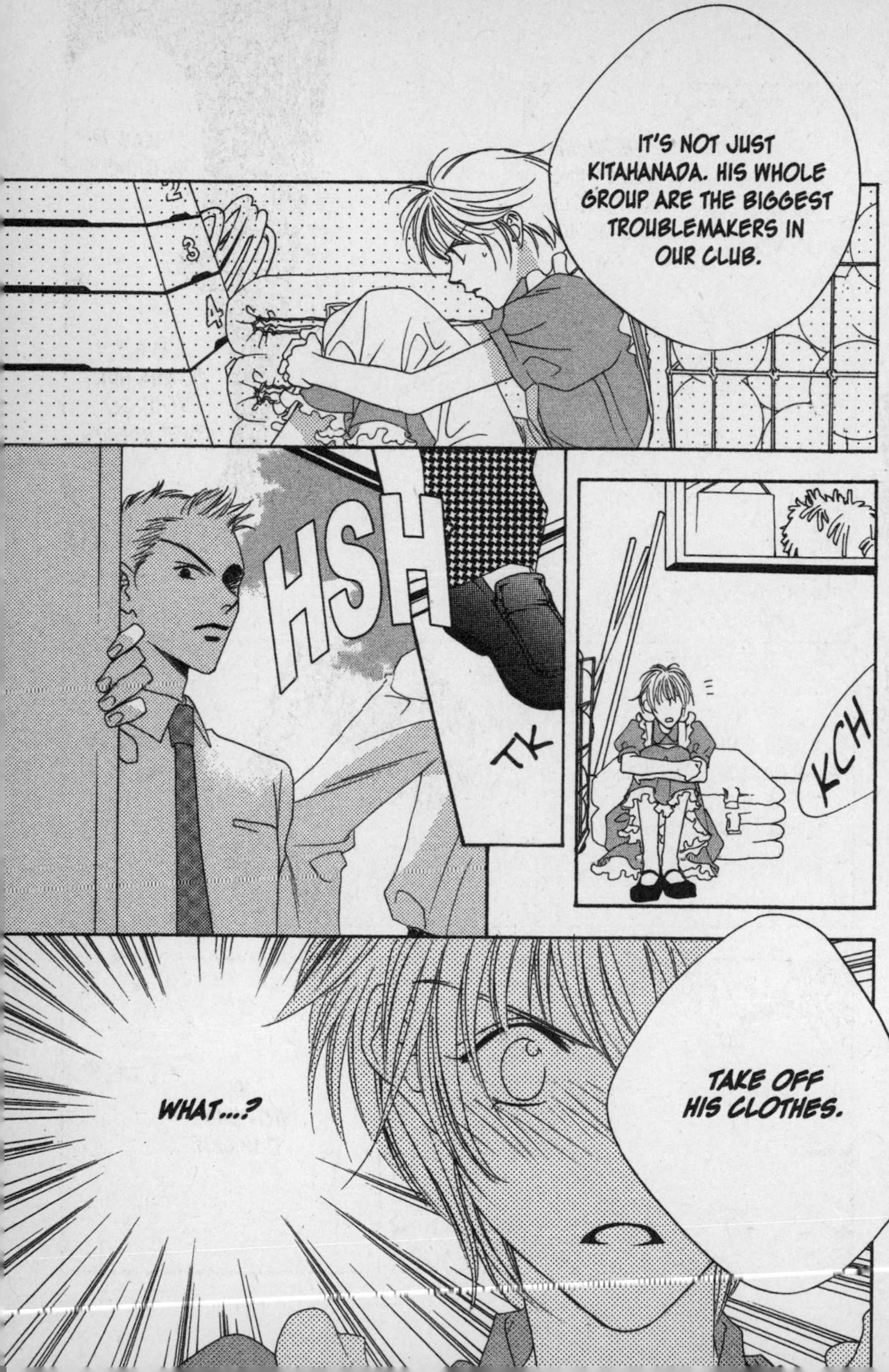
IT'S NOT JUST KITAHANADA. HIS WHOLE GROUP ARE THE BIGGEST TROUBLEMAKERS IN OUR CLUB.
KCH
HSH
TK
TAKE OFF HIS CLOTHES.
WHAT...?

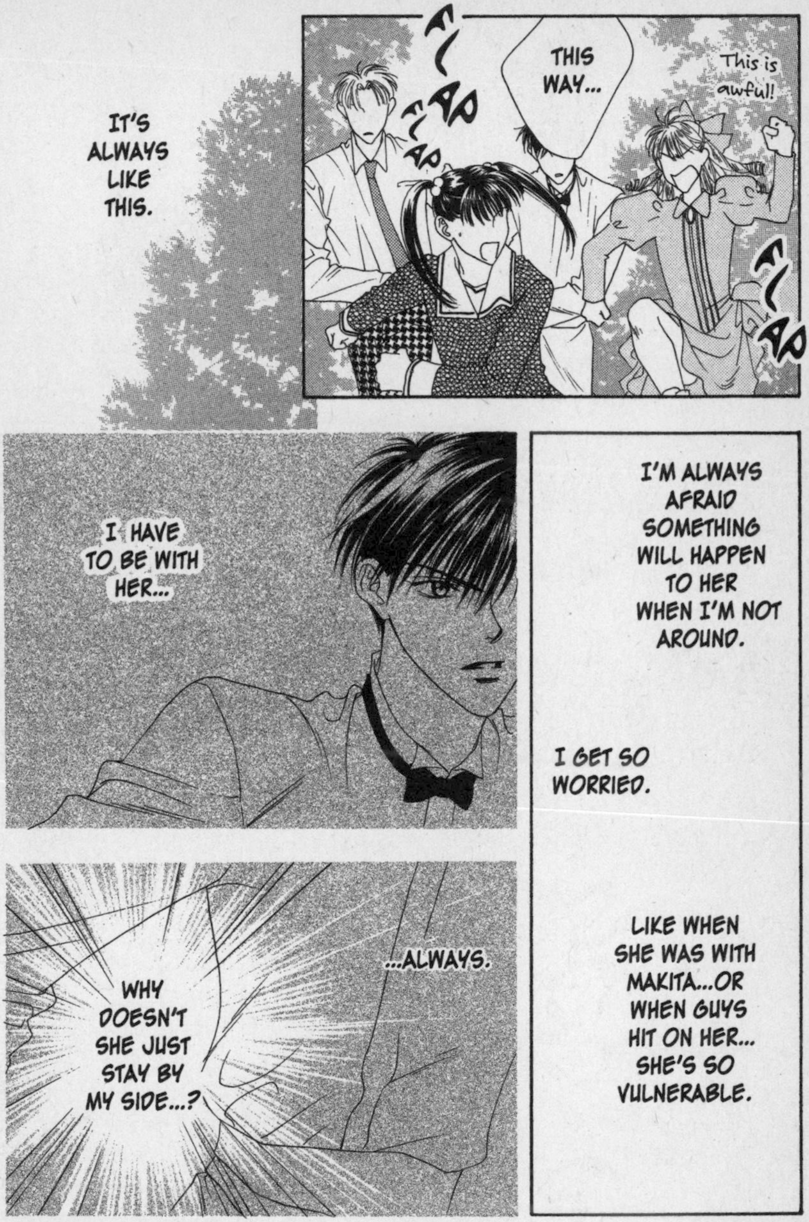
This is awful!
THIS WAY...
FLAP FLAP
FLAP
IT'S ALWAYS LIKE THIS.
I'M ALWAYS AFRAID SOMETHING WILL HAPPEN TO HER WHEN I'M NOT AROUND.
I GET SO WORRIED.
LIKE WHEN SHE WAS WITH MAKITA...OR WHEN GUYS HIT ON HER... SHE'S SO VULNERABLE.
I HAVE TO BE WITH HER...
...ALWAYS.
WHY DOESN'T SHE JUST STAY BY MY SIDE...?

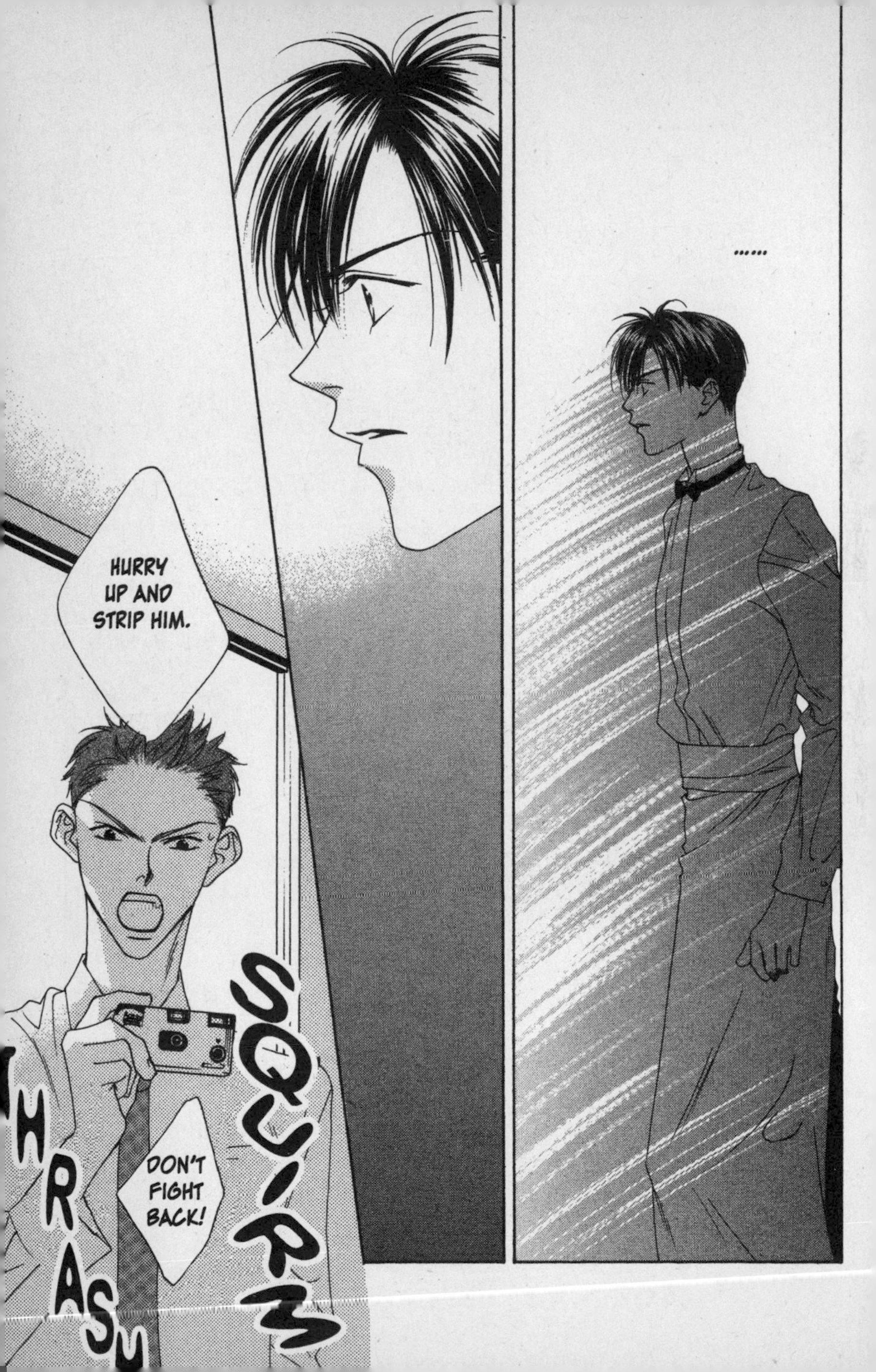
......
HURRY UP AND STRIP HIM.
SQUIRM
DON'T FIGHT BACK!
THRAS

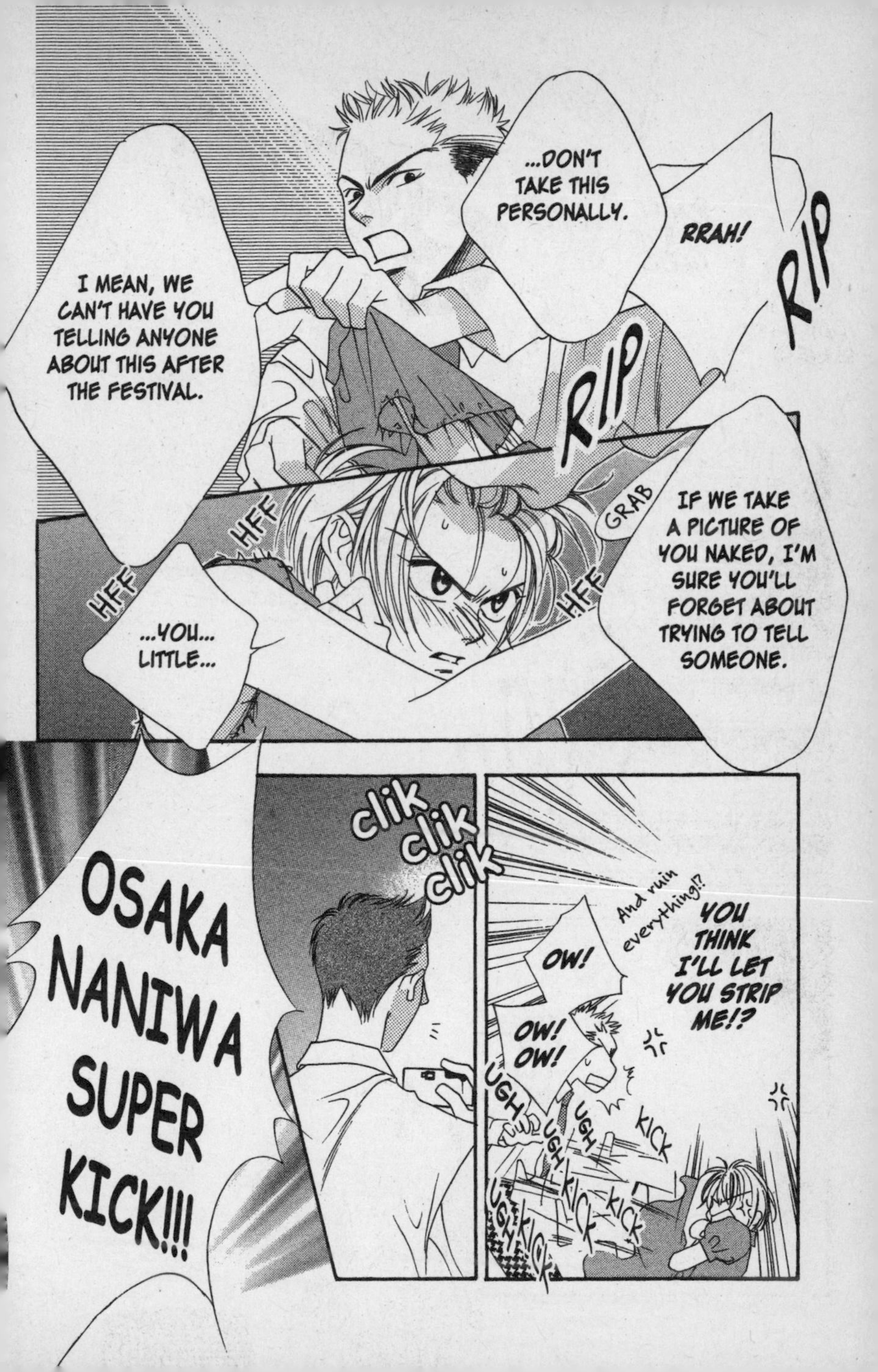
RIP
RRAH!
...DON'T TAKE THIS PERSONALLY.
RIP
I MEAN, WE CAN'T HAVE YOU TELLING ANYONE ABOUT THIS AFTER THE FESTIVAL.
IF WE TAKE A PICTURE OF YOU NAKED, I'M SURE YOU'LL FORGET ABOUT TRYING TO TELL SOMEONE.
GRAB
HFF
HFF
HFF
...YOU... LITTLE...
HFF
YOU THINK I'LL LET YOU STRIP ME!?
And ruin everything!?
OW!
OW! OW!
UGH
UGH
UGH
UGH
KICK
KICK
KICK
KICK
KICK
clik clik clik
OSAKA NANIWA SUPER KICK!!!

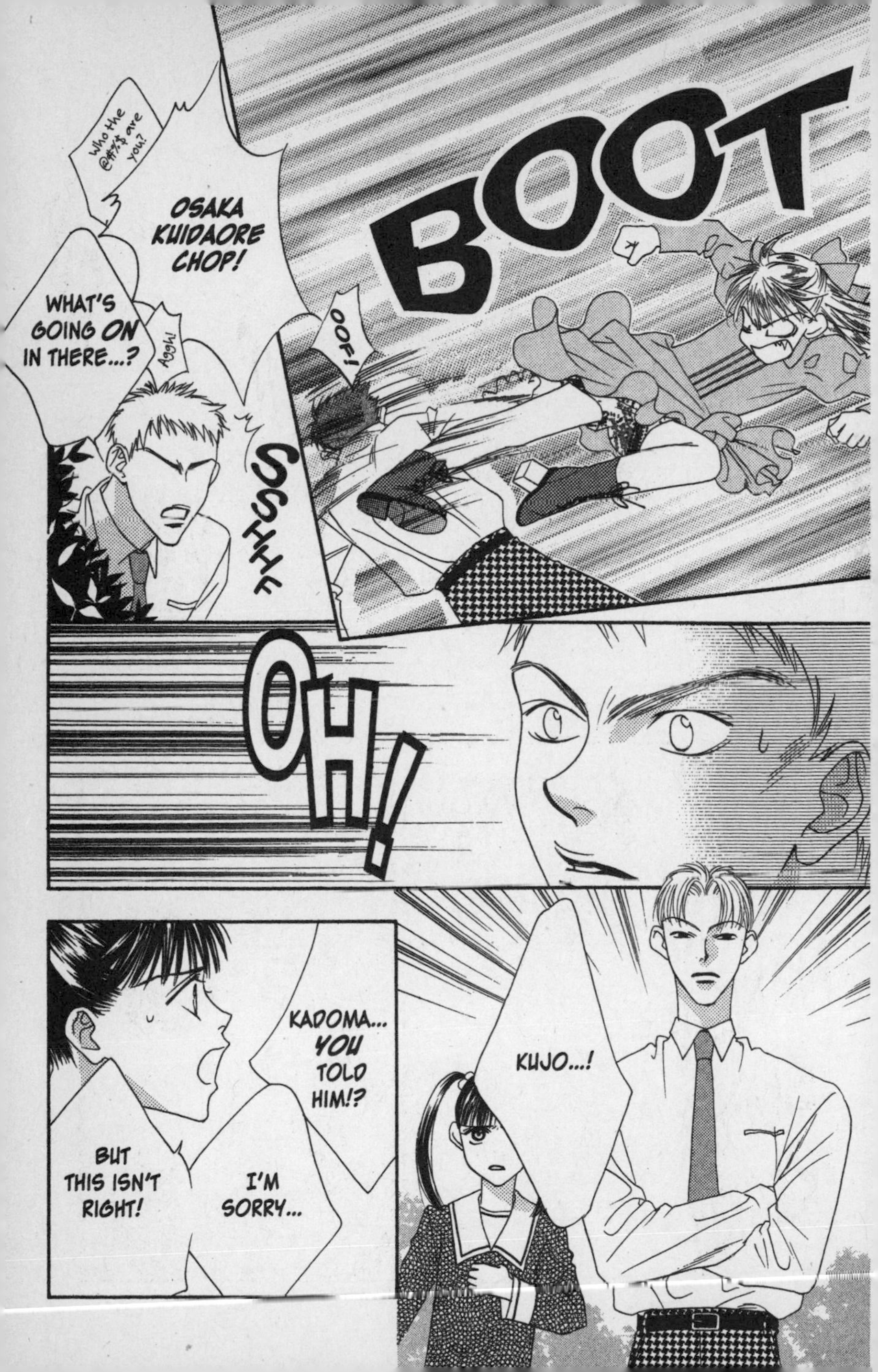
BOOT
OOF!
OSAKA KUIDAORE CHOP!
Who the @#%$ are you?
Aggh!
SSHHF
WHAT'S GOING ON IN THERE...?
OH!
KUJO...!
KADOMA... YOU TOLD HIM!?
I'M SORRY...
BUT THIS ISN'T RIGHT!

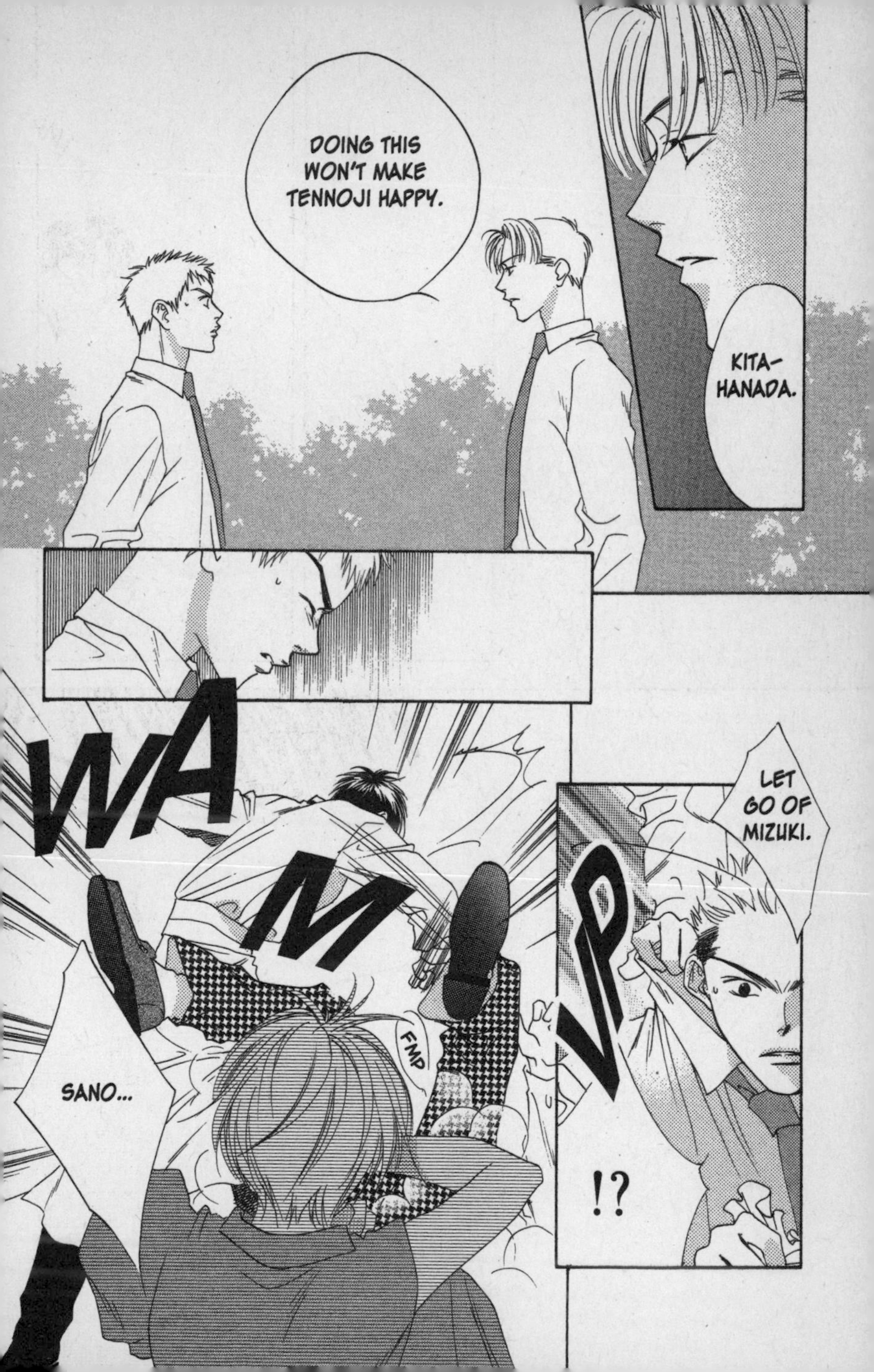
KITA-
HANADA.
DOING THIS WON'T MAKE TENNOJI HAPPY.
LET GO OF MIZUKI.
!?
WAMP
FMP
SANO...

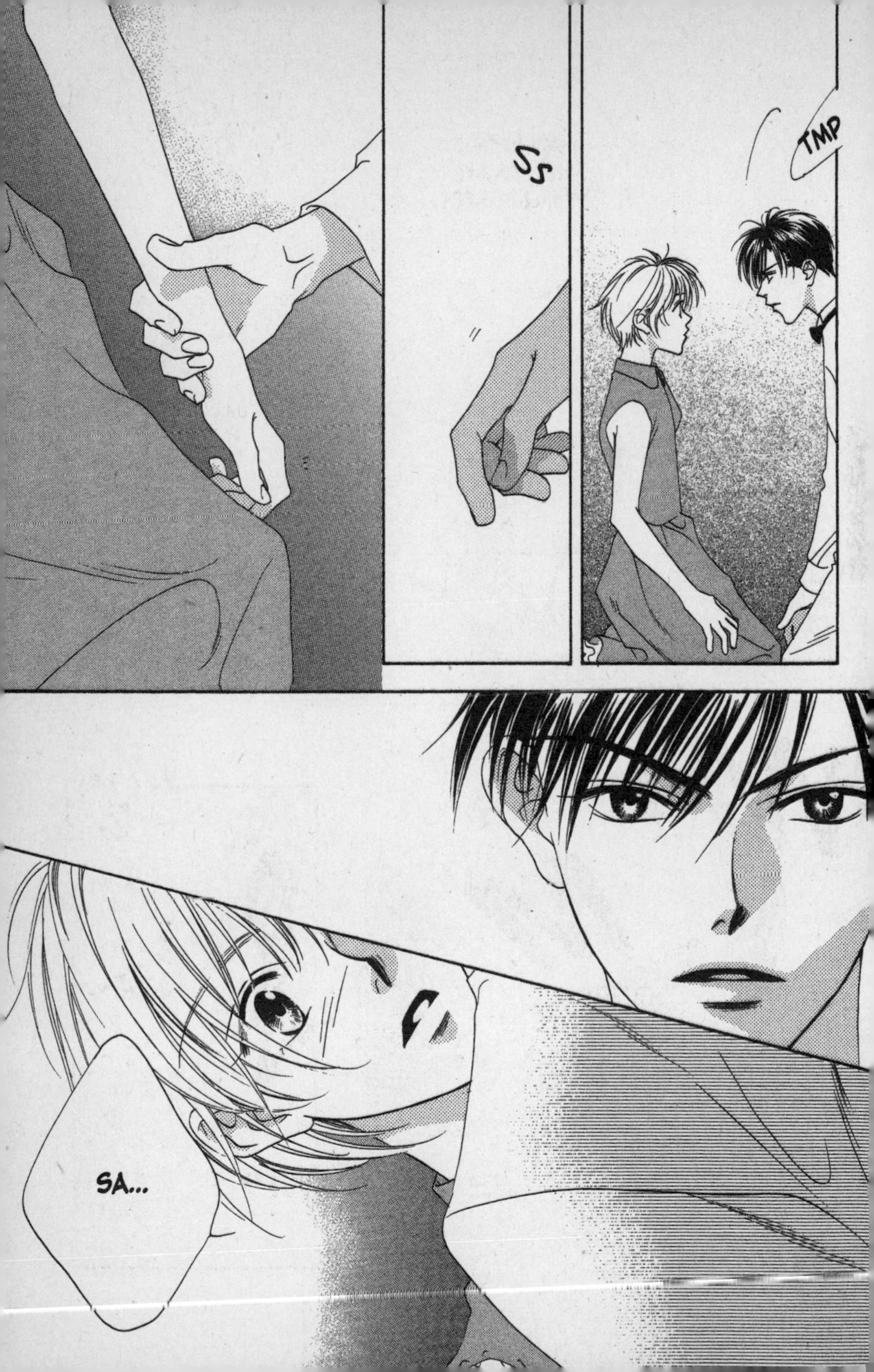
TMP
Ss
SA...

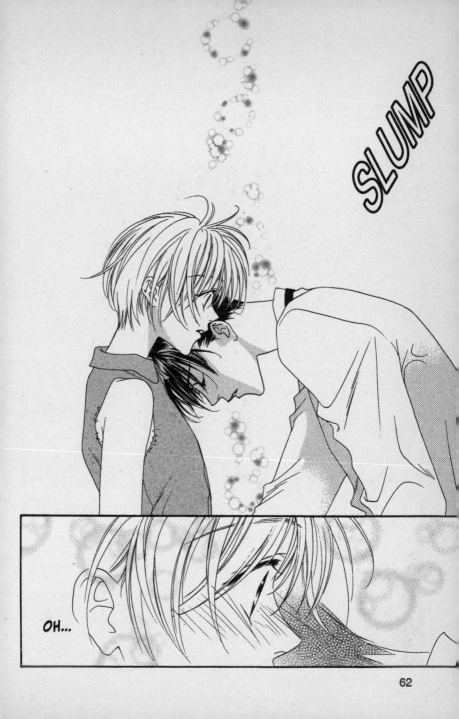

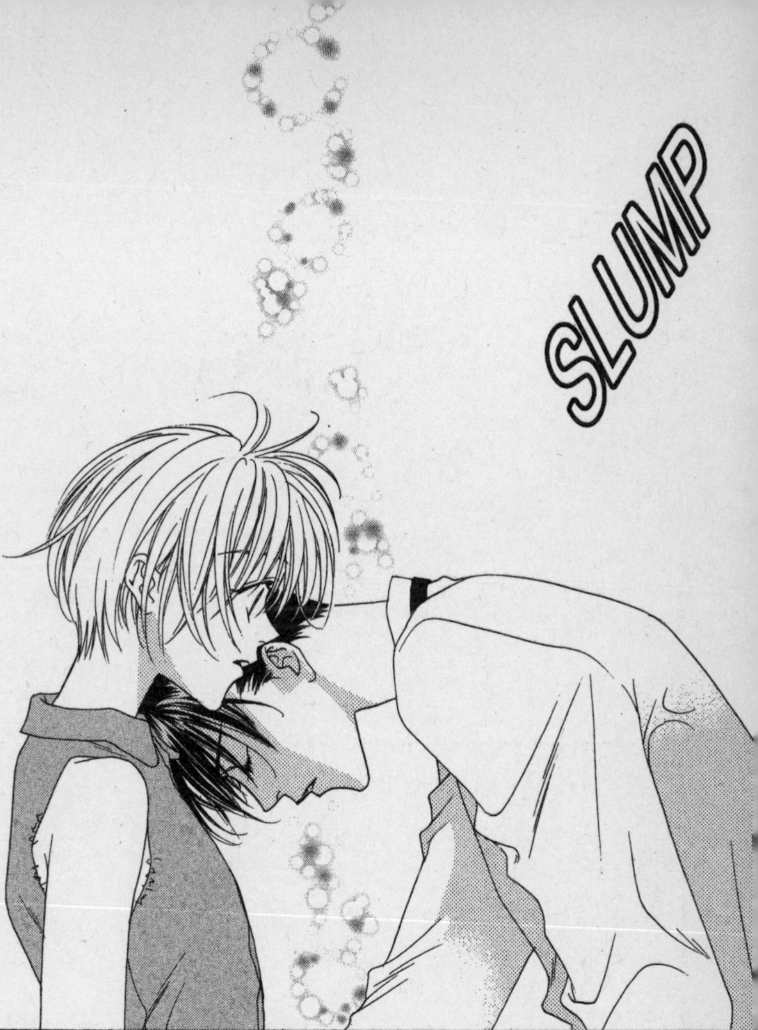
SLUMP
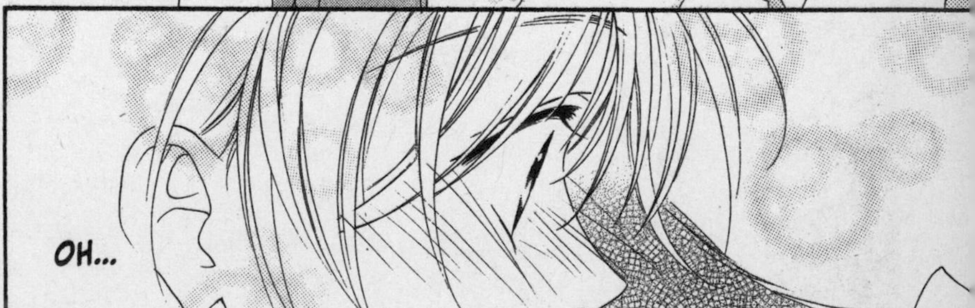
OH...

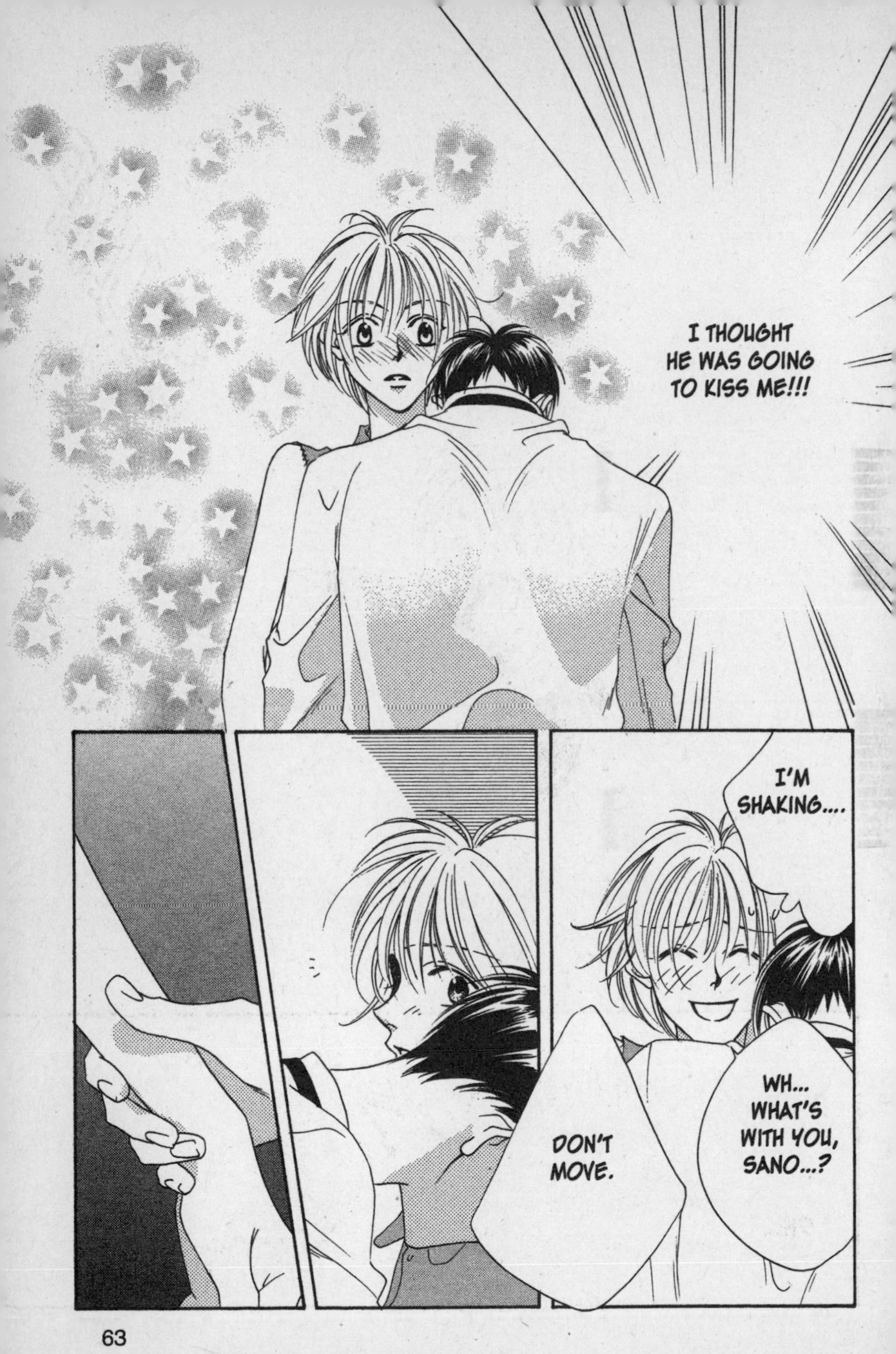
I THOUGHT HE WAS GOING TO KISS ME!!!
I'M SHAKING....
WH... WHAT'S WITH YOU, SANO...?
DON'T MOVE.

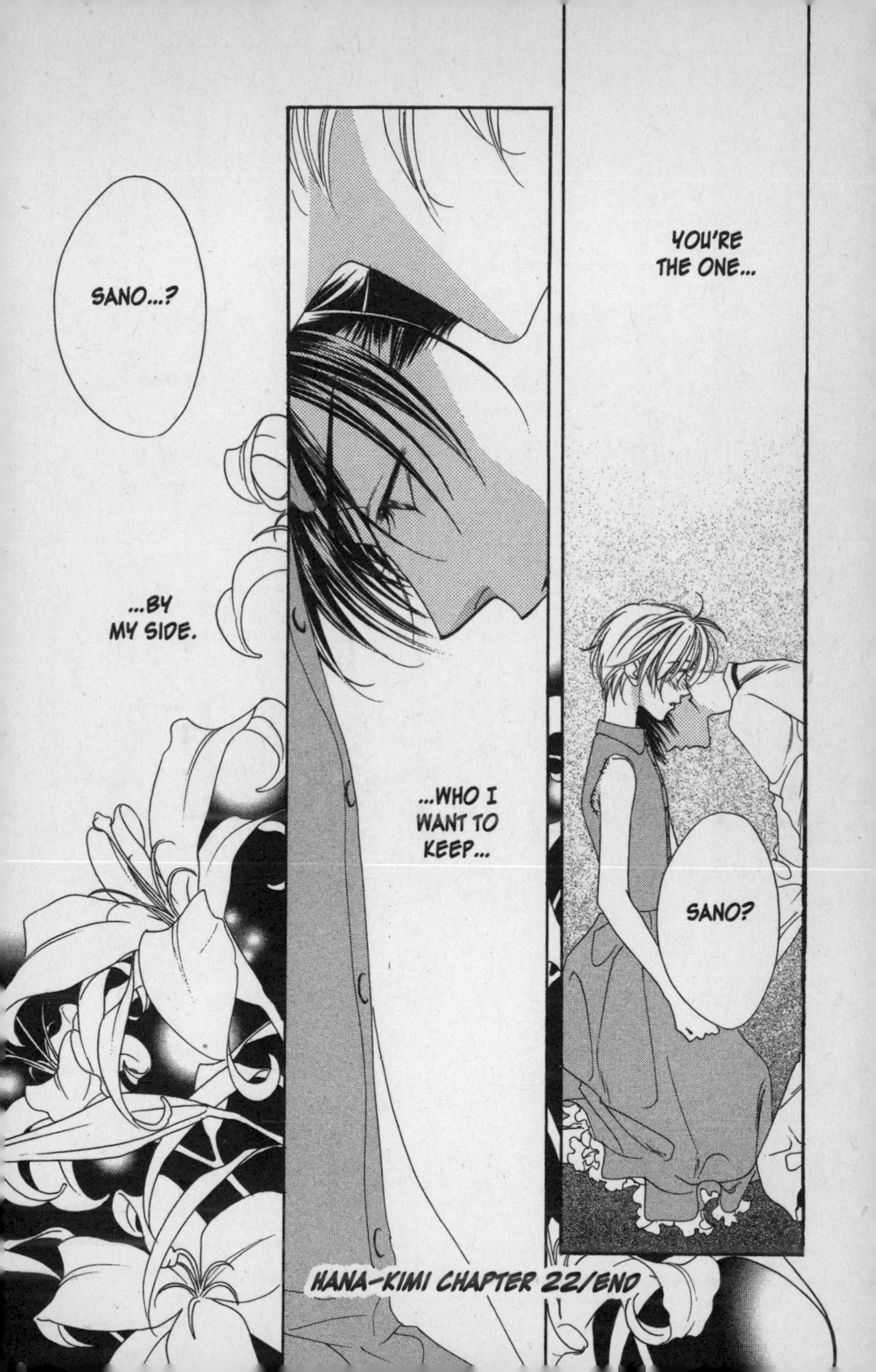
YOU'RE THE ONE...
SANO?
...WHO I WANT TO KEEP...
SANO...?
...BY MY SIDE.
HANA-KIMI CHAPTER 22/END

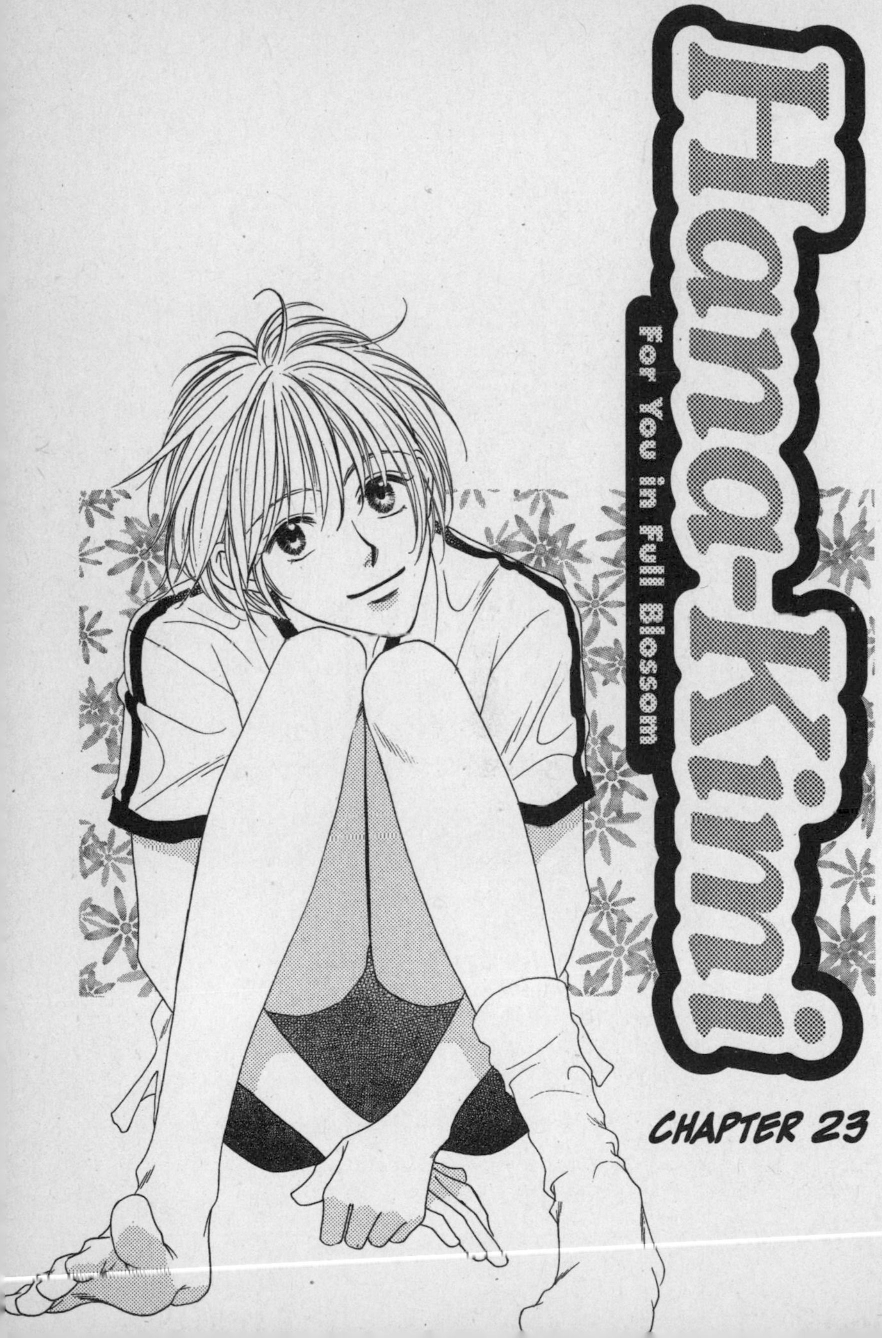
Hana-Kimi
For You in Full Blossom
CHAPTER 23

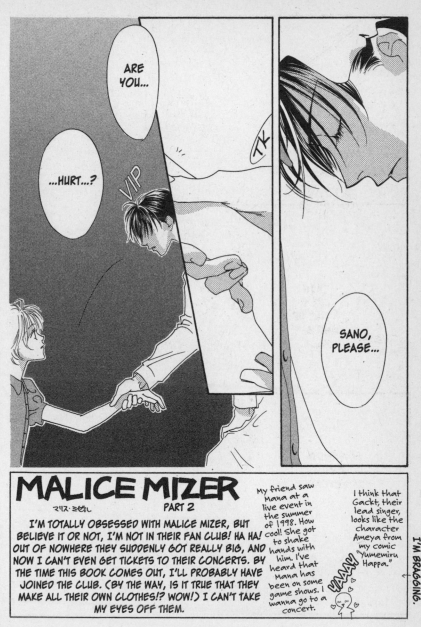

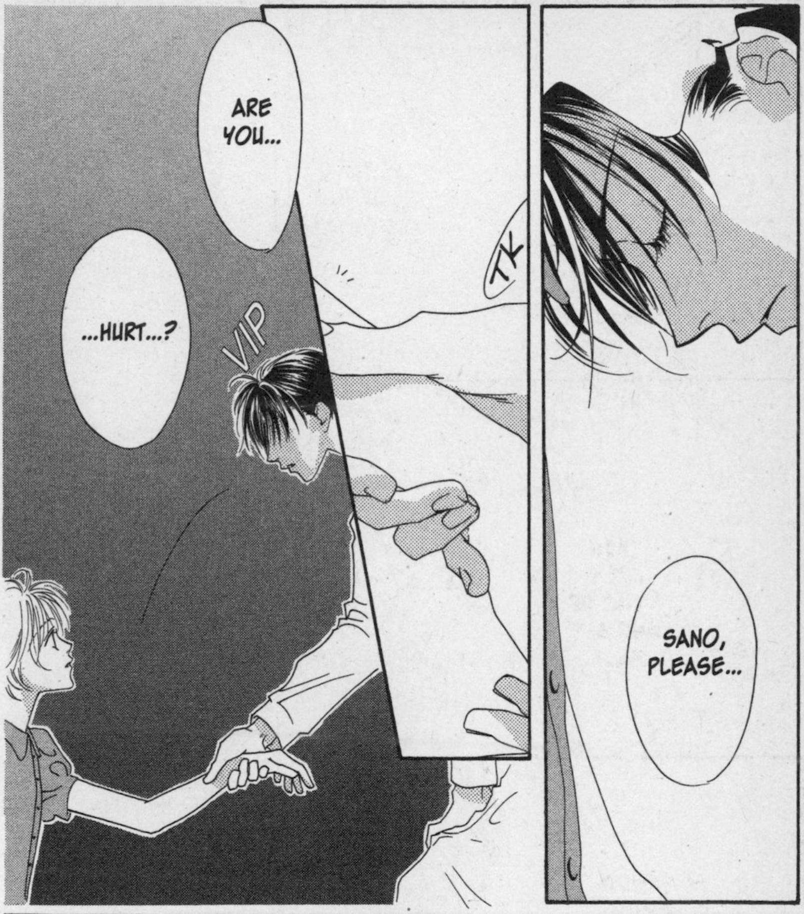
SANO, PLEASE...
TK
ARE YOU...
...HURT...?
VIP

MALICE MIZER

マリス・ミゼル

PART 2

I'M TOTALLY OBSESSED WITH MALICE MIZER, BUT BELIEVE IT OR NOT, I'M NOT IN THEIR FAN CLUB! HA HA! OUT OF NOWHERE THEY SUDDENLY GOT REALLY BIG, AND NOW I CAN'T EVEN GET TICKETS TO THEIR CONCERTS. BY THE TIME THIS BOOK COMES OUT, I'LL PROBABLY HAVE JOINED THE CLUB. (BY THE WAY, IS IT TRUE THAT THEY MAKE ALL THEIR OWN CLOTHES!? WOW!) I CAN'T TAKE MY EYES OFF THEM.

My friend saw Mana at a live event in the summer of 1998. How cool! She got to shake hands with him. I've heard that Mana has been on some game shows. I wanna go to a concert.

I think that Gackt, their lead singer, looks like the character Ameya from my comic "Yumemiru Happa."

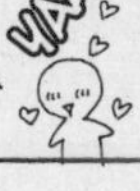
WAAAY

← I'M BRAGGING.

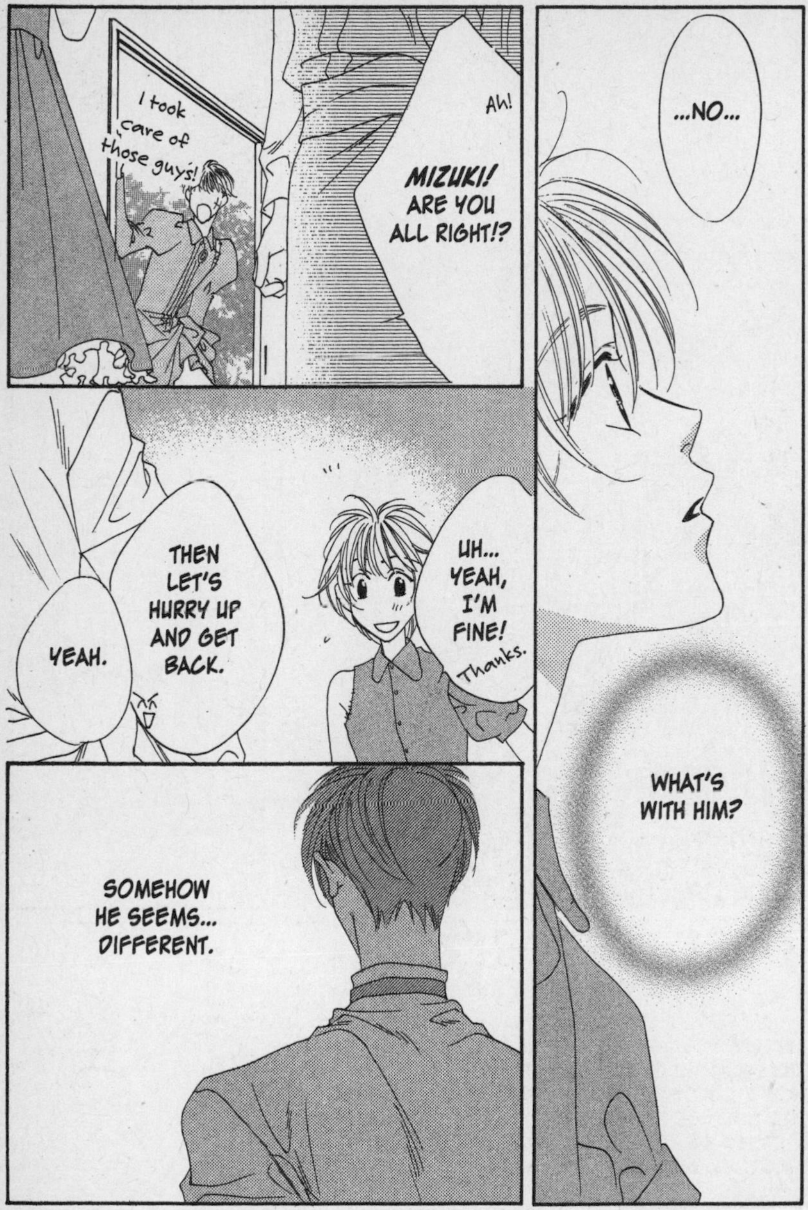
...NO...
WHAT'S WITH HIM?
Ah!
MIZUKI! ARE YOU ALL RIGHT!?
I took care of those guys!
UH... YEAH, I'M FINE!
Thanks.
THEN LET'S HURRY UP AND GET BACK.
YEAH.
SOMEHOW HE SEEMS... DIFFERENT.

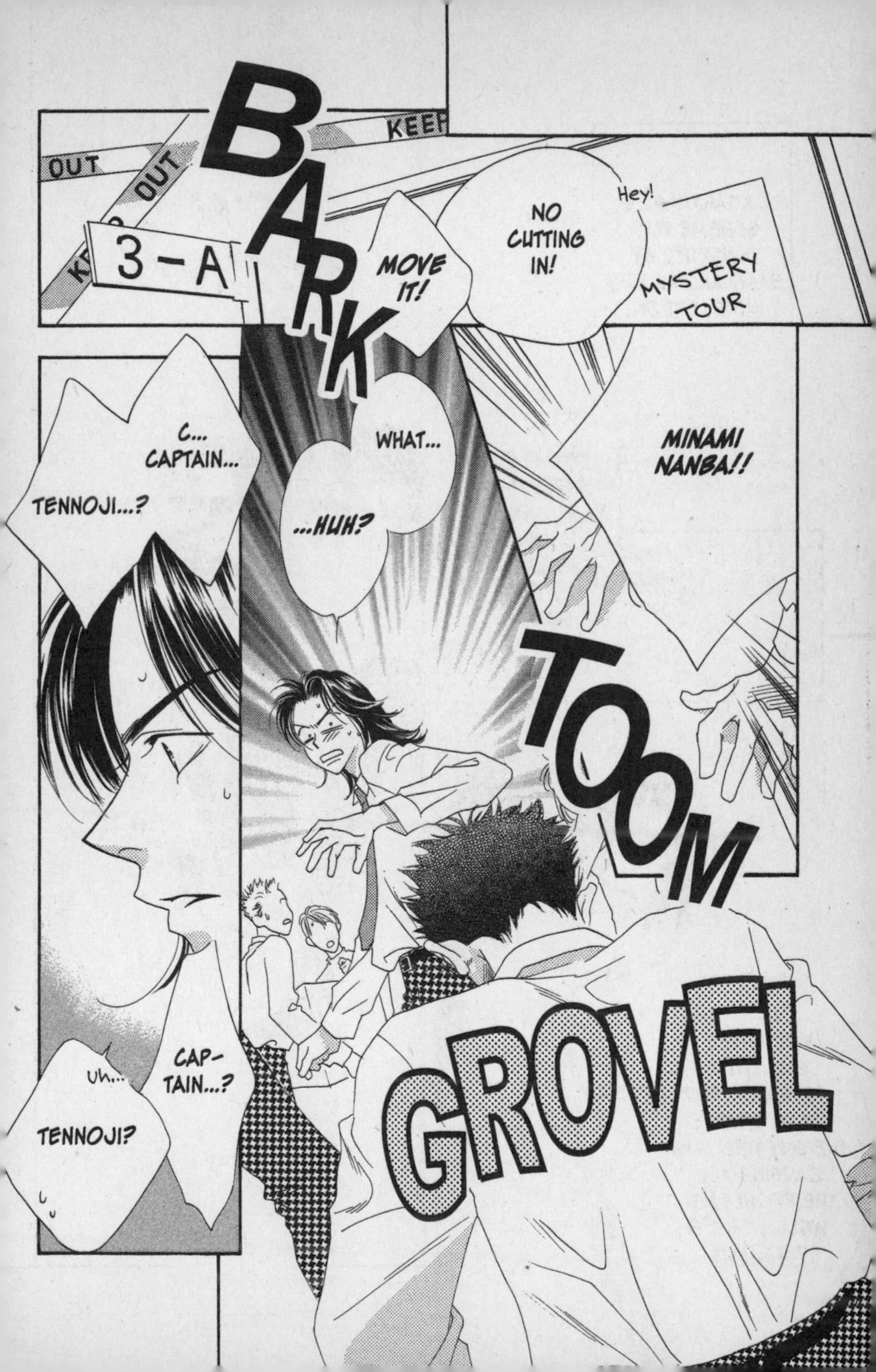
Hey!
NO CUTTING IN!
MYSTERY TOUR
MOVE IT!
BARK
3-A
KEEP
OUT
OUT
MINAMI NANBA!!
TOOOM
GROVEL
WHAT...
...HUH?
C... CAPTAIN...
TENNOJI...?
CAP-TAIN...?
Uh...
TENNOJI?

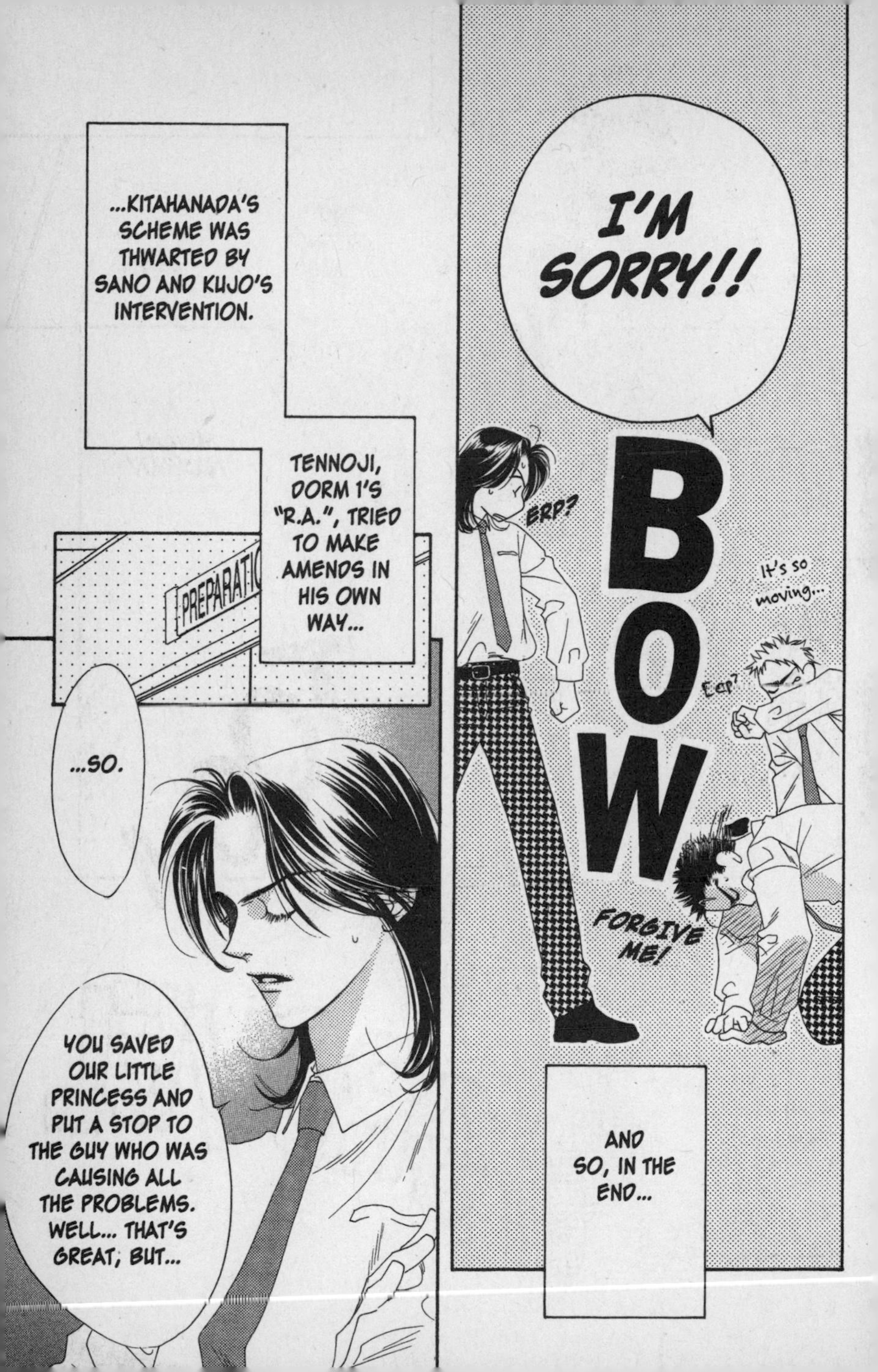
I'M SORRY!!
BOW
ERP?
It's so moving...
Erp?
FORGIVE ME!
AND SO, IN THE END...
...KITAHANADA'S SCHEME WAS THWARTED BY SANO AND KUJO'S INTERVENTION.
TENNOJI, DORM 1'S "R.A.", TRIED TO MAKE AMENDS IN HIS OWN WAY...
PREPARATI
...SO.
YOU SAVED OUR LITTLE PRINCESS AND PUT A STOP TO THE GUY WHO WAS CAUSING ALL THE PROBLEMS. WELL... THAT'S GREAT, BUT...

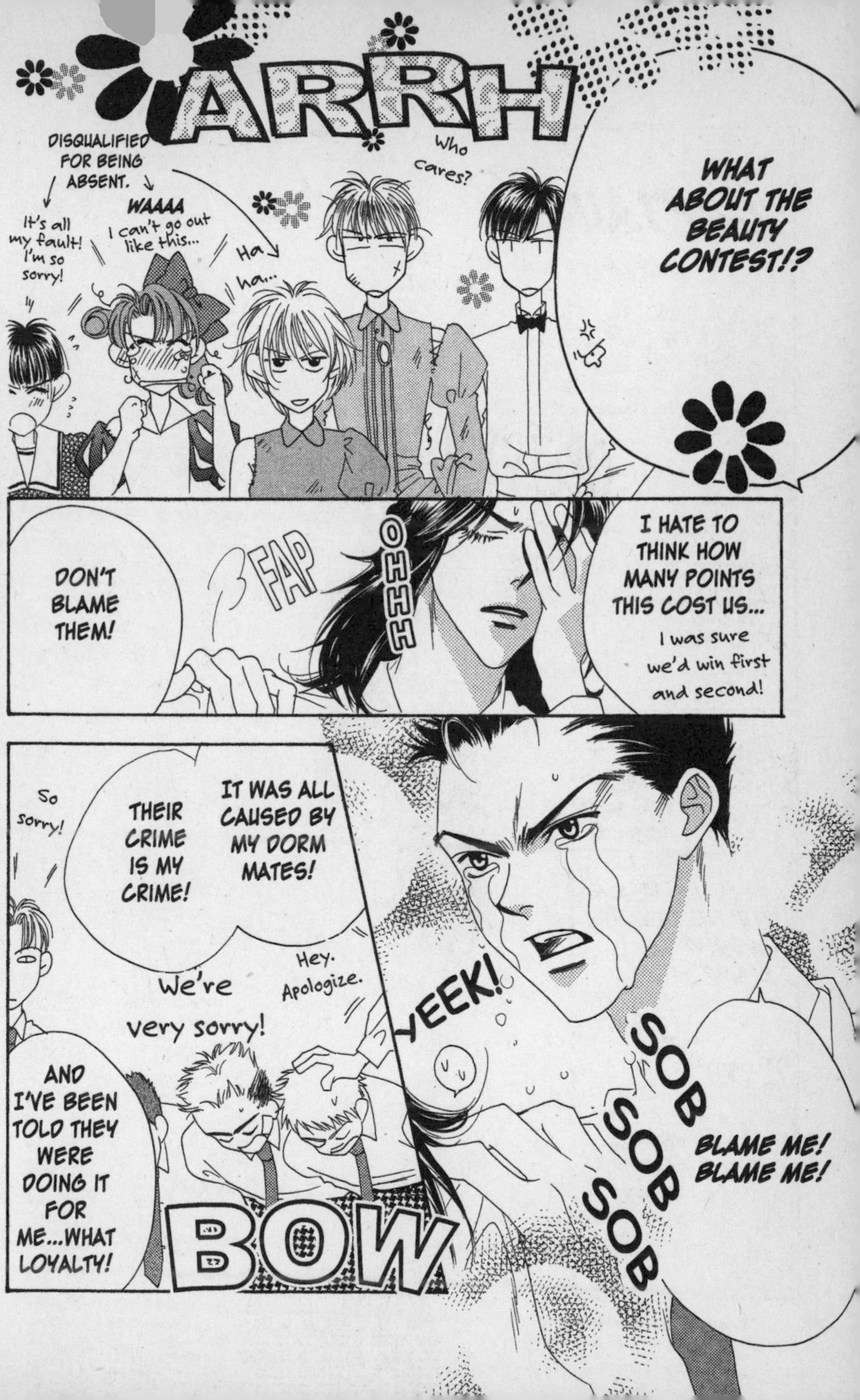
ARRH
WHAT ABOUT THE BEAUTY CONTEST!?
Who cares?
Ha ha...
DISQUALIFIED FOR BEING ABSENT.
WAAAA I can't go out like this...
It's all my fault! I'm so sorry!
I HATE TO THINK HOW MANY POINTS THIS COST US...
I was sure we'd win first and second!
OHHHH
FAP
DON'T BLAME THEM!
BLAME ME! BLAME ME!
SOB SOB SOB
YEEK!
IT WAS ALL CAUSED BY MY DORM MATES!
THEIR CRIME IS MY CRIME!
So sorry!
Hey. Apologize.
We're very sorry!
BOW
AND I'VE BEEN TOLD THEY WERE DOING IT FOR ME...WHAT LOYALTY!

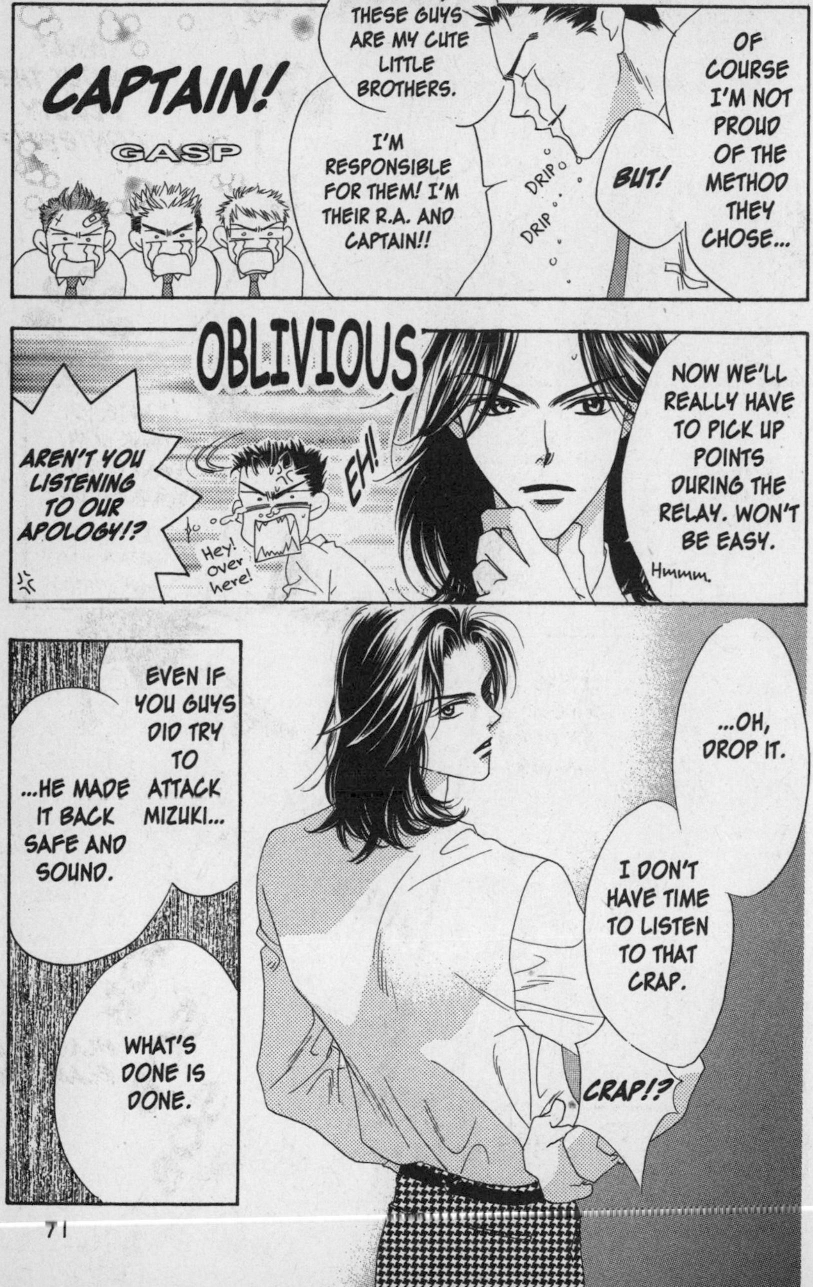
OF COURSE I'M NOT PROUD OF THE METHOD THEY CHOSE...
BUT!
DRIP DRIP
...TO ME, THESE GUYS ARE MY CUTE LITTLE BROTHERS.
I'M RESPONSIBLE FOR THEM! I'M THEIR R.A. AND CAPTAIN!!
CAPTAIN!
GASP
NOW WE'LL REALLY HAVE TO PICK UP POINTS DURING THE RELAY. WON'T BE EASY.
Hmmm.
OBLIVIOUS
EH!
AREN'T YOU LISTENING TO OUR APOLOGY!?
Hey! over here!
...OH, DROP IT.
I DON'T HAVE TIME TO LISTEN TO THAT CRAP.
CRAP!?
EVEN IF YOU GUYS DID TRY TO ATTACK MIZUKI...
...HE MADE IT BACK SAFE AND SOUND.
WHAT'S DONE IS DONE.

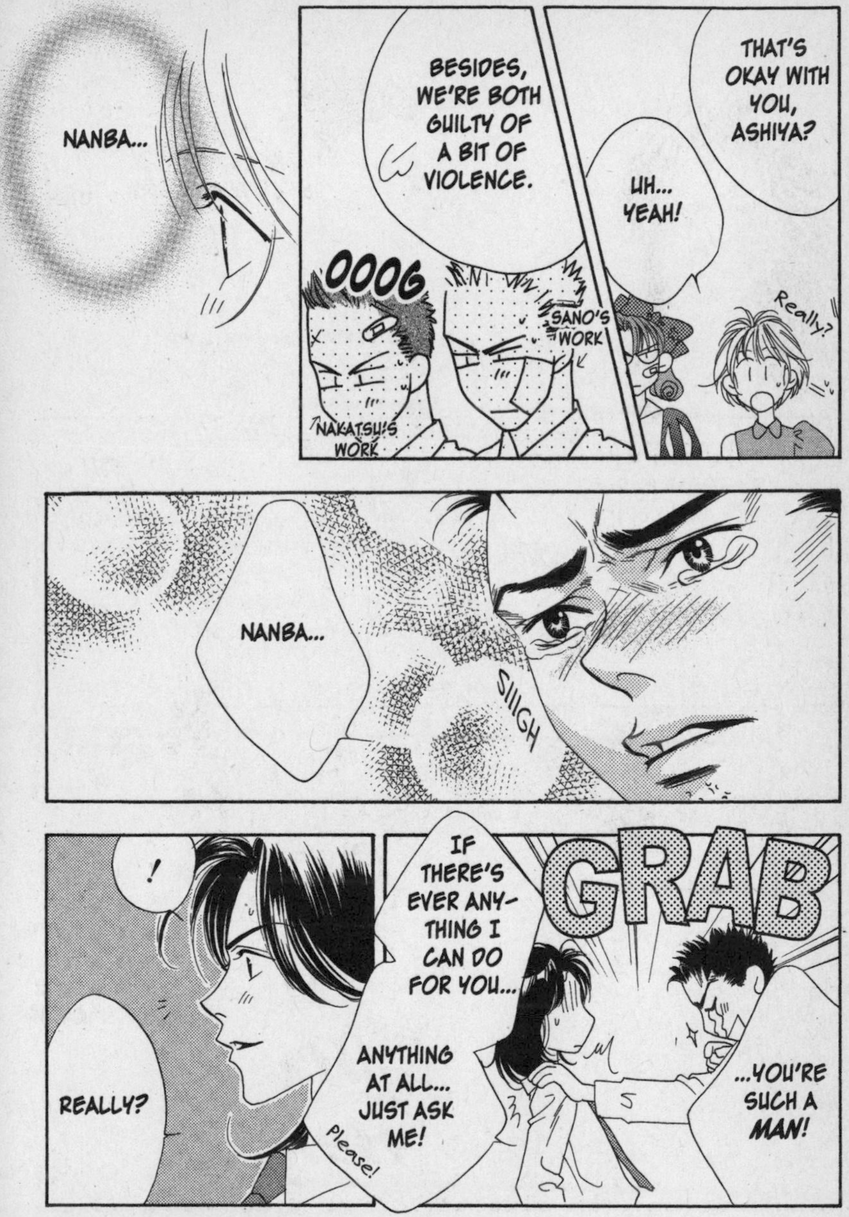
THAT'S OKAY WITH YOU, ASHIYA?
UH... YEAH!
Really?
BESIDES, WE'RE BOTH GUILTY OF A BIT OF VIOLENCE.
OOOG
SANO'S WORK
NAKATSU'S WORK
NANBA...
NANBA...
SIIIGH
GRAB
...YOU'RE SUCH A *MAN*!
IF THERE'S EVER ANYTHING I CAN DO FOR YOU...
ANYTHING AT ALL... JUST ASK ME!
Please!
!
REALLY?

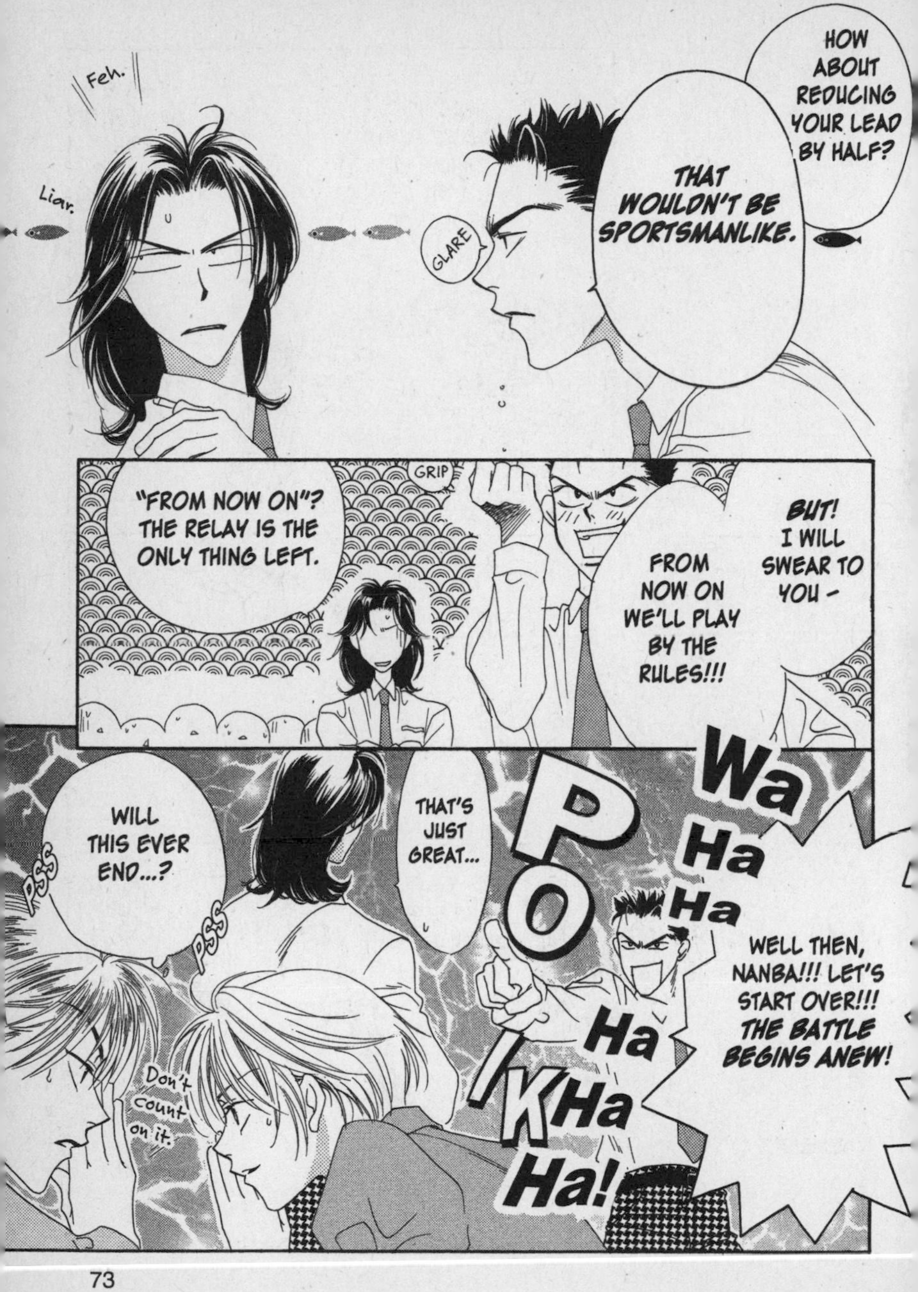
HOW ABOUT REDUCING YOUR LEAD BY HALF?
THAT WOULDN'T BE SPORTSMANLIKE.
GLARE
Feh.
Liar.
BUT! I WILL SWEAR TO YOU -
FROM NOW ON WE'LL PLAY BY THE RULES!!!
GRIP
"FROM NOW ON"? THE RELAY IS THE ONLY THING LEFT.
Wa Ha Ha Ha Ha Ha Ha!
WELL THEN, NANBA!!! LET'S START OVER!!! THE BATTLE BEGINS ANEW!
POIK
THAT'S JUST GREAT...
WILL THIS EVER END...?
PSS
PSS
Don't count on it.

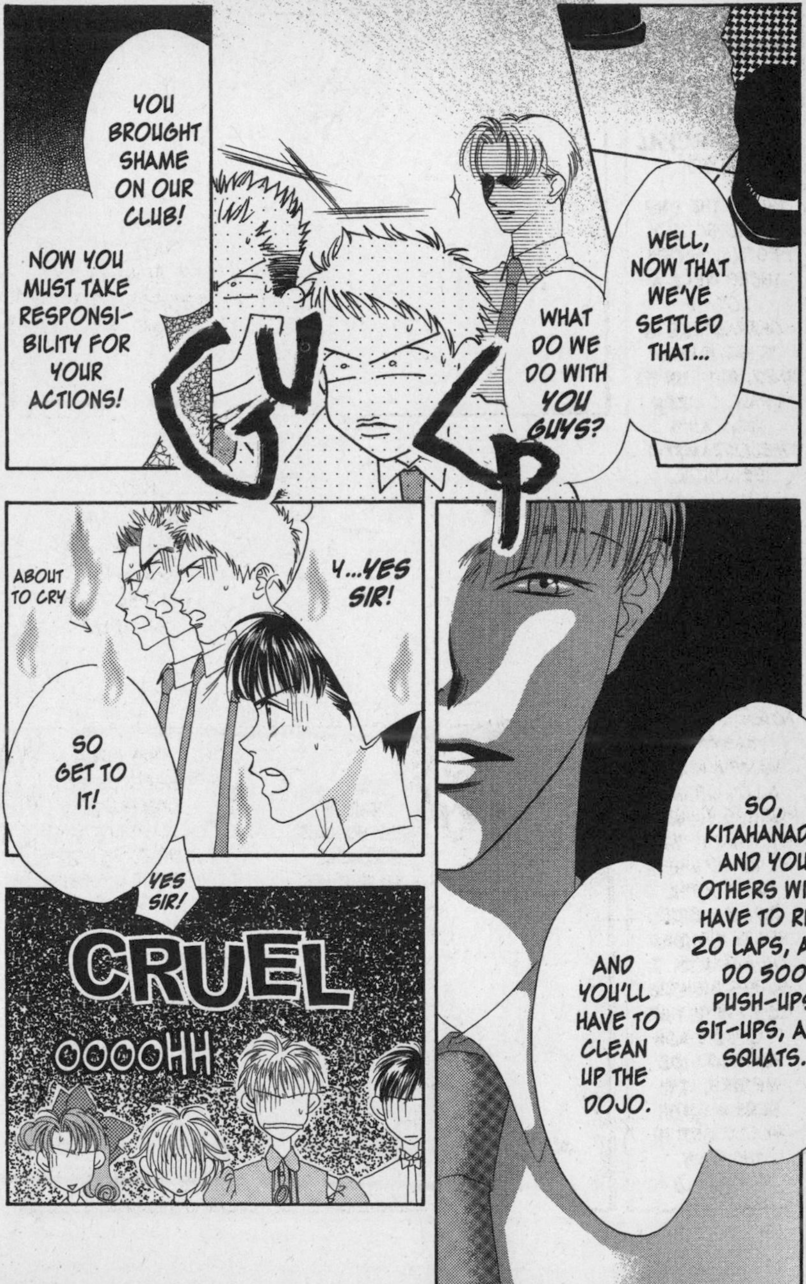
WELL, NOW THAT WE'VE SETTLED THAT...
WHAT DO WE DO WITH YOU GUYS?
GULP
YOU BROUGHT SHAME ON OUR CLUB!
NOW YOU MUST TAKE RESPONSI-BILITY FOR YOUR ACTIONS!
SO, KITAHANADA AND YOU OTHERS WILL HAVE TO RUN 20 LAPS, AND DO 500 PUSH-UPS, SIT-UPS, AND SQUATS.
AND YOU'LL HAVE TO CLEAN UP THE DOJO.
Y...YES SIR!
ABOUT TO CRY
SO GET TO IT!
YES SIR!
CRUEL
OOOOHH

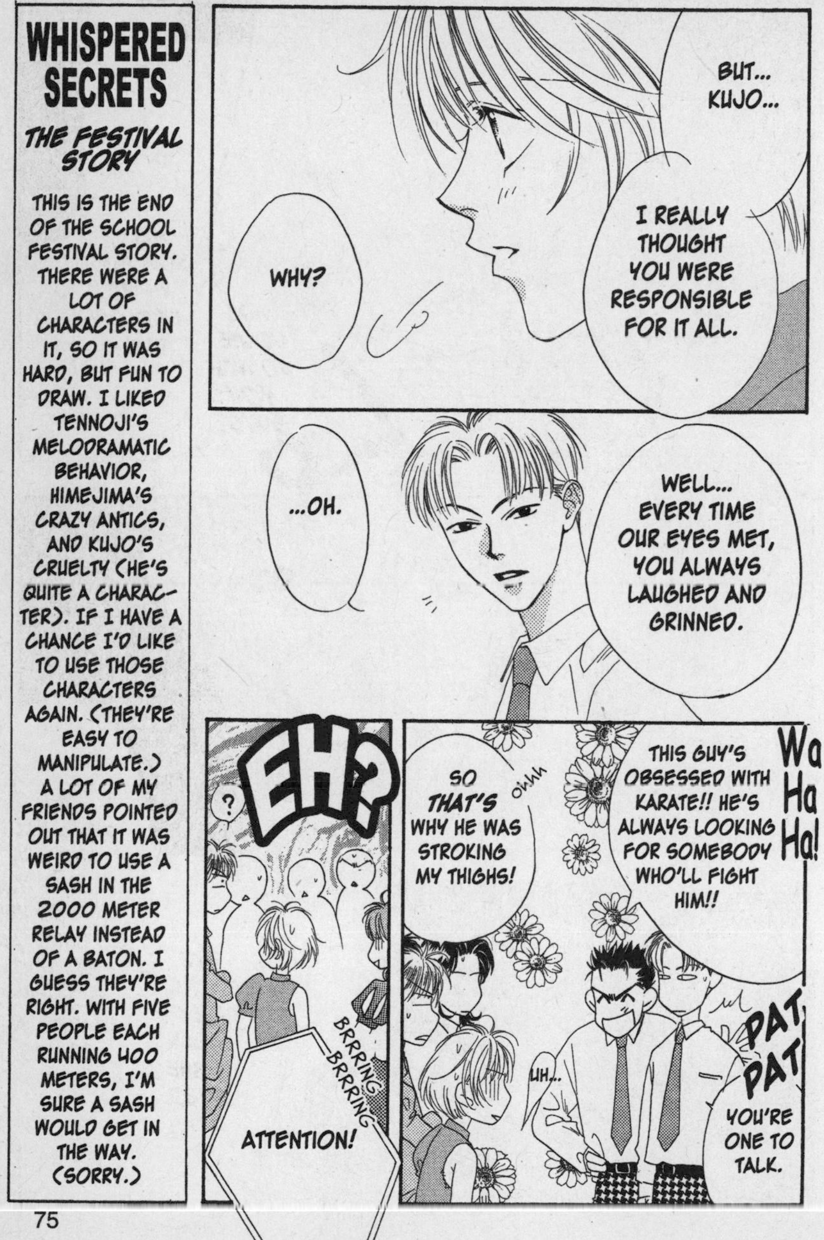
BUT... KUJO...
I REALLY THOUGHT YOU WERE RESPONSIBLE FOR IT ALL.
WHY?
WELL... EVERY TIME OUR EYES MET, YOU ALWAYS LAUGHED AND GRINNED.
...OH.
Wa Ha Ha!
THIS GUY'S OBSESSED WITH KARATE!! HE'S ALWAYS LOOKING FOR SOMEBODY WHO'LL FIGHT HIM!!
SO THAT'S WHY HE WAS STROKING MY THIGHS!
PAT PAT
YOU'RE ONE TO TALK.
UH...
EH?
?
BRRRING BRRRING
ATTENTION!

WHISPERED SECRETS

THE FESTIVAL STORY

THIS IS THE END OF THE SCHOOL FESTIVAL STORY. THERE WERE A LOT OF CHARACTERS IN IT, SO IT WAS HARD, BUT FUN TO DRAW. I LIKED TENNOJI'S MELODRAMATIC BEHAVIOR, HIMEJIMA'S CRAZY ANTICS, AND KUJO'S CRUELTY (HE'S QUITE A CHARACTER). IF I HAVE A CHANCE I'D LIKE TO USE THOSE CHARACTERS AGAIN. (THEY'RE EASY TO MANIPULATE.) A LOT OF MY FRIENDS POINTED OUT THAT IT WAS WEIRD TO USE A SASH IN THE 2000 METER RELAY INSTEAD OF A BATON. I GUESS THEY'RE RIGHT. WITH FIVE PEOPLE EACH RUNNING 400 METERS, I'M SURE A SASH WOULD GET IN THE WAY. (SORRY.)

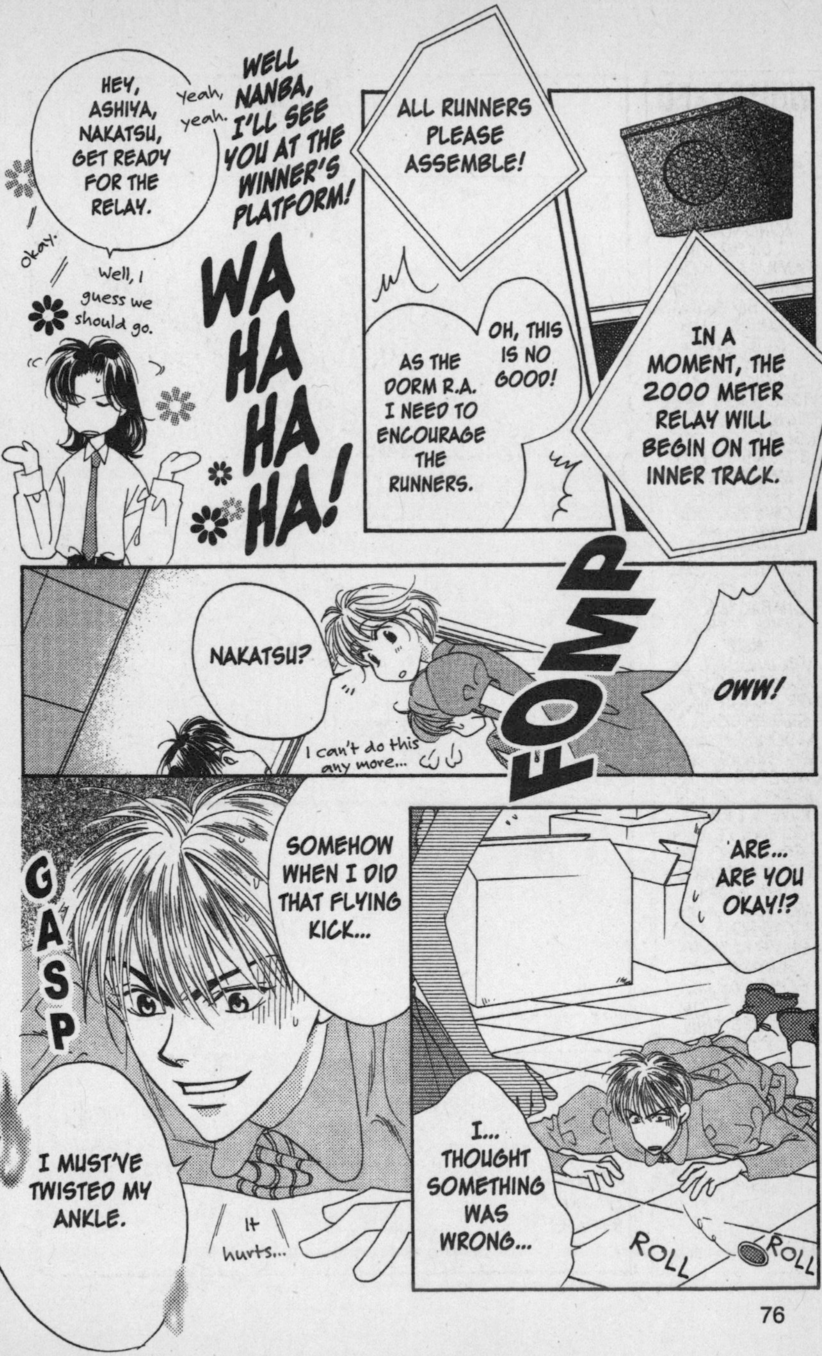
ALL RUNNERS PLEASE ASSEMBLE!
IN A MOMENT, THE 2000 METER RELAY WILL BEGIN ON THE INNER TRACK.
OH, THIS IS NO GOOD!
AS THE DORM R.A. I NEED TO ENCOURAGE THE RUNNERS.
WELL NANBA, I'LL SEE YOU AT THE WINNER'S PLATFORM!
WA HA HA HA HA!
HEY, ASHIYA, NAKATSU, GET READY FOR THE RELAY.
Yeah, yeah.
Okay.
Well, I guess we should go.
OWW!
FOMP
NAKATSU?
I can't do this any more...
ARE... ARE YOU OKAY!?
I... THOUGHT SOMETHING WAS WRONG...
ROLL
ROLL
SOMEHOW WHEN I DID THAT FLYING KICK...
GASP
I MUST'VE TWISTED MY ANKLE.
It hurts...

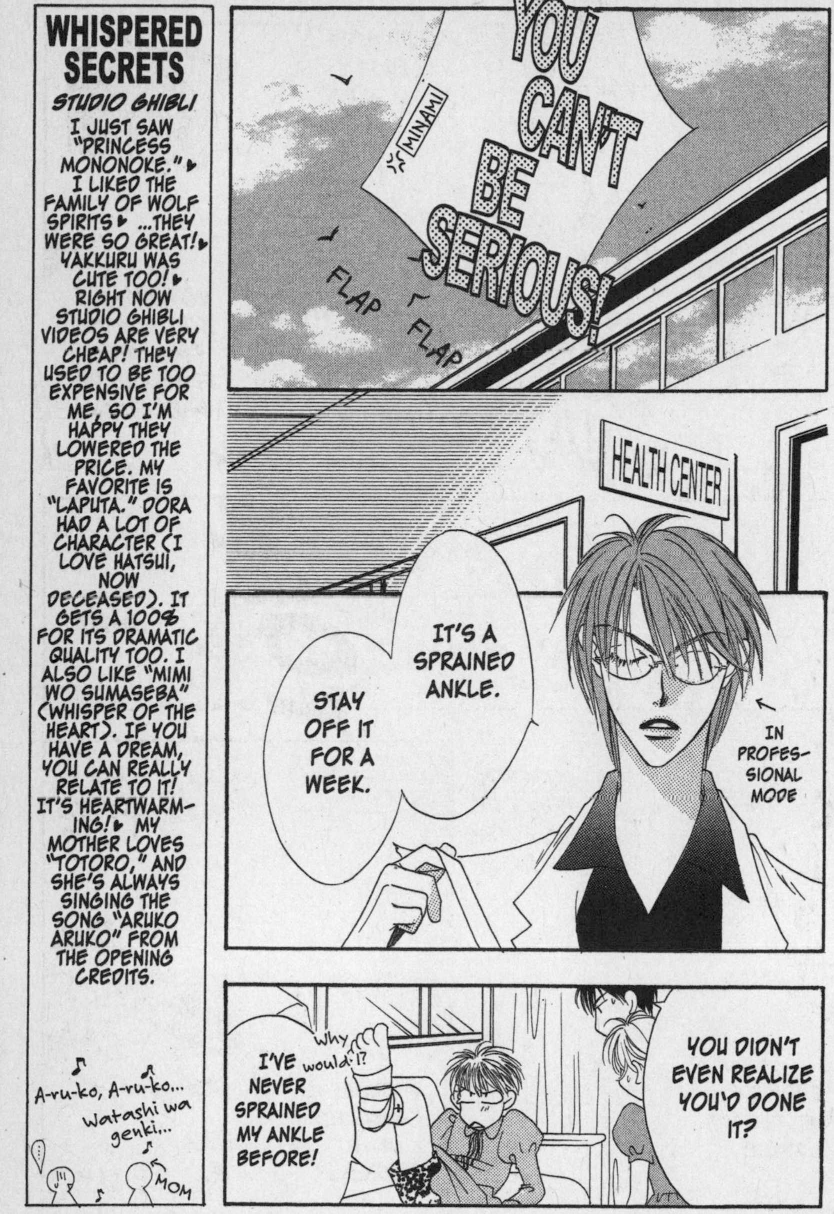
YOU CAN'T BE SERIOUS!
MINAMI
FLAP
FLAP
HEALTH CENTER
IT'S A SPRAINED ANKLE.
STAY OFF IT FOR A WEEK.
IN PROFES-SIONAL MODE
YOU DIDN'T EVEN REALIZE YOU'D DONE IT?
Why would I?
I'VE NEVER SPRAINED MY ANKLE BEFORE!

WHISPERED SECRETS

STUDIO GHIBLI

I JUST SAW "PRINCESS MONONOKE." ♥ I LIKED THE FAMILY OF WOLF SPIRITS ♥ ...THEY WERE SO GREAT! ♥ YAKKURU WAS CUTE TOO! ♥ RIGHT NOW STUDIO GHIBLI VIDEOS ARE VERY CHEAP! THEY USED TO BE TOO EXPENSIVE FOR ME, SO I'M HAPPY THEY LOWERED THE PRICE. MY FAVORITE IS "LAPUTA." DORA HAD A LOT OF CHARACTER (I LOVE HATSUI, NOW DECEASED). IT GETS A 100% FOR ITS DRAMATIC QUALITY TOO. I ALSO LIKE "MIMI WO SUMASEBA" (WHISPER OF THE HEART). IF YOU HAVE A DREAM, YOU CAN REALLY RELATE TO IT! IT'S HEARTWARMING! ♥ MY MOTHER LOVES "TOTORO," AND SHE'S ALWAYS SINGING THE SONG "ARUKO ARUKO" FROM THE OPENING CREDITS.

♪ A-ru-ko, A-ru-ko... ♪

Watashi wa genki... ♪

MOM

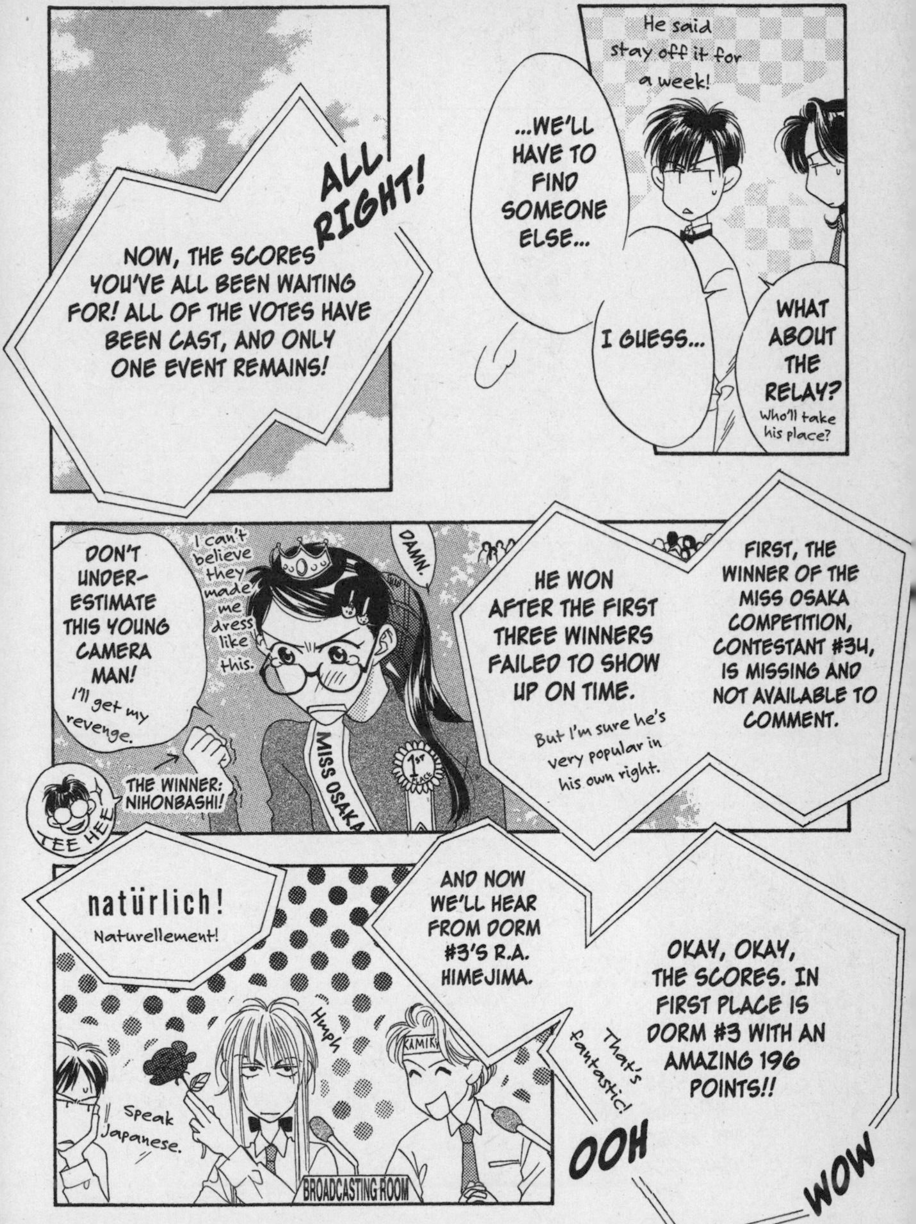

WHAT ABOUT THE RELAY? Who'll take his place?
He said stay off it for a week!
...WE'LL HAVE TO FIND SOMEONE ELSE...
I GUESS...
ALL RIGHT!
NOW, THE SCORES YOU'VE ALL BEEN WAITING FOR! ALL OF THE VOTES HAVE BEEN CAST, AND ONLY ONE EVENT REMAINS!
FIRST, THE WINNER OF THE MISS OSAKA COMPETITION, CONTESTANT #34, IS MISSING AND NOT AVAILABLE TO COMMENT.
HE WON AFTER THE FIRST THREE WINNERS FAILED TO SHOW UP ON TIME.
But I'm sure he's very popular in his own right.
DAMN.
I can't believe they made me dress like this.
DON'T UNDER-ESTIMATE THIS YOUNG CAMERA MAN!
I'll get my revenge.
MISS OSAKA
THE WINNER: NIHONBASHI!
TEE HEE
OKAY, OKAY, THE SCORES. IN FIRST PLACE IS DORM #3 WITH AN AMAZING 196 POINTS!!
WOW
OOH
That's fantastic!
AND NOW WE'LL HEAR FROM DORM #3'S R.A. HIMEJIMA.
Hmph
natürlich!
Naturellement!
Speak Japanese.
BROADCASTING ROOM

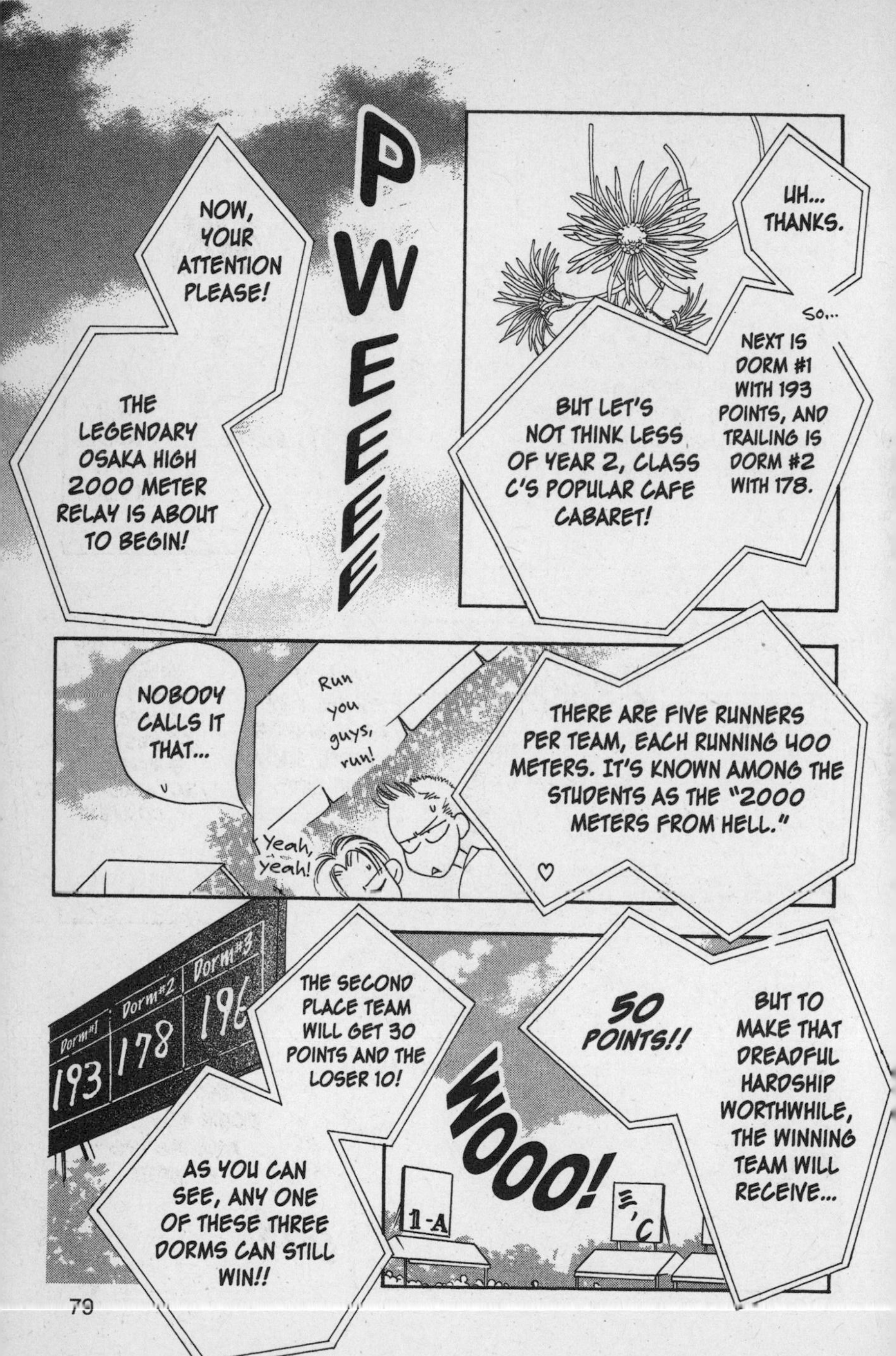
UH... THANKS.
So...
NEXT IS DORM #1 WITH 193 POINTS, AND TRAILING IS DORM #2 WITH 178.
BUT LET'S NOT THINK LESS OF YEAR 2, CLASS C'S POPULAR CAFE CABARET!
PWEEEE
NOW, YOUR ATTENTION PLEASE!
THE LEGENDARY OSAKA HIGH 2000 METER RELAY IS ABOUT TO BEGIN!
THERE ARE FIVE RUNNERS PER TEAM, EACH RUNNING 400 METERS. IT'S KNOWN AMONG THE STUDENTS AS THE "2000 METERS FROM HELL."
Run you guys, run!
NOBODY CALLS IT THAT...
Yeah, yeah!
BUT TO MAKE THAT DREADFUL HARDSHIP WORTHWHILE, THE WINNING TEAM WILL RECEIVE...
50 POINTS!!
WOOO!
THE SECOND PLACE TEAM WILL GET 30 POINTS AND THE LOSER 10!
AS YOU CAN SEE, ANY ONE OF THESE THREE DORMS CAN STILL WIN!!
Dorm#3 196
Dorm#2 178
Dorm#1 193
1-A

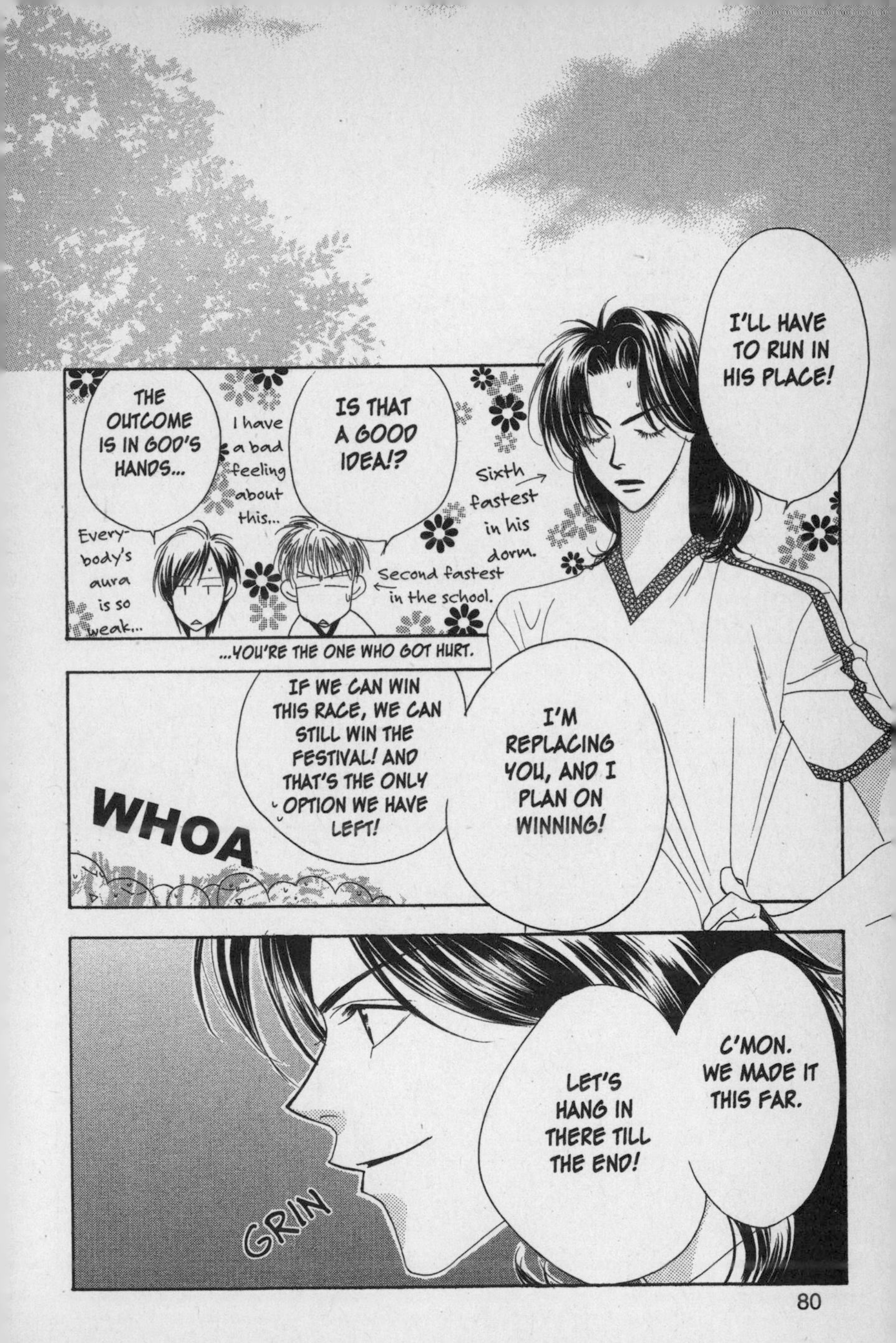
I'LL HAVE TO RUN IN HIS PLACE!
IS THAT A GOOD IDEA!?
Sixth fastest in his dorm.
Second fastest in the school.
I have a bad feeling about this...
THE OUTCOME IS IN GOD'S HANDS...
Every-body's aura is so weak...
...YOU'RE THE ONE WHO GOT HURT.
I'M REPLACING YOU, AND I PLAN ON WINNING!
IF WE CAN WIN THIS RACE, WE CAN STILL WIN THE FESTIVAL! AND THAT'S THE ONLY OPTION WE HAVE LEFT!
WHOA
C'MON. WE MADE IT THIS FAR.
LET'S HANG IN THERE TILL THE END!
GRIN

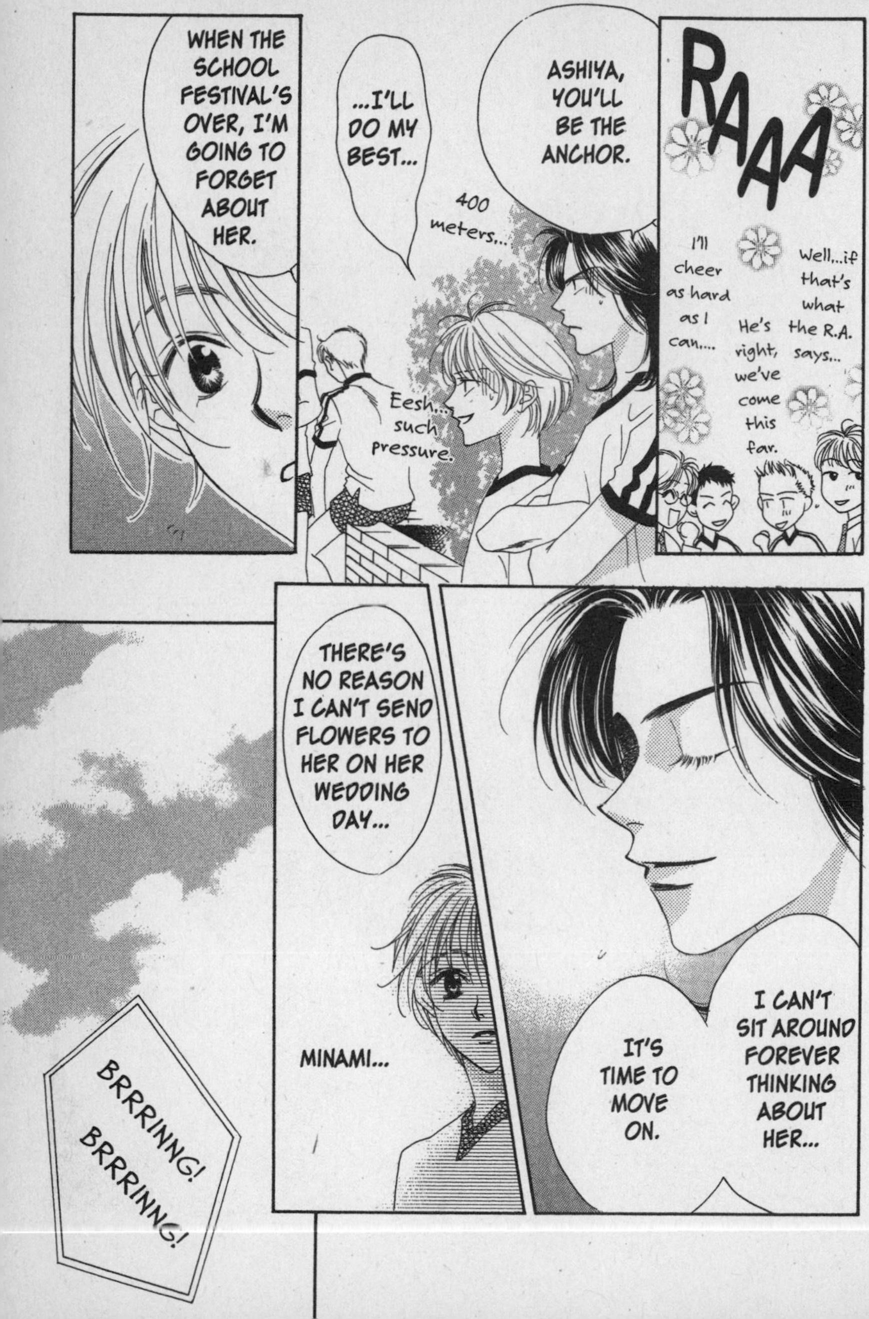
RAAA
Well...if that's what the R.A. says...
He's right, we've come this far.
I'll cheer as hard as I can....
ASHIYA, YOU'LL BE THE ANCHOR.
400 meters...
...I'LL DO MY BEST...
Eesh... such pressure.
WHEN THE SCHOOL FESTIVAL'S OVER, I'M GOING TO FORGET ABOUT HER.
I CAN'T SIT AROUND FOREVER THINKING ABOUT HER...
IT'S TIME TO MOVE ON.
THERE'S NO REASON I CAN'T SEND FLOWERS TO HER ON HER WEDDING DAY...
MINAMI...
BRRRINNG! BRRRINNG!

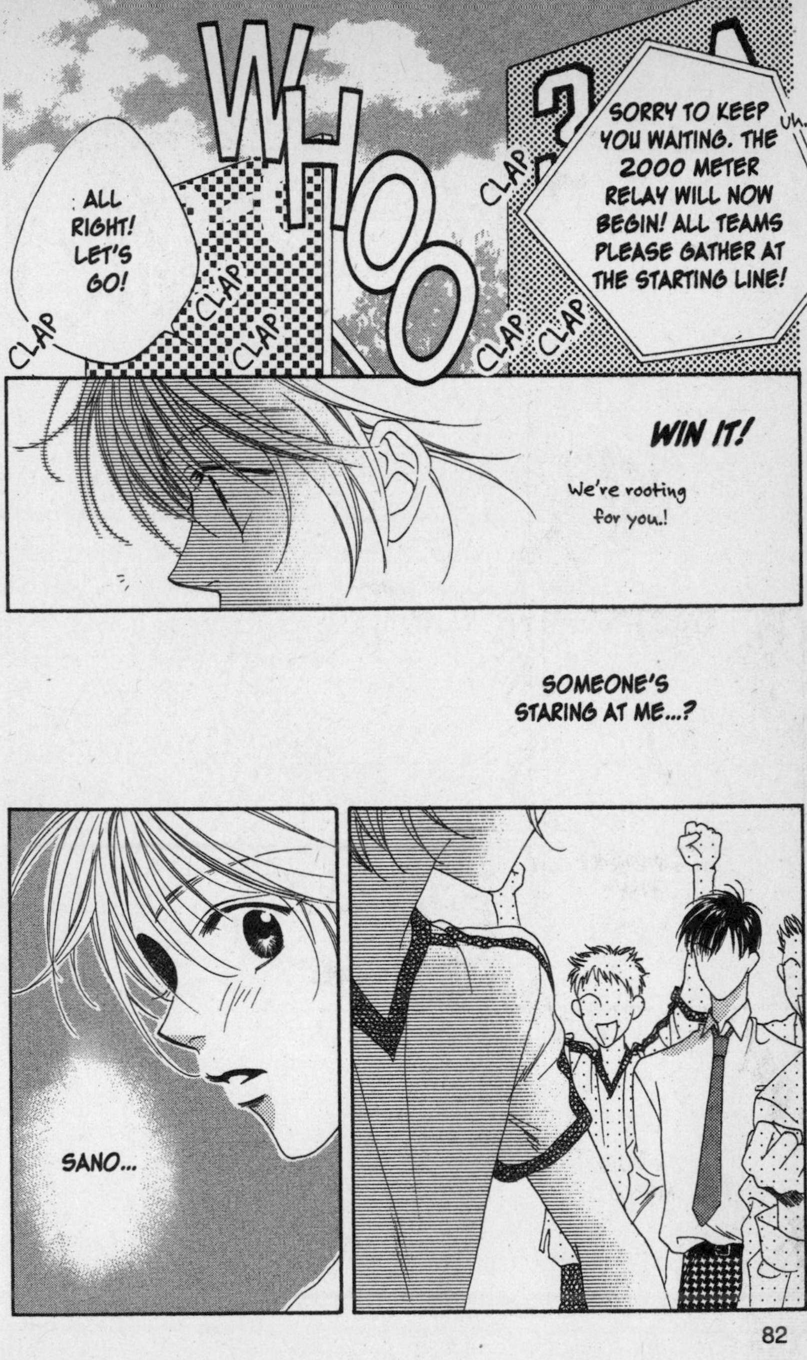
?
uh...
SORRY TO KEEP YOU WAITING. THE 2000 METER RELAY WILL NOW BEGIN! ALL TEAMS PLEASE GATHER AT THE STARTING LINE!
CLAP
CLAP CLAP
WHOO
CLAP CLAP
CLAP
ALL RIGHT! LET'S GO!
WIN IT!
We're rooting for you.!
SOMEONE'S STARING AT ME...?
SANO...

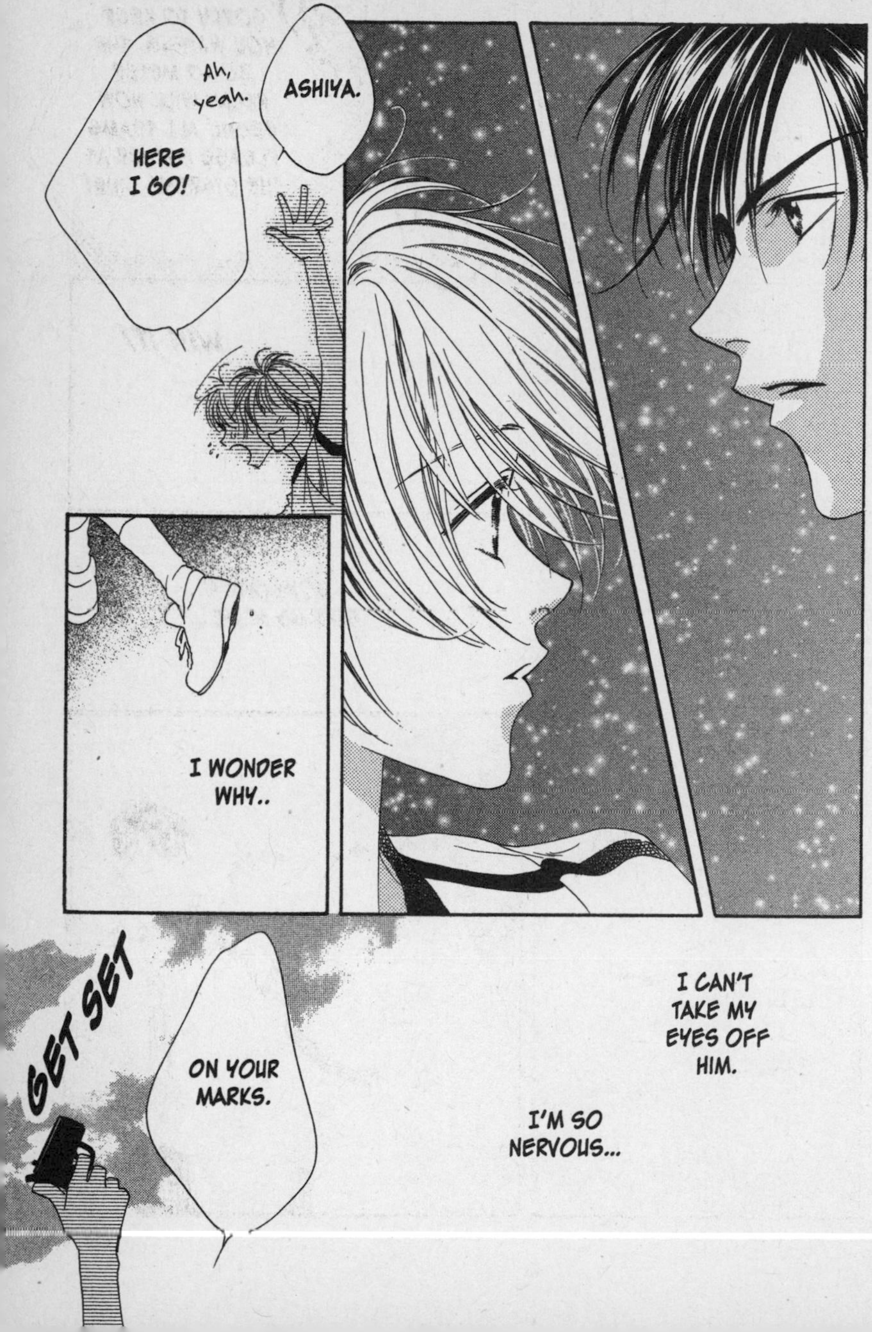
ASHIYA.
Ah, yeah.
HERE I GO!
I WONDER WHY..
I CAN'T TAKE MY EYES OFF HIM.
I'M SO NERVOUS...
ON YOUR MARKS.
GET SET

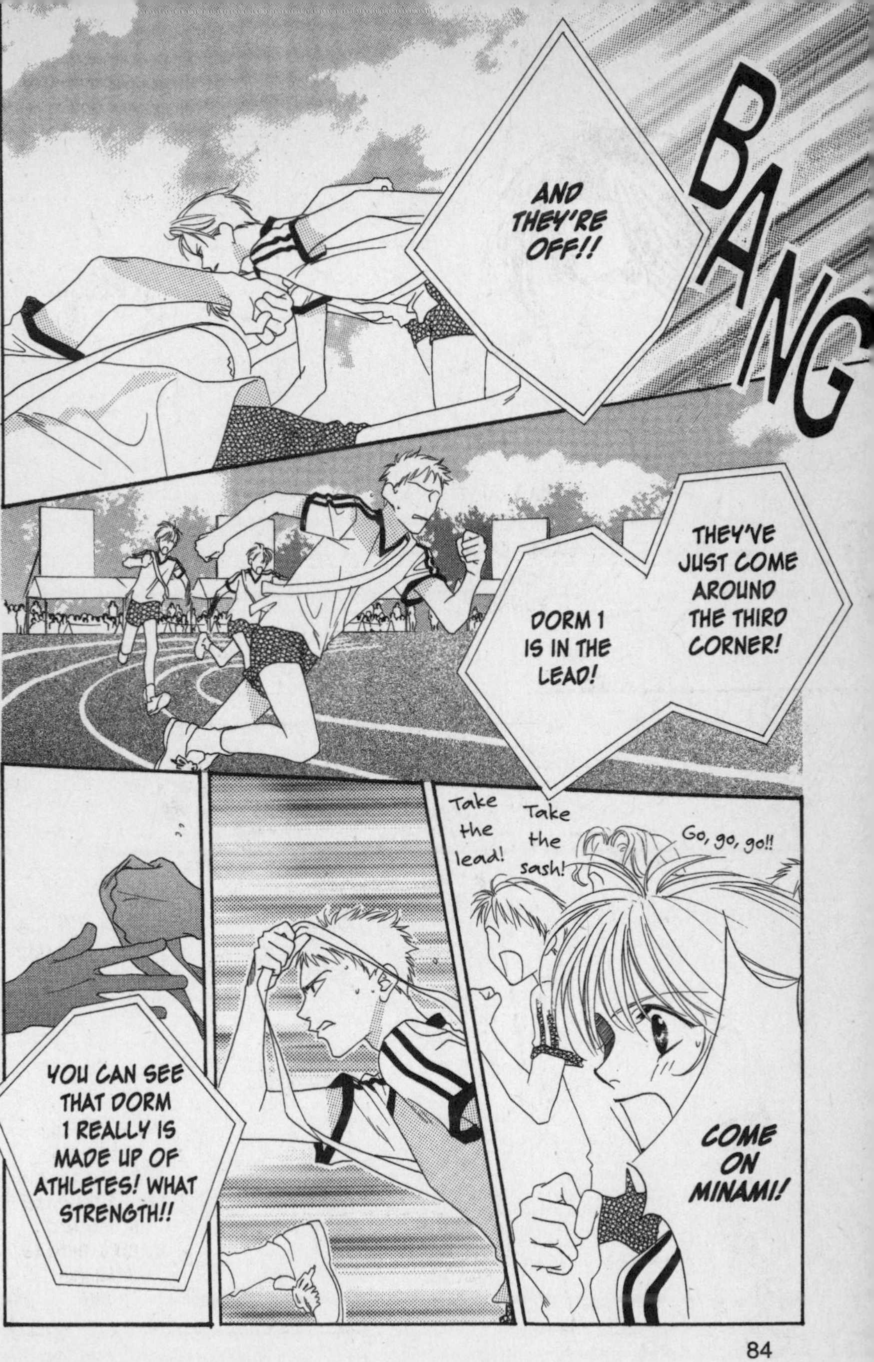
BANG
AND THEY'RE OFF!!
THEY'VE JUST COME AROUND THE THIRD CORNER!
DORM 1 IS IN THE LEAD!
Go, go, go!!
Take the sash!
Take the lead!
COME ON MINAMI!
YOU CAN SEE THAT DORM 1 REALLY IS MADE UP OF ATHLETES! WHAT STRENGTH!!

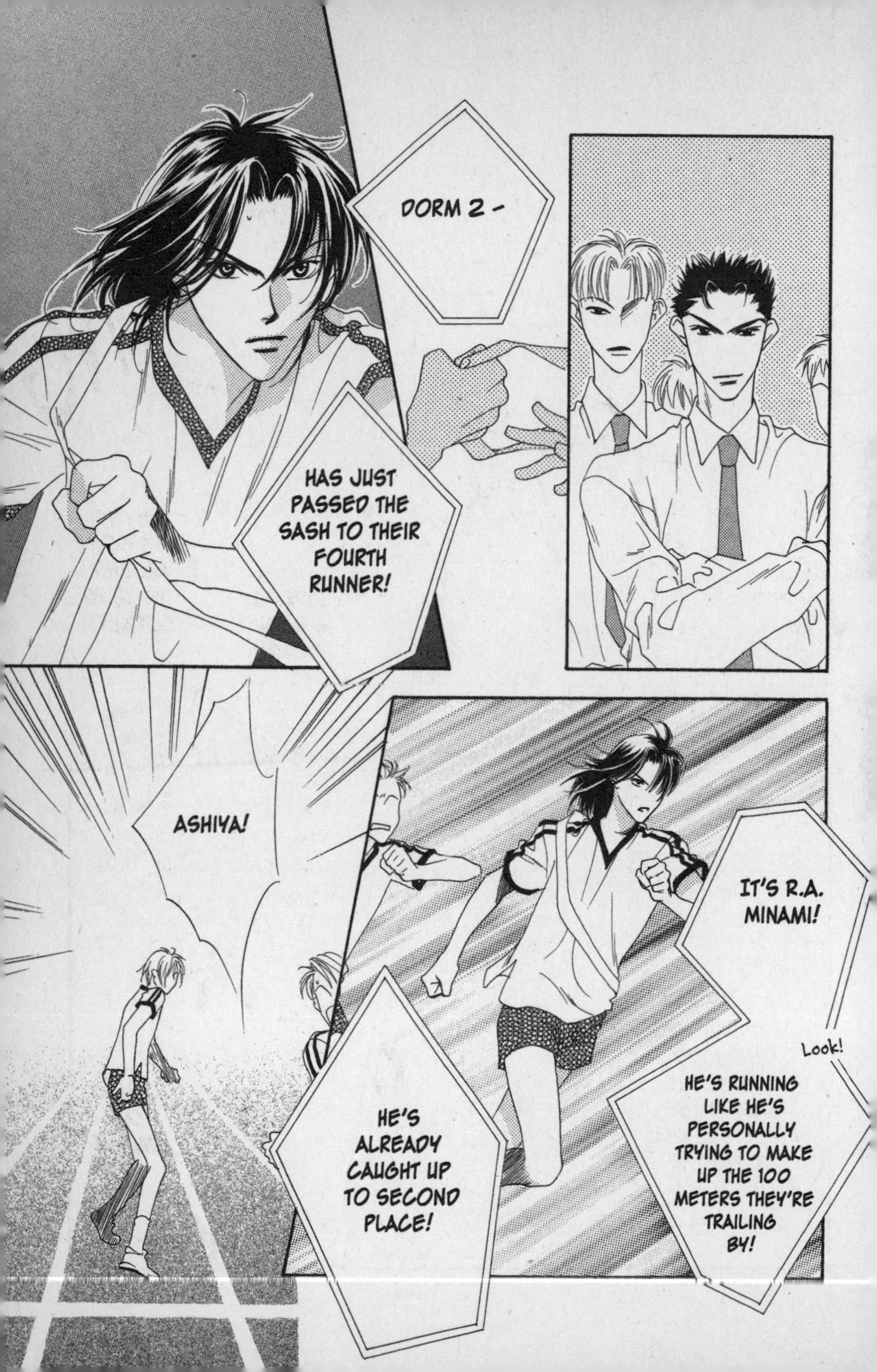
DORM 2 -
HAS JUST PASSED THE SASH TO THEIR FOURTH RUNNER!
IT'S R.A. MINAMI!
Look!
HE'S RUNNING LIKE HE'S PERSONALLY TRYING TO MAKE UP THE 100 METERS THEY'RE TRAILING BY!
HE'S ALREADY CAUGHT UP TO SECOND PLACE!
ASHIYA!

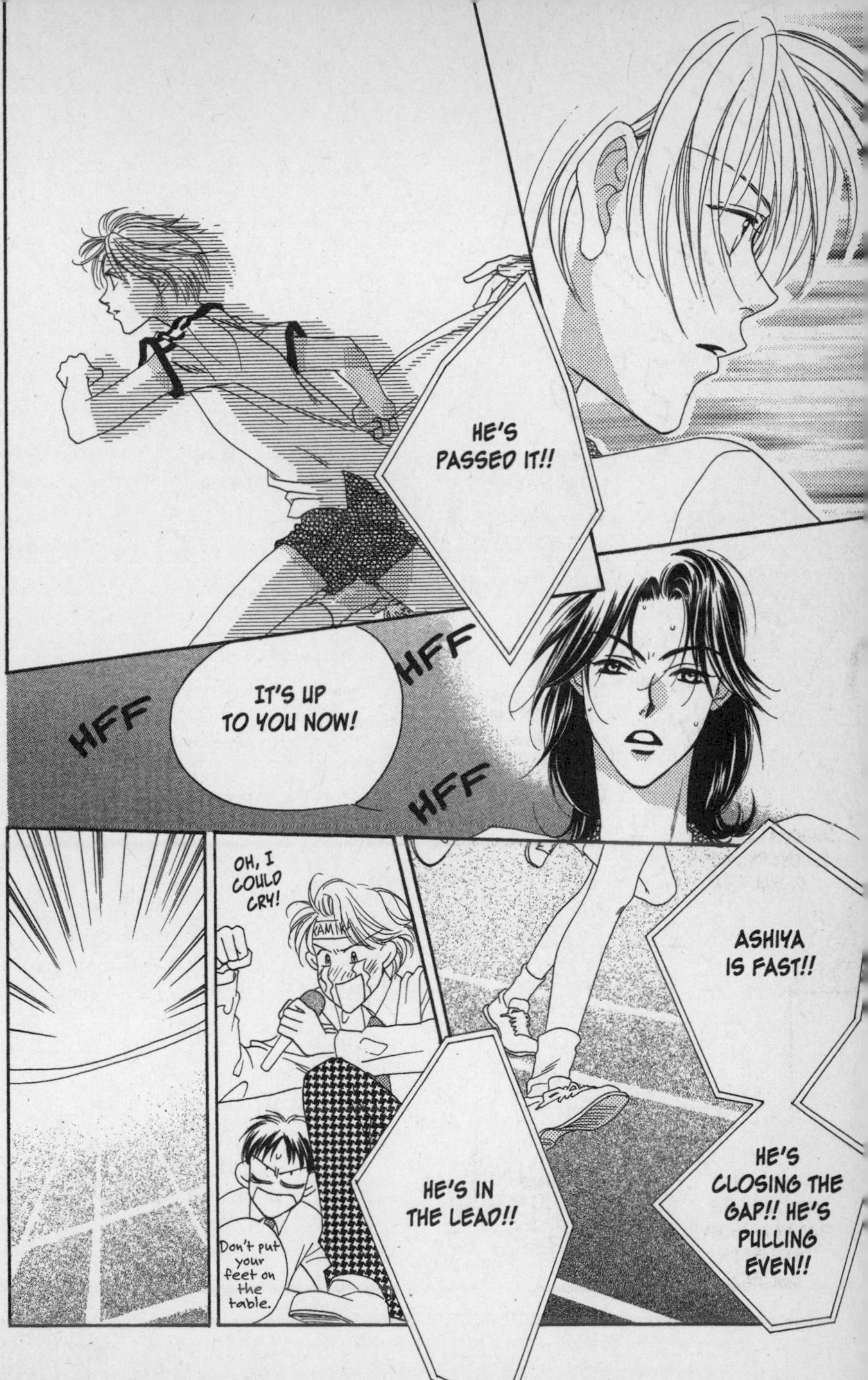
HE'S PASSED IT!!
HFF
IT'S UP TO YOU NOW!
HFF
HFF
ASHIYA IS FAST!!
HE'S CLOSING THE GAP!! HE'S PULLING EVEN!!
HE'S IN THE LEAD!!
OH, I COULD CRY!
Don't put your feet on the table.

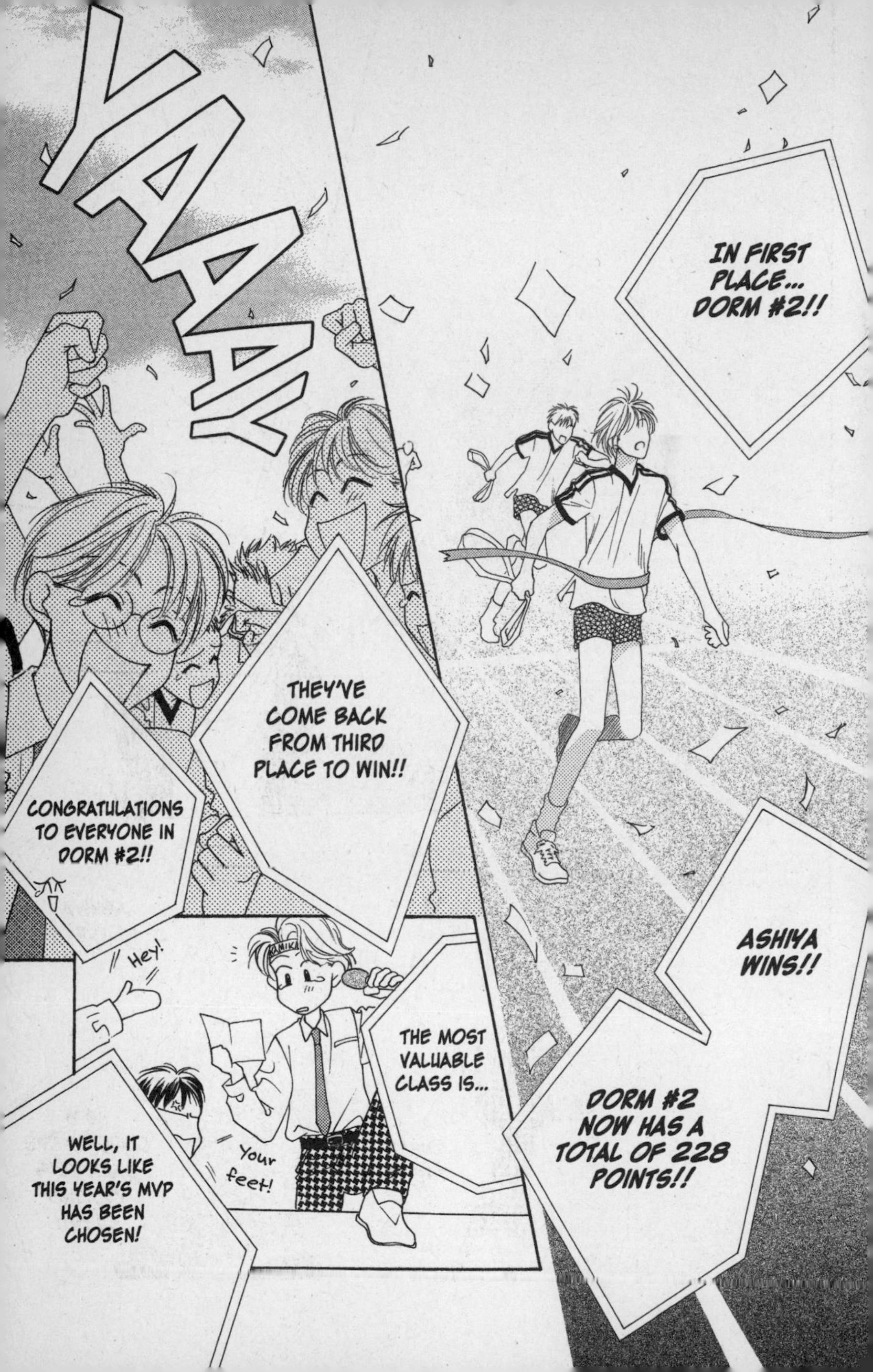
IN FIRST PLACE... DORM #2!!
ASHIYA WINS!!
DORM #2 NOW HAS A TOTAL OF 228 POINTS!!
YAAAAY
THEY'VE COME BACK FROM THIRD PLACE TO WIN!!
CONGRATULATIONS TO EVERYONE IN DORM #2!!
THE MOST VALUABLE CLASS IS...
Hey!
Your feet!
WELL, IT LOOKS LIKE THIS YEAR'S MVP HAS BEEN CHOSEN!

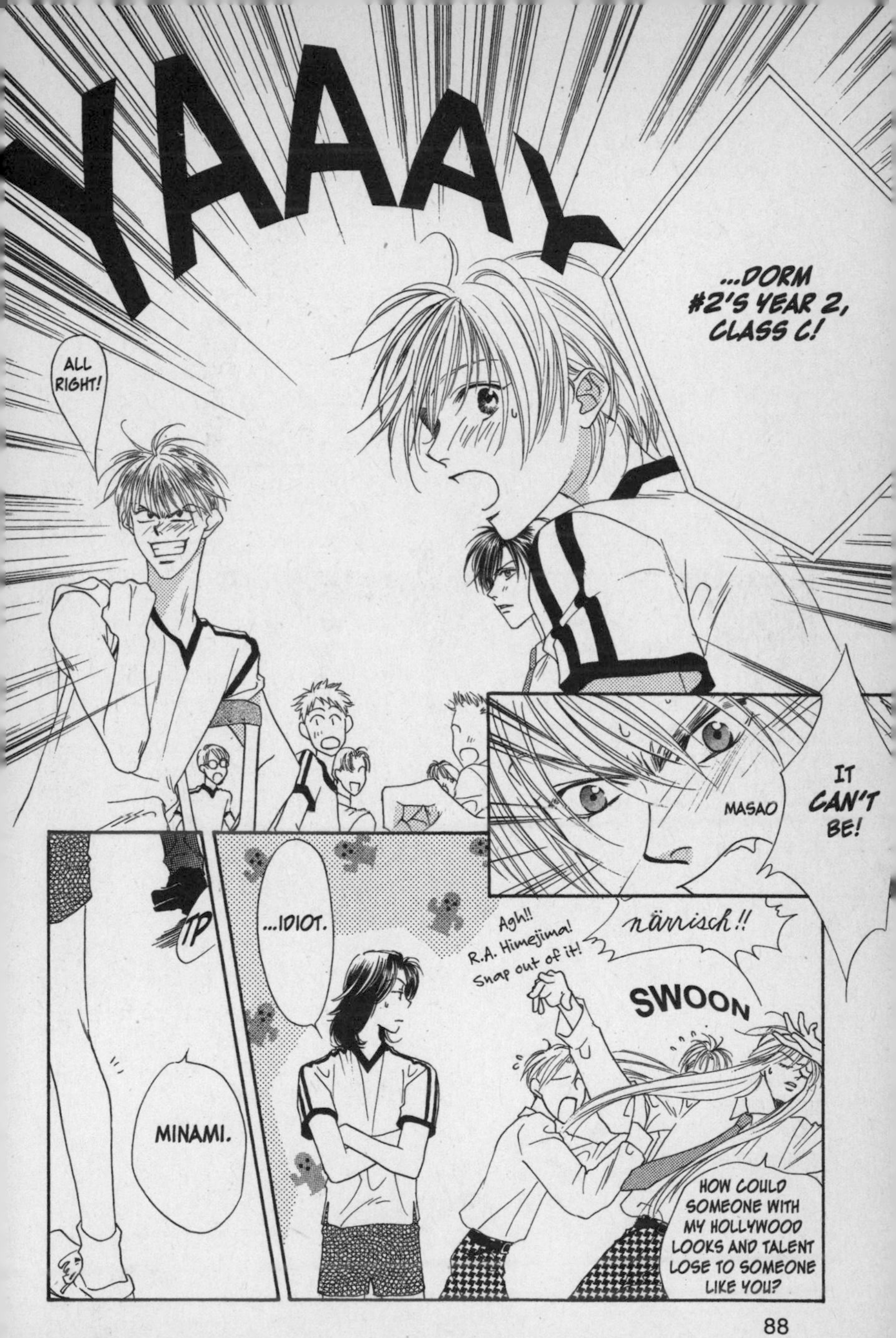
YAAAY
...DORM #2'S YEAR 2, CLASS C!
ALL RIGHT!
MASAO
IT CAN'T BE!
närrisch!!
Agh!! R.A. Himejima! Snap out of it!
SWOON
HOW COULD SOMEONE WITH MY HOLLYWOOD LOOKS AND TALENT LOSE TO SOMEONE LIKE YOU?
...IDIOT.
TP
MINAMI.

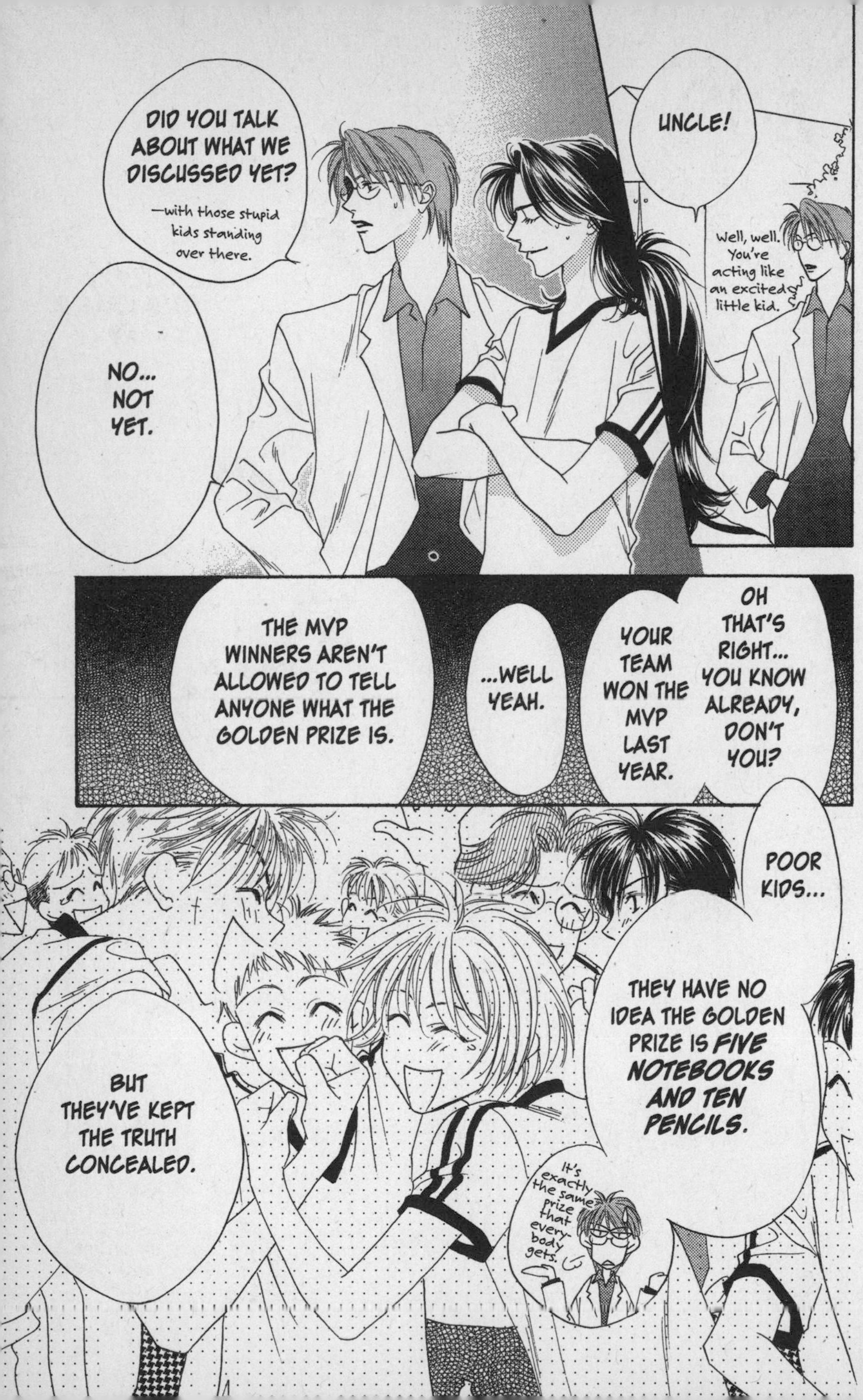

UNCLE!
Well, well. You're acting like an excited little kid.
DID YOU TALK ABOUT WHAT WE DISCUSSED YET?
—with those stupid kids standing over there.
NO... NOT YET.
OH THAT'S RIGHT... YOU KNOW ALREADY, DON'T YOU?
YOUR TEAM WON THE MVP LAST YEAR.
...WELL YEAH.
THE MVP WINNERS AREN'T ALLOWED TO TELL ANYONE WHAT THE GOLDEN PRIZE IS.
POOR KIDS...
THEY HAVE NO IDEA THE GOLDEN PRIZE IS *FIVE NOTEBOOKS AND TEN PENCILS*.
It's exactly the same prize that everybody gets.
BUT THEY'VE KEPT THE TRUTH CONCEALED.

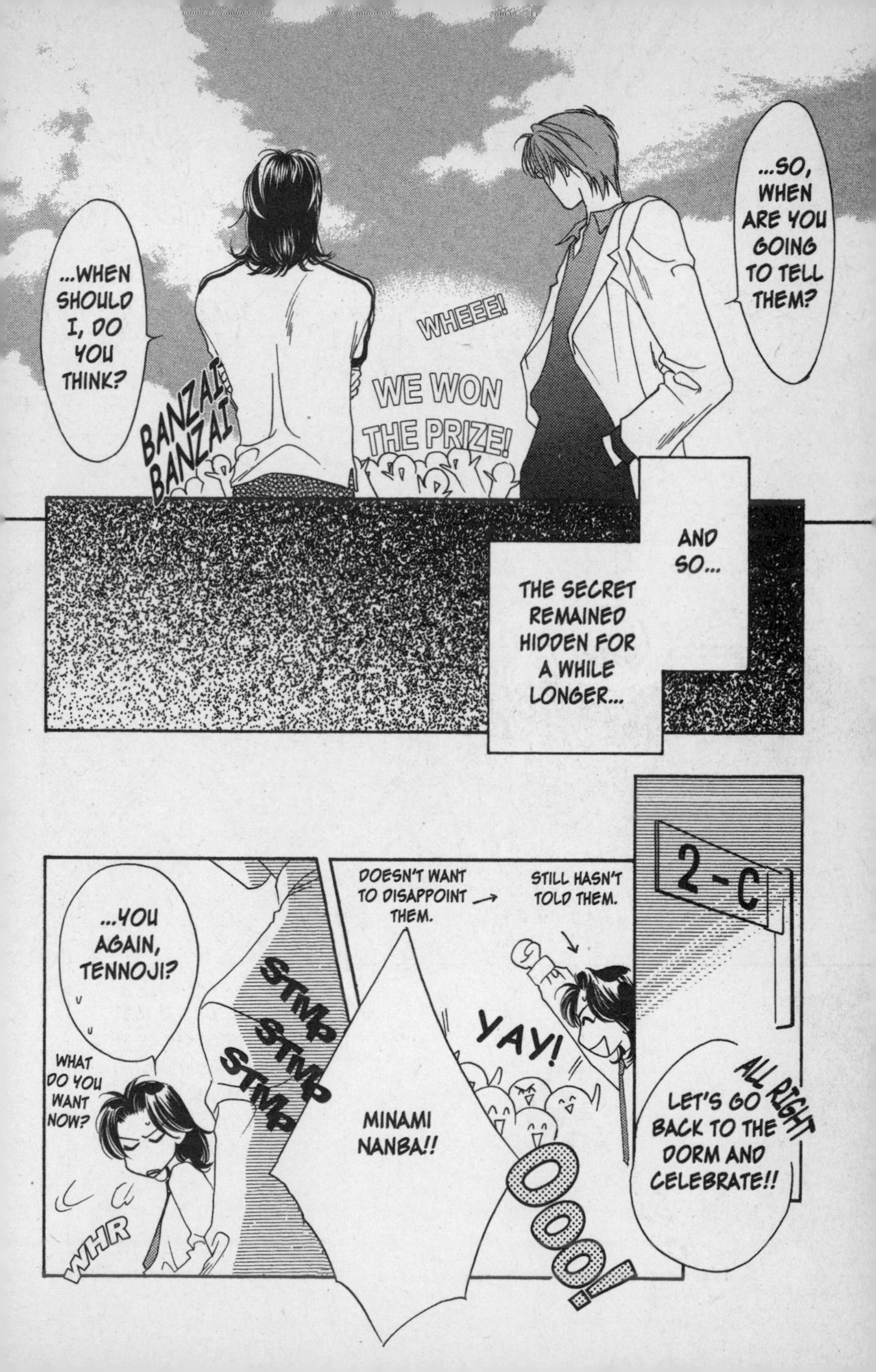
...SO, WHEN ARE YOU GOING TO TELL THEM?
WHEEE!
WE WON THE PRIZE!
BANZAI BANZAI
...WHEN SHOULD I, DO YOU THINK?
AND SO...
THE SECRET REMAINED HIDDEN FOR A WHILE LONGER...
2-C
ALL RIGHT
LET'S GO BACK TO THE DORM AND CELEBRATE!!
STILL HASN'T TOLD THEM.
YAY!
DOESN'T WANT TO DISAPPOINT THEM.
MINAMI NANBA!!
OOOO!
STMP STMP STMP
...YOU AGAIN, TENNOJI?
WHAT DO YOU WANT NOW?
WHR

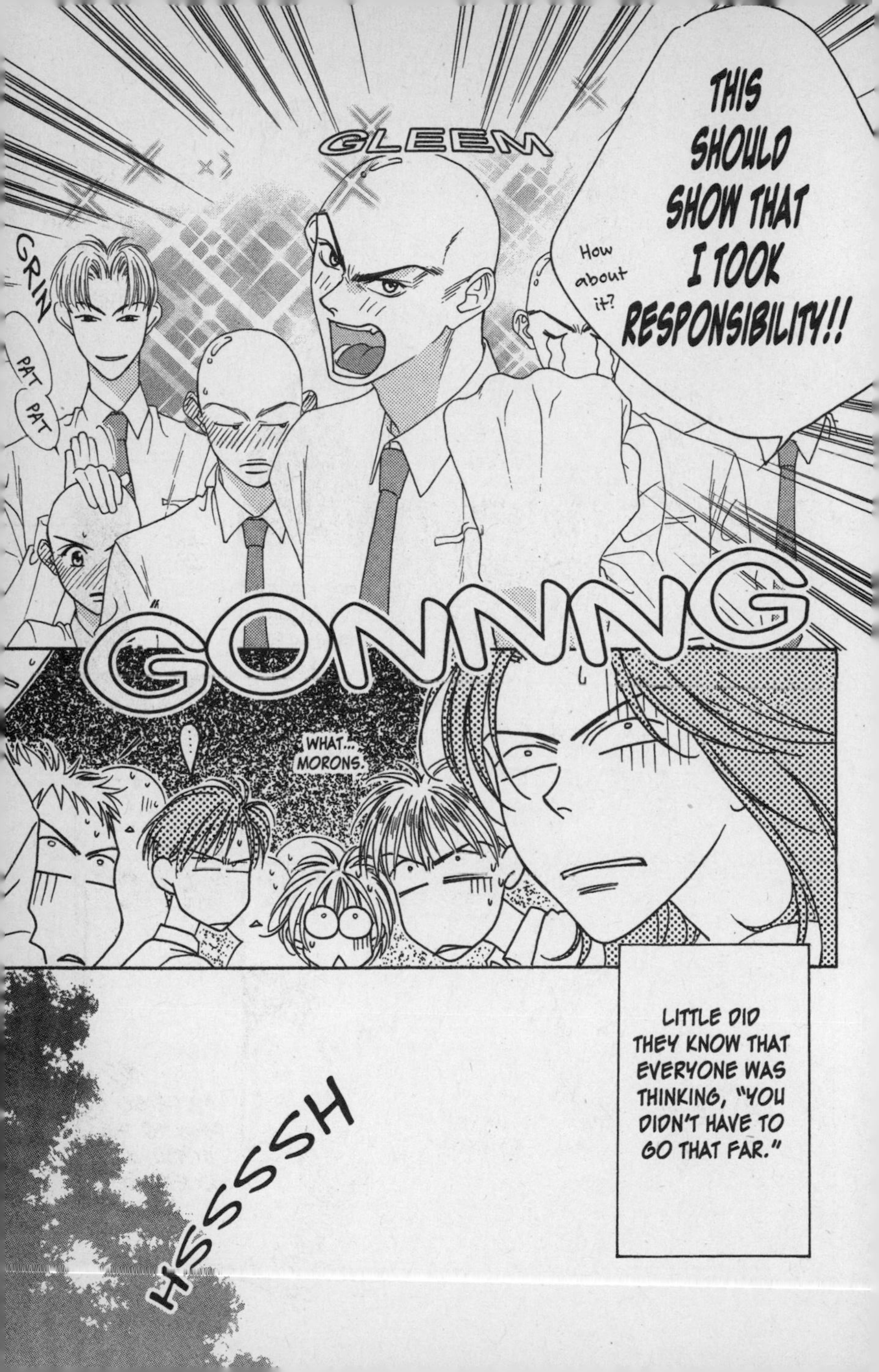
THIS SHOULD SHOW THAT I TOOK RESPONSIBILITY!!
How about it?
GLEEM
GRIN
PAT PAT
GONNNG
WHAT... MORONS.
!
LITTLE DID THEY KNOW THAT EVERYONE WAS THINKING, "YOU DIDN'T HAVE TO GO THAT FAR."
HSSSSH

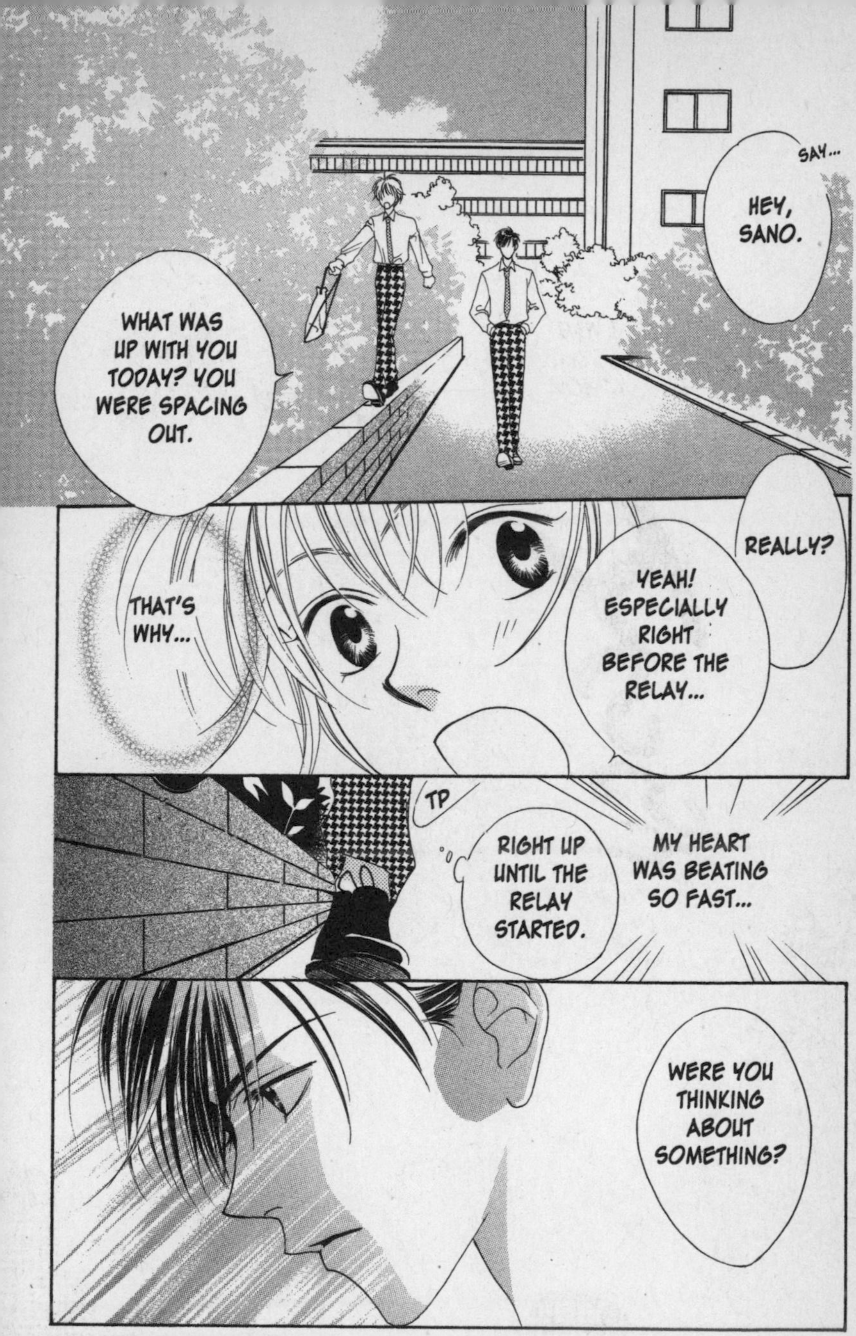
SAY...
HEY, SANO.
WHAT WAS UP WITH YOU TODAY? YOU WERE SPACING OUT.
REALLY?
YEAH! ESPECIALLY RIGHT BEFORE THE RELAY...
THAT'S WHY...
MY HEART WAS BEATING SO FAST...
RIGHT UP UNTIL THE RELAY STARTED.
TP
WERE YOU THINKING ABOUT SOMETHING?

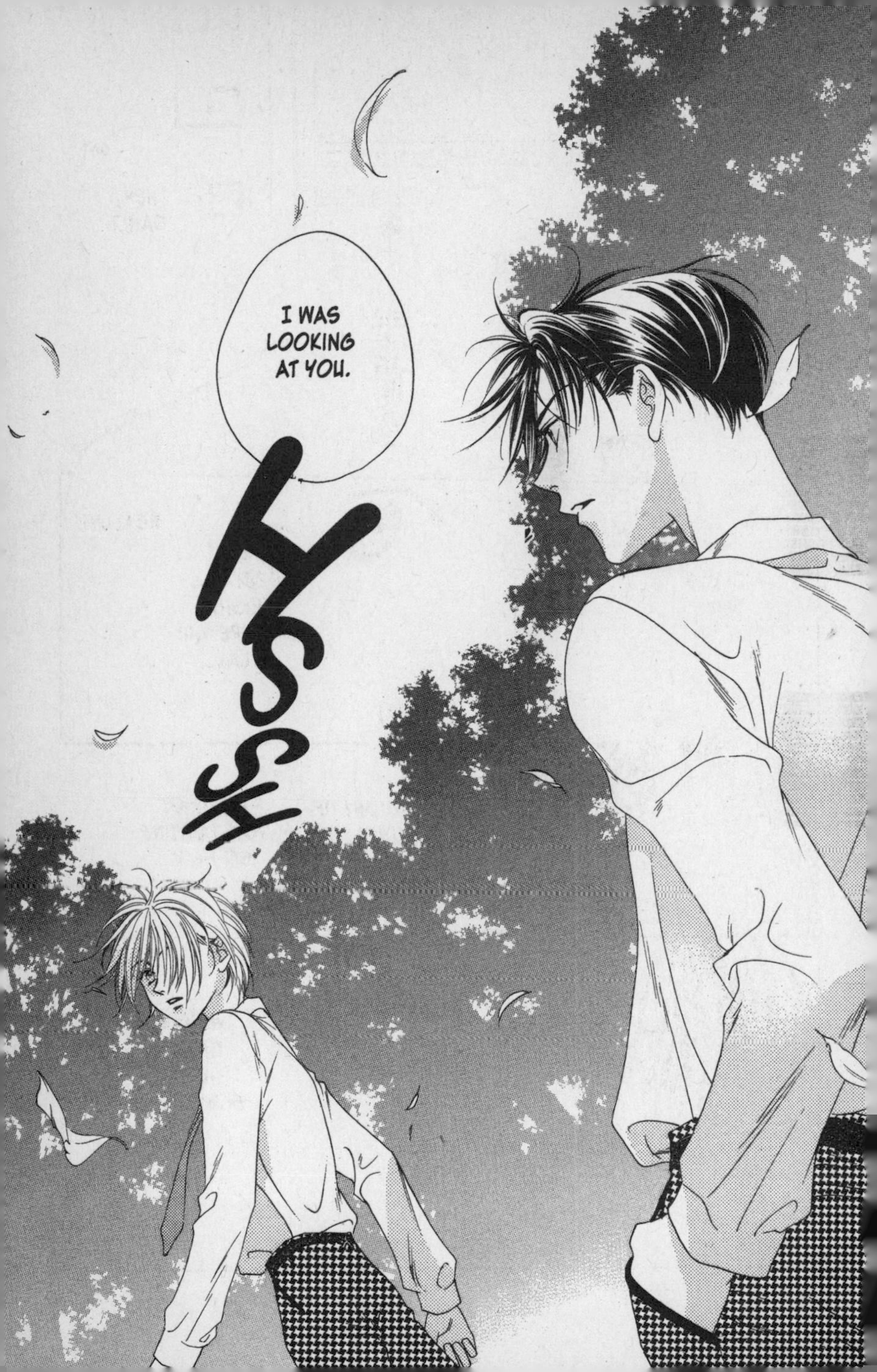
I WAS LOOKING AT YOU.
HSSH

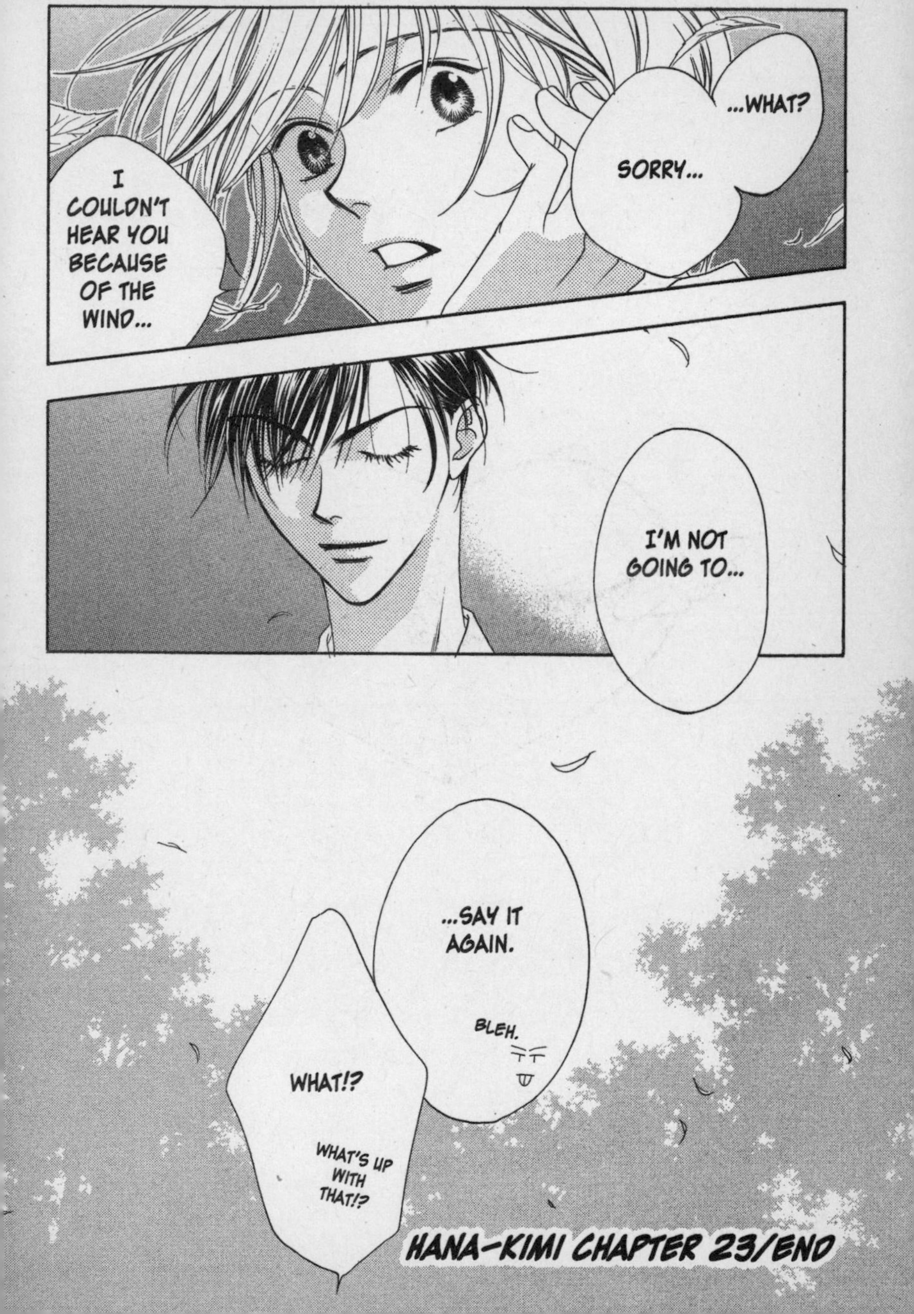
...WHAT? SORRY...
I COULDN'T HEAR YOU BECAUSE OF THE WIND...
I'M NOT GOING TO...
...SAY IT AGAIN.
BLEH.
WHAT!?
WHAT'S UP WITH THAT!?
HANA-KIMI CHAPTER 23/END

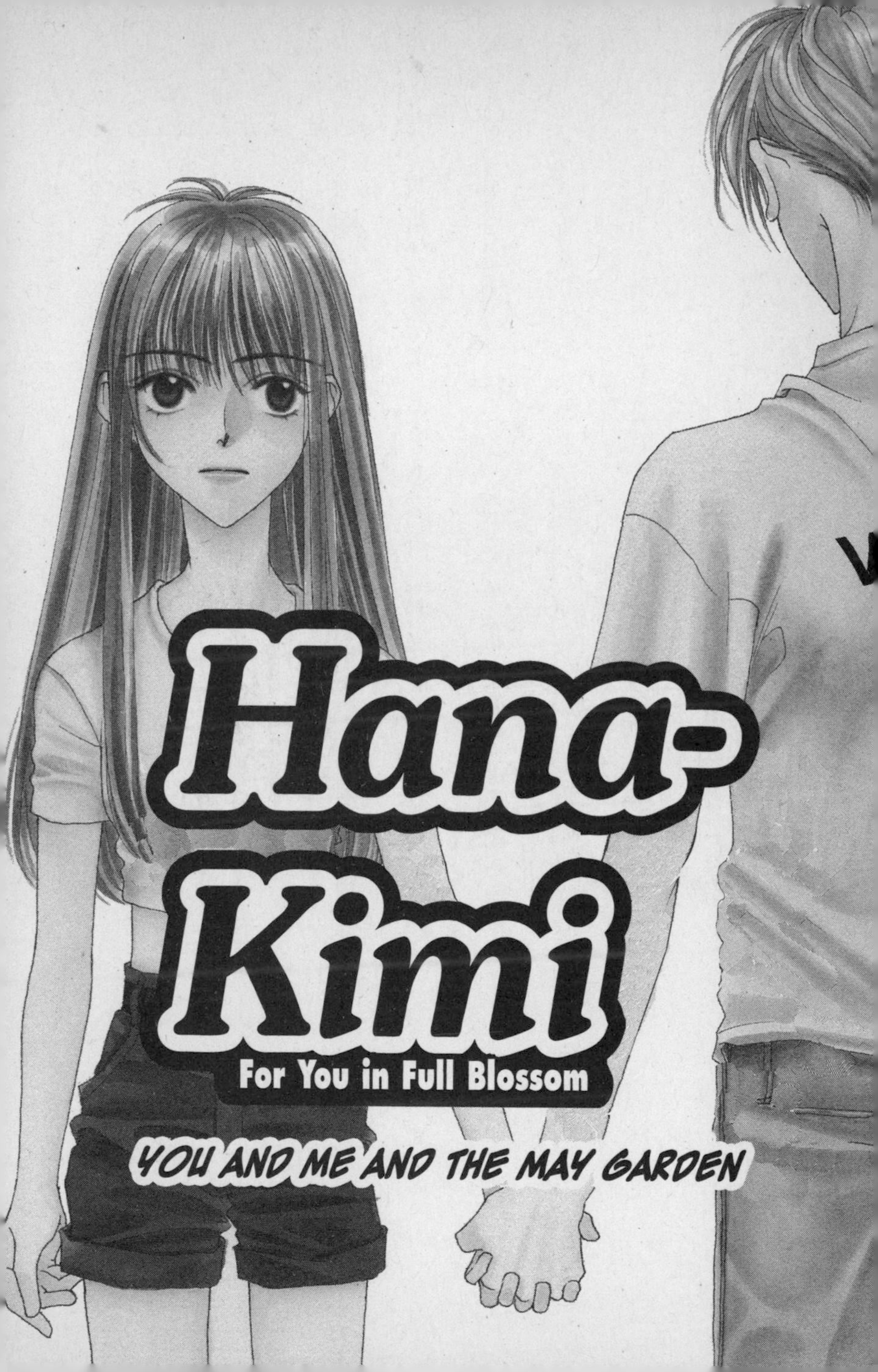
Hana-Kimi
For You in Full Blossom
YOU AND ME AND THE MAY GARDEN

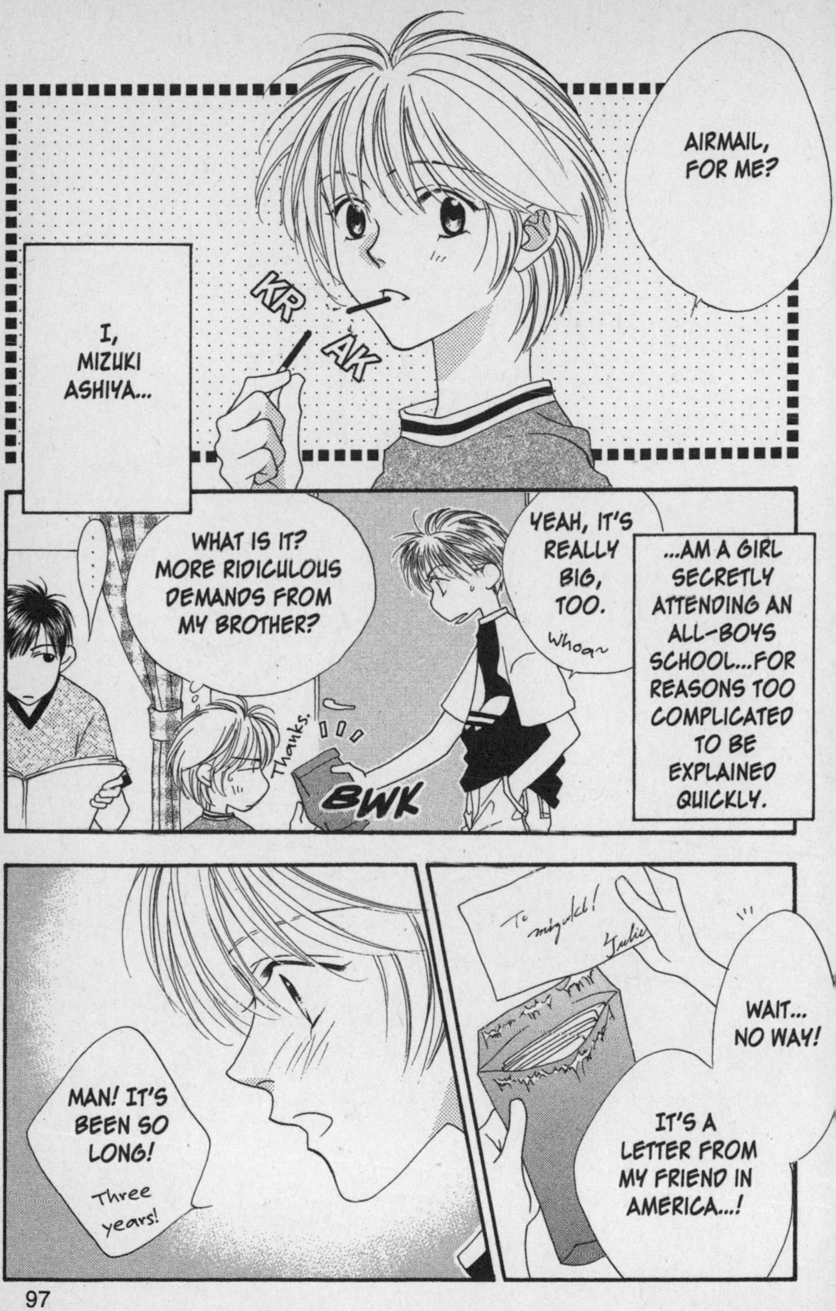
AIRMAIL, FOR ME?
KRAK
I, MIZUKI ASHIYA...
...AM A GIRL SECRETLY ATTENDING AN ALL-BOYS SCHOOL...FOR REASONS TOO COMPLICATED TO BE EXPLAINED QUICKLY.
YEAH, IT'S REALLY BIG, TOO.
Whoa~
BWK
Thanks.
WHAT IS IT? MORE RIDICULOUS DEMANDS FROM MY BROTHER?
WAIT... NO WAY!
IT'S A LETTER FROM MY FRIEND IN AMERICA...!
MAN! IT'S BEEN SO LONG!
Three years!

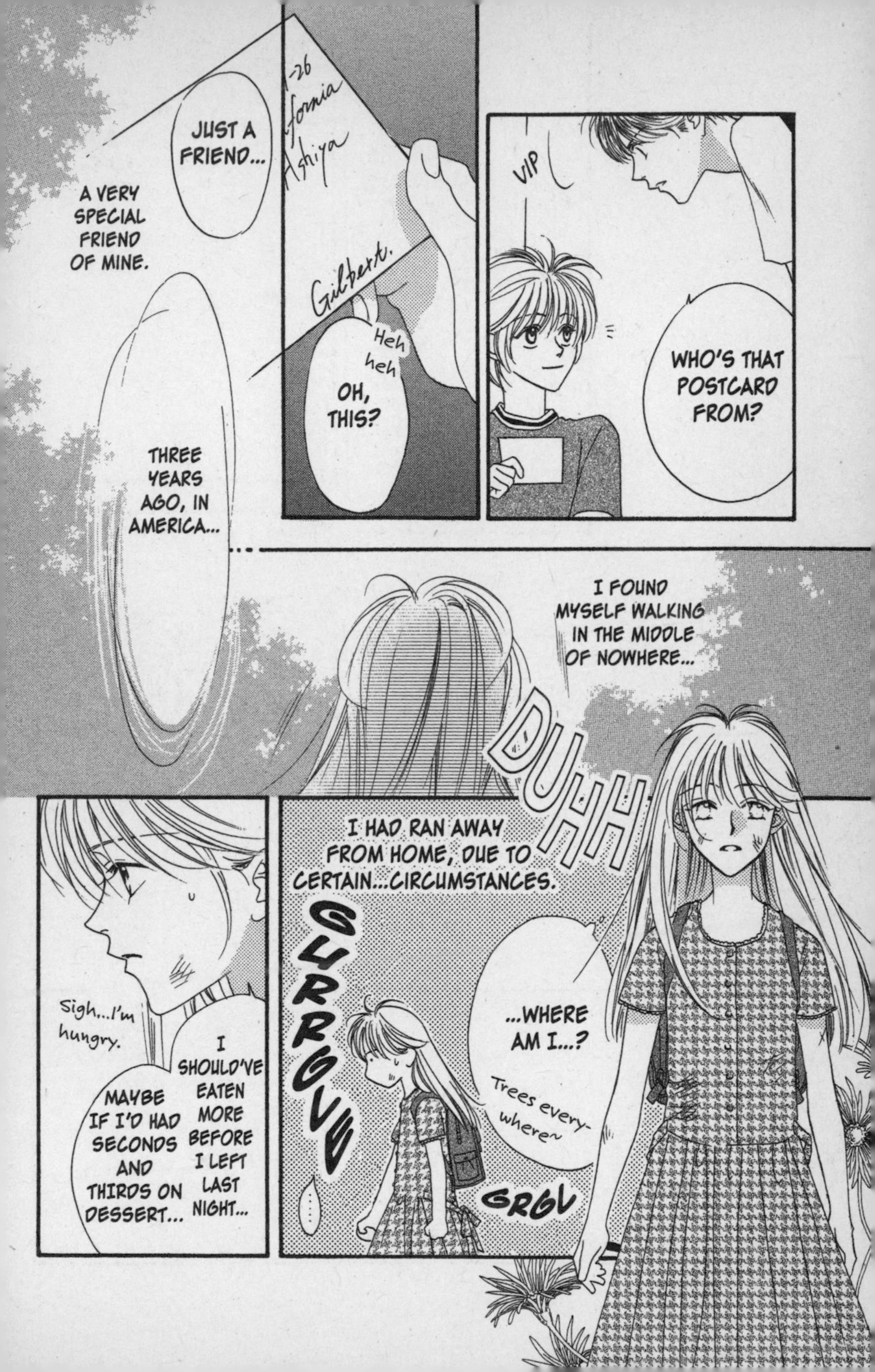
VIP
WHO'S THAT POSTCARD FROM?
Heh heh
OH, THIS?
1-26
fornia
Ashiya
Gilbert.
JUST A FRIEND...
A VERY SPECIAL FRIEND OF MINE.
THREE YEARS AGO, IN AMERICA...
I FOUND MYSELF WALKING IN THE MIDDLE OF NOWHERE...
DUHH
I HAD RAN AWAY FROM HOME, DUE TO CERTAIN...CIRCUMSTANCES.
...WHERE AM I...?
Trees every-where~
GURRGVV
GRGV
...
Sigh...I'm hungry.
I SHOULD'VE EATEN MORE BEFORE I LEFT LAST NIGHT...
MAYBE IF I'D HAD SECONDS AND THIRDS ON DESSERT...

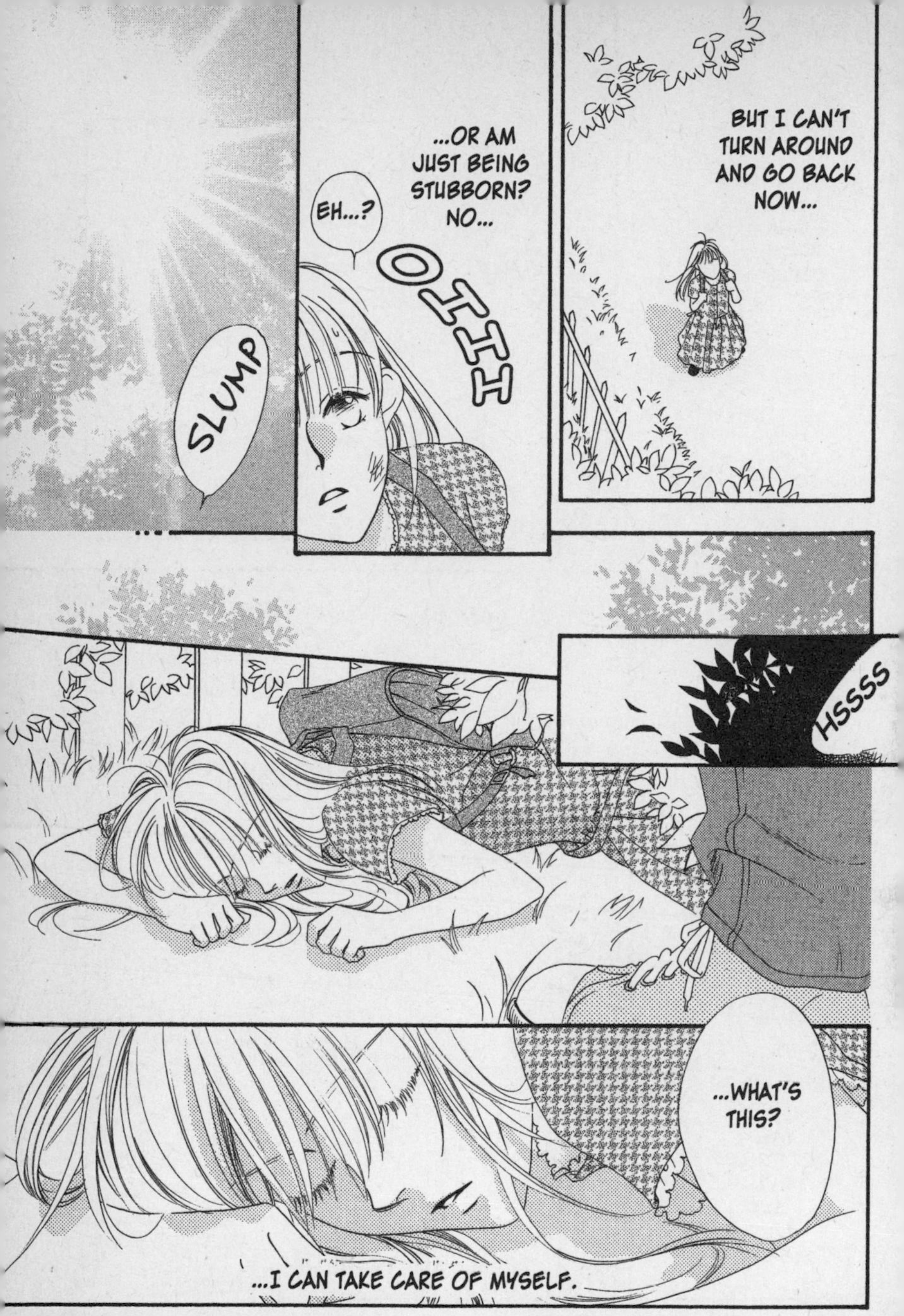
BUT I CAN'T TURN AROUND AND GO BACK NOW...
...OR AM JUST BEING STUBBORN? NO...
EH...?
OTTO
SLUMP
...
HSSSS
...WHAT'S THIS?
...I CAN TAKE CARE OF MYSELF.

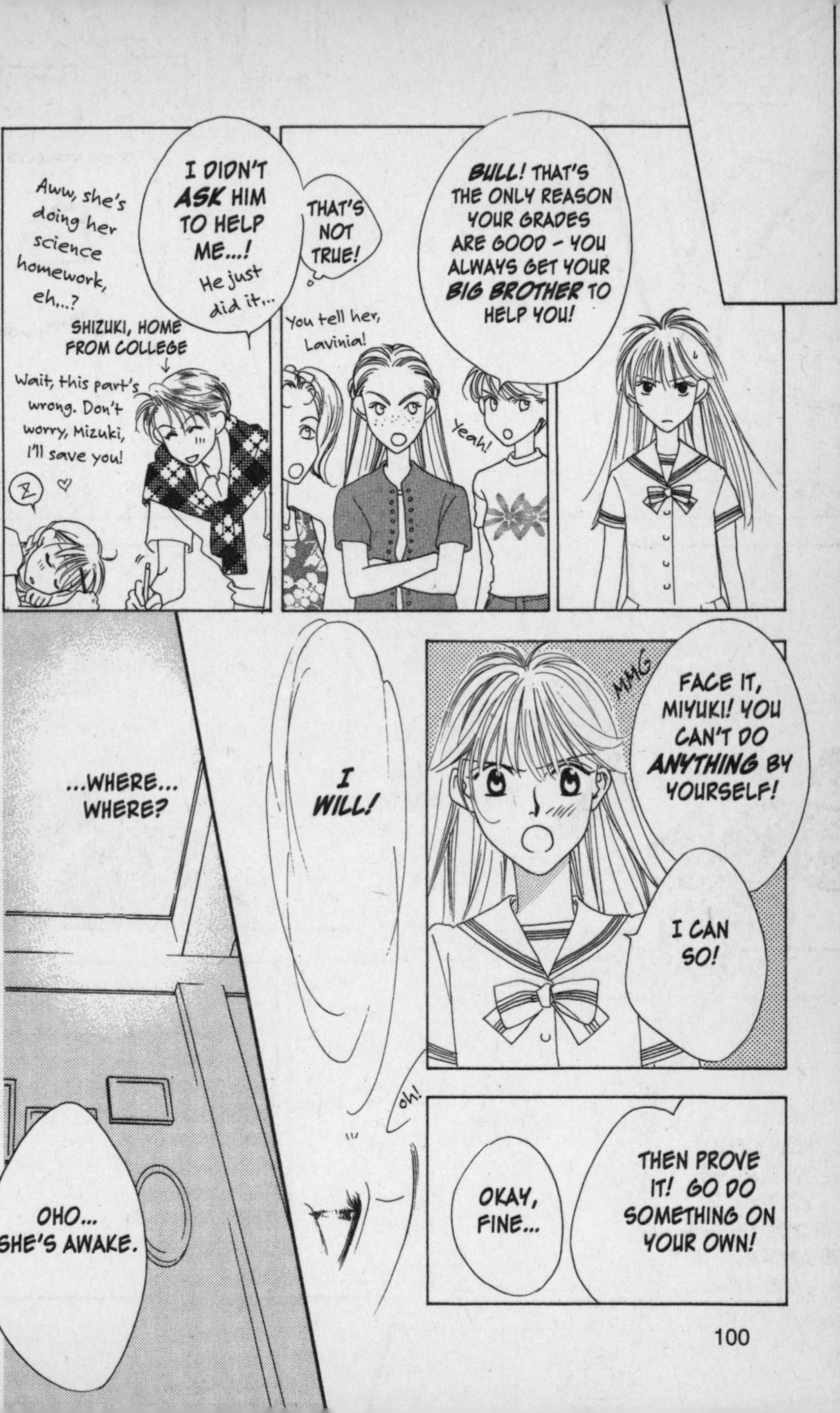
BULL! THAT'S THE ONLY REASON YOUR GRADES ARE GOOD - YOU ALWAYS GET YOUR BIG BROTHER TO HELP YOU!
THAT'S NOT TRUE!
Yeah!
You tell her, Lavinia!
I DIDN'T ASK HIM TO HELP ME...!
He just did it...
Aww, she's doing her science homework, eh...?
SHIZUKI, HOME FROM COLLEGE
Wait, this part's wrong. Don't worry, Mizuki, I'll save you!
Z
FACE IT, MIYUKI! YOU CAN'T DO ANYTHING BY YOURSELF!
MMG
I CAN SO!
THEN PROVE IT! GO DO SOMETHING ON YOUR OWN!
OKAY, FINE...
I WILL!
oh!
...WHERE... WHERE?
OHO... SHE'S AWAKE.

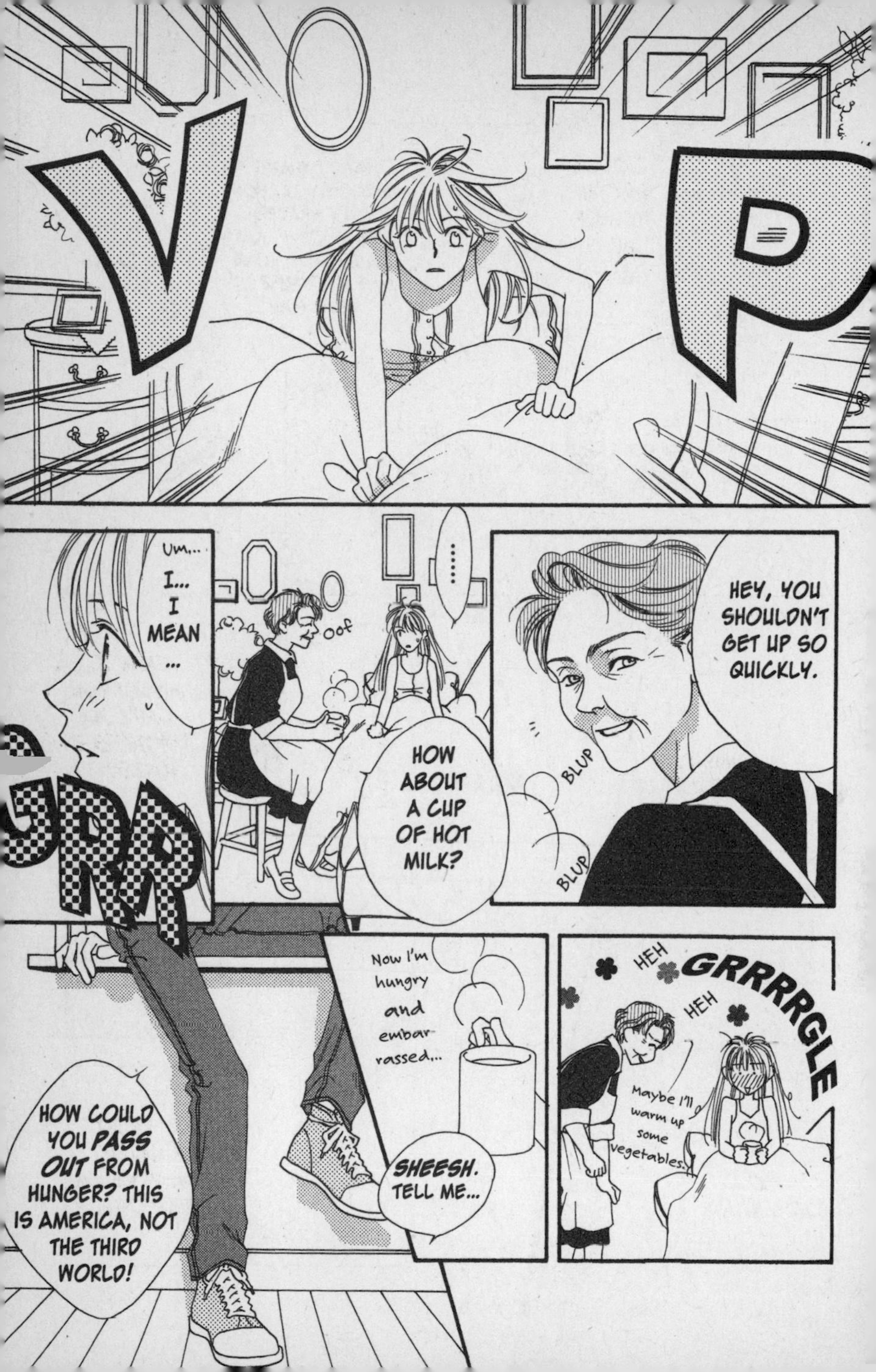

VP
HEY, YOU SHOULDN'T GET UP SO QUICKLY.
BLUP
BLUP
......
Oof
HOW ABOUT A CUP OF HOT MILK?
Um... I... I MEAN ...
HEH
HEH
GRRRRGLE
Maybe I'll warm up some vegetables.
Now I'm hungry and embarrassed...
SHEESH. TELL ME...
HOW COULD YOU *PASS OUT* FROM HUNGER? THIS IS AMERICA, NOT THE THIRD WORLD!

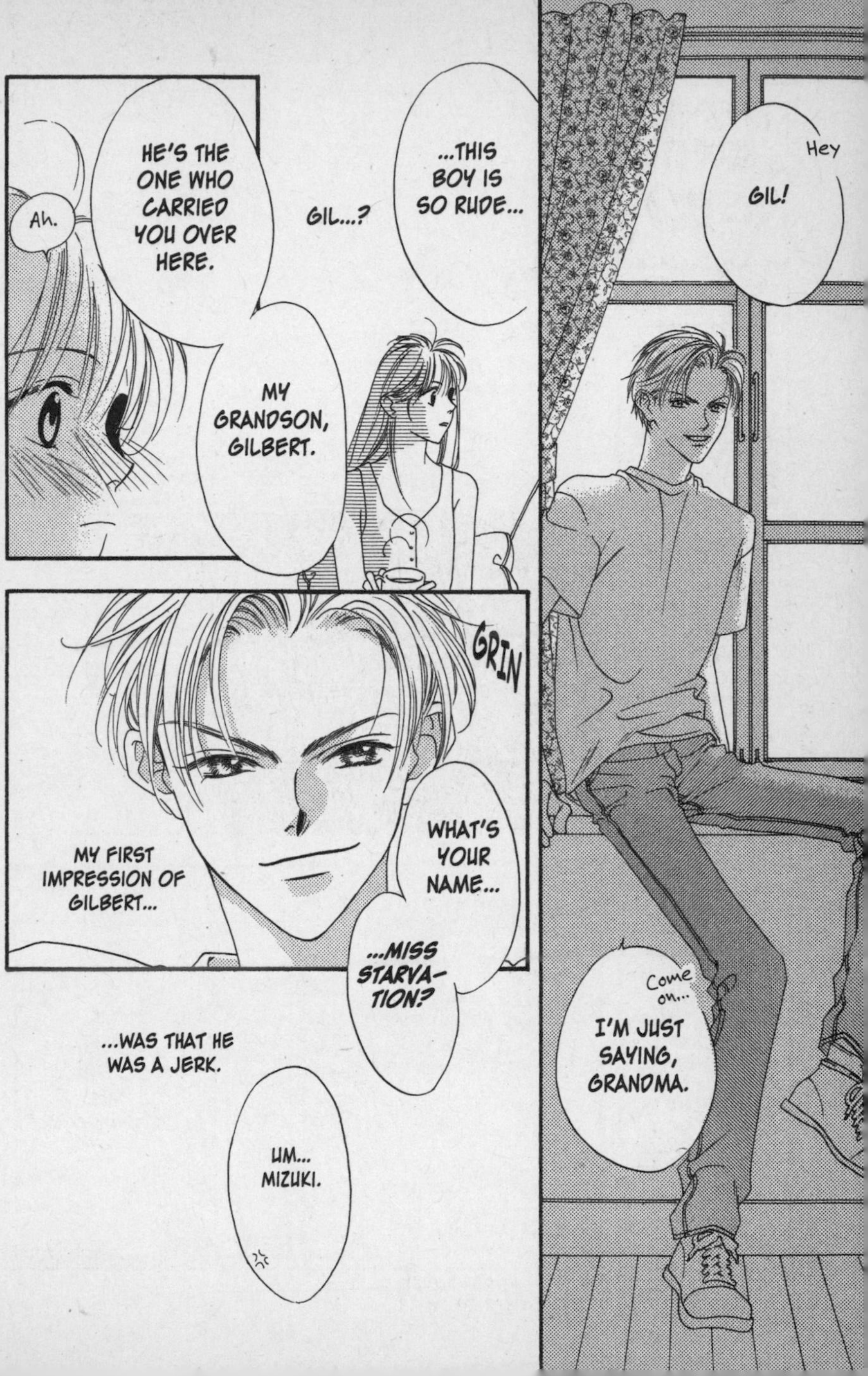
Hey
GIL!
Come on...
I'M JUST SAYING, GRANDMA.
...THIS BOY IS SO RUDE...
GIL...?
HE'S THE ONE WHO CARRIED YOU OVER HERE.
Ah.
MY GRANDSON, GILBERT.
GRIN
WHAT'S YOUR NAME...
...MISS STARVATION?
MY FIRST IMPRESSION OF GILBERT...
...WAS THAT HE WAS A JERK.
UM... MIZUKI.

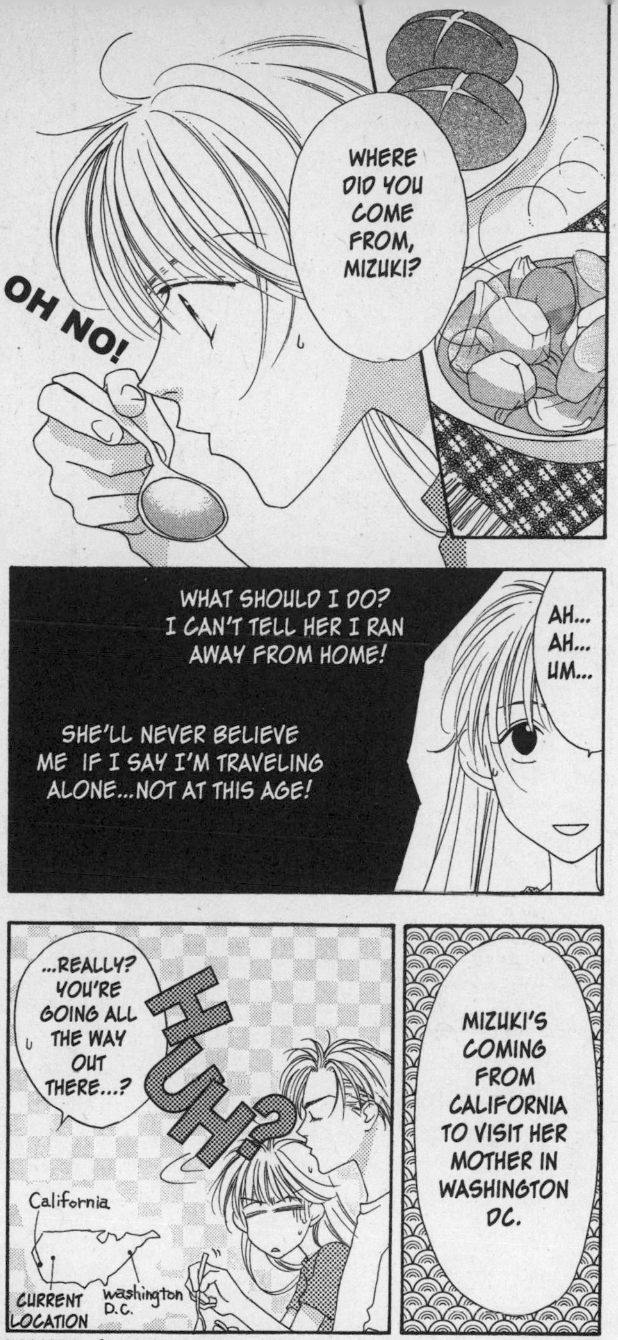
WHERE DID YOU COME FROM, MIZUKI?
OH NO!
AH... AH... UM...
WHAT SHOULD I DO? I CAN'T TELL HER I RAN AWAY FROM HOME!
SHE'LL NEVER BELIEVE ME IF I SAY I'M TRAVELING ALONE...NOT AT THIS AGE!
MIZUKI'S COMING FROM CALIFORNIA TO VISIT HER MOTHER IN WASHINGTON DC.
HUH?
...REALLY? YOU'RE GOING ALL THE WAY OUT THERE...?
California
CURRENT LOCATION
washington D.C.

WHISPERED SECRETS

THE MAN IN THE MASK

THE CHARACTER GILBERT WHO APPEARS IN THIS STORY WAS MODELED AFTER LEONARDO DICAPRIO! AT THE TIME I WROTE THIS, MY EDITOR LOVED DICAPRIO, AND I SORT OF PICKED THAT UP. AT THAT TIME, HE WASN'T TOO FAMOUS YET, ALTHOUGH HE'D BEEN IN "ROMEO & JULIET" AND "TOTAL ECLIPSE." I'M NOT IN LOVE WITH HIM, BUT I THINK HE'S A SUPERB ACTOR. "TITANIC," THOUGH...A LOT OF ACTORS COULD'VE PLAYED HIS ROLE. THE STORY WAS OKAY, BUT THE ROMANTIC PART WAS TOO CHEESY. I WAS DISAPPOINTED. AT THE THEATER, I WAS LIKE, "AM I SUPPOSED TO CRY NOW?", AND THE PERSON NEXT TO ME WAS SOBBING. IT WAS EMBARRASSING.

↑ IF YOU WANT TO SEE DICAPRIO'S TRUE TALENT, THEN WATCH THIS!!

I GUESS EVERYBODY'S DIFFERENT. (I DON'T WANT TO BE RUDE TO ALL THE PEOPLE WHO LIKED THE MOVIE.)

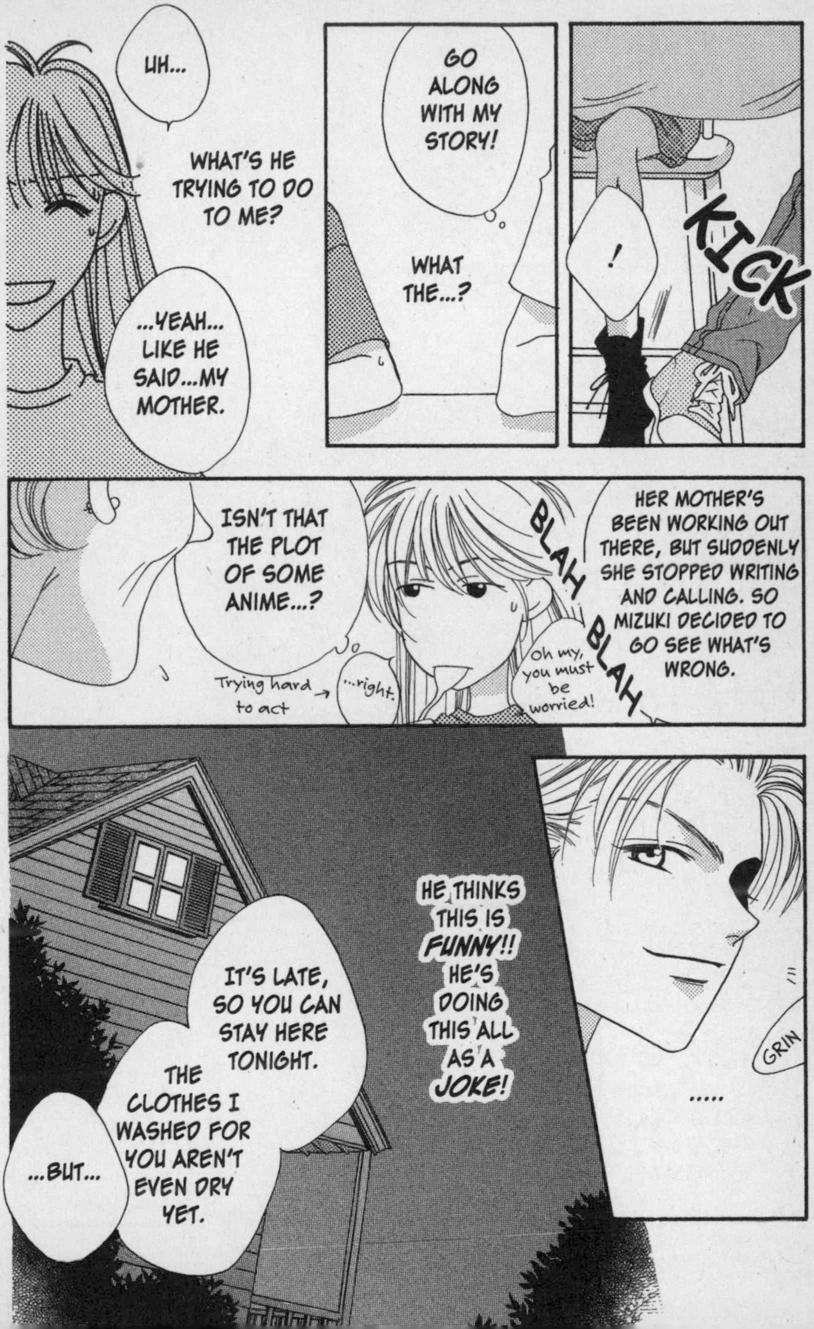
!
KICK
GO ALONG WITH MY STORY!
WHAT THE...?
UH...
WHAT'S HE TRYING TO DO TO ME?
...YEAH... LIKE HE SAID...MY MOTHER.
HER MOTHER'S BEEN WORKING OUT THERE, BUT SUDDENLY SHE STOPPED WRITING AND CALLING. SO MIZUKI DECIDED TO GO SEE WHAT'S WRONG.
BLAH BLAH
Oh my, you must be worried!
...right.
Trying hard to act
ISN'T THAT THE PLOT OF SOME ANIME...?
GRIN
.....
HE THINKS THIS IS FUNNY!! HE'S DOING THIS ALL AS A JOKE!
IT'S LATE, SO YOU CAN STAY HERE TONIGHT.
THE CLOTHES I WASHED FOR YOU AREN'T EVEN DRY YET.
...BUT...

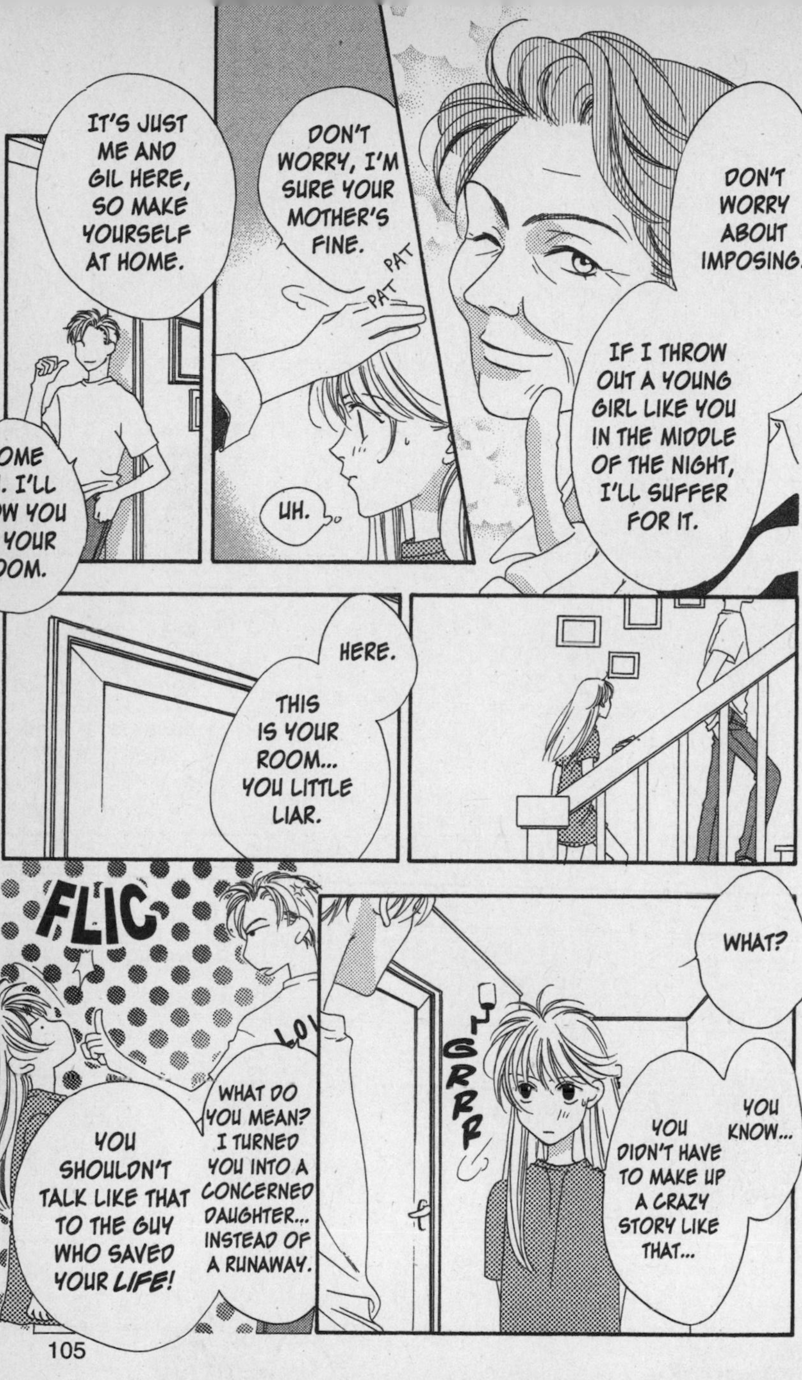
DON'T WORRY ABOUT IMPOSING.
IF I THROW OUT A YOUNG GIRL LIKE YOU IN THE MIDDLE OF THE NIGHT, I'LL SUFFER FOR IT.
DON'T WORRY, I'M SURE YOUR MOTHER'S FINE.
PAT PAT
UH.
IT'S JUST ME AND GIL HERE, SO MAKE YOURSELF AT HOME.
COME ON. I'LL SHOW YOU TO YOUR ROOM.
HERE.
THIS IS YOUR ROOM... YOU LITTLE LIAR.
WHAT?
YOU KNOW...
YOU DIDN'T HAVE TO MAKE UP A CRAZY STORY LIKE THAT...
GRRR
FLIC
WHAT DO YOU MEAN? I TURNED YOU INTO A CONCERNED DAUGHTER... INSTEAD OF A RUNAWAY.
YOU SHOULDN'T TALK LIKE THAT TO THE GUY WHO SAVED YOUR LIFE!

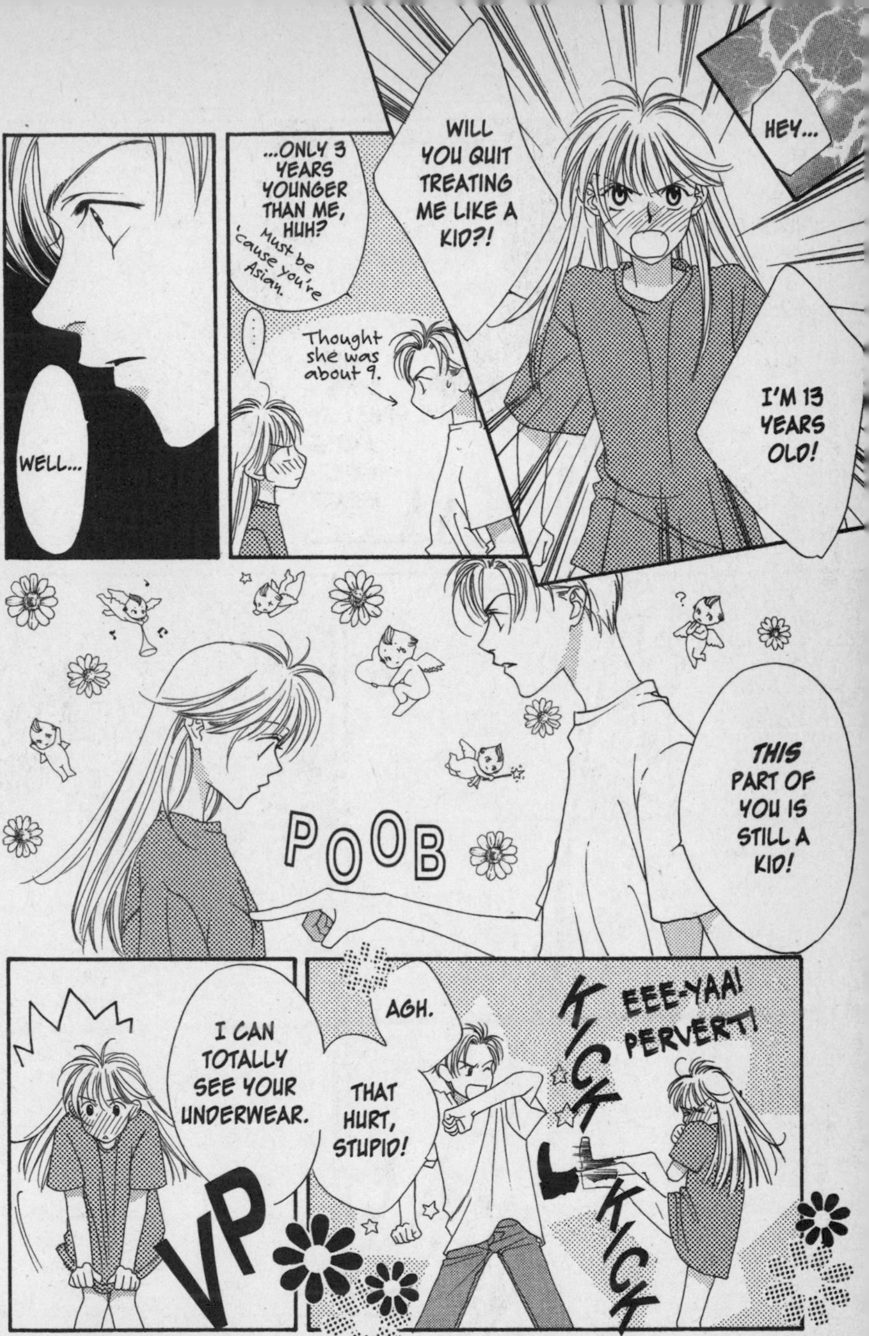
HEY...
WILL YOU QUIT TREATING ME LIKE A KID?!
I'M 13 YEARS OLD!
...ONLY 3 YEARS YOUNGER THAN ME, HUH?
Must be 'cause you're Asian.
...
Thought she was about 9.
WELL...
THIS PART OF YOU IS STILL A KID!
POOB
EEE-YAA! PERVERT!
KICK
KICK
AGH.
THAT HURT, STUPID!
I CAN TOTALLY SEE YOUR UNDERWEAR.
VP

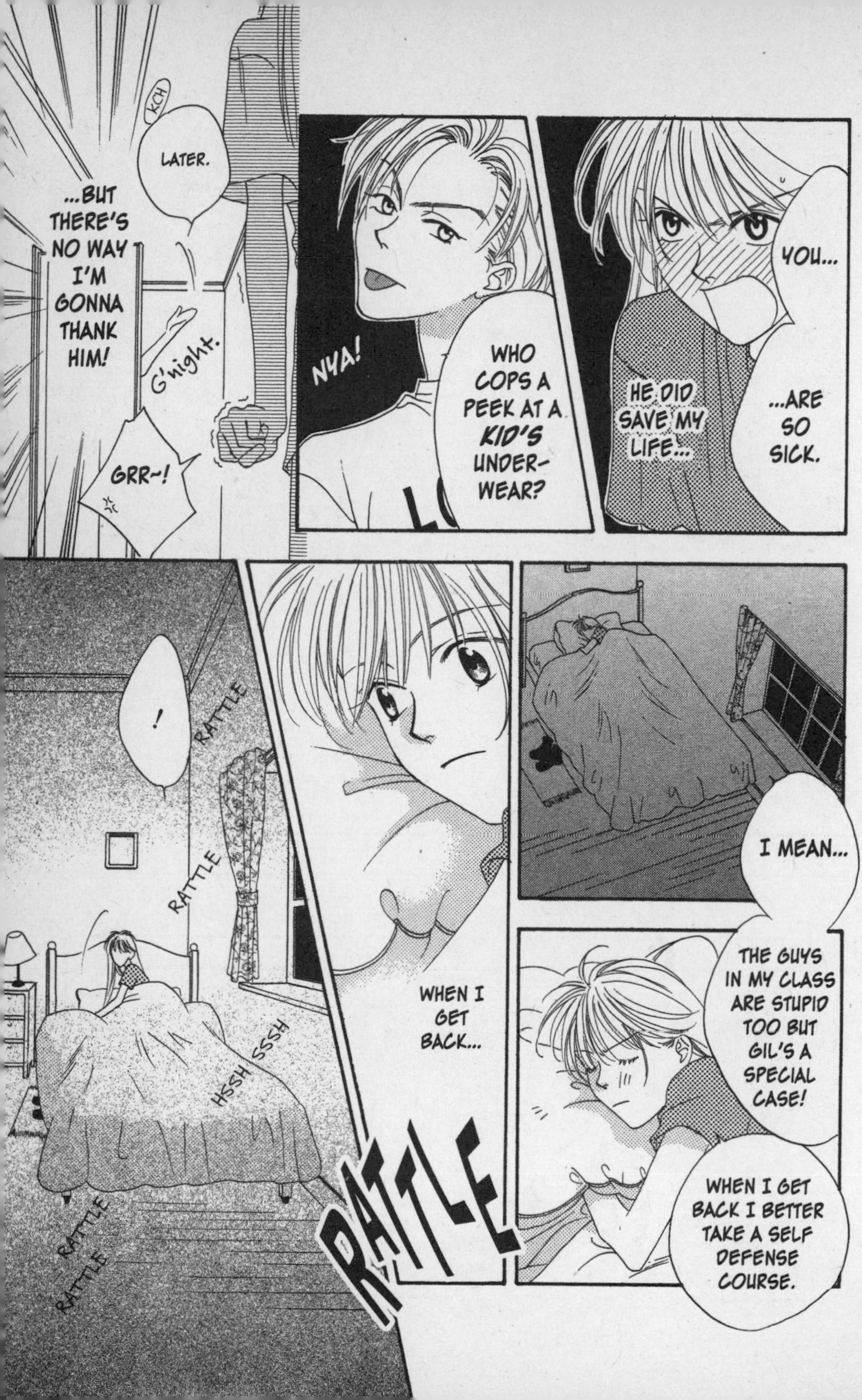
YOU...
...ARE SO SICK.
HE DID SAVE MY LIFE...
NYA!
WHO COPS A PEEK AT A KID'S UNDER-WEAR?
KCH
LATER.
G'night.
GRR~!
...BUT THERE'S NO WAY I'M GONNA THANK HIM!
I MEAN...
THE GUYS IN MY CLASS ARE STUPID TOO BUT GIL'S A SPECIAL CASE!
WHEN I GET BACK I BETTER TAKE A SELF DEFENSE COURSE.
WHEN I GET BACK...
RATTLE
!
RATTLE
RATTLE
HSSH SSSH
RATTLE
RATTLE

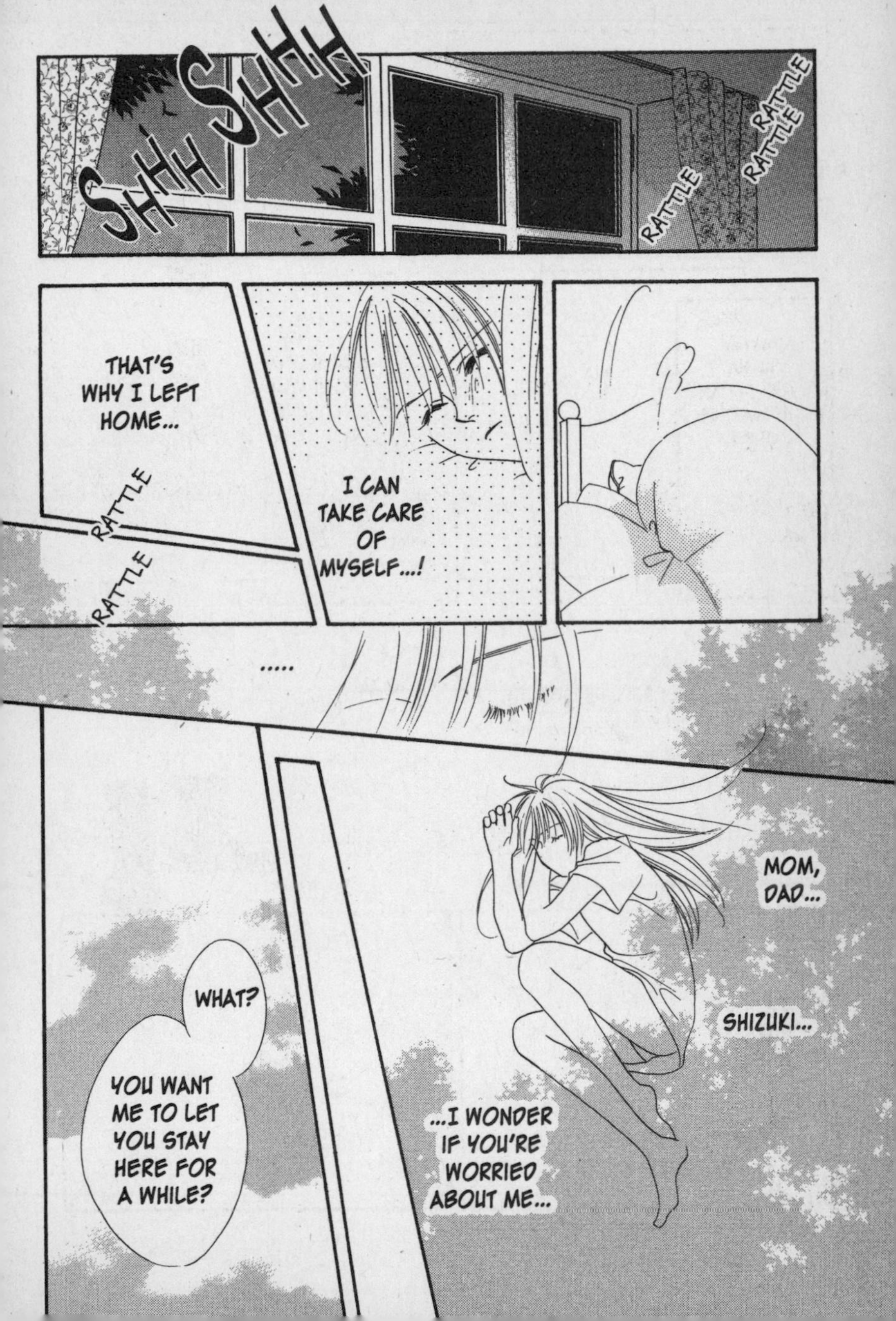
RATTLE RATTLE
RATTLE
SHHH SHHH
I CAN TAKE CARE OF MYSELF...!
THAT'S WHY I LEFT HOME...
RATTLE RATTLE
.....
MOM, DAD...
SHIZUKI...
...I WONDER IF YOU'RE WORRIED ABOUT ME...
WHAT?
YOU WANT ME TO LET YOU STAY HERE FOR A WHILE?

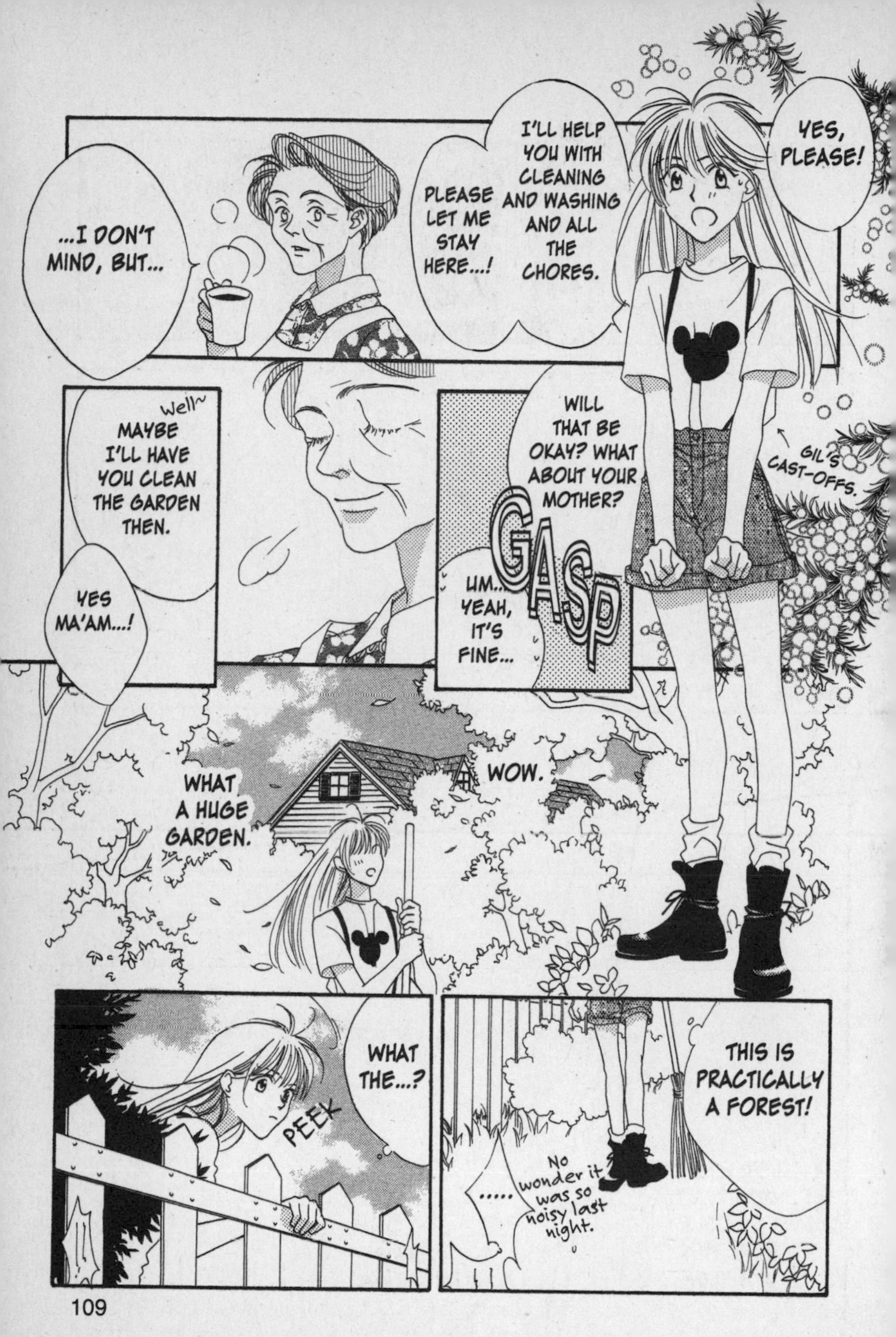
YES, PLEASE!
GIL'S CAST-OFFS.
I'LL HELP YOU WITH CLEANING AND WASHING AND ALL THE CHORES.
PLEASE LET ME STAY HERE...!
...I DON'T MIND, BUT...
WILL THAT BE OKAY? WHAT ABOUT YOUR MOTHER?
GASP
UM... YEAH, IT'S FINE...
Well~
MAYBE I'LL HAVE YOU CLEAN THE GARDEN THEN.
YES MA'AM...!
WOW.
WHAT A HUGE GARDEN.
THIS IS PRACTICALLY A FOREST!
.....
No wonder it was so noisy last night.
WHAT THE...?
PEEK

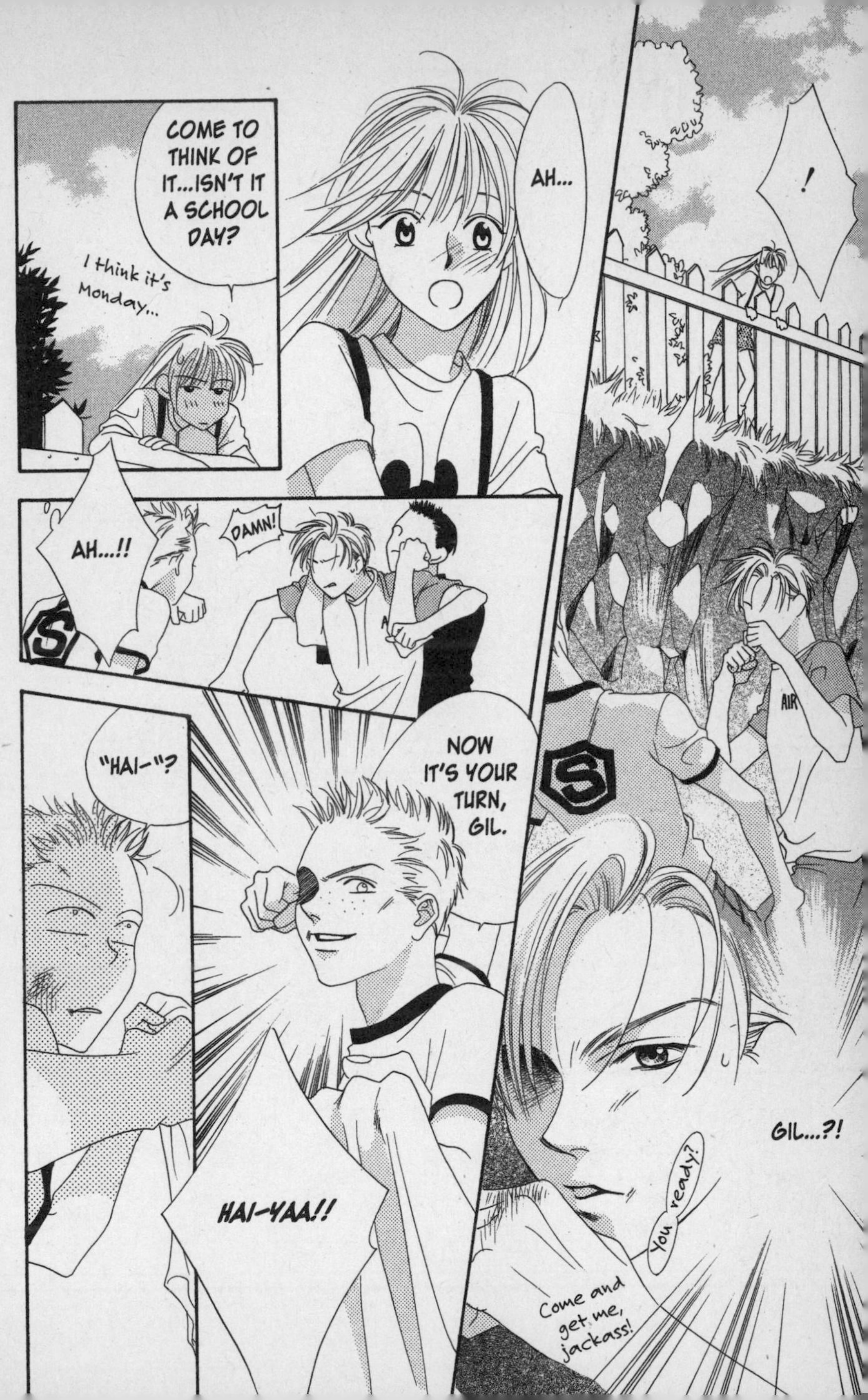
!
GIL...?!
You ready?
Come and get me, jackass!
AH...
COME TO THINK OF IT...ISN'T IT A SCHOOL DAY?
I think it's Monday...
DAMN!
AH...!!
NOW IT'S YOUR TURN, GIL.
"HAI-"?
HAI-YAA!!

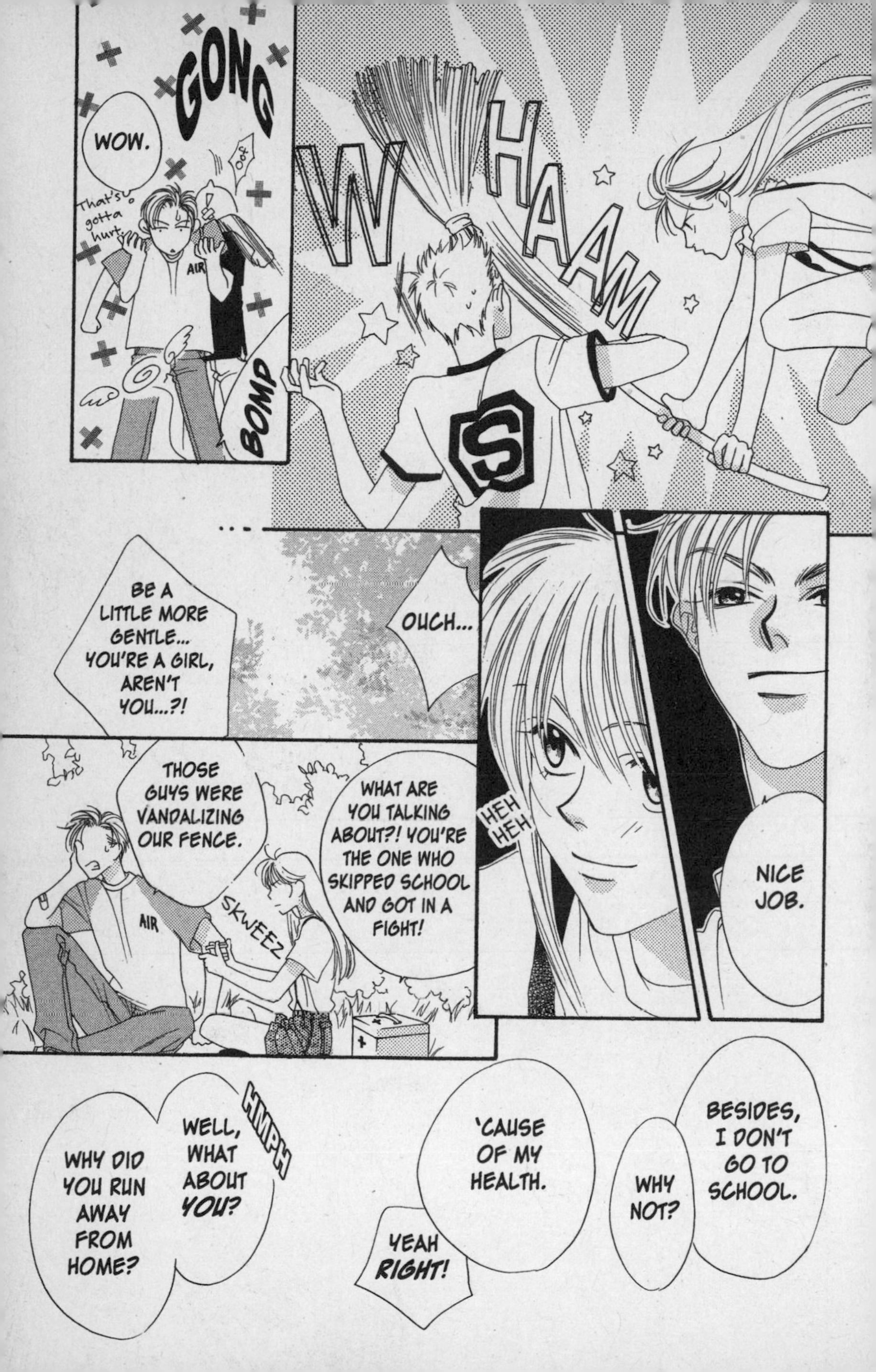
WHAAM
GONG
oof
WOW.
That's gotta hurt.
BOMP
...
HEH HEH
NICE JOB.
OUCH...
BE A LITTLE MORE GENTLE... YOU'RE A GIRL, AREN'T YOU...?!
WHAT ARE YOU TALKING ABOUT?! YOU'RE THE ONE WHO SKIPPED SCHOOL AND GOT IN A FIGHT!
THOSE GUYS WERE VANDALIZING OUR FENCE.
SKWEEZ
BESIDES, I DON'T GO TO SCHOOL.
WHY NOT?
'CAUSE OF MY HEALTH.
YEAH RIGHT!
WELL, WHAT ABOUT YOU?
HMPH
WHY DID YOU RUN AWAY FROM HOME?

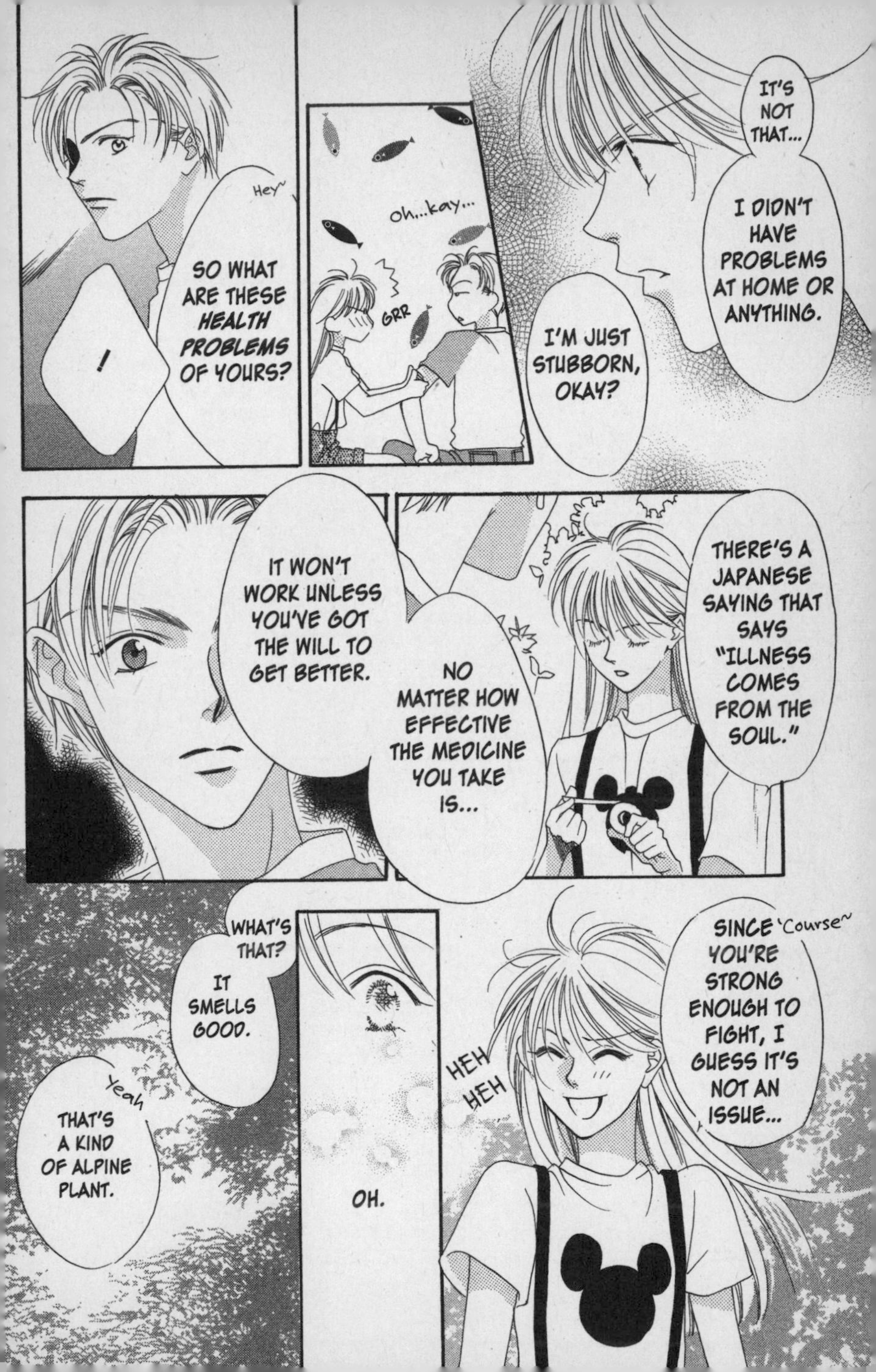
IT'S NOT THAT...
I DIDN'T HAVE PROBLEMS AT HOME OR ANYTHING.
I'M JUST STUBBORN, OKAY?
Oh...kay...
GRR
Hey~
SO WHAT ARE THESE HEALTH PROBLEMS OF YOURS?
!
THERE'S A JAPANESE SAYING THAT SAYS "ILLNESS COMES FROM THE SOUL."
NO MATTER HOW EFFECTIVE THE MEDICINE YOU TAKE IS...
IT WON'T WORK UNLESS YOU'VE GOT THE WILL TO GET BETTER.
SINCE YOU'RE STRONG ENOUGH TO FIGHT, I GUESS IT'S NOT AN ISSUE...
'Course~
HEH HEH
OH.
WHAT'S THAT? IT SMELLS GOOD.
Yeah
THAT'S A KIND OF ALPINE PLANT.

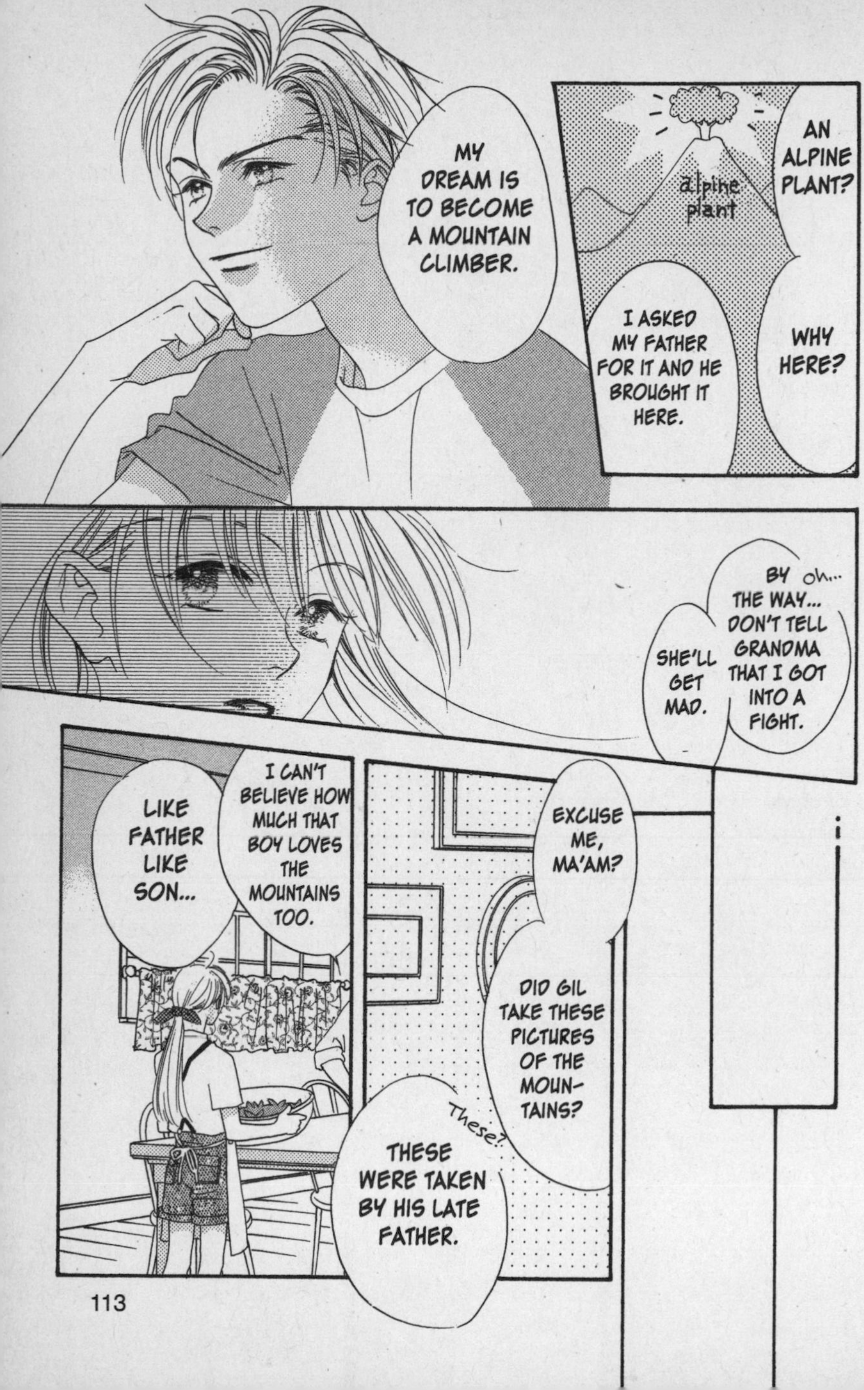
AN ALPINE PLANT?
alpine plant
WHY HERE?
I ASKED MY FATHER FOR IT AND HE BROUGHT IT HERE.
MY DREAM IS TO BECOME A MOUNTAIN CLIMBER.
BY THE WAY... DON'T TELL GRANDMA THAT I GOT INTO A FIGHT.
oh...
SHE'LL GET MAD.
EXCUSE ME, MA'AM?
DID GIL TAKE THESE PICTURES OF THE MOUN-TAINS?
These?
THESE WERE TAKEN BY HIS LATE FATHER.
I CAN'T BELIEVE HOW MUCH THAT BOY LOVES THE MOUNTAINS TOO.
LIKE FATHER LIKE SON...

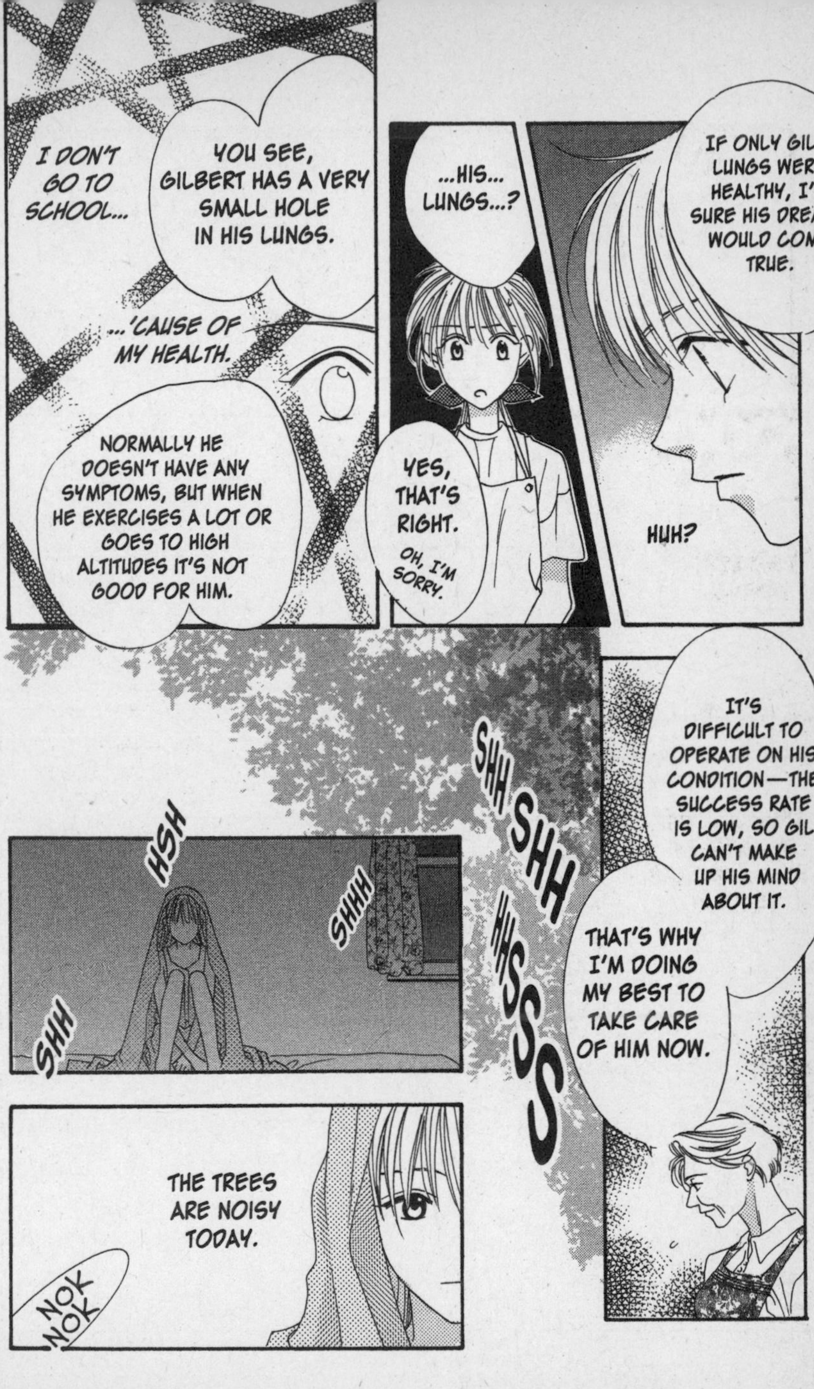
IF ONLY GIL'S LUNGS WERE HEALTHY, I'M SURE HIS DREAMS WOULD COME TRUE.
HUH?
...HIS... LUNGS...?
YES, THAT'S RIGHT.
OH, I'M SORRY.
YOU SEE, GILBERT HAS A VERY SMALL HOLE IN HIS LUNGS.
NORMALLY HE DOESN'T HAVE ANY SYMPTOMS, BUT WHEN HE EXERCISES A LOT OR GOES TO HIGH ALTITUDES IT'S NOT GOOD FOR HIM.
I DON'T GO TO SCHOOL...
...'CAUSE OF MY HEALTH.
IT'S DIFFICULT TO OPERATE ON HIS CONDITION—THE SUCCESS RATE IS LOW, SO GIL CAN'T MAKE UP HIS MIND ABOUT IT.
THAT'S WHY I'M DOING MY BEST TO TAKE CARE OF HIM NOW.
SHH SHH HHSSS
HSH
SHHH
SHH
THE TREES ARE NOISY TODAY.
NOK NOK

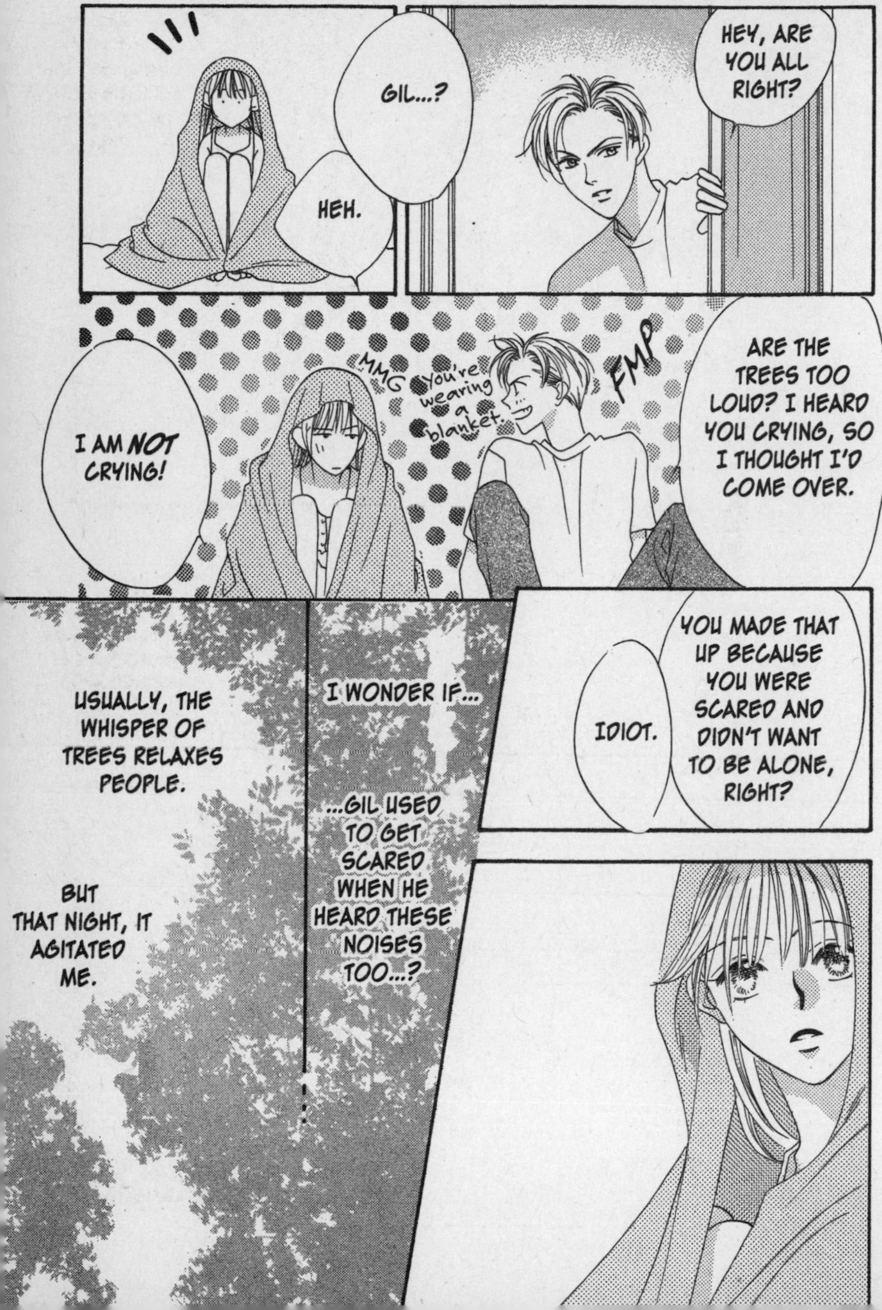
HEY, ARE YOU ALL RIGHT?
GIL...?
HEH.
ARE THE TREES TOO LOUD? I HEARD YOU CRYING, SO I THOUGHT I'D COME OVER.
FMP
You're wearing a blanket.
MMG
I AM NOT CRYING!
YOU MADE THAT UP BECAUSE YOU WERE SCARED AND DIDN'T WANT TO BE ALONE, RIGHT?
IDIOT.
I WONDER IF...
...GIL USED TO GET SCARED WHEN HE HEARD THESE NOISES TOO...?
USUALLY, THE WHISPER OF TREES RELAXES PEOPLE.
BUT THAT NIGHT, IT AGITATED ME.

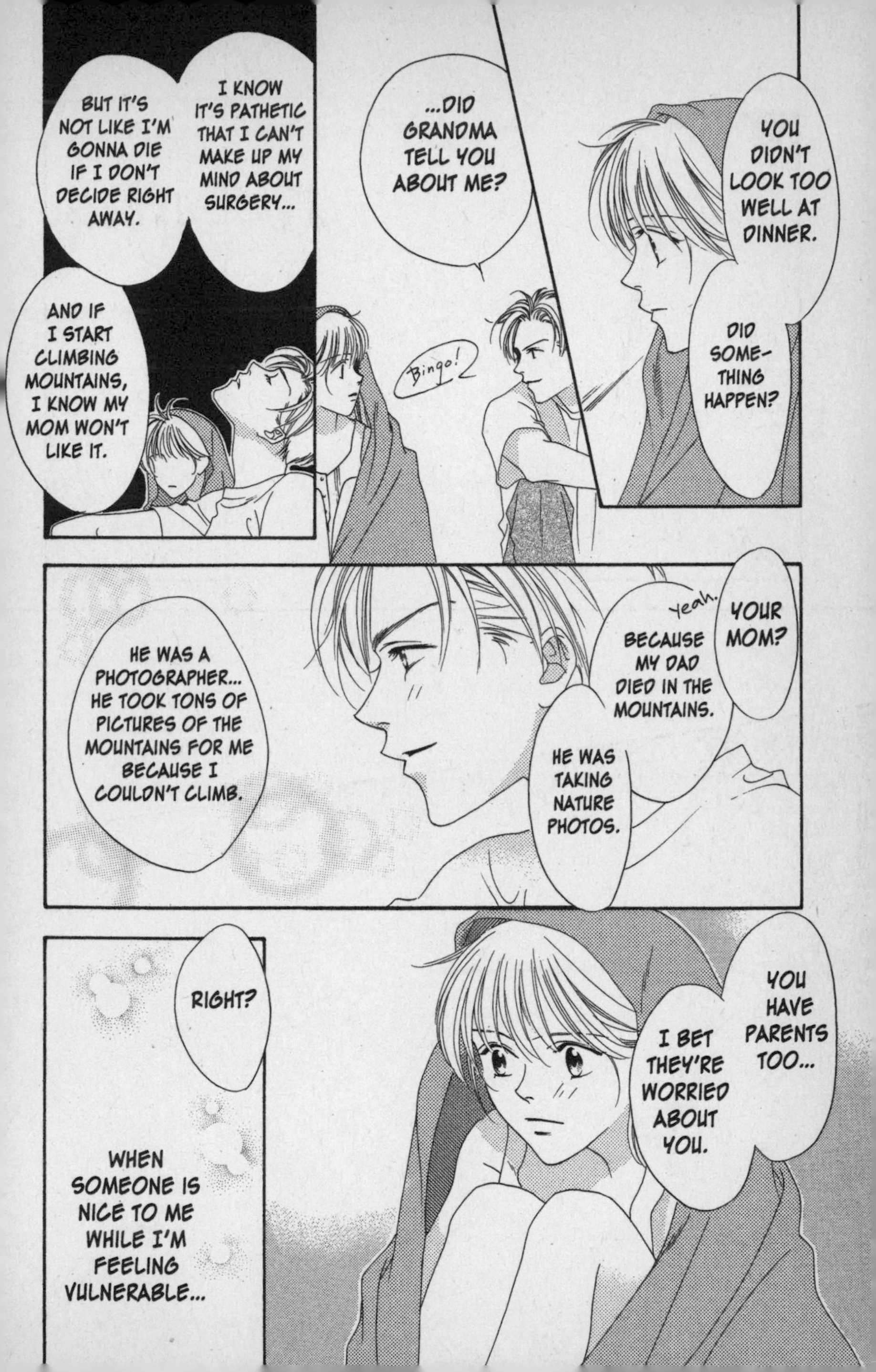
YOU DIDN'T LOOK TOO WELL AT DINNER.
DID SOMETHING HAPPEN?
...DID GRANDMA TELL YOU ABOUT ME?
Bingo!
I KNOW IT'S PATHETIC THAT I CAN'T MAKE UP MY MIND ABOUT SURGERY...
BUT IT'S NOT LIKE I'M GONNA DIE IF I DON'T DECIDE RIGHT AWAY.
AND IF I START CLIMBING MOUNTAINS, I KNOW MY MOM WON'T LIKE IT.
YOUR MOM?
Yeah.
BECAUSE MY DAD DIED IN THE MOUNTAINS.
HE WAS TAKING NATURE PHOTOS.
HE WAS A PHOTOGRAPHER... HE TOOK TONS OF PICTURES OF THE MOUNTAINS FOR ME BECAUSE I COULDN'T CLIMB.
YOU HAVE PARENTS TOO...
I BET THEY'RE WORRIED ABOUT YOU.
RIGHT?
WHEN SOMEONE IS NICE TO ME WHILE I'M FEELING VULNERABLE...

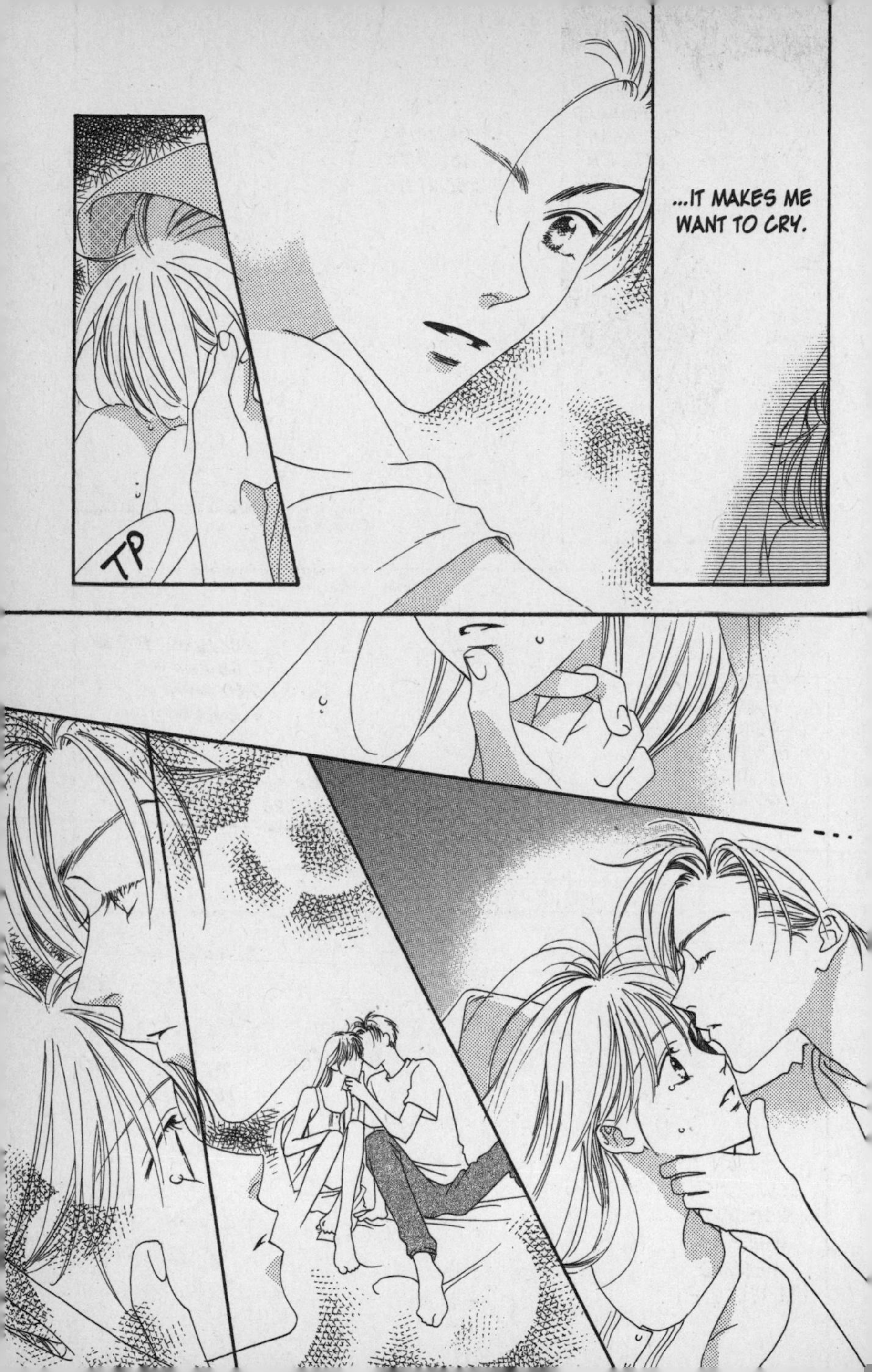
...IT MAKES ME WANT TO CRY.
TP
...

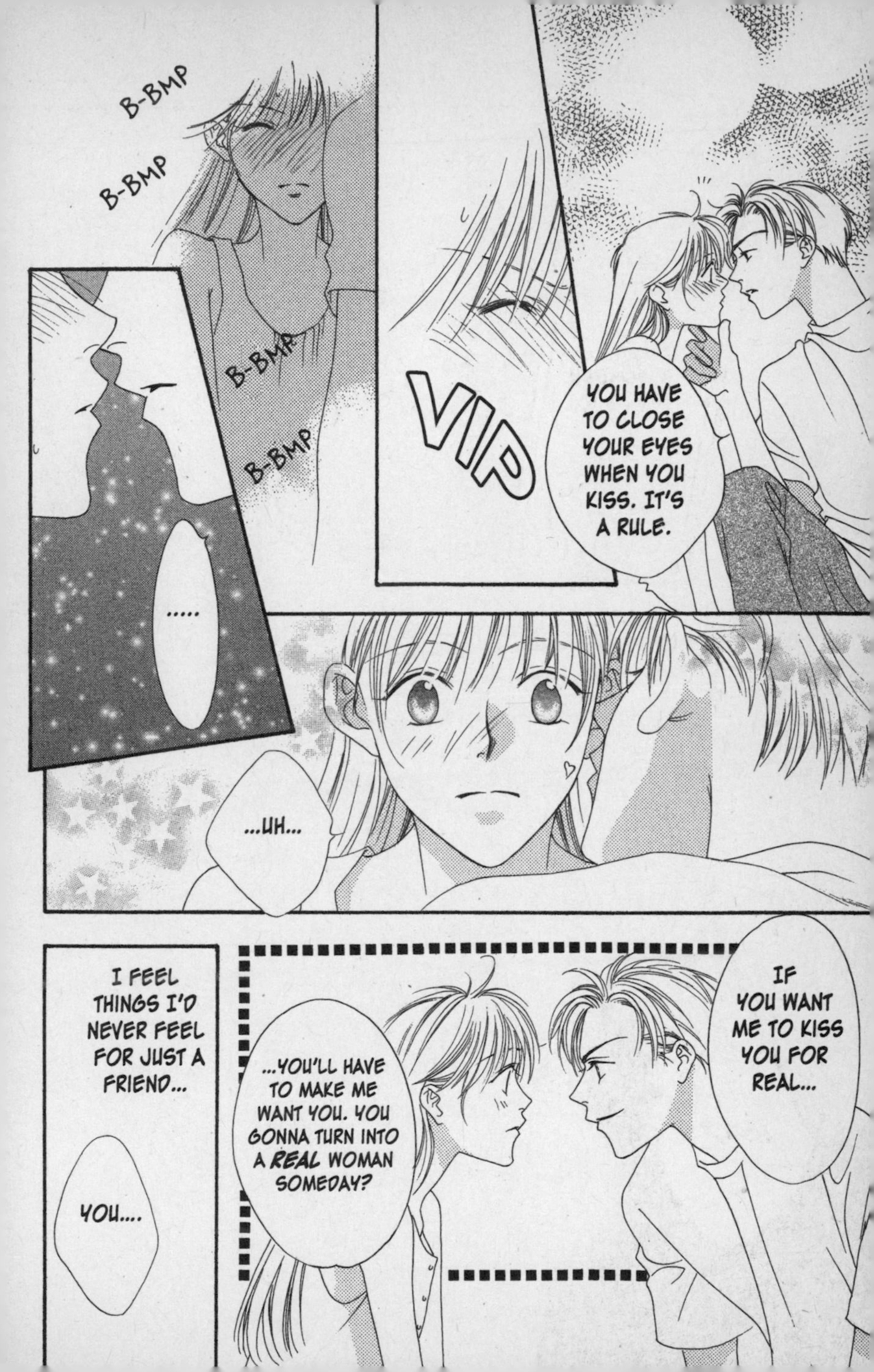
YOU HAVE TO CLOSE YOUR EYES WHEN YOU KISS. IT'S A RULE.
VIP
B-BMP
B-BMP
B-BMP
B-BMP
.....
...UH...
IF YOU WANT ME TO KISS YOU FOR REAL...
...YOU'LL HAVE TO MAKE ME WANT YOU. YOU GONNA TURN INTO A *REAL* WOMAN SOMEDAY?
I FEEL THINGS I'D NEVER FEEL FOR JUST A FRIEND...
YOU....

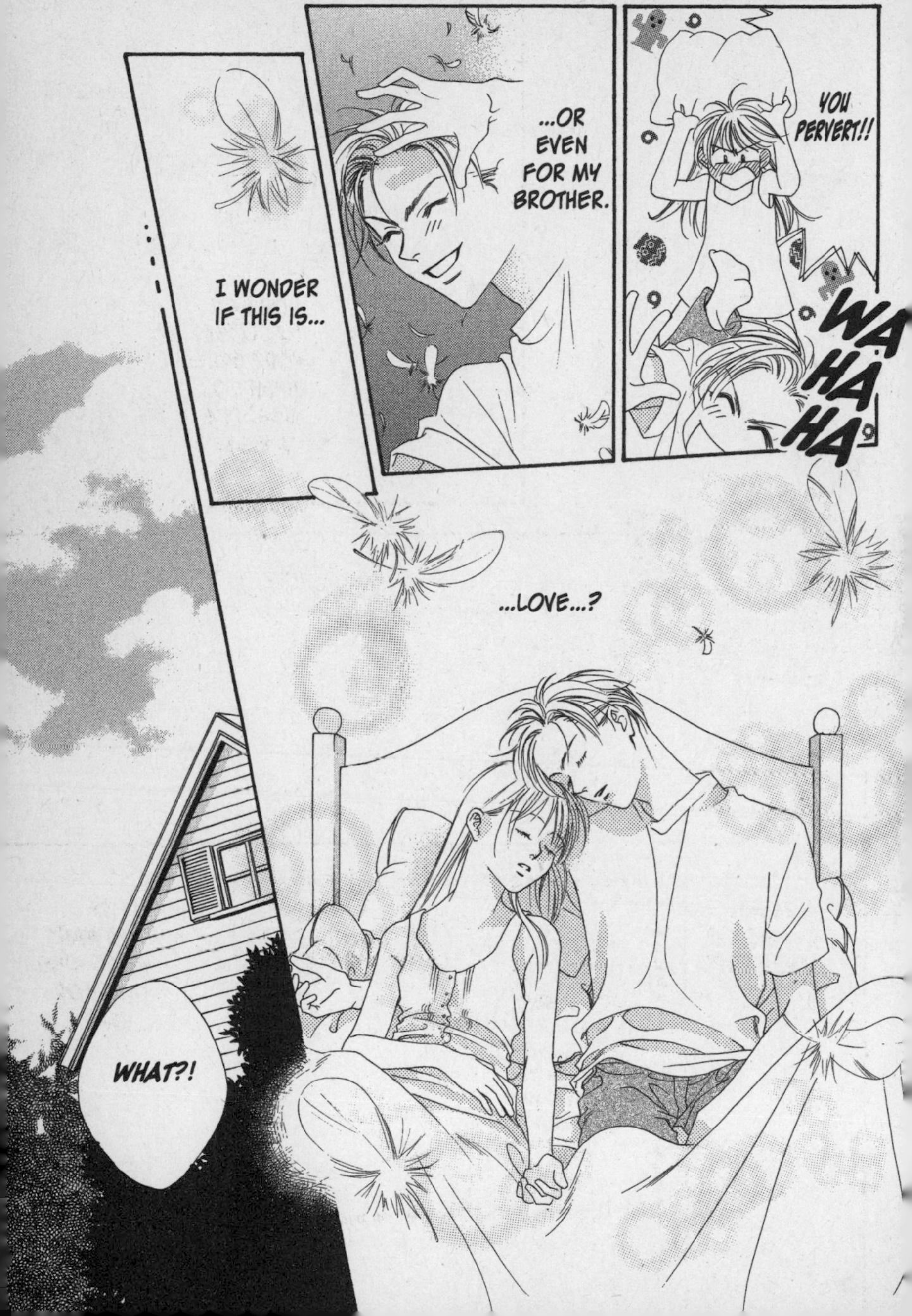
YOU PERVERT!!
WAHAHAHA
...OR EVEN FOR MY BROTHER.
I WONDER IF THIS IS...
...LOVE...?
WHAT?!

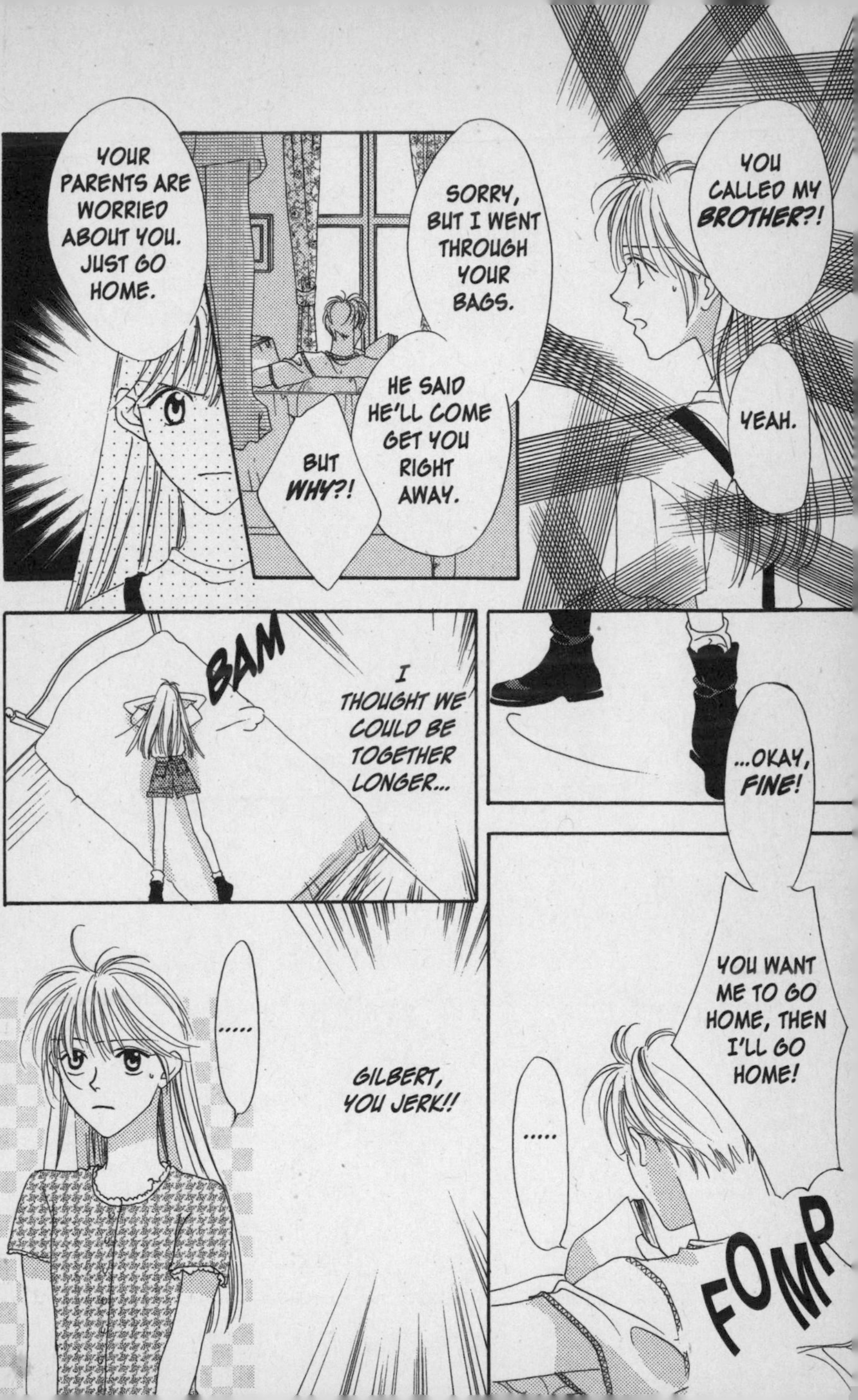
YOU CALLED MY BROTHER?!
YEAH.
SORRY, BUT I WENT THROUGH YOUR BAGS.
HE SAID HE'LL COME GET YOU RIGHT AWAY.
BUT WHY?!
YOUR PARENTS ARE WORRIED ABOUT YOU. JUST GO HOME.
...OKAY, FINE!
YOU WANT ME TO GO HOME, THEN I'LL GO HOME!
.....
FOMP
BAM
I THOUGHT WE COULD BE TOGETHER LONGER...
.....
GILBERT, YOU JERK!!

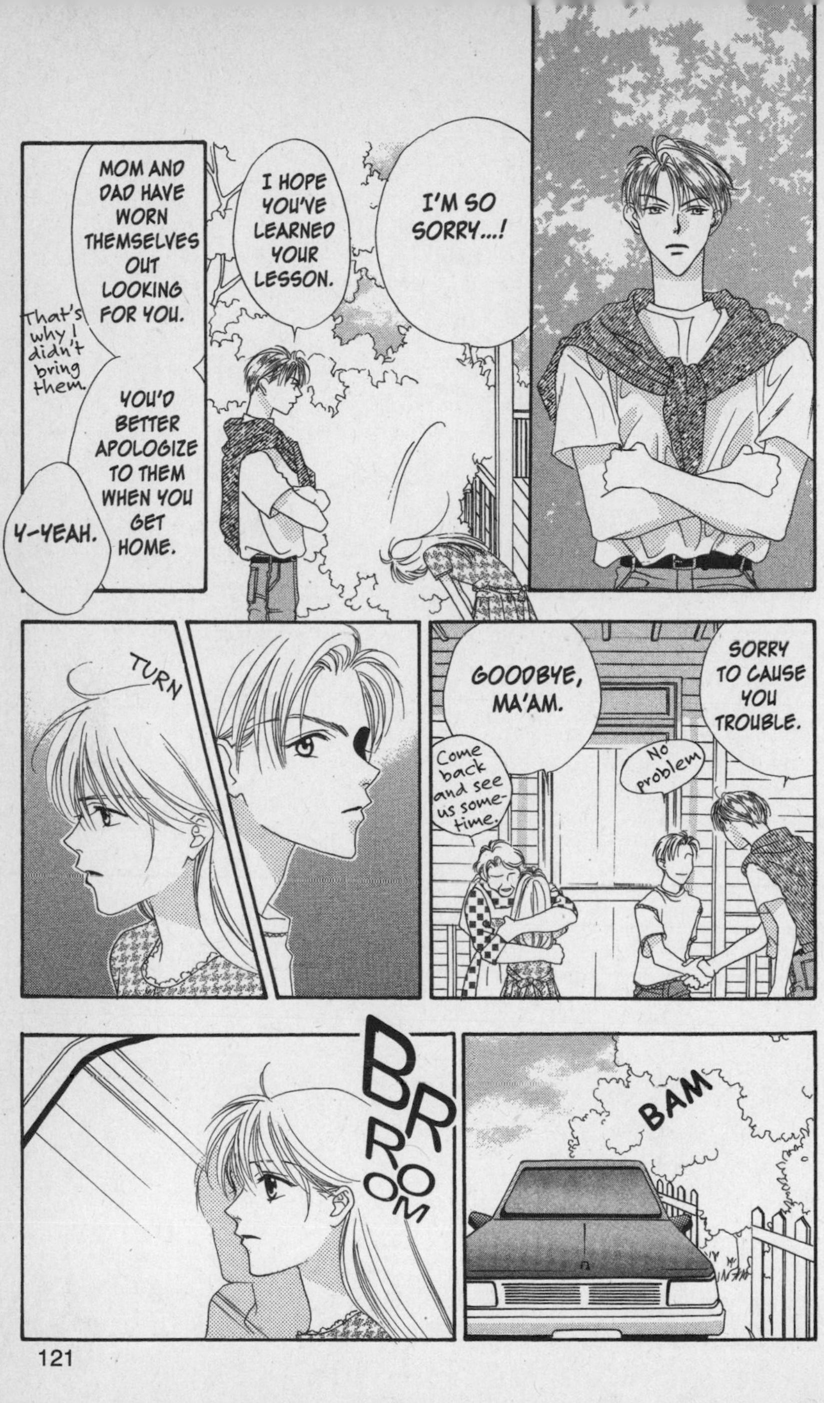
I'M SO SORRY...!
I HOPE YOU'VE LEARNED YOUR LESSON.
MOM AND DAD HAVE WORN THEMSELVES OUT LOOKING FOR YOU.
That's why I didn't bring them.
YOU'D BETTER APOLOGIZE TO THEM WHEN YOU GET HOME.
Y-YEAH.
SORRY TO CAUSE YOU TROUBLE.
No problem
GOODBYE, MA'AM.
Come back and see us some-time.
TURN
BAM
BRROOM

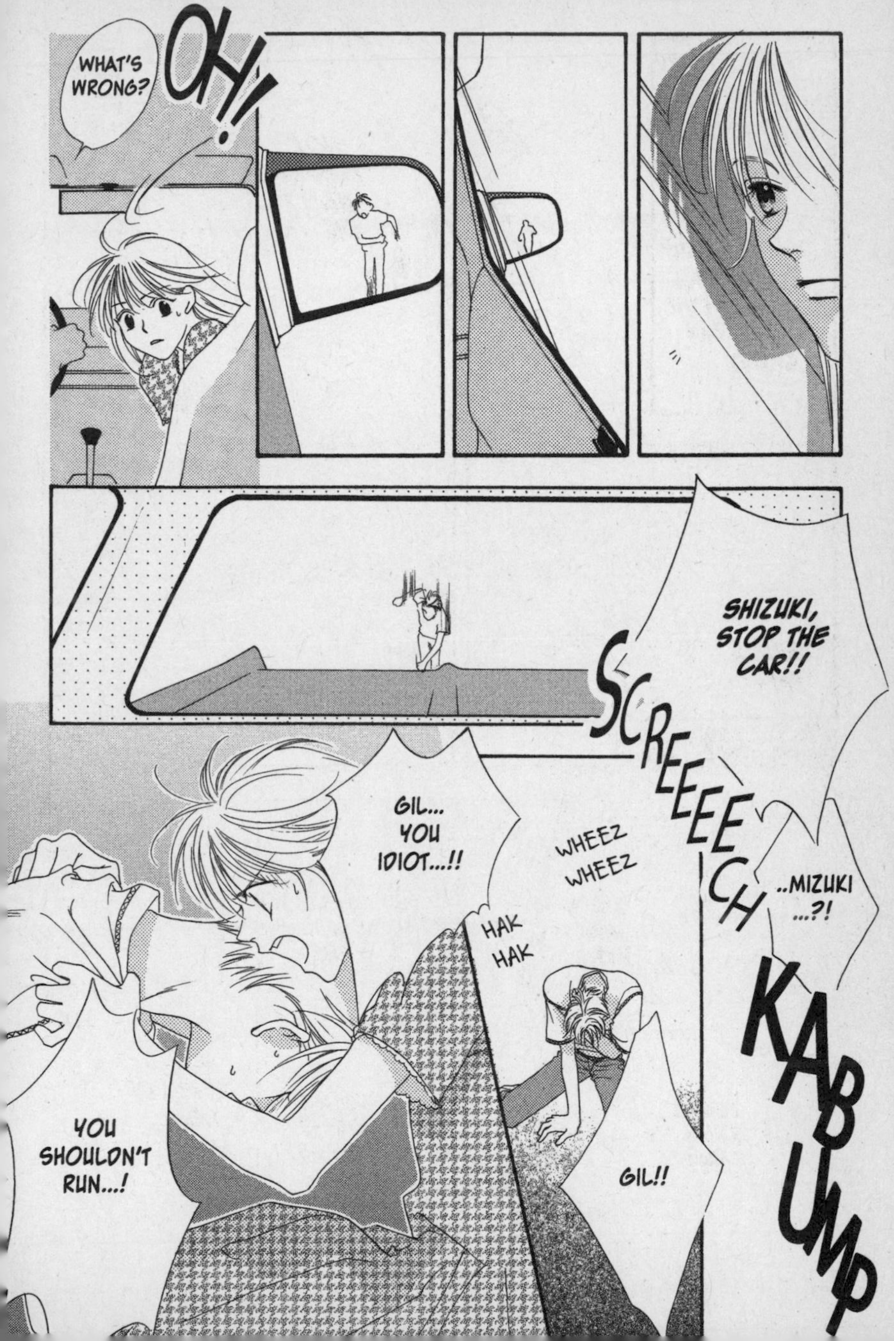
OH!!
WHAT'S WRONG?
SHIZUKI, STOP THE CAR!!
SCREEEEECH
KABUMP
..MIZUKI ...?!
GIL!!
HAK HAK
WHEEZ WHEEZ
GIL... YOU IDIOT...!!
YOU SHOULDN'T RUN...!

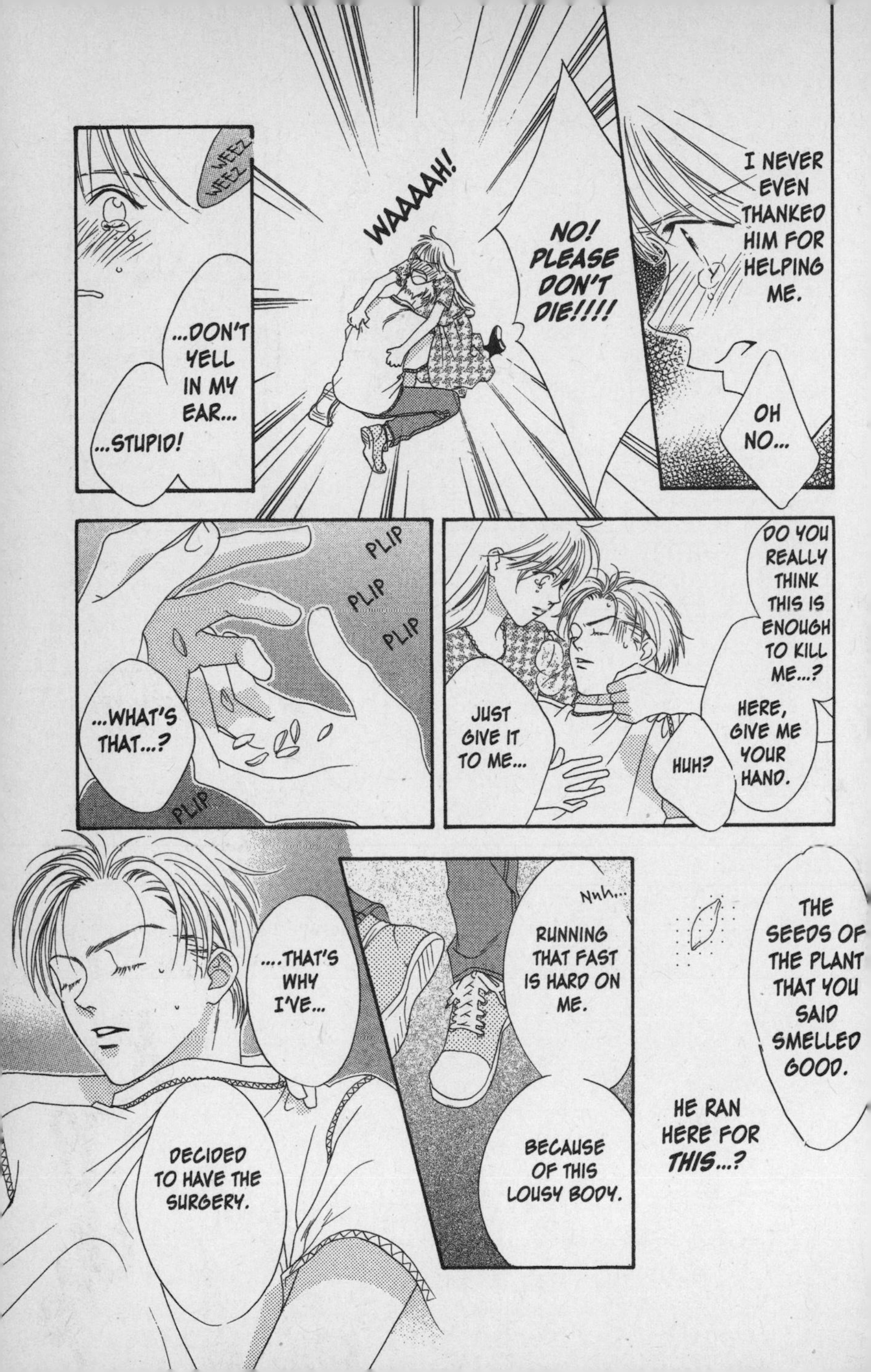
I NEVER EVEN THANKED HIM FOR HELPING ME.
OH NO...
WAAAAH!
NO! PLEASE DON'T DIE!!!!
WEEZ WEEZ
...DON'T YELL IN MY EAR...
...STUPID!
DO YOU REALLY THINK THIS IS ENOUGH TO KILL ME...?
HERE, GIVE ME YOUR HAND.
HUH?
JUST GIVE IT TO ME...
PLIP
PLIP
PLIP
...WHAT'S THAT...?
PLIP
THE SEEDS OF THE PLANT THAT YOU SAID SMELLED GOOD.
HE RAN HERE FOR THIS...?
Nnh...
RUNNING THAT FAST IS HARD ON ME.
BECAUSE OF THIS LOUSY BODY.
....THAT'S WHY I'VE...
DECIDED TO HAVE THE SURGERY.

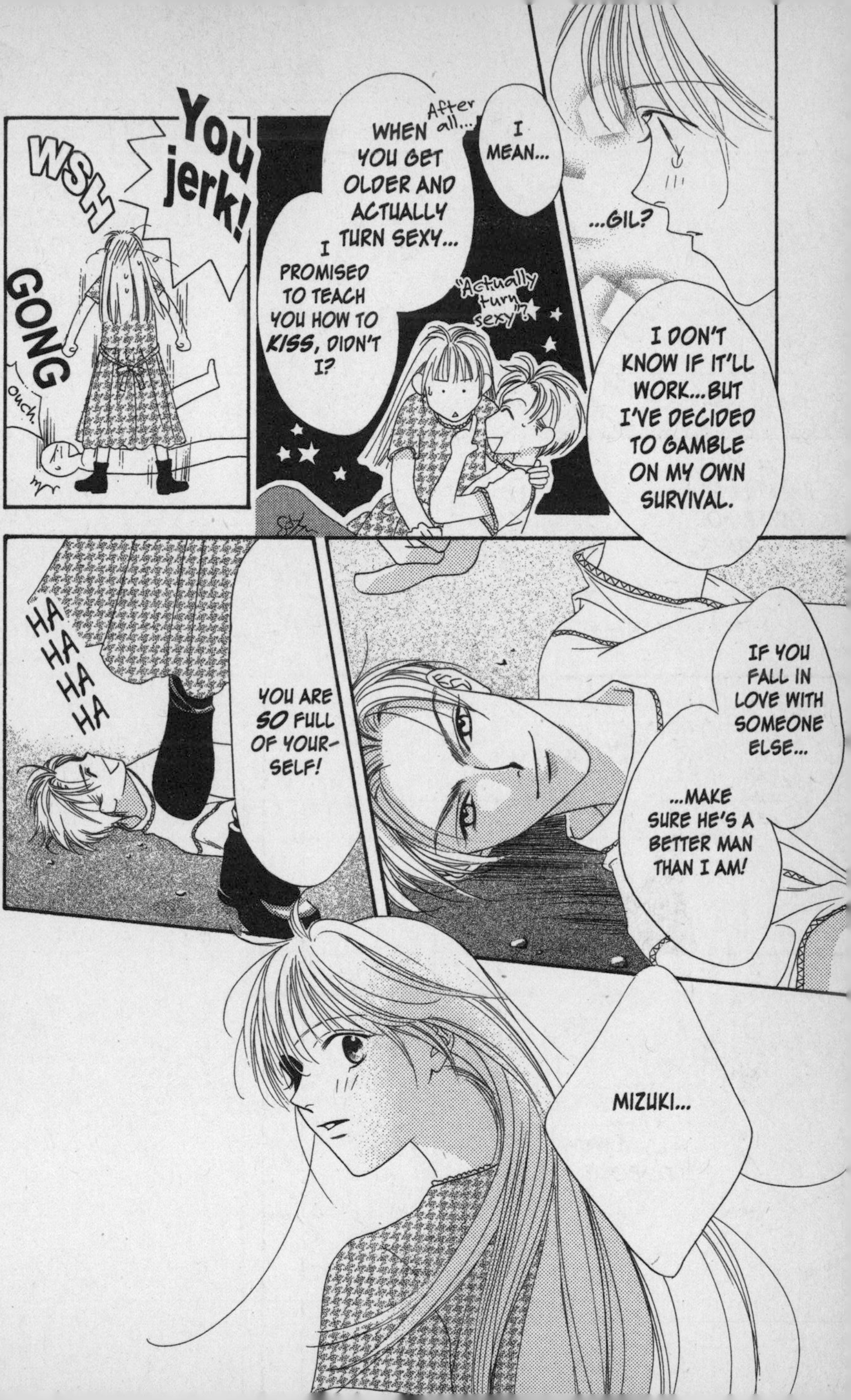
...GIL?
I DON'T KNOW IF IT'LL WORK...BUT I'VE DECIDED TO GAMBLE ON MY OWN SURVIVAL.
I MEAN...
After all...
WHEN YOU GET OLDER AND ACTUALLY TURN SEXY...
I PROMISED TO TEACH YOU HOW TO *KISS*, DIDN'T I?
'Actually turn sexy'?
You jerk!
WSH
GONG
ouch.
IF YOU FALL IN LOVE WITH SOMEONE ELSE...
...MAKE SURE HE'S A BETTER MAN THAN I AM!
YOU ARE *SO* FULL OF YOUR-SELF!
HA HA HA HA
MIZUKI...

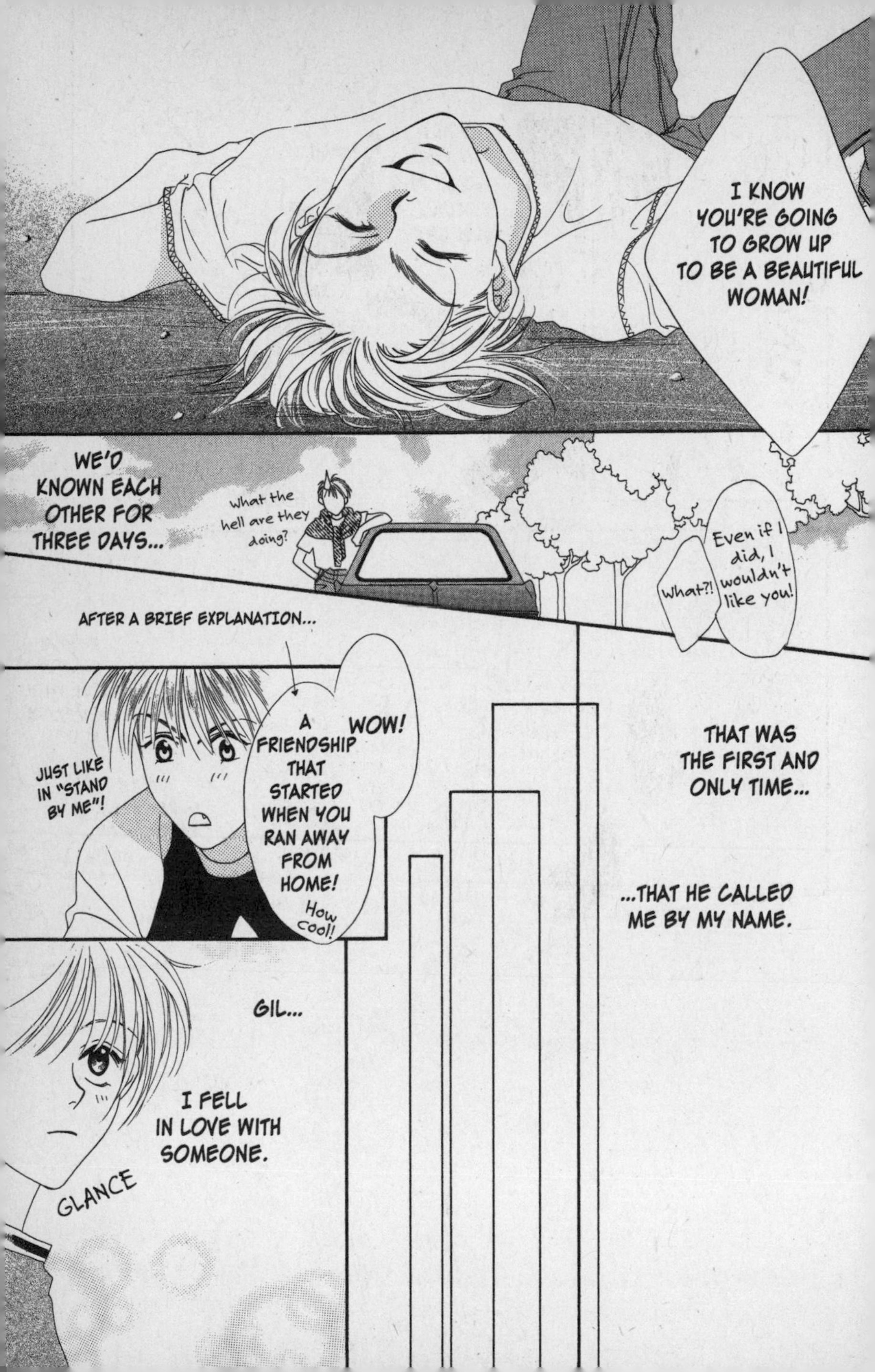
I KNOW YOU'RE GOING TO GROW UP TO BE A BEAUTIFUL WOMAN!
Even if I did, I wouldn't like you!
What?!
what the hell are they doing?
WE'D KNOWN EACH OTHER FOR THREE DAYS...
THAT WAS THE FIRST AND ONLY TIME...
...THAT HE CALLED ME BY MY NAME.
AFTER A BRIEF EXPLANATION...
WOW!
A FRIENDSHIP THAT STARTED WHEN YOU RAN AWAY FROM HOME!
How cool!
JUST LIKE IN "STAND BY ME"!
GIL...
I FELL IN LOVE WITH SOMEONE.
GLANCE

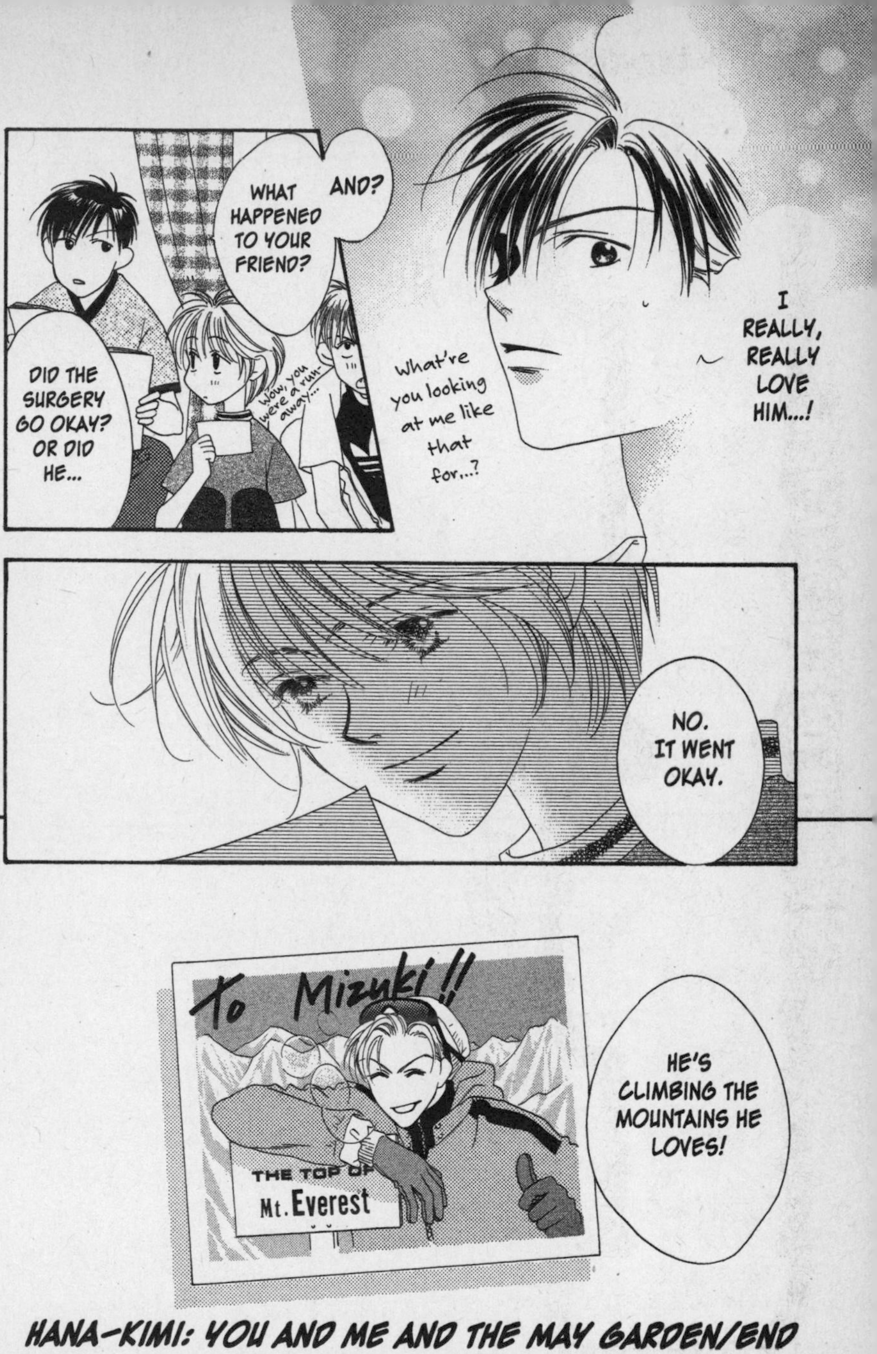
I REALLY, REALLY LOVE HIM...!
What're you looking at me like that for...?
AND?
WHAT HAPPENED TO YOUR FRIEND?
Wow, you were a run-away...
DID THE SURGERY GO OKAY? OR DID HE...
NO. IT WENT OKAY.
HE'S CLIMBING THE MOUNTAINS HE LOVES!
To Mizuki!!
THE TOP
Mt. Everest

HANA-KIMI: YOU AND ME AND THE MAY GARDEN/END

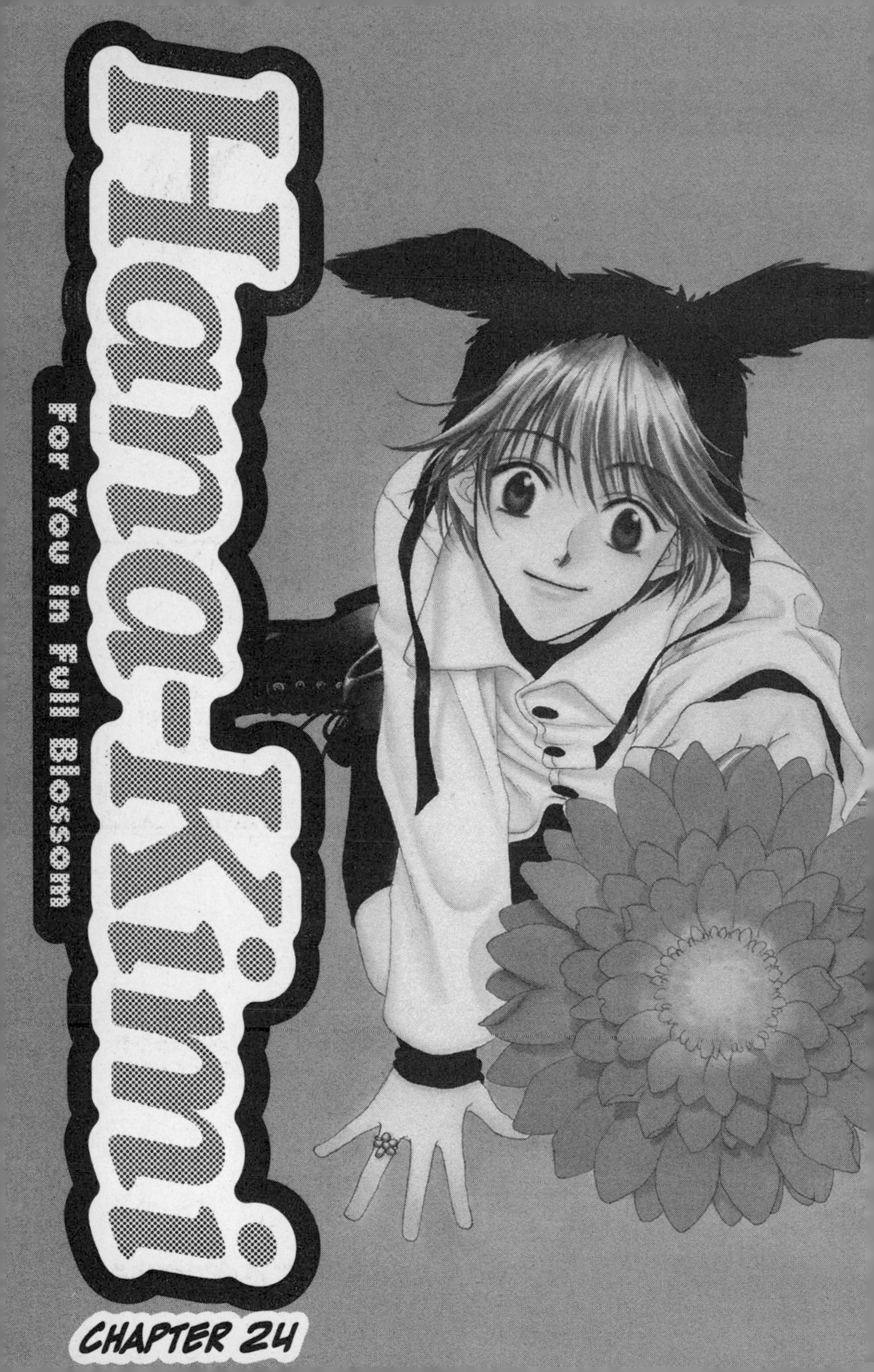
Hana-Kimi!
For You in Full Blossom
CHAPTER 24

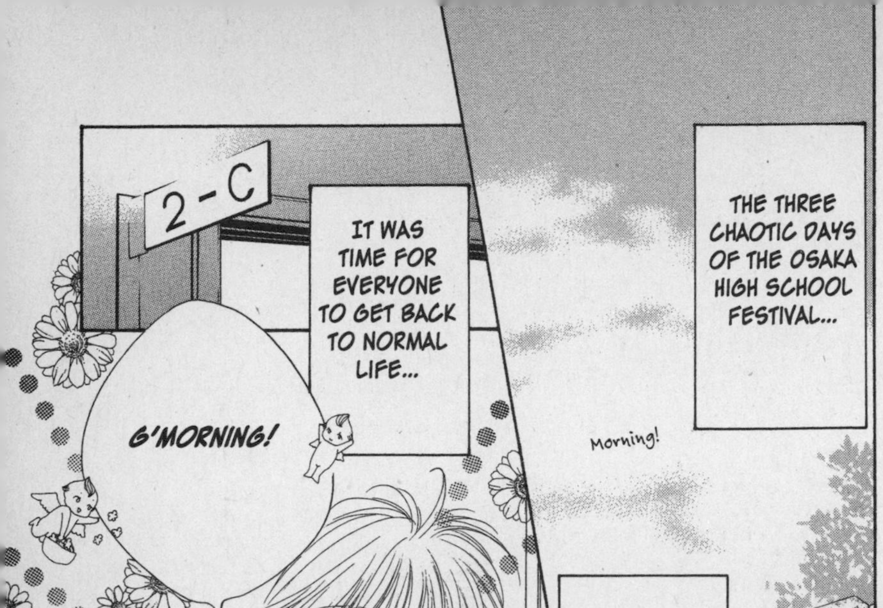
THE THREE CHAOTIC DAYS OF THE OSAKA HIGH SCHOOL FESTIVAL...
Morning!
...ENDED WITH DORM #2'S COMEBACK VICTORY.
Hey, can I borrow your notes?
Aww, damn it...
2-C
IT WAS TIME FOR EVERYONE TO GET BACK TO NORMAL LIFE...
G'MORNING!
TA DA!

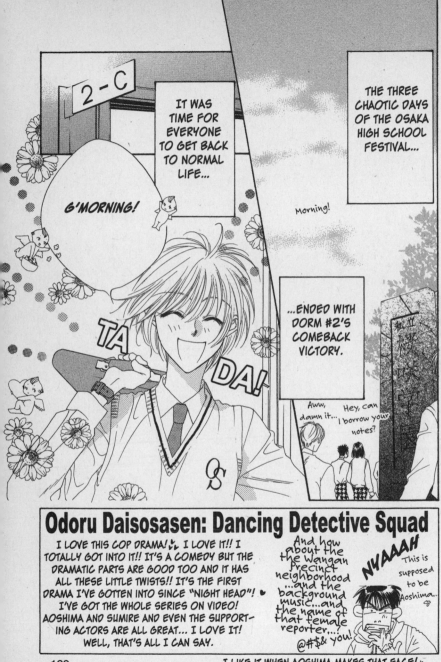

Odoru Daisosasen: Dancing Detective Squad

I LOVE THIS COP DRAMA! I LOVE IT!! I TOTALLY GOT INTO IT!! IT'S A COMEDY BUT THE DRAMATIC PARTS ARE GOOD TOO AND IT HAS ALL THESE LITTLE TWISTS!! IT'S THE FIRST DRAMA I'VE GOTTEN INTO SINCE "NIGHT HEAD"! I'VE GOT THE WHOLE SERIES ON VIDEO! AOSHIMA AND SUMIRE AND EVEN THE SUPPORTING ACTORS ARE ALL GREAT... I LOVE IT! WELL, THAT'S ALL I CAN SAY.

And how about the the Wangan Precinct neighborhood ...and the background music...and the name of that female reporter...? @#$& you!

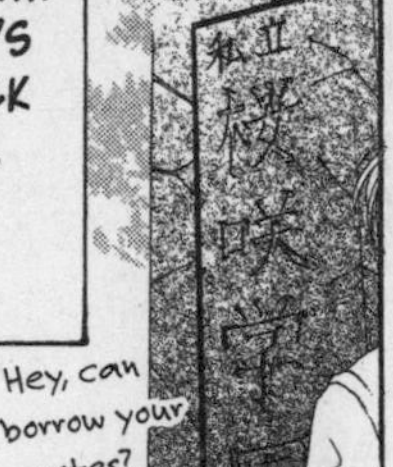
NYAAAH
This is supposed to be Aoshima...

I LIKE IT WHEN AOSHIMA MAKES THAT FACE!

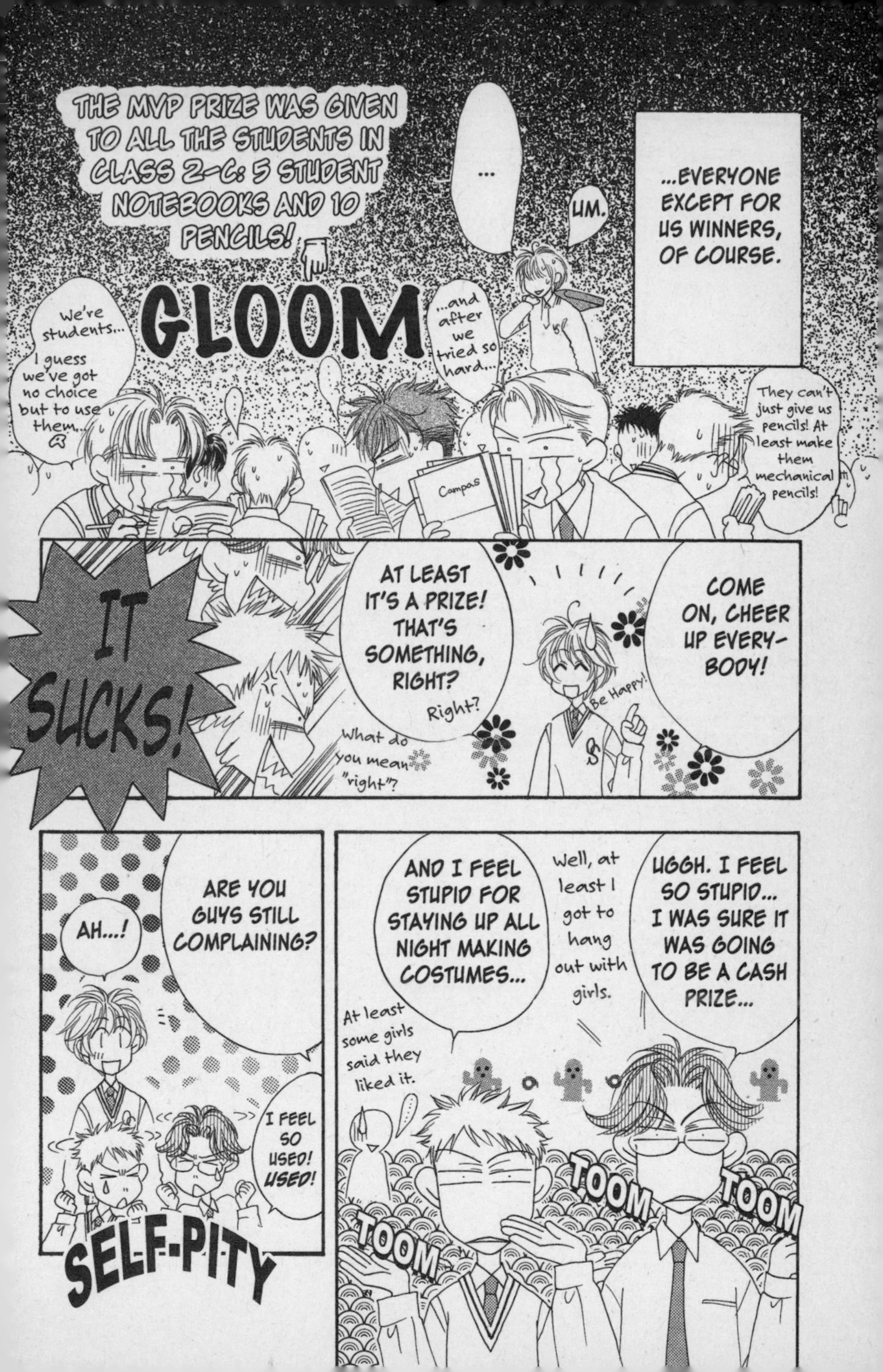
...EVERYONE EXCEPT FOR US WINNERS, OF COURSE.
UM.
...
THE MVP PRIZE WAS GIVEN TO ALL THE STUDENTS IN CLASS 2-C: 5 STUDENT NOTEBOOKS AND 10 PENCILS!
They can't just give us pencils! At least make them mechanical pencils!
...and after we tried so hard...
GLOOM
We're students...
I guess we've got no choice but to use them...
Campas
COME ON, CHEER UP EVERY-BODY!
Be Happy!
AT LEAST IT'S A PRIZE! THAT'S SOMETHING, RIGHT?
Right?
What do you mean "right"?
IT SUCKS!
UGGH. I FEEL SO STUPID... I WAS SURE IT WAS GOING TO BE A CASH PRIZE...
Well, at least I got to hang out with girls.
AND I FEEL STUPID FOR STAYING UP ALL NIGHT MAKING COSTUMES...
At least some girls said they liked it.
TOOM
TOOM
TOOM
ARE YOU GUYS STILL COMPLAINING?
AH...!
I FEEL SO USED! USED!
SELF-PITY

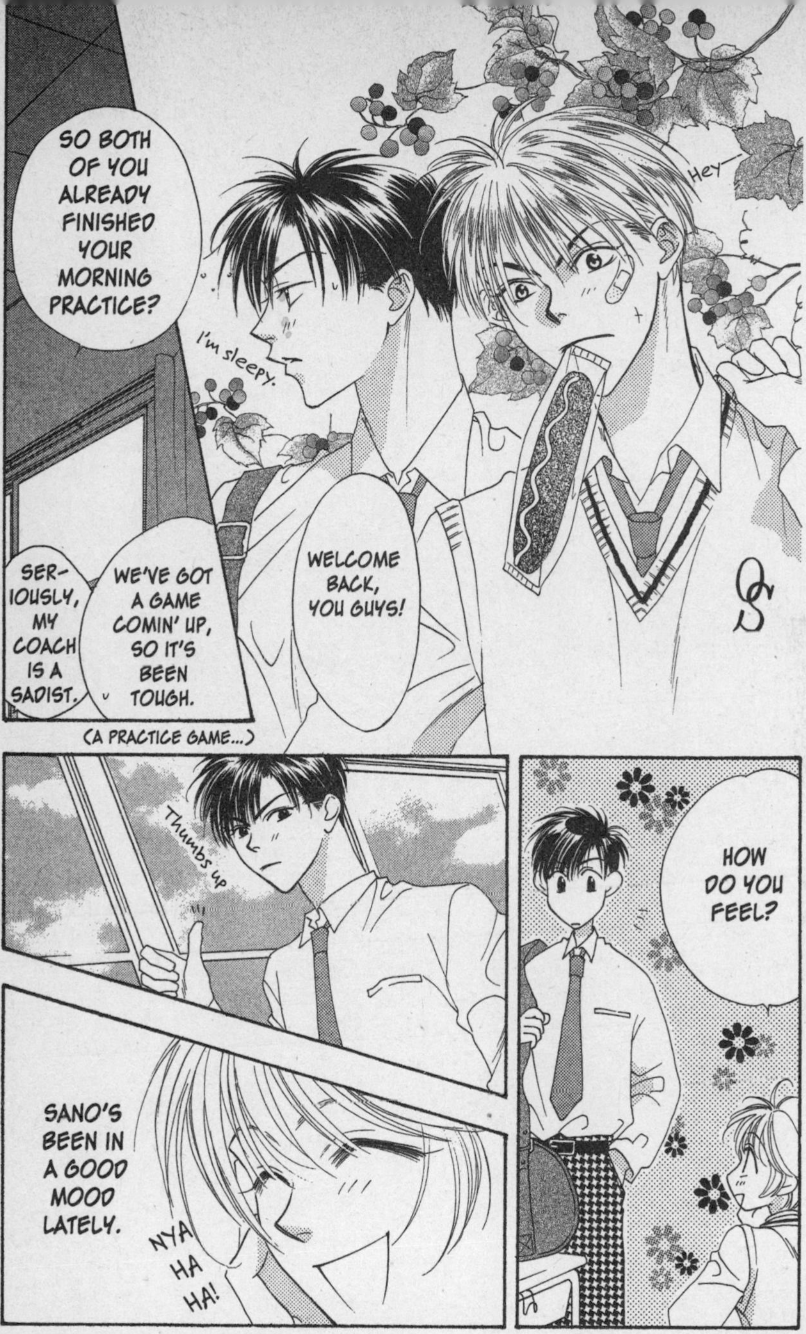
Hey—
SO BOTH OF YOU ALREADY FINISHED YOUR MORNING PRACTICE?
I'm sleepy.
WELCOME BACK, YOU GUYS!
WE'VE GOT A GAME COMIN' UP, SO IT'S BEEN TOUGH.
SER-IOUSLY, MY COACH IS A SADIST.
(A PRACTICE GAME...)
HOW DO YOU FEEL?
Thumbs up
SANO'S BEEN IN A GOOD MOOD LATELY.
NYA HA HA!

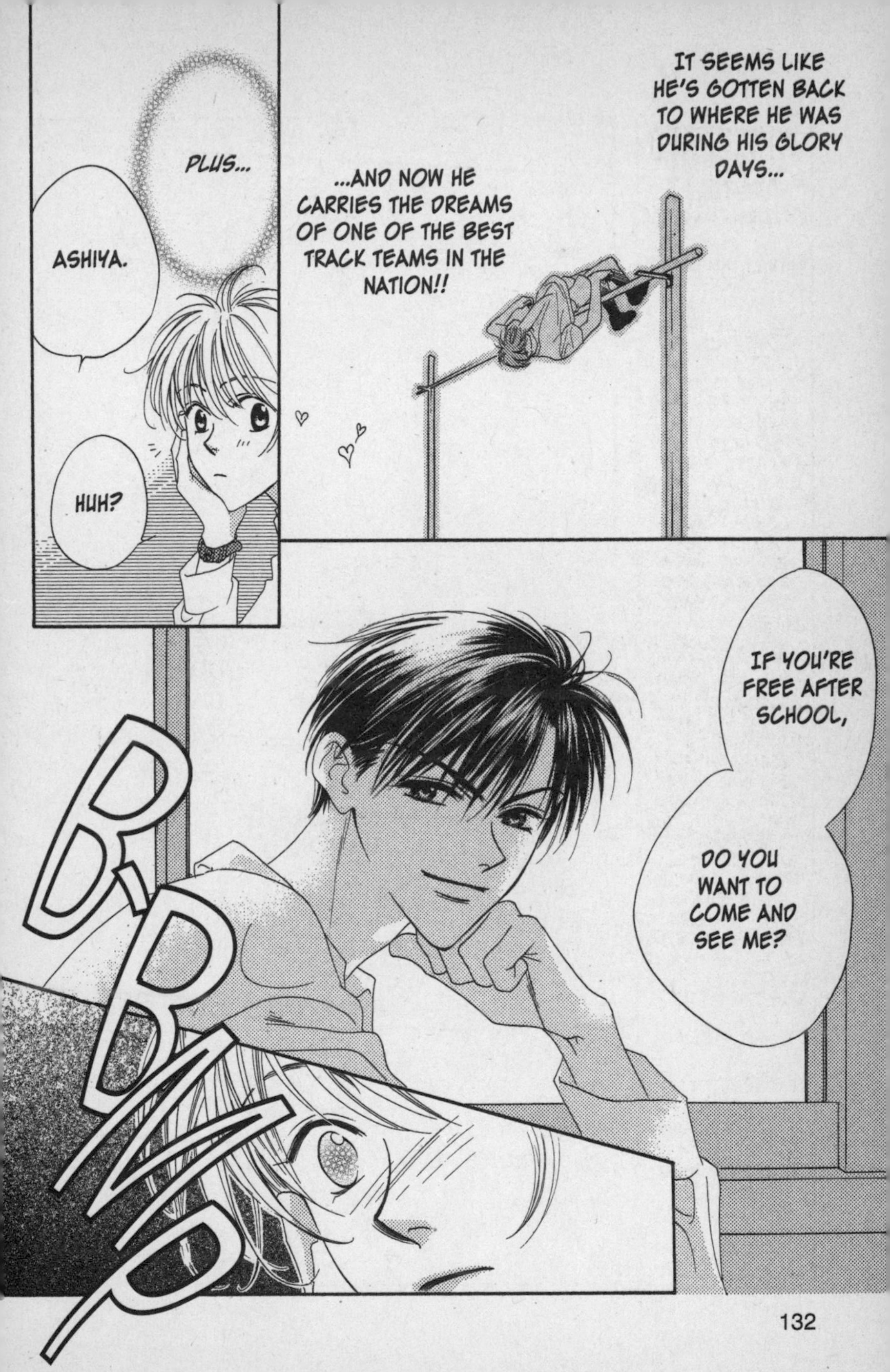
IT SEEMS LIKE HE'S GOTTEN BACK TO WHERE HE WAS DURING HIS GLORY DAYS...
...AND NOW HE CARRIES THE DREAMS OF ONE OF THE BEST TRACK TEAMS IN THE NATION!!
PLUS...
ASHIYA.
HUH?
IF YOU'RE FREE AFTER SCHOOL,
DO YOU WANT TO COME AND SEE ME?
B-BUMP

WHISPERED SECRETS
(STRANGE PAIR)

THIS IS THE STORY OF NAKATSU'S EMOTIONAL JOURNEY OF LOVE (HA HA). IZUMI HAS ALREADY RECOGNIZED HIS OWN FEELINGS, SO NOW IT'S NAKATSU'S TURN. I'M ALWAYS HARD ON NAKATSU (HEH), BUT SOMETIMES I NEED TO SHOW HIM IN A GOOD LIGHT. THIS TIME IT WASN'T NAKATSU BUT RATHER "THOSE TWO" WHO STOLE THE SPOTLIGHT. (SEE PAGE 141...BUT DON'T SKIP TO IT.) YOU MIGHT BE LEFT WITH SOME DOUBTS AND ASK, "WHY IS HE DOING CHIROPRACTICS NAKED?" WELL, IT'S JUST A LITTLE FAN SERVICE.♡ HEH. I HEARD THERE'S A RUMOR ABOUT "UMEDA + KUJO." OH NO! IS THERE REALLY?!

...IS THAT WHAT EVERYBODY WANTS TO READ ABOUT?

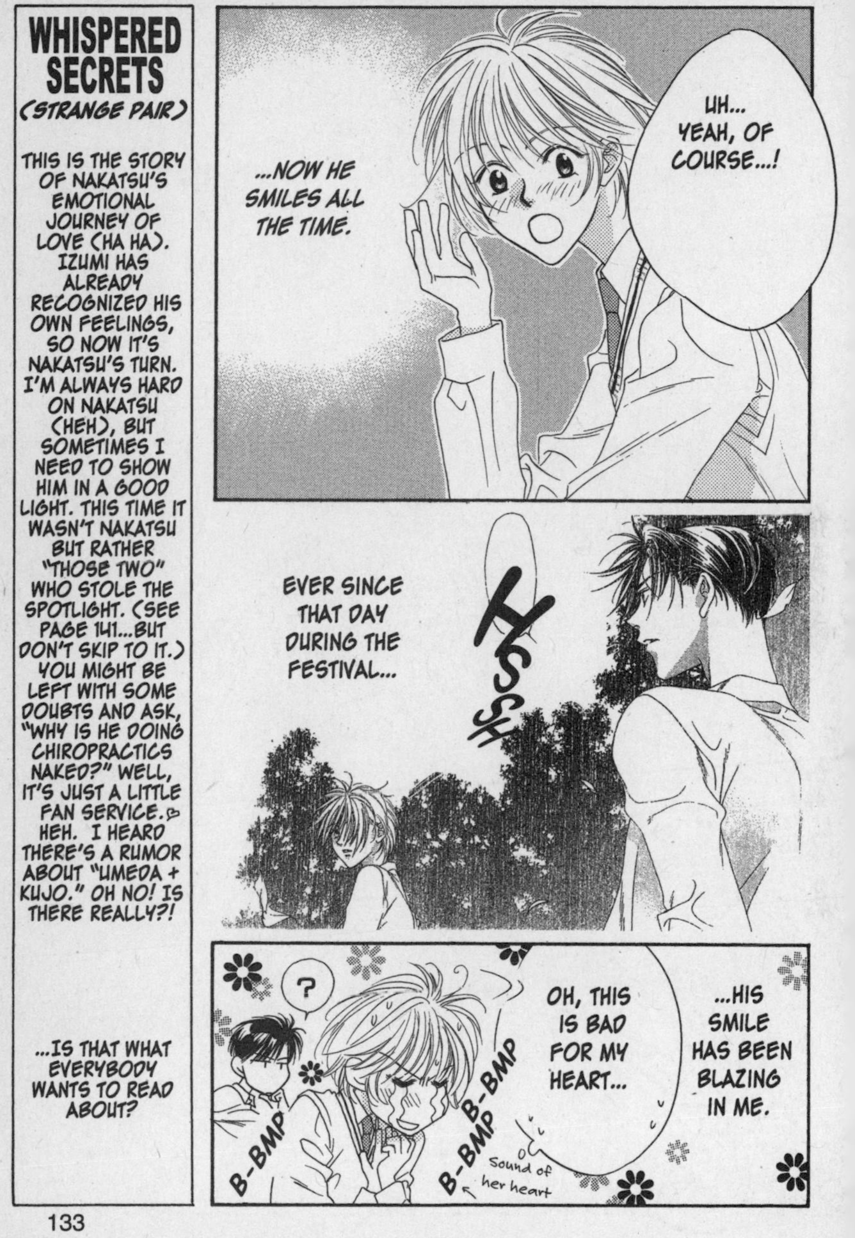
UH... YEAH, OF COURSE...!
...NOW HE SMILES ALL THE TIME.
HSSSH
EVER SINCE THAT DAY DURING THE FESTIVAL...
...HIS SMILE HAS BEEN BLAZING IN ME.
OH, THIS IS BAD FOR MY HEART...
?
B-BMP B-BMP
B-BMP
Sound of her heart

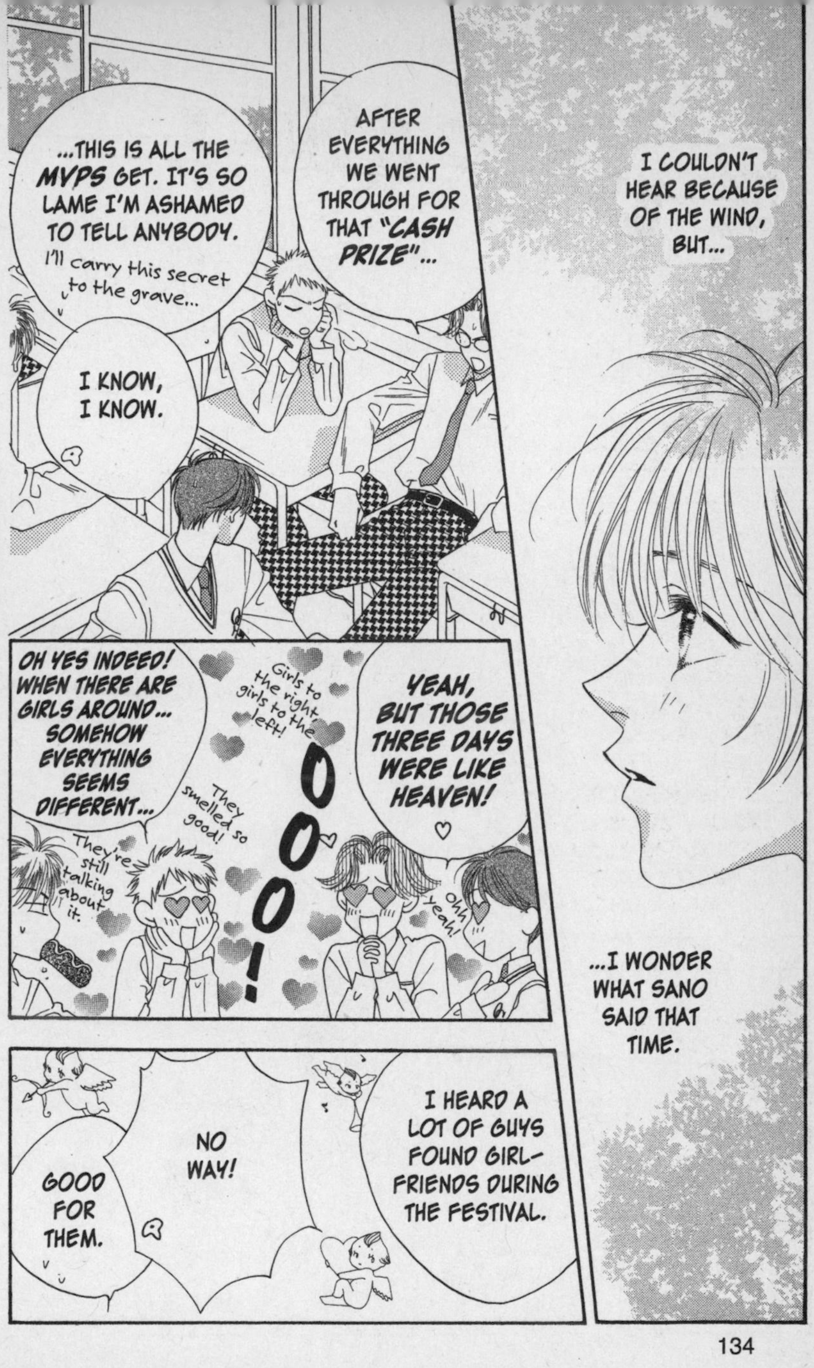
I COULDN'T HEAR BECAUSE OF THE WIND, BUT...
...I WONDER WHAT SANO SAID THAT TIME.
AFTER EVERYTHING WE WENT THROUGH FOR THAT "CASH PRIZE"...
...THIS IS ALL THE MVPS GET. IT'S SO LAME I'M ASHAMED TO TELL ANYBODY.
I'll carry this secret to the grave...
I KNOW, I KNOW.
YEAH, BUT THOSE THREE DAYS WERE LIKE HEAVEN! ♡
Ohh yeah!
OOO!
Girls to the right, girls to the left!
OH YES INDEED! WHEN THERE ARE GIRLS AROUND... SOMEHOW EVERYTHING SEEMS DIFFERENT...
They smelled so good!
They're still talking about it.
I HEARD A LOT OF GUYS FOUND GIRL-FRIENDS DURING THE FESTIVAL.
NO WAY!
GOOD FOR THEM.

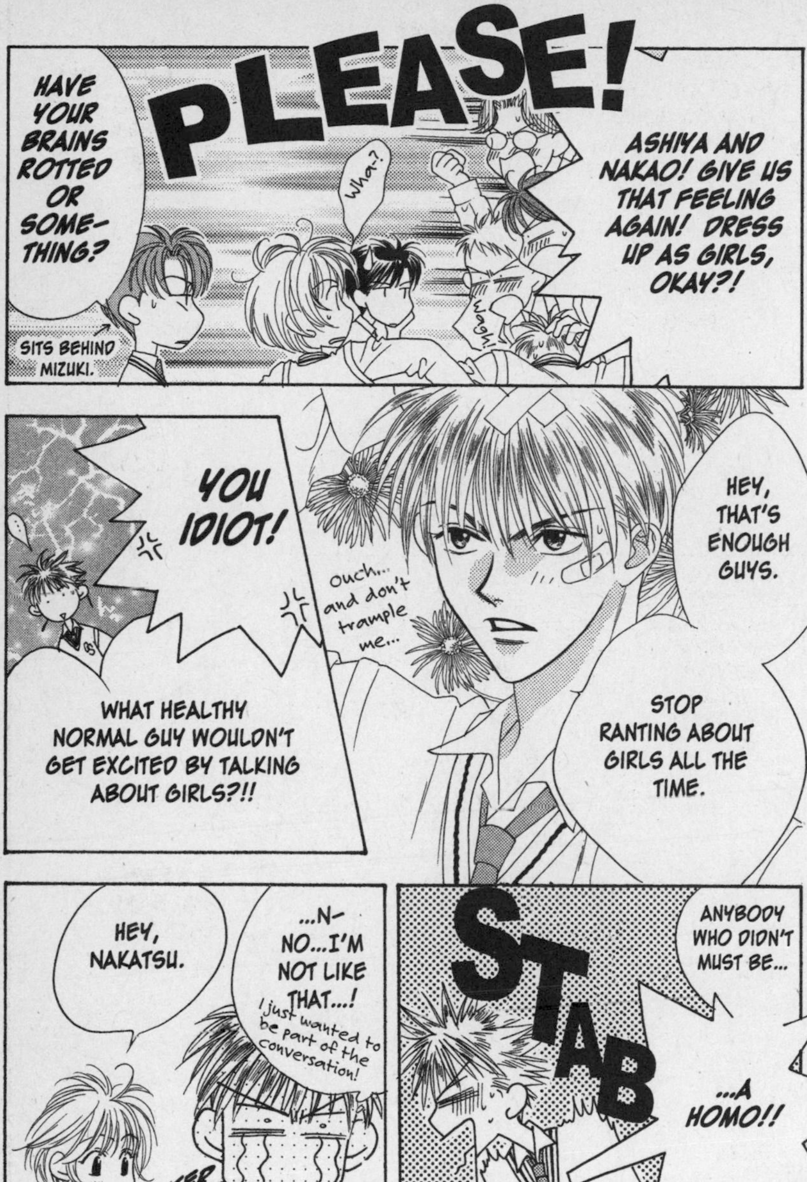
ASHIYA AND NAKAO! GIVE US THAT FEELING AGAIN! DRESS UP AS GIRLS, OKAY?!
PLEASE!
Wagh!
Wha-?
HAVE YOUR BRAINS ROTTED OR SOME-THING?
SITS BEHIND MIZUKI.
HEY, THAT'S ENOUGH GUYS.
STOP RANTING ABOUT GIRLS ALL THE TIME.
ouch... and don't trample me...
YOU IDIOT!
WHAT HEALTHY NORMAL GUY WOULDN'T GET EXCITED BY TALKING ABOUT GIRLS?!!
ANYBODY WHO DIDN'T MUST BE...
STAB
...A HOMO!!
...N-NO...I'M NOT LIKE THAT...!
I just wanted to be part of the conversation!
HEY, NAKATSU.
MUTTER
MUTTER

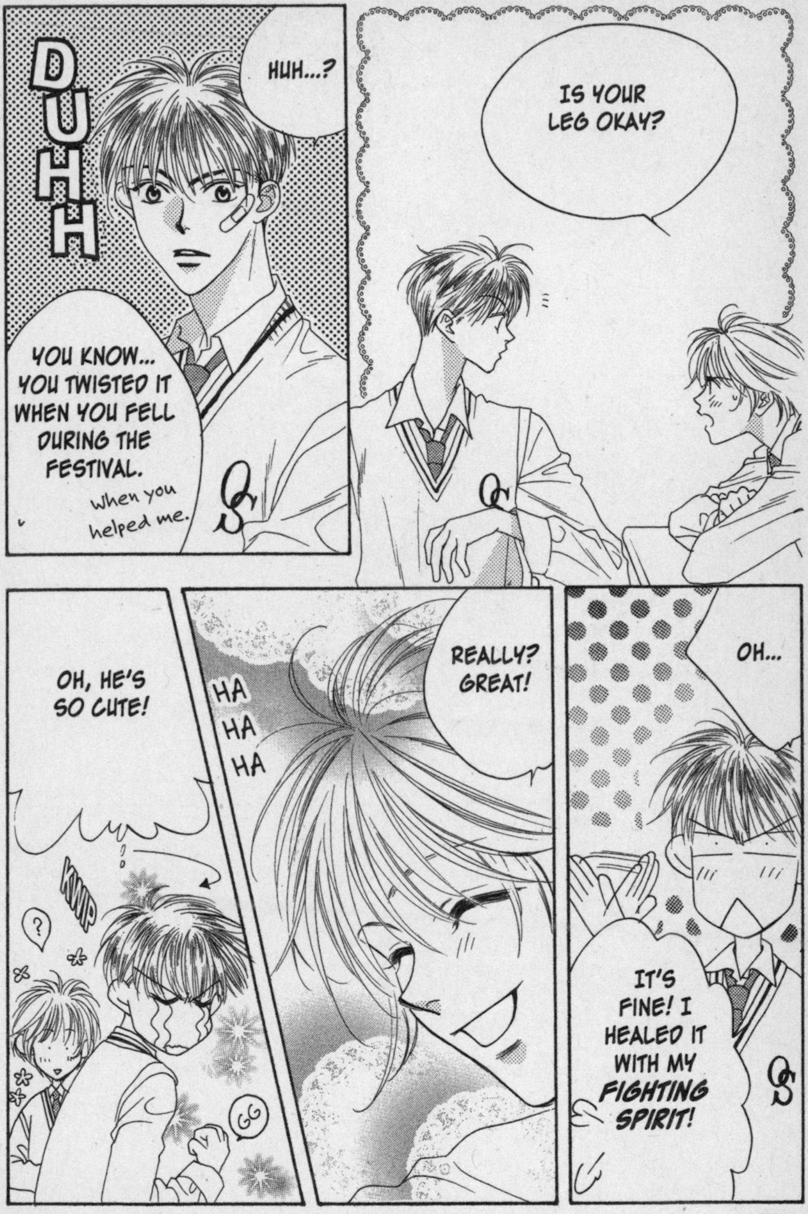
IS YOUR LEG OKAY?
HUH...?
DUHH
YOU KNOW... YOU TWISTED IT WHEN YOU FELL DURING THE FESTIVAL.
when you helped me.
OH...
IT'S FINE! I HEALED IT WITH MY FIGHTING SPIRIT!
REALLY? GREAT!
HA HA HA
OH, HE'S SO CUTE!
KWIP
?
GG

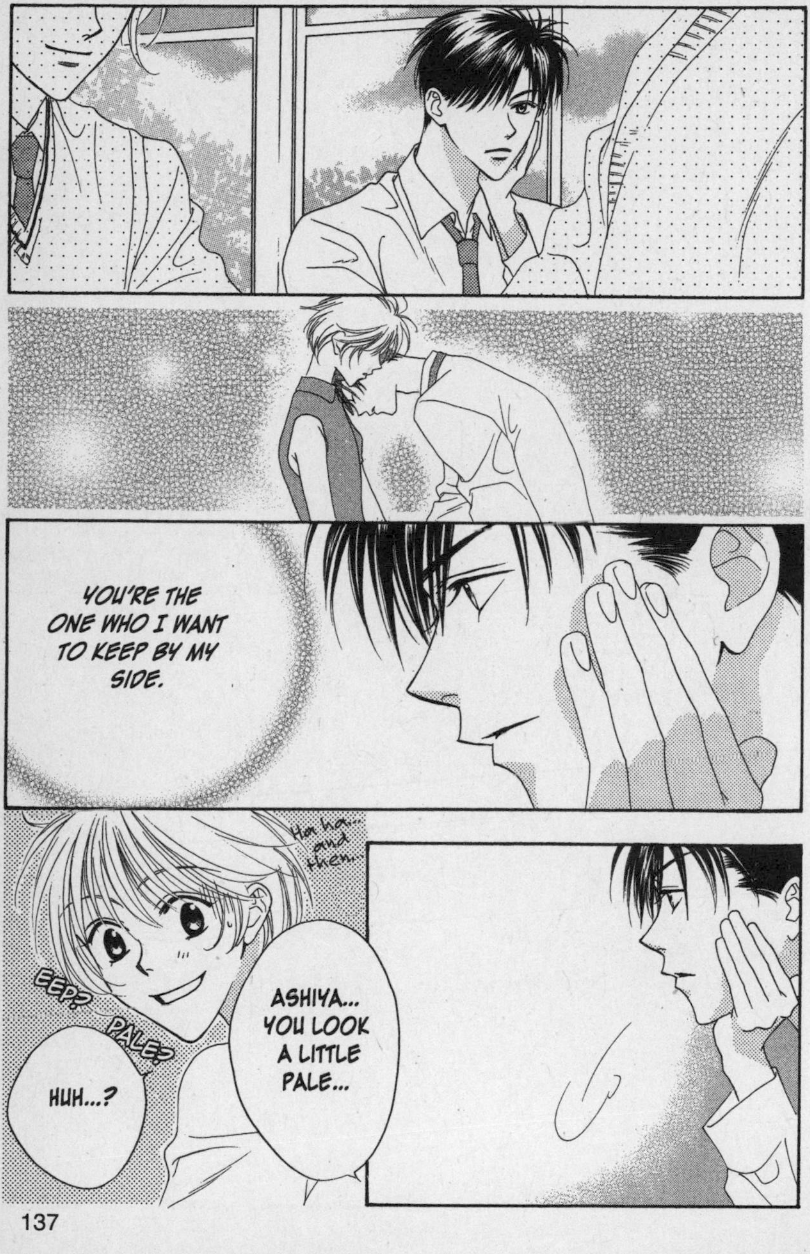
YOU'RE THE ONE WHO I WANT TO KEEP BY MY SIDE.
Ha ha... and then...
ASHIYA... YOU LOOK A LITTLE PALE...
EEP? PALE?
HUH...?

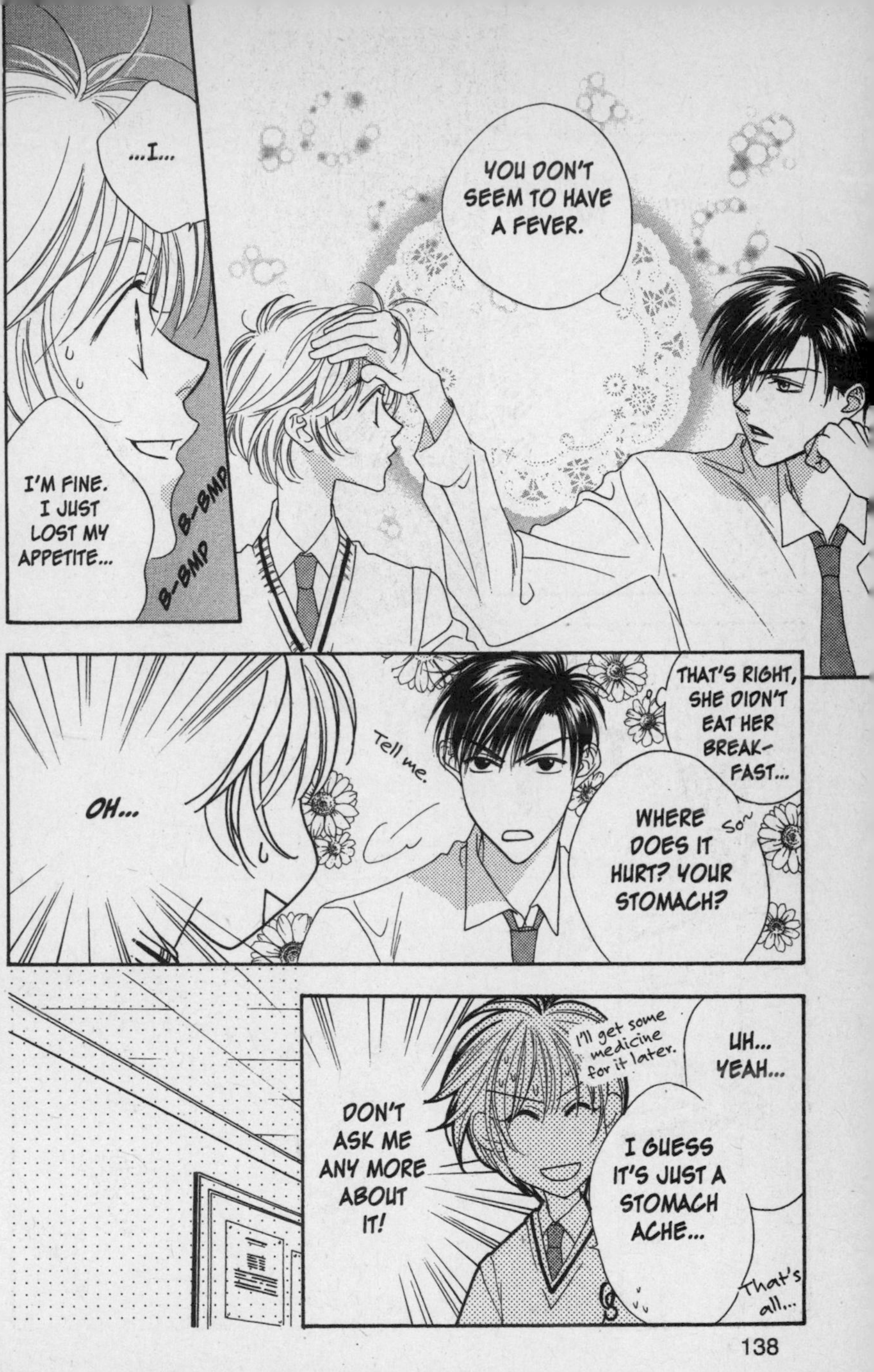
YOU DON'T SEEM TO HAVE A FEVER.
...I...
I'M FINE. I JUST LOST MY APPETITE...
B-BMP
B-BMP
THAT'S RIGHT, SHE DIDN'T EAT HER BREAK-FAST...
WHERE DOES IT HURT? YOUR STOMACH?
So~
Tell me.
OH...
UH... YEAH...
I'll get some medicine for it later.
I GUESS IT'S JUST A STOMACH ACHE...
That's all...
DON'T ASK ME ANY MORE ABOUT IT!

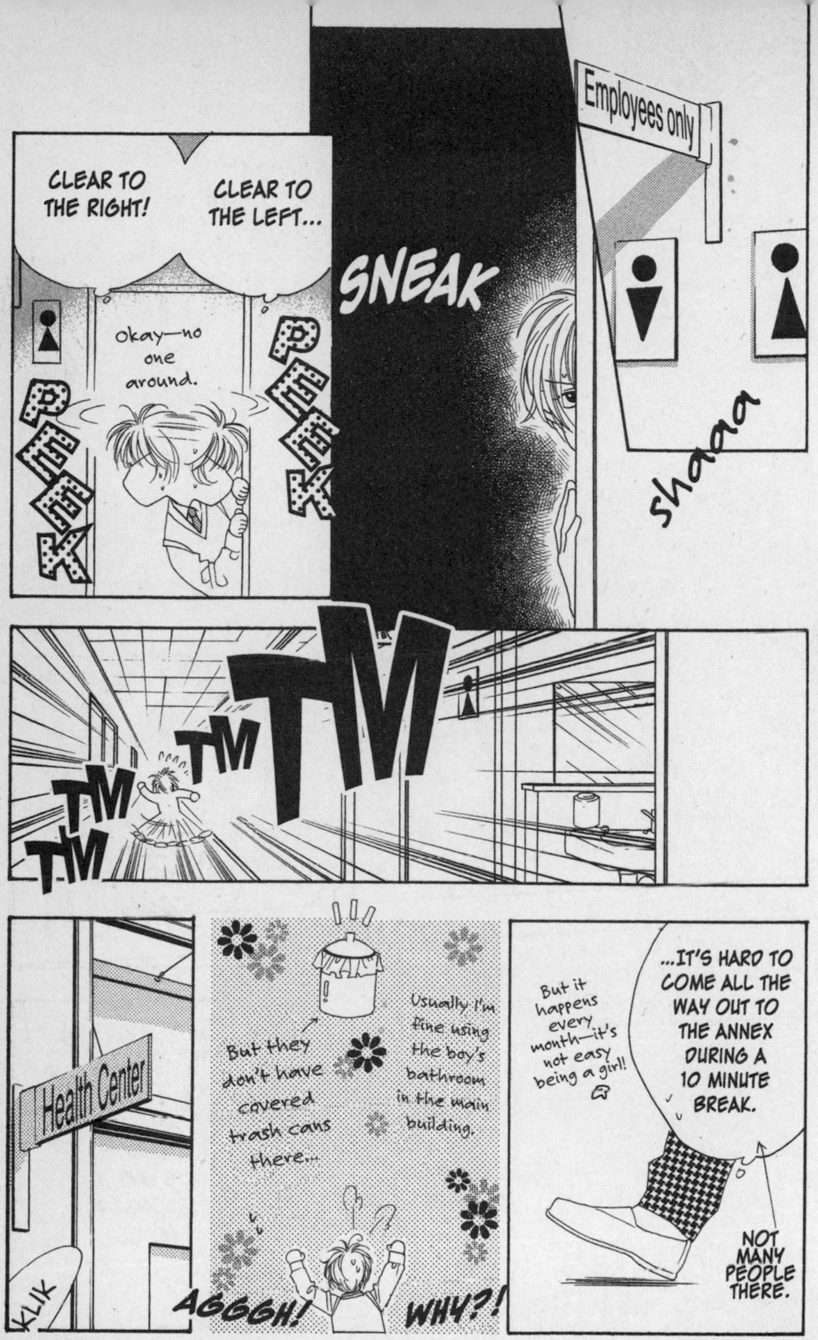
Employees only
SNEAK
shaaa
CLEAR TO THE RIGHT!
CLEAR TO THE LEFT...
PEEK
PEEK
Okay—no one around.
TM
TM
TM
TM
...IT'S HARD TO COME ALL THE WAY OUT TO THE ANNEX DURING A 10 MINUTE BREAK.
But it happens every month—it's not easy being a girl!
NOT MANY PEOPLE THERE.
Usually I'm fine using the boy's bathroom in the main building.
But they don't have covered trash cans there...
AGGGH!
WHY?!
Health Center
KLIK

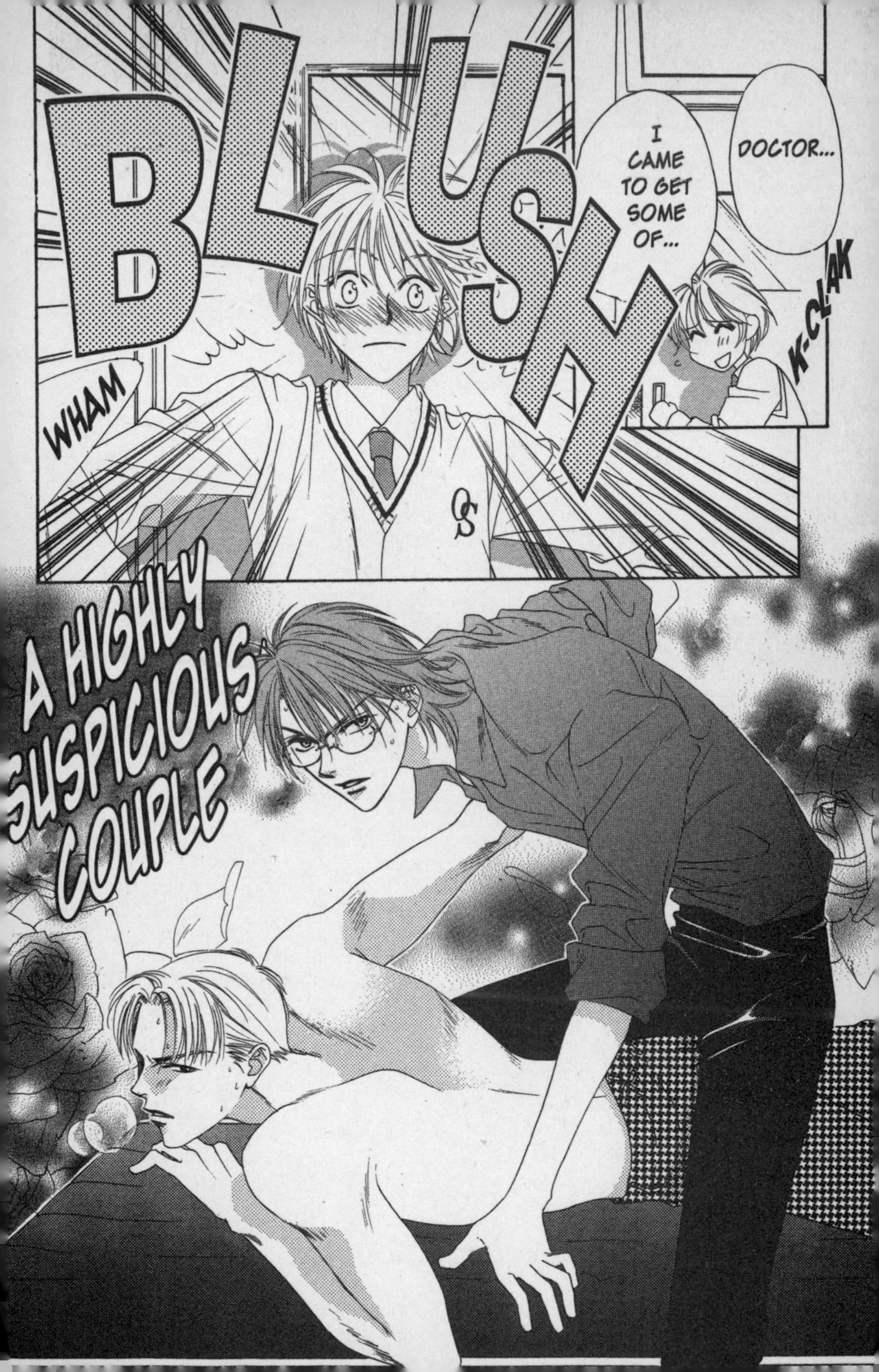
DOCTOR...
I CAME TO GET SOME OF...
K-CLAK
BLUSH
WHAM
A HIGHLY SUSPICIOUS COUPLE

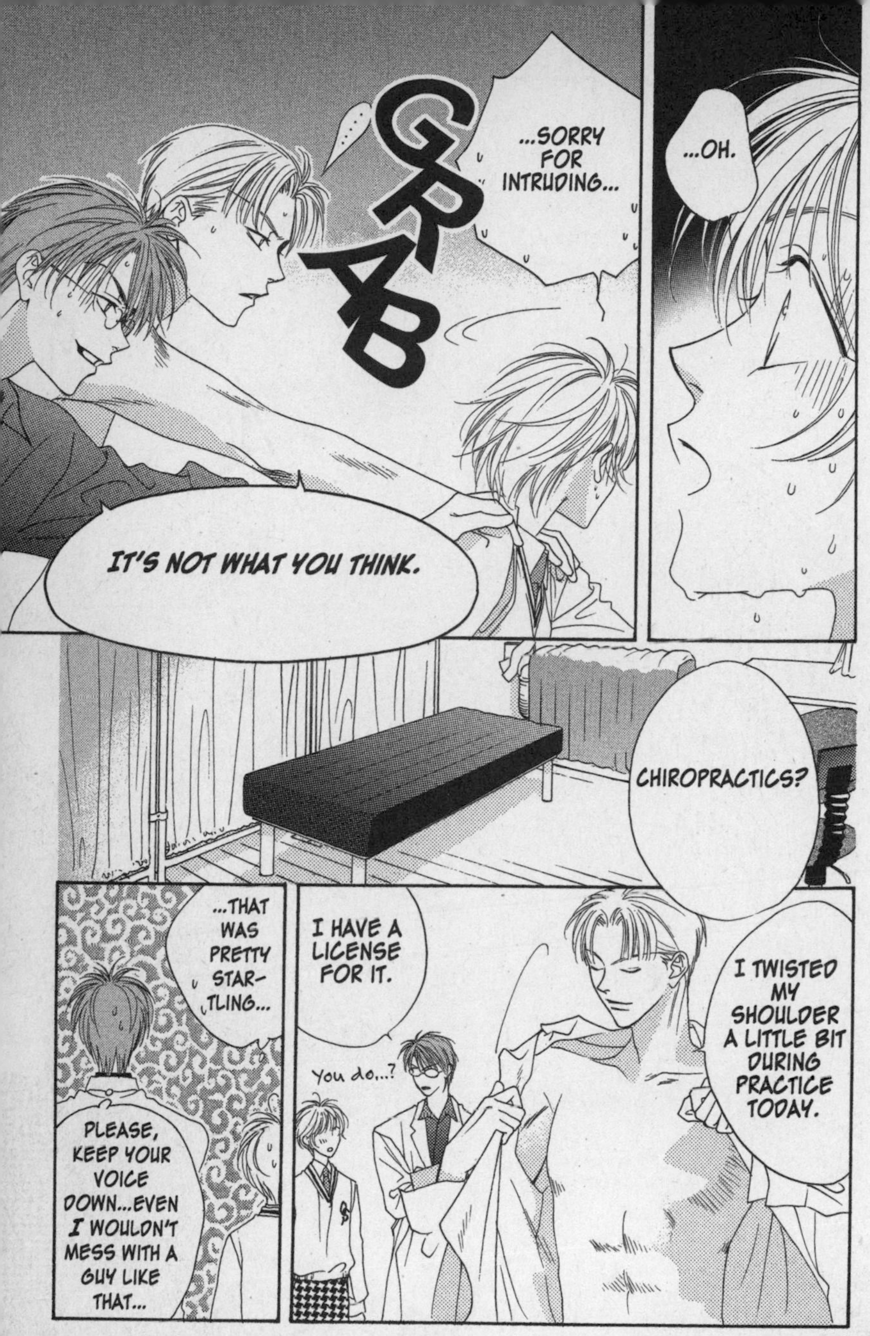
...OH.
...SORRY FOR INTRUDING...
GRAB
...
IT'S NOT WHAT YOU THINK.
CHIROPRACTICS?
I TWISTED MY SHOULDER A LITTLE BIT DURING PRACTICE TODAY.
I HAVE A LICENSE FOR IT.
You do...?
...THAT WAS PRETTY STAR-TLING...
PLEASE, KEEP YOUR VOICE DOWN...EVEN I WOULDN'T MESS WITH A GUY LIKE THAT...

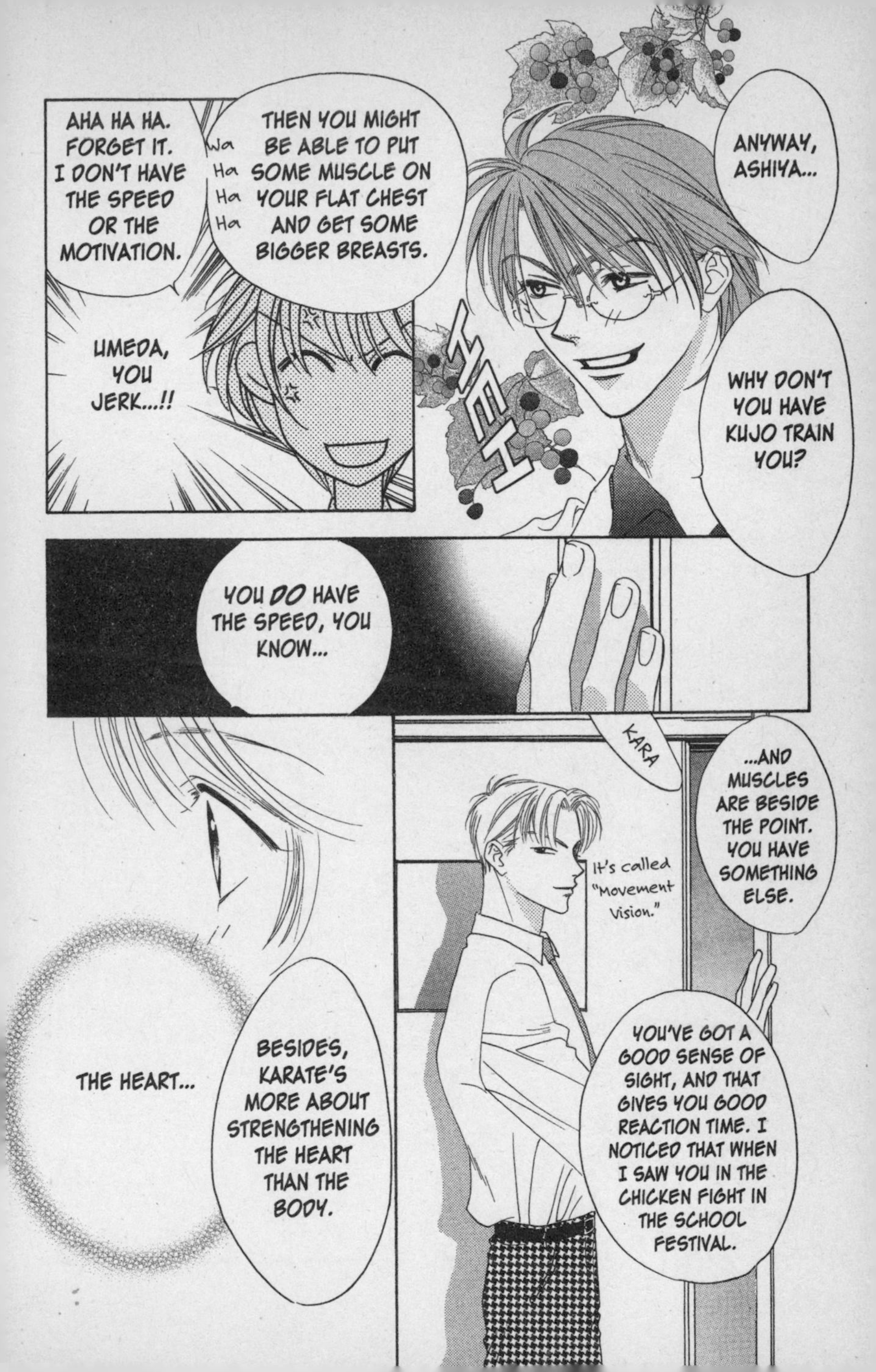
ANYWAY, ASHIYA...
WHY DON'T YOU HAVE KUJO TRAIN YOU?
HEH
THEN YOU MIGHT BE ABLE TO PUT SOME MUSCLE ON YOUR FLAT CHEST AND GET SOME BIGGER BREASTS.
Wa Ha Ha Ha
AHA HA HA. FORGET IT. I DON'T HAVE THE SPEED OR THE MOTIVATION.
UMEDA, YOU JERK...!!
YOU *DO* HAVE THE SPEED, YOU KNOW...
KARA
...AND MUSCLES ARE BESIDE THE POINT. YOU HAVE SOMETHING ELSE.
It's called "Movement Vision."
YOU'VE GOT A GOOD SENSE OF SIGHT, AND THAT GIVES YOU GOOD REACTION TIME. I NOTICED THAT WHEN I SAW YOU IN THE CHICKEN FIGHT IN THE SCHOOL FESTIVAL.
BESIDES, KARATE'S MORE ABOUT STRENGTHENING THE HEART THAN THE BODY.
THE HEART...

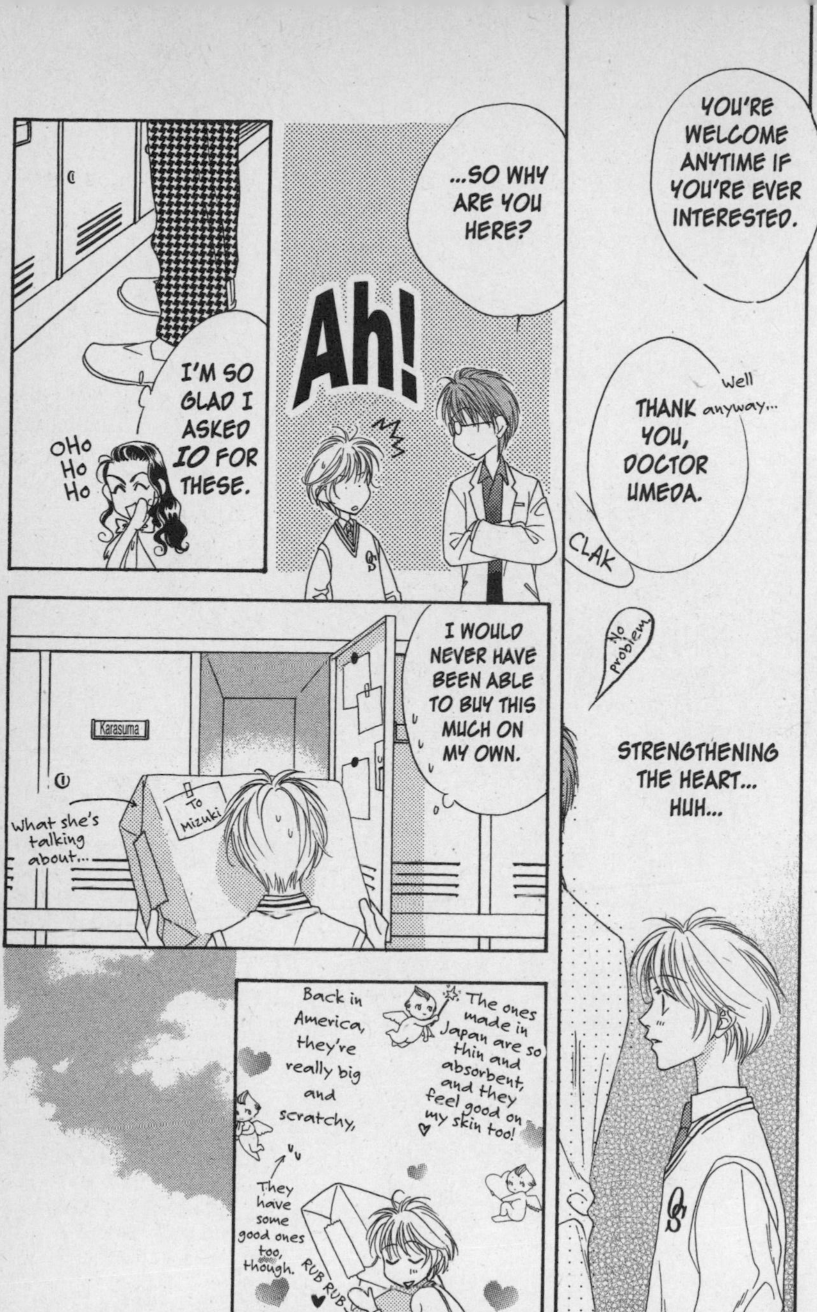
YOU'RE WELCOME ANYTIME IF YOU'RE EVER INTERESTED.
Well anyway...
THANK YOU, DOCTOR UMEDA.
CLAK
No problem
STRENGTHENING THE HEART... HUH...
...SO WHY ARE YOU HERE?
Ah!
I'M SO GLAD I ASKED IO FOR THESE.
OHo Ho Ho
I WOULD NEVER HAVE BEEN ABLE TO BUY THIS MUCH ON MY OWN.
Karasuma
To Mizuki
What she's talking about...
The ones made in Japan are so thin and absorbent, and they feel good on my skin too!
Back in America, they're really big and scratchy,
They have some good ones too, though.
RUB RUB

PUT THE BOX AWAY BEFORE SOMEONE SEES YOU...

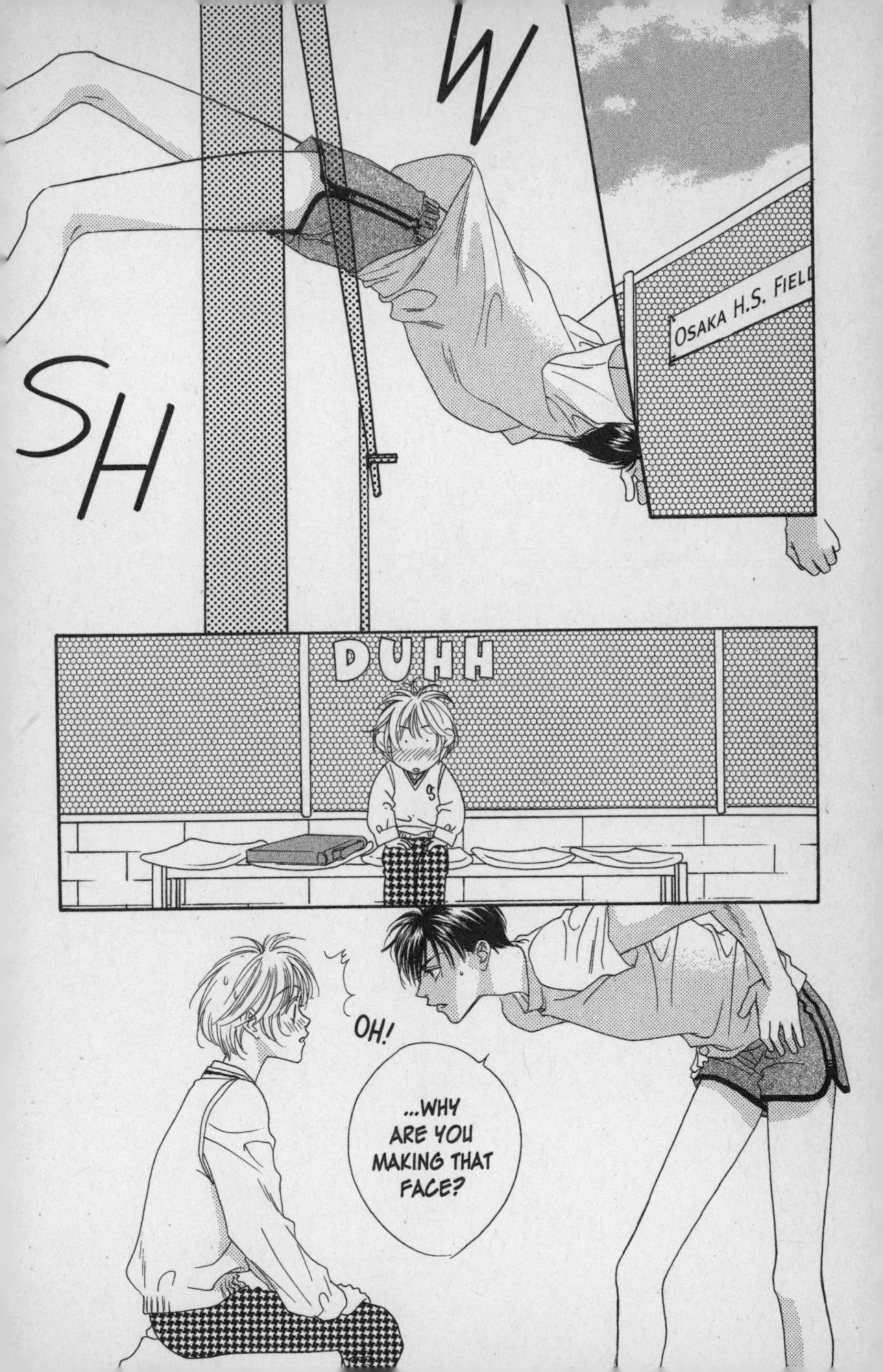
W
SH
OSAKA H.S. FIELD
DUHH
OH!
...WHY ARE YOU MAKING THAT FACE?

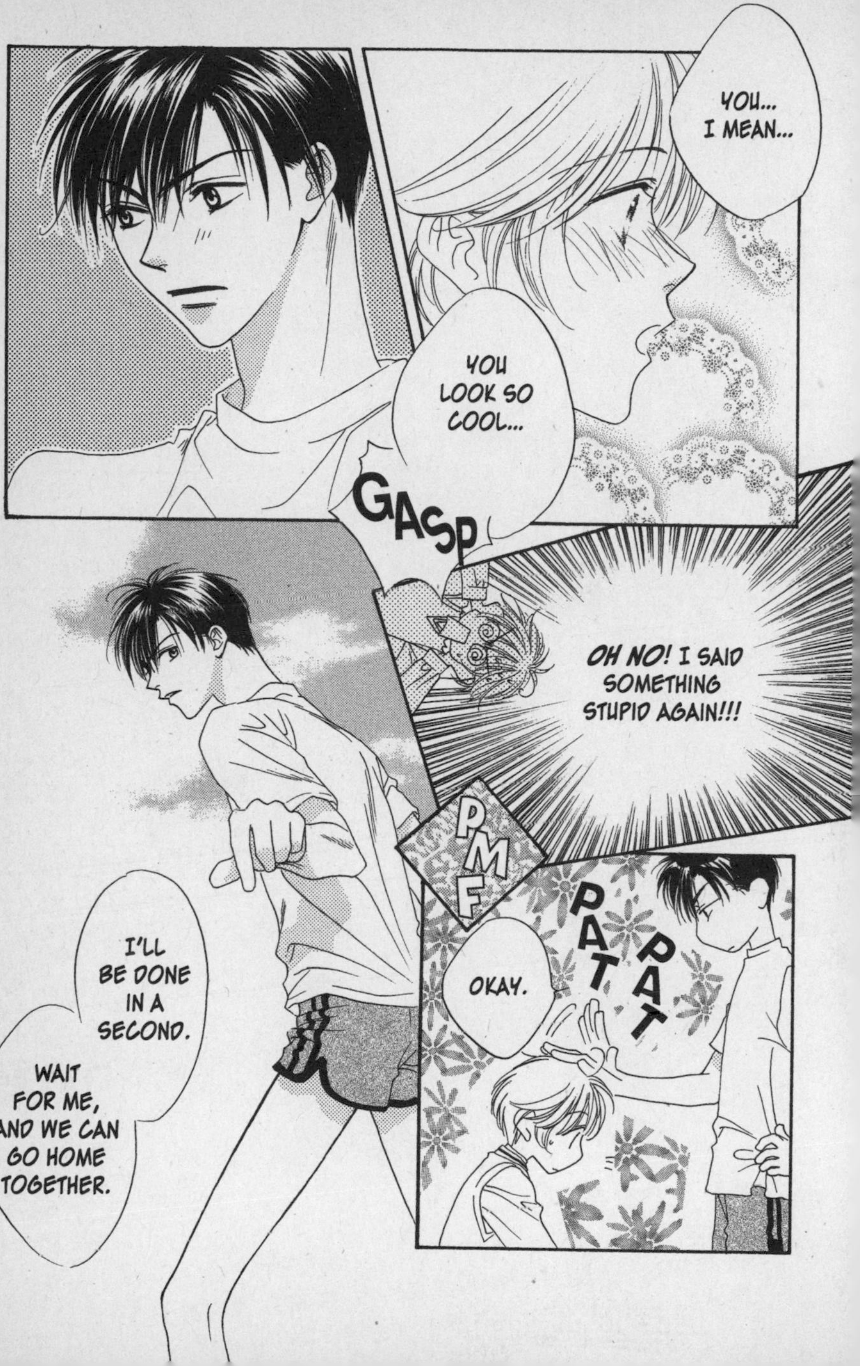
YOU... I MEAN...
YOU LOOK SO COOL...
GASP
OH NO! I SAID SOMETHING STUPID AGAIN!!!
PMF
PAT PAT
OKAY.
I'LL BE DONE IN A SECOND.
WAIT FOR ME, AND WE CAN GO HOME TOGETHER.

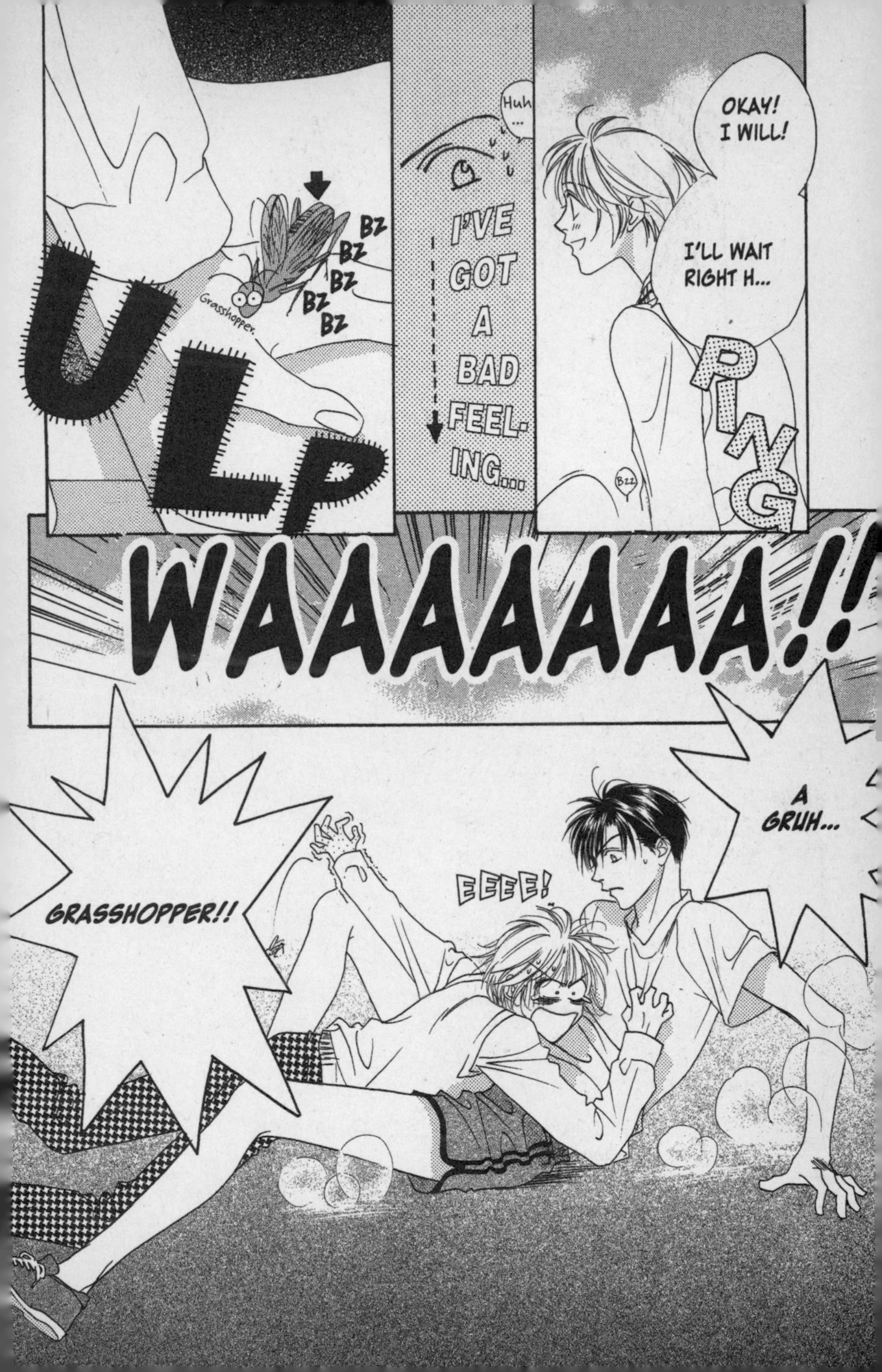
OKAY! I WILL!
I'LL WAIT RIGHT H...
PING
Bzz
Huh...
I'VE GOT A BAD FEELING...
BZ
BZ
BZ
BZ
BZ
Grasshopper.
ULP
WAAAAAAA!!
A GRUH...
EEEE!
GRASSHOPPER!!

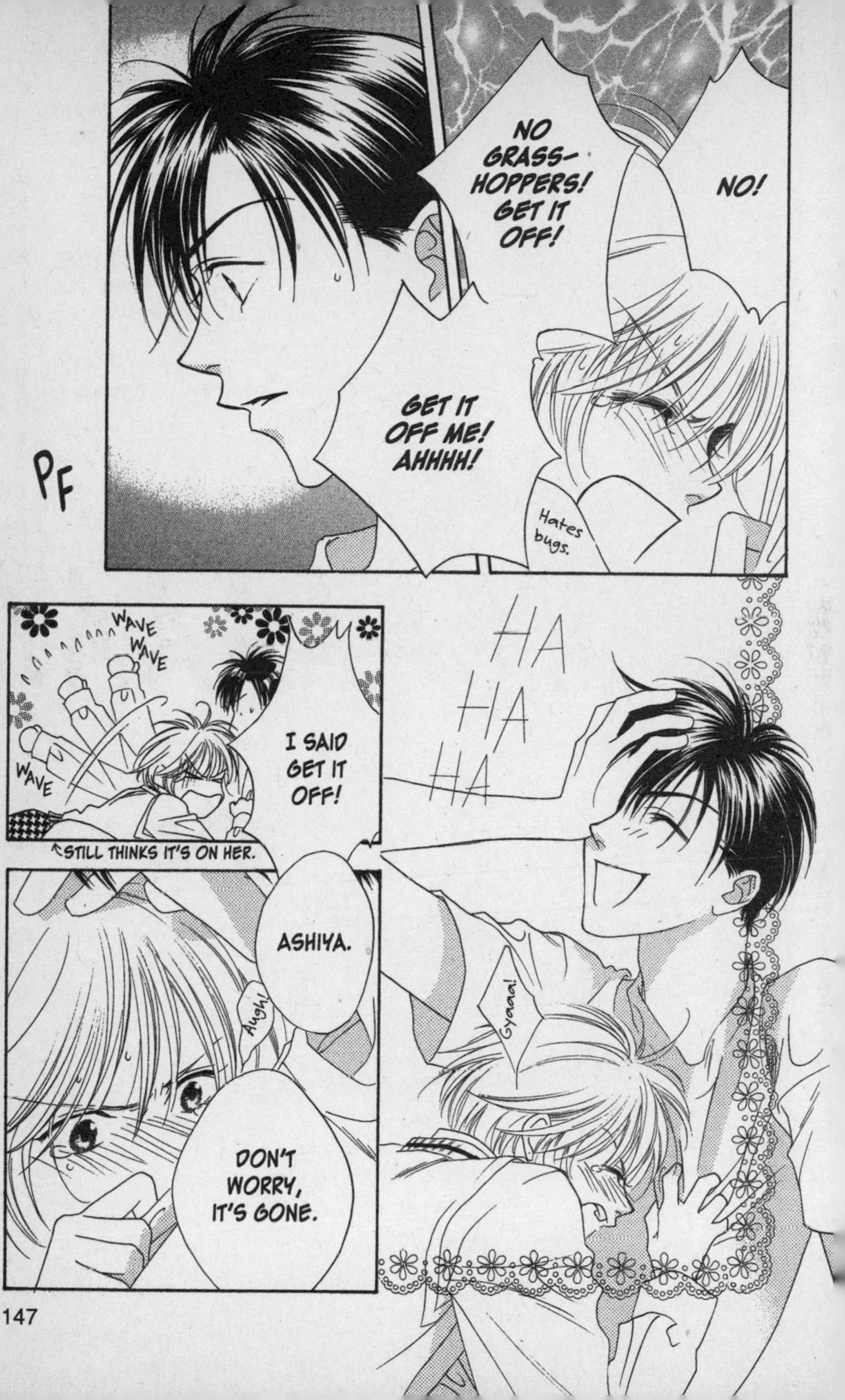
NO!
NO GRASS-HOPPERS! GET IT OFF!
GET IT OFF ME! AHHHH!
Hates bugs.
PF
HA HA HA
Gyaaa!
WAVE WAVE
WAVE
I SAID GET IT OFF!
↖STILL THINKS IT'S ON HER.
ASHIYA.
Augh!
DON'T WORRY, IT'S GONE.

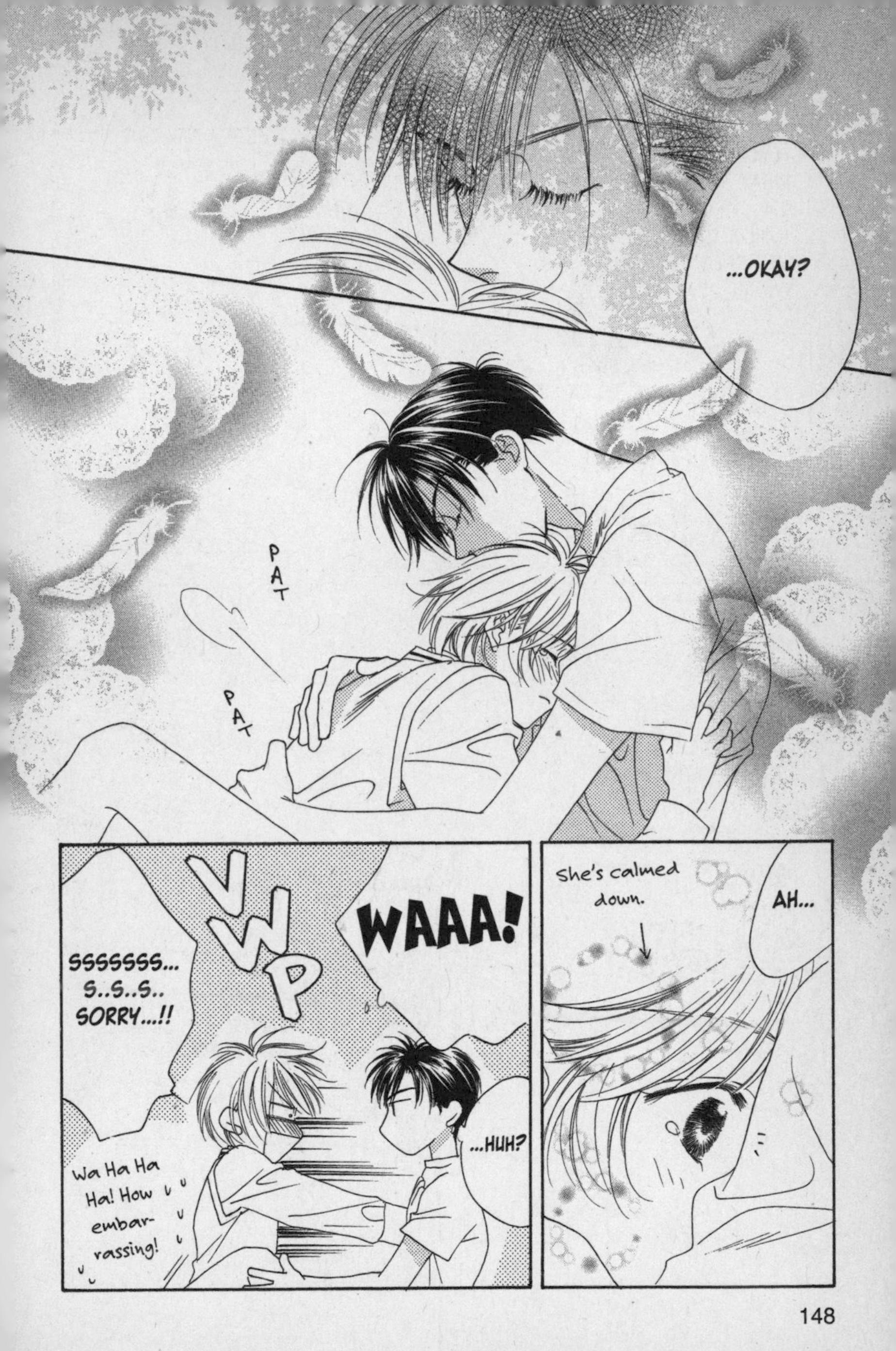
...OKAY?
PAT
PAT
AH...
She's calmed down.
WAAA!
VWP
SSSSSSS... S..S..S.. SORRY...!!
...HUH?
Wa Ha Ha Ha! How embarrassing!

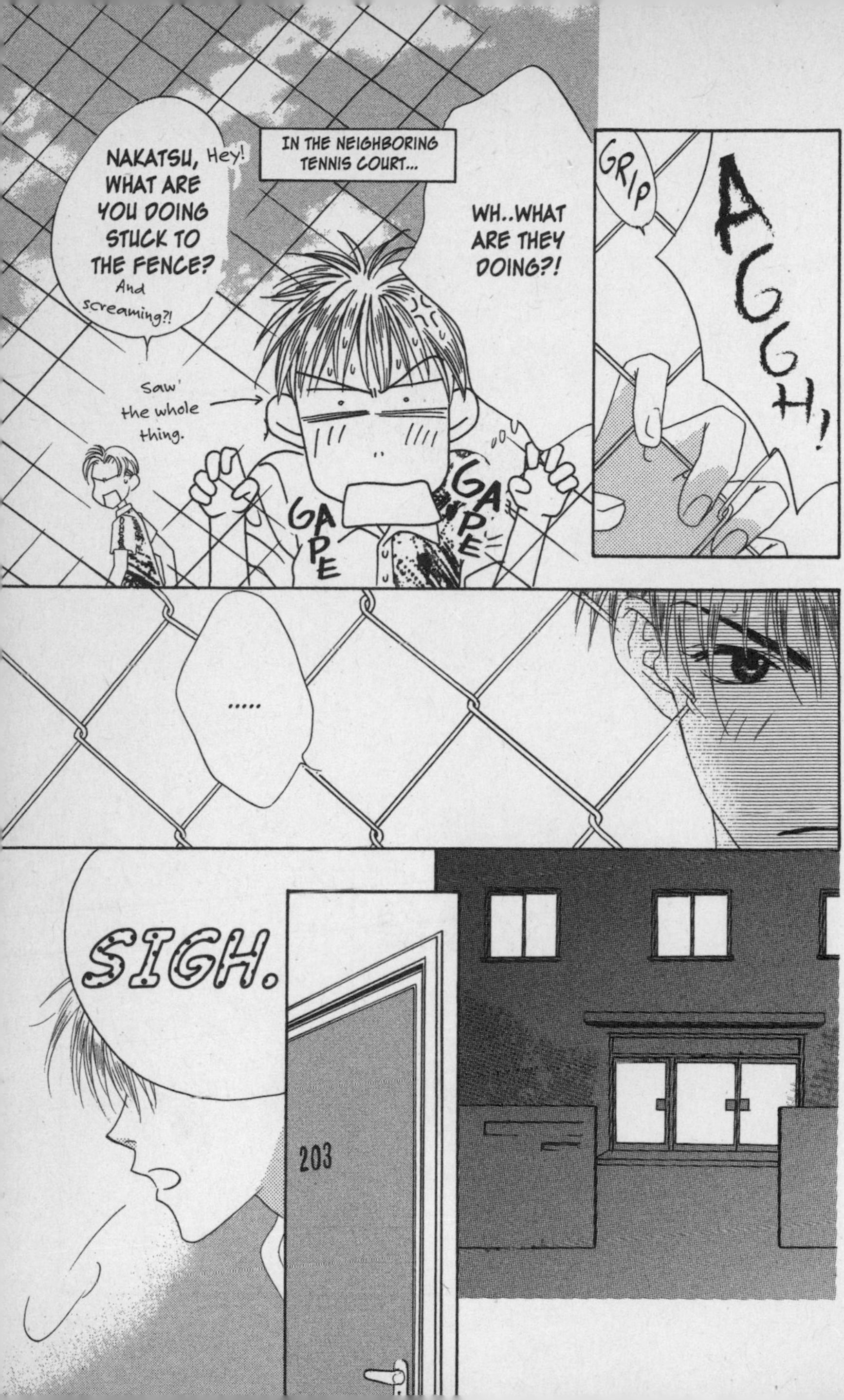
GRIP
AGGH!
IN THE NEIGHBORING TENNIS COURT...
WH..WHAT ARE THEY DOING?!
Hey!
NAKATSU, WHAT ARE YOU DOING STUCK TO THE FENCE?
And screaming?!
GAPE
GAPE
Saw the whole thing.
.....
SIGH.
203

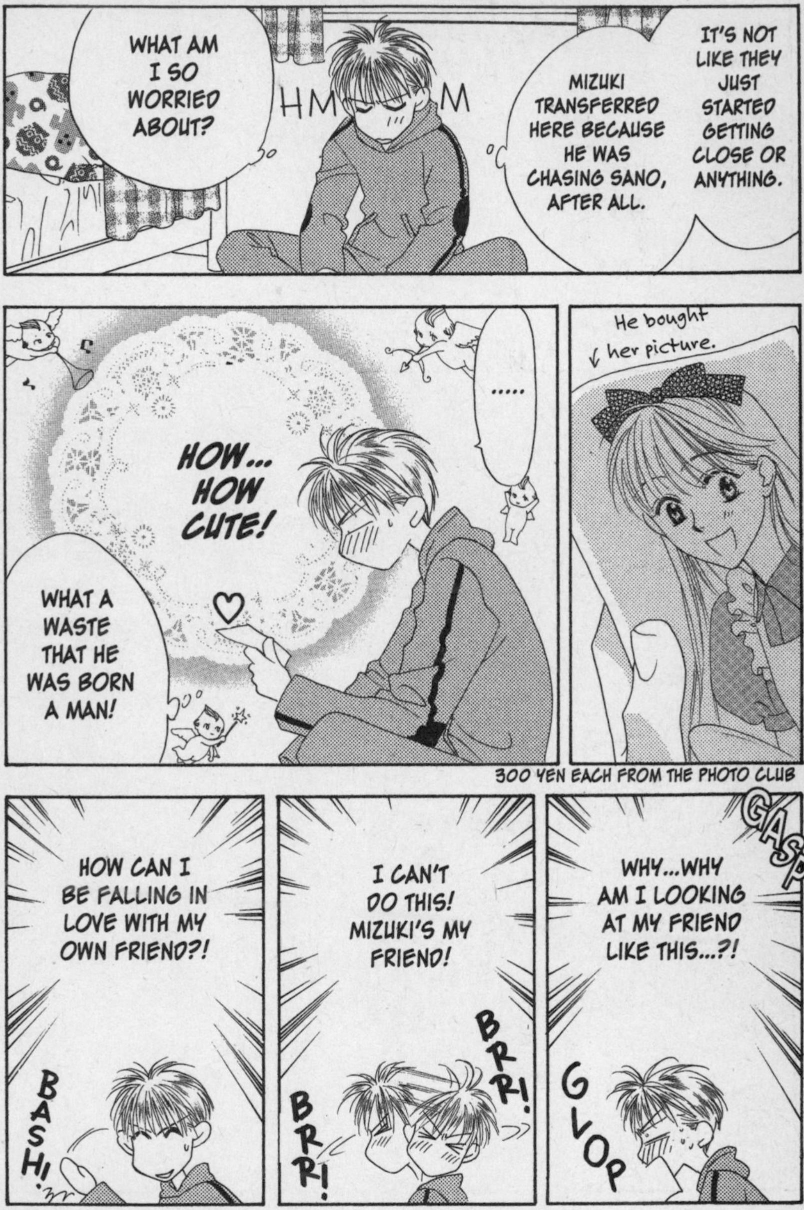
IT'S NOT LIKE THEY JUST STARTED GETTING CLOSE OR ANYTHING.
MIZUKI TRANSFERRED HERE BECAUSE HE WAS CHASING SANO, AFTER ALL.
HMMM
WHAT AM I SO WORRIED ABOUT?
He bought her picture.
300 YEN EACH FROM THE PHOTO CLUB
.....
HOW... HOW CUTE!
WHAT A WASTE THAT HE WAS BORN A MAN!
GASP
WHY...WHY AM I LOOKING AT MY FRIEND LIKE THIS...?!
GVOP
BRRR!
I CAN'T DO THIS! MIZUKI'S MY FRIEND!
BRRR!
HOW CAN I BE FALLING IN LOVE WITH MY OWN FRIEND?!
BASH!

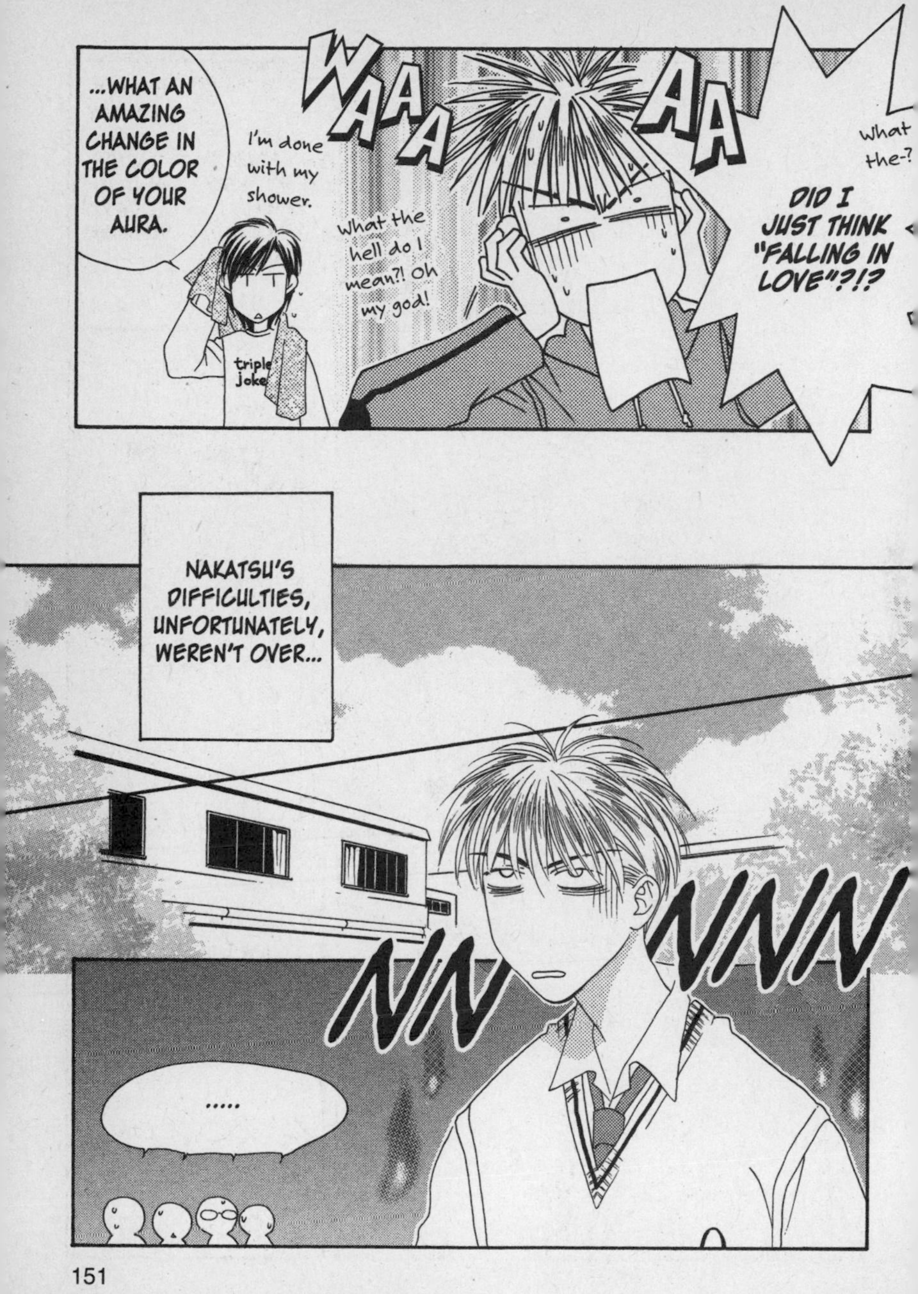
WAAAAAA
what the-?
DID I JUST THINK "FALLING IN LOVE"?!?
what the hell do I mean?! Oh my god!
I'm done with my shower.
...WHAT AN AMAZING CHANGE IN THE COLOR OF YOUR AURA.
triple joke
NAKATSU'S DIFFICULTIES, UNFORTUNATELY, WEREN'T OVER...
NNNNN
.....

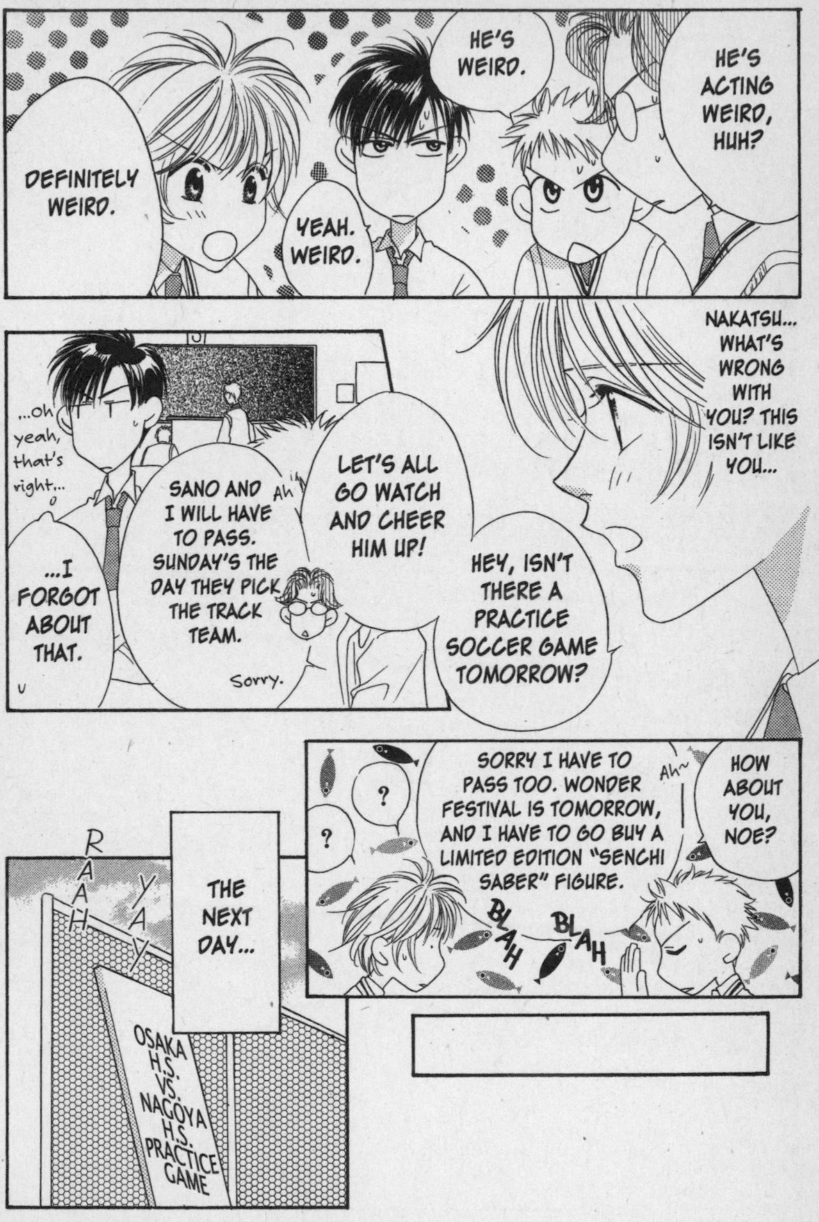
HE'S ACTING WEIRD, HUH?
HE'S WEIRD.
YEAH. WEIRD.
DEFINITELY WEIRD.
NAKATSU... WHAT'S WRONG WITH YOU? THIS ISN'T LIKE YOU...
HEY, ISN'T THERE A PRACTICE SOCCER GAME TOMORROW?
LET'S ALL GO WATCH AND CHEER HIM UP!
Ah
SANO AND I WILL HAVE TO PASS. SUNDAY'S THE DAY THEY PICK THE TRACK TEAM.
Sorry.
...oh yeah, that's right...
...I FORGOT ABOUT THAT.
HOW ABOUT YOU, NOE?
Ah~
SORRY I HAVE TO PASS TOO. WONDER FESTIVAL IS TOMORROW, AND I HAVE TO GO BUY A LIMITED EDITION "SENCHI SABER" FIGURE.
?
?
BLAH BLAH
THE NEXT DAY...
RAAH
YAY
OSAKA H.S. VS. NAGOYA H.S. PRACTICE GAME

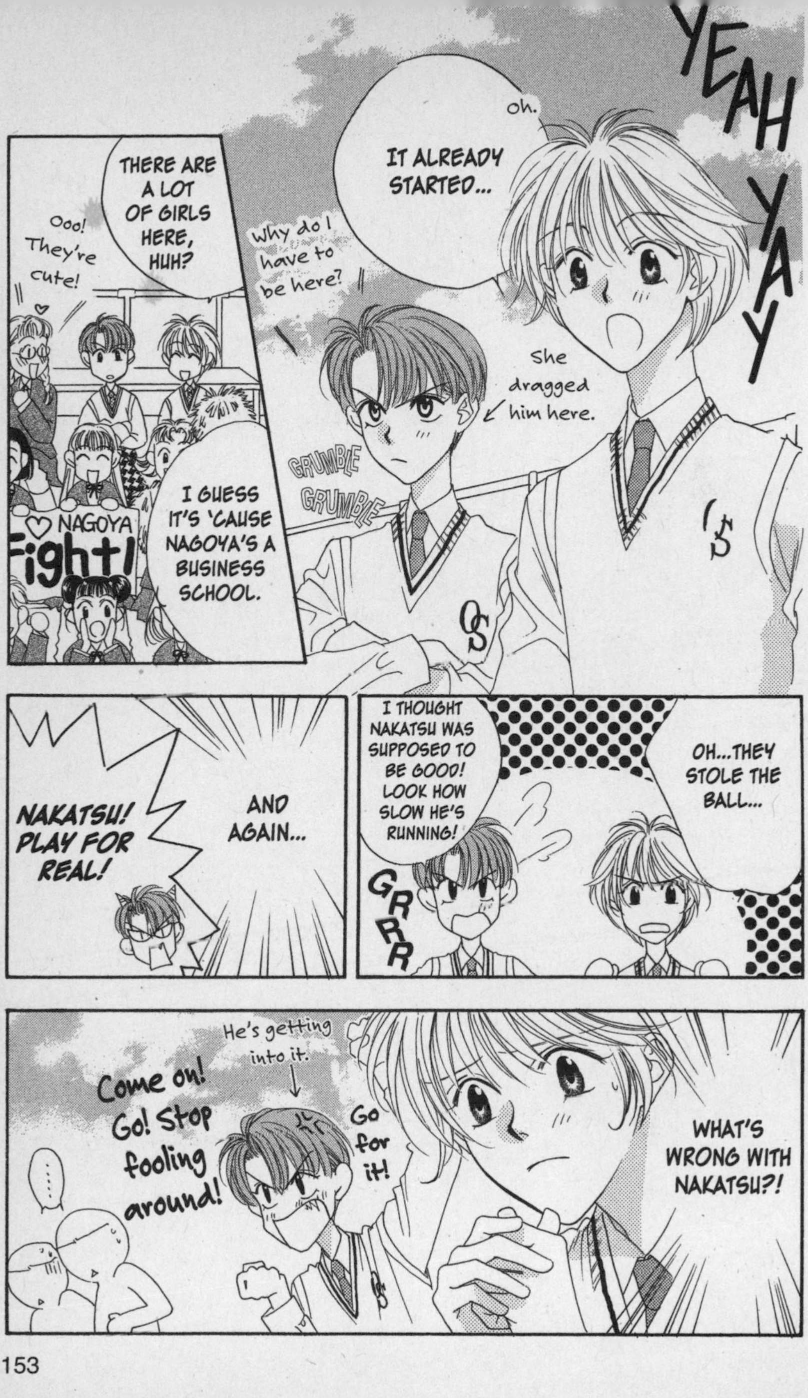
YEAH YAY
Oh.
IT ALREADY STARTED...
She dragged him here.
Why do I have to be here?
GRUMBLE GRUMBLE
THERE ARE A LOT OF GIRLS HERE, HUH?
Ooo! They're cute!
I GUESS IT'S 'CAUSE NAGOYA'S A BUSINESS SCHOOL.
NAGOYA Fight!
OH...THEY STOLE THE BALL...
I THOUGHT NAKATSU WAS SUPPOSED TO BE GOOD! LOOK HOW SLOW HE'S RUNNING!
GRRR
AND AGAIN...
NAKATSU! PLAY FOR REAL!
WHAT'S WRONG WITH NAKATSU?!
Go for it!
He's getting into it.
Come on! Go! Stop fooling around!
......

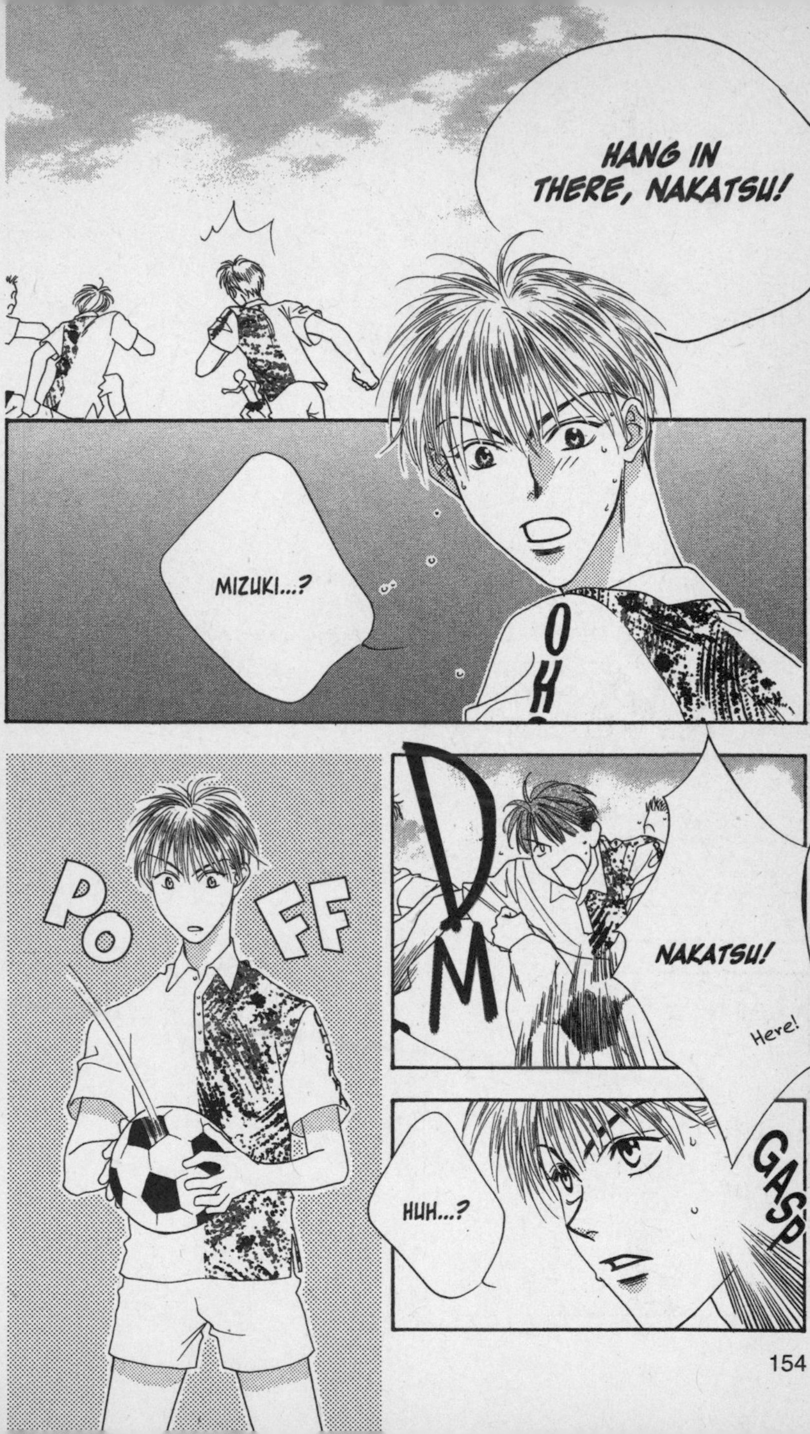
HANG IN THERE, NAKATSU!
MIZUKI...?
DM
NAKATSU!
Here!
GASP
HUH...?
POFF

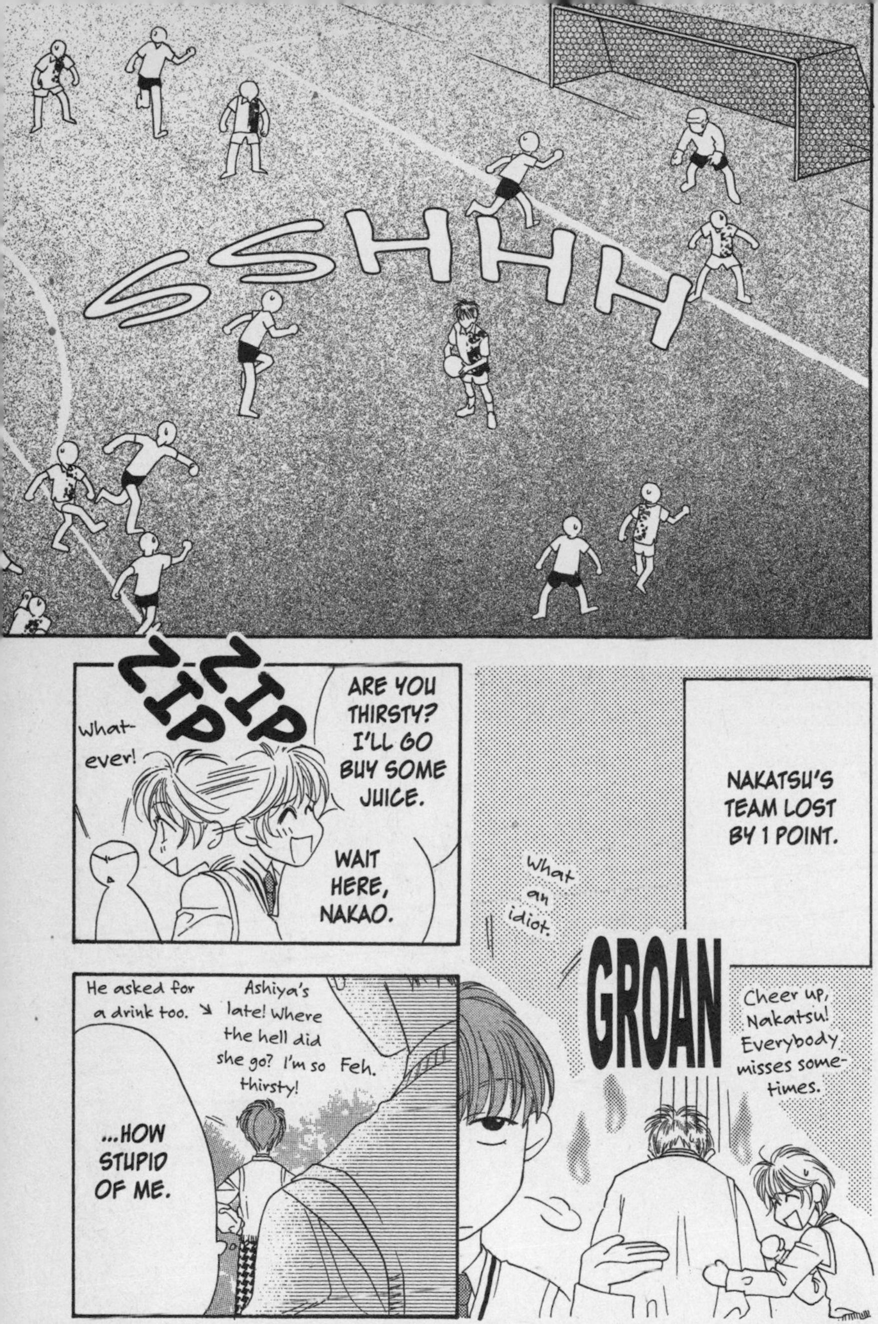
SSHHH
NAKATSU'S TEAM LOST BY 1 POINT.
What an idiot.
GROAN
Cheer up, Nakatsu! Everybody misses sometimes.
ZIP ZIP
ARE YOU THIRSTY? I'LL GO BUY SOME JUICE.
WAIT HERE, NAKAO.
What-ever!
Ashiya's late! Where the hell did she go? I'm so thirsty!
Feh.
He asked for a drink too.
...HOW STUPID OF ME.

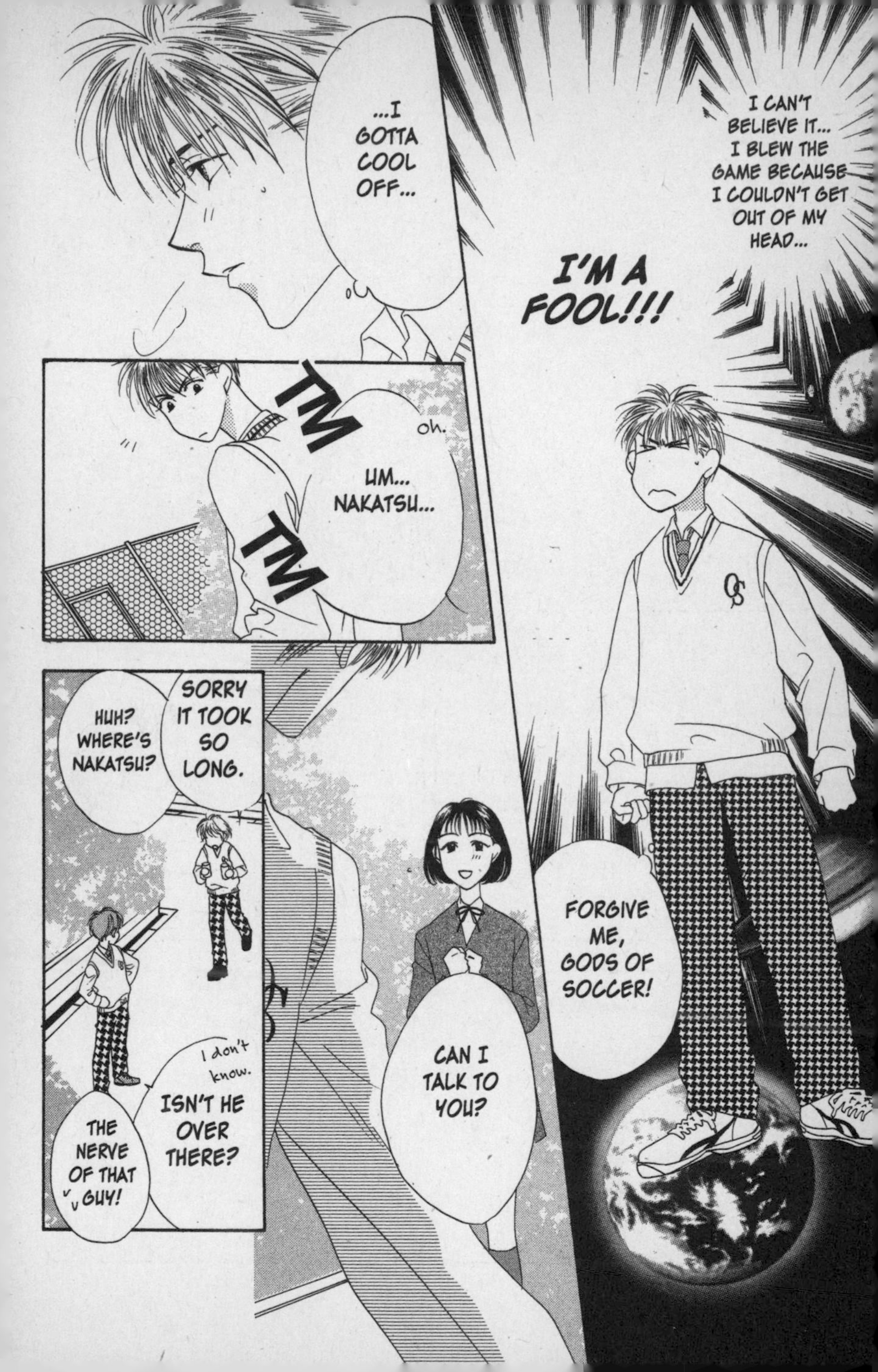
I CAN'T BELIEVE IT... I BLEW THE GAME BECAUSE I COULDN'T GET OUT OF MY HEAD...
I'M A FOOL!!!
FORGIVE ME, GODS OF SOCCER!
...I GOTTA COOL OFF...
TM TM
oh.
UM... NAKATSU...
CAN I TALK TO YOU?
SORRY IT TOOK SO LONG.
HUH? WHERE'S NAKATSU?
I don't know.
ISN'T HE OVER THERE?
THE NERVE OF THAT GUY!

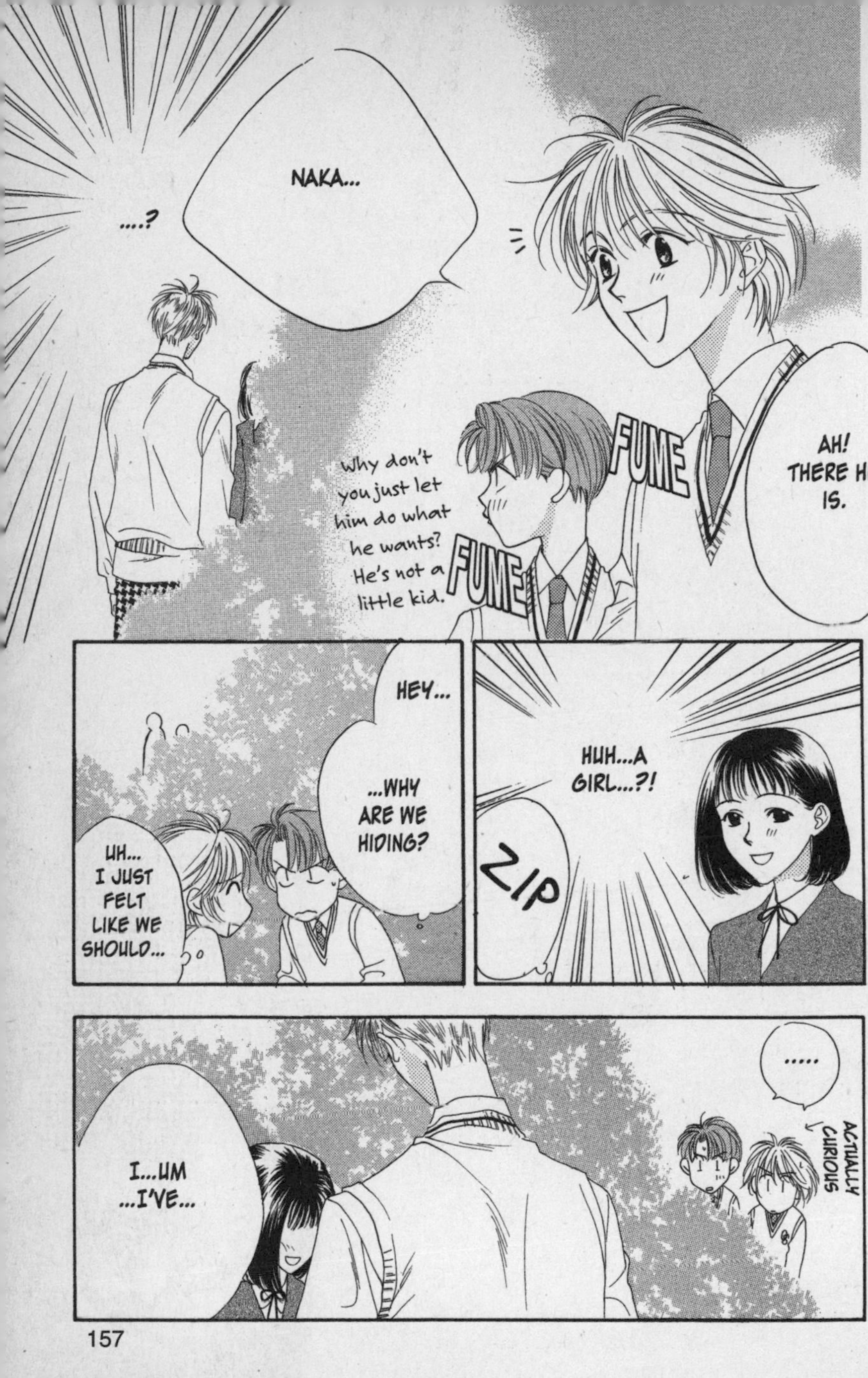
AH! THERE HE IS.
FUME
FUME
Why don't you just let him do what he wants? He's not a little kid.
NAKA...
....?
HUH...A GIRL...?!
ZIP
HEY...
...WHY ARE WE HIDING?
UH... I JUST FELT LIKE WE SHOULD...
.....
ACTUALLY CURIOUS
I...UM ...I'VE...

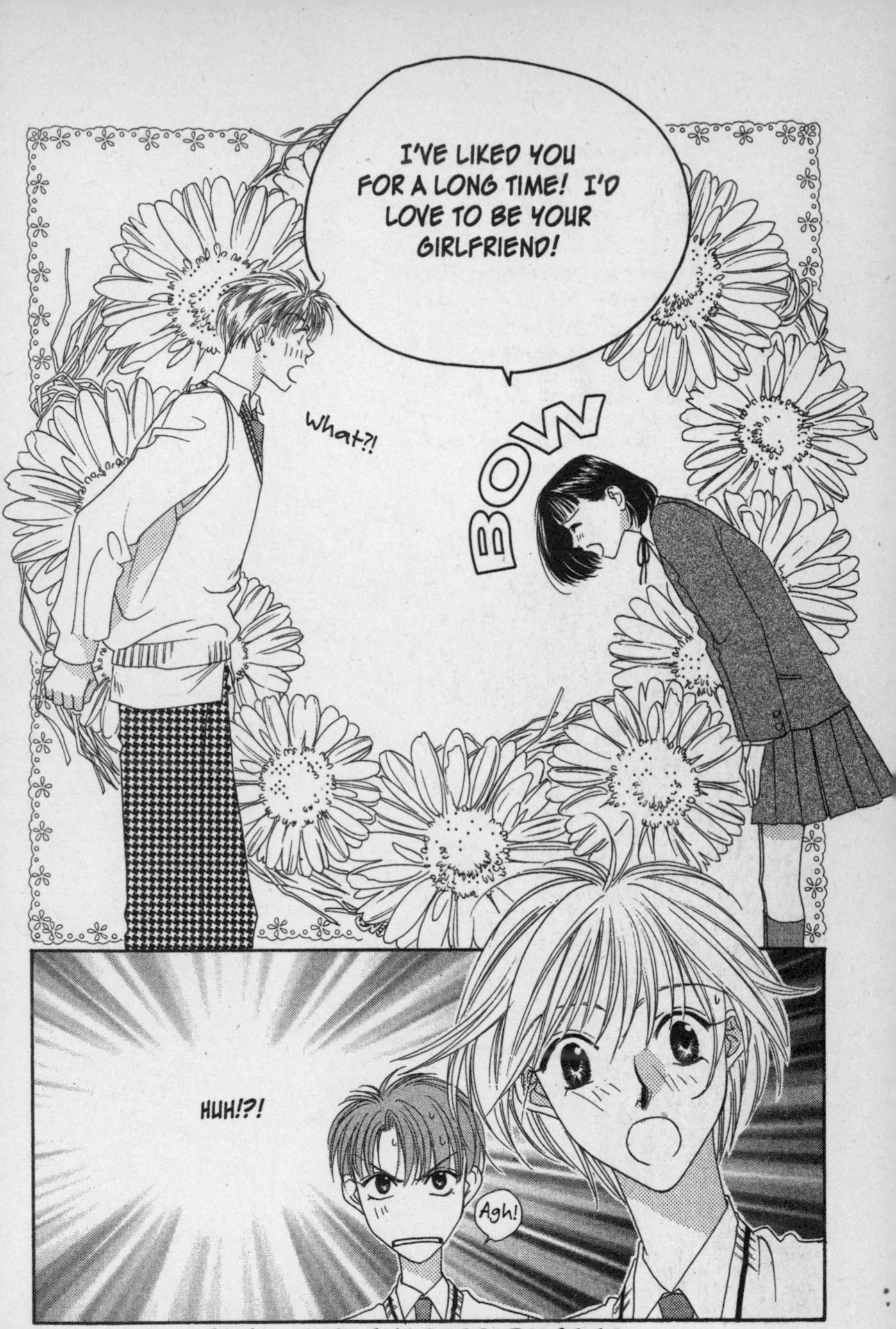
I'VE LIKED YOU FOR A LONG TIME! I'D LOVE TO BE YOUR GIRLFRIEND!
BOW
What?!
HUH!?!
Agh!

HANA-KIMI CHAPTER 24/END

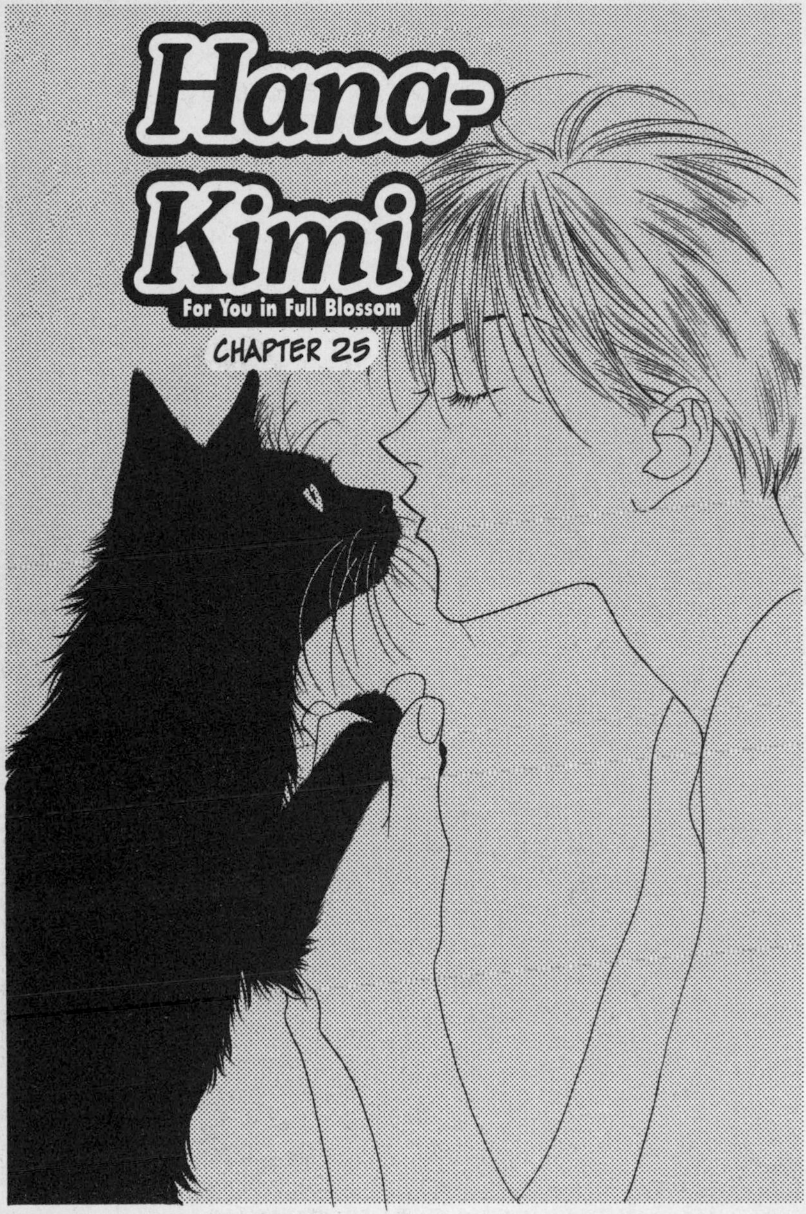
Hana-
Kimi
For You in Full Blossom
CHAPTER 25

HUH?
WHAT...?
BLAH YADA
BLAH YADA
What's all the noise?
.....
It's class 2-C.
THAT'S MY CLASS.

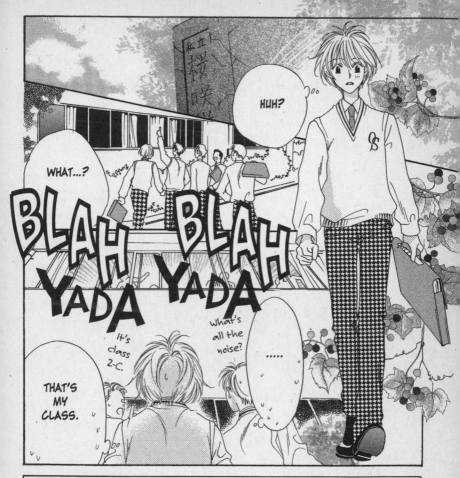

Yappari Neko ga Suki: Yes, I Love Cats

DOES ANYBODY ELSE KNOW THIS SHOW? IT WAS A FUJI TV DRAMA FROM ABOUT 10 YEARS AGO (WRITTEN BY KOKI MITANI). IT'S THE STORY OF THE THREE ONDA SISTERS. (THOSE ARE THE ONLY THREE CHARACTERS, AND THEN THERE'S SACHIKO THE CAT.) IT'S A FAMILY DRAMA. THE OLDER SISTER IS KAYANO (MASAKO MOTAI), THE NEXT IS REIKO (SHIGERU MUROI), AND THE YOUNGEST IS KIMIE (SATOMI KOBAYASHI). THEIR RELATIONSHIPS ARE VERY INTERESTING♥. THERE ARE 26 EPISODES OUT ON VIDEO. (A NEW ONE CAME OUT THIS YEAR TOO.)

See it if you get a chance!

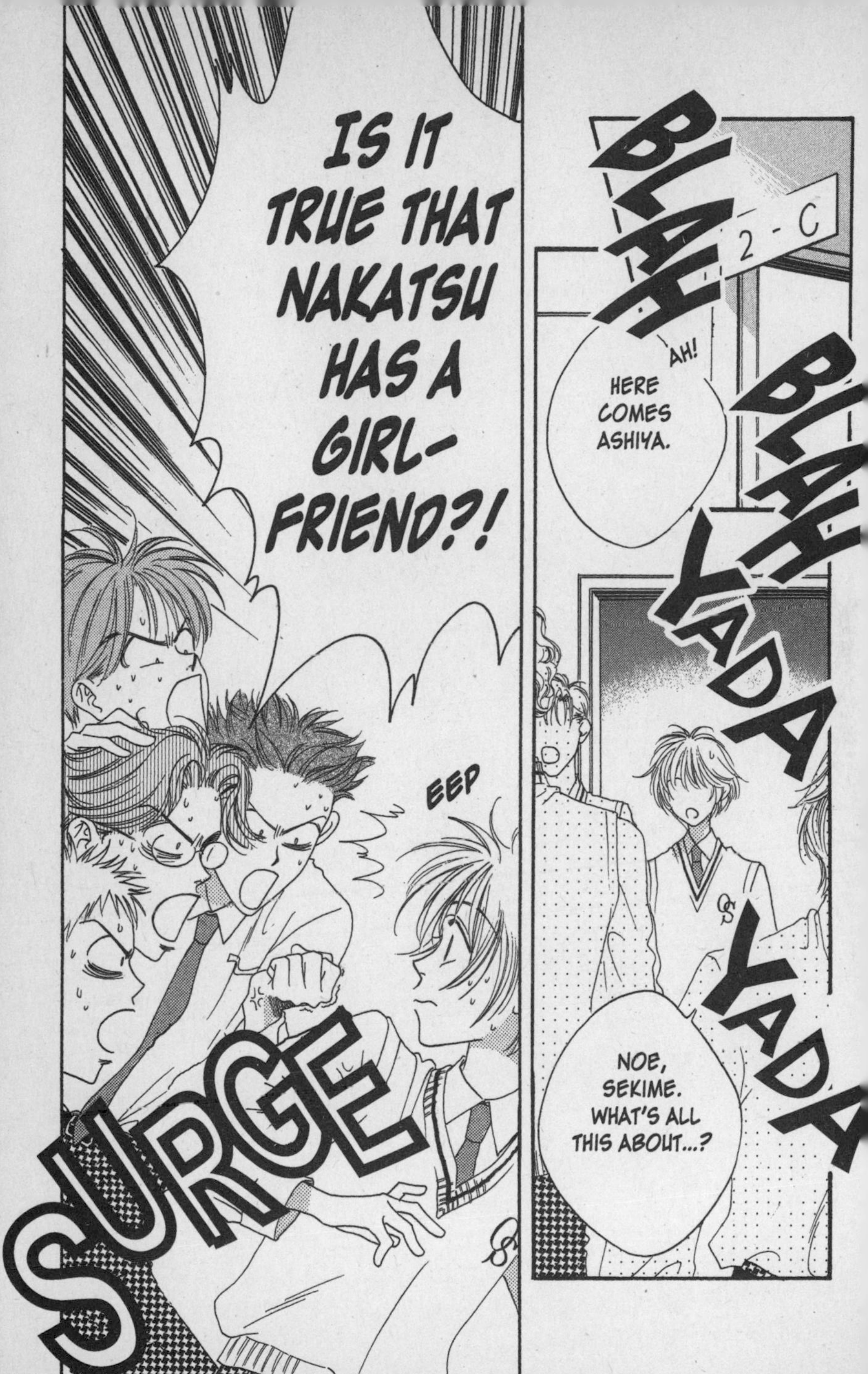
BLAH
BLAH
AH!
HERE COMES ASHIYA.
YADA
YADA
NOE, SEKIME. WHAT'S ALL THIS ABOUT...?
IS IT TRUE THAT NAKATSU HAS A GIRL-FRIEND?!
EEP
SURGE

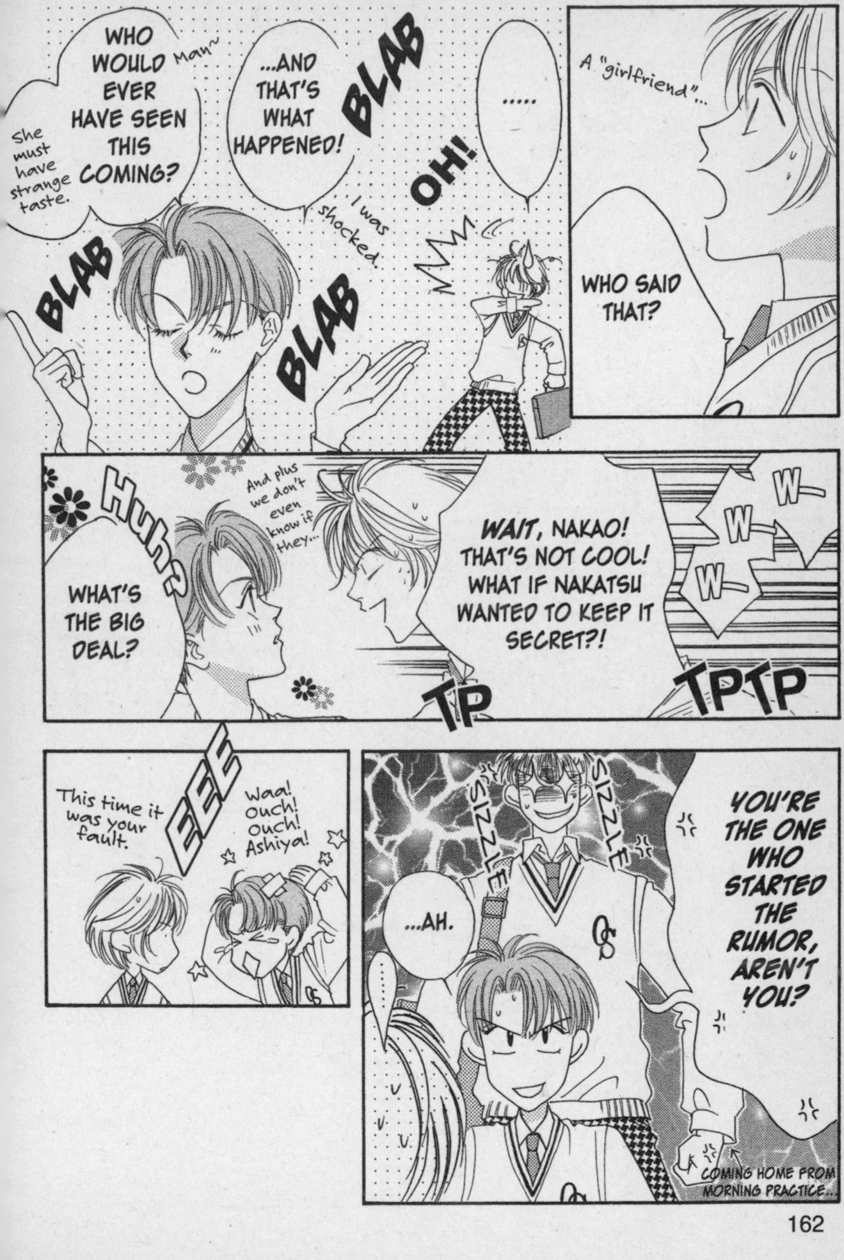
A "girlfriend"...
WHO SAID THAT?
.....
OH!
BLAB
...AND THAT'S WHAT HAPPENED!
I was shocked.
WHO WOULD EVER HAVE SEEN THIS COMING?
Man~
She must have strange taste.
BLAB
BLAB
W—
W—
W—
TPTP
WAIT, NAKAO! THAT'S NOT COOL! WHAT IF NAKATSU WANTED TO KEEP IT SECRET?!
TP
And plus we don't even know if they...
Huh?
WHAT'S THE BIG DEAL?
YOU'RE THE ONE WHO STARTED THE RUMOR, AREN'T YOU?
SIZZLE
SIZZLE
...AH.
COMING HOME FROM MORNING PRACTICE...
Waa! Ouch! Ouch! Ashiya!
EEE
This time it was your fault.

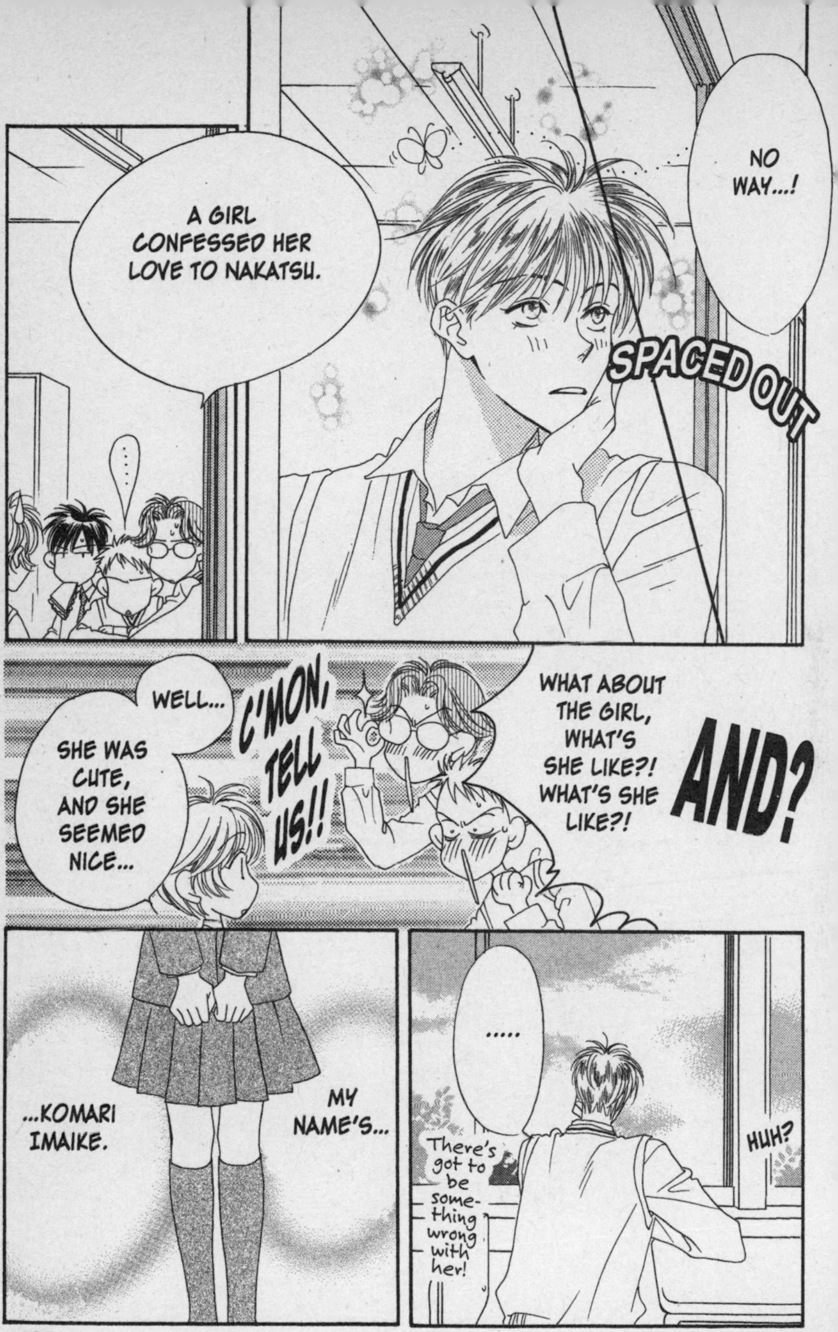
NO WAY...!
SPACED OUT
A GIRL CONFESSED HER LOVE TO NAKATSU.
.....
AND?
WHAT ABOUT THE GIRL, WHAT'S SHE LIKE?! WHAT'S SHE LIKE?!
C'MON, TELL US!!
WELL...
SHE WAS CUTE, AND SHE SEEMED NICE...
HUH?
.....
There's got to be something wrong with her!
MY NAME'S...
...KOMARI IMAIKE.

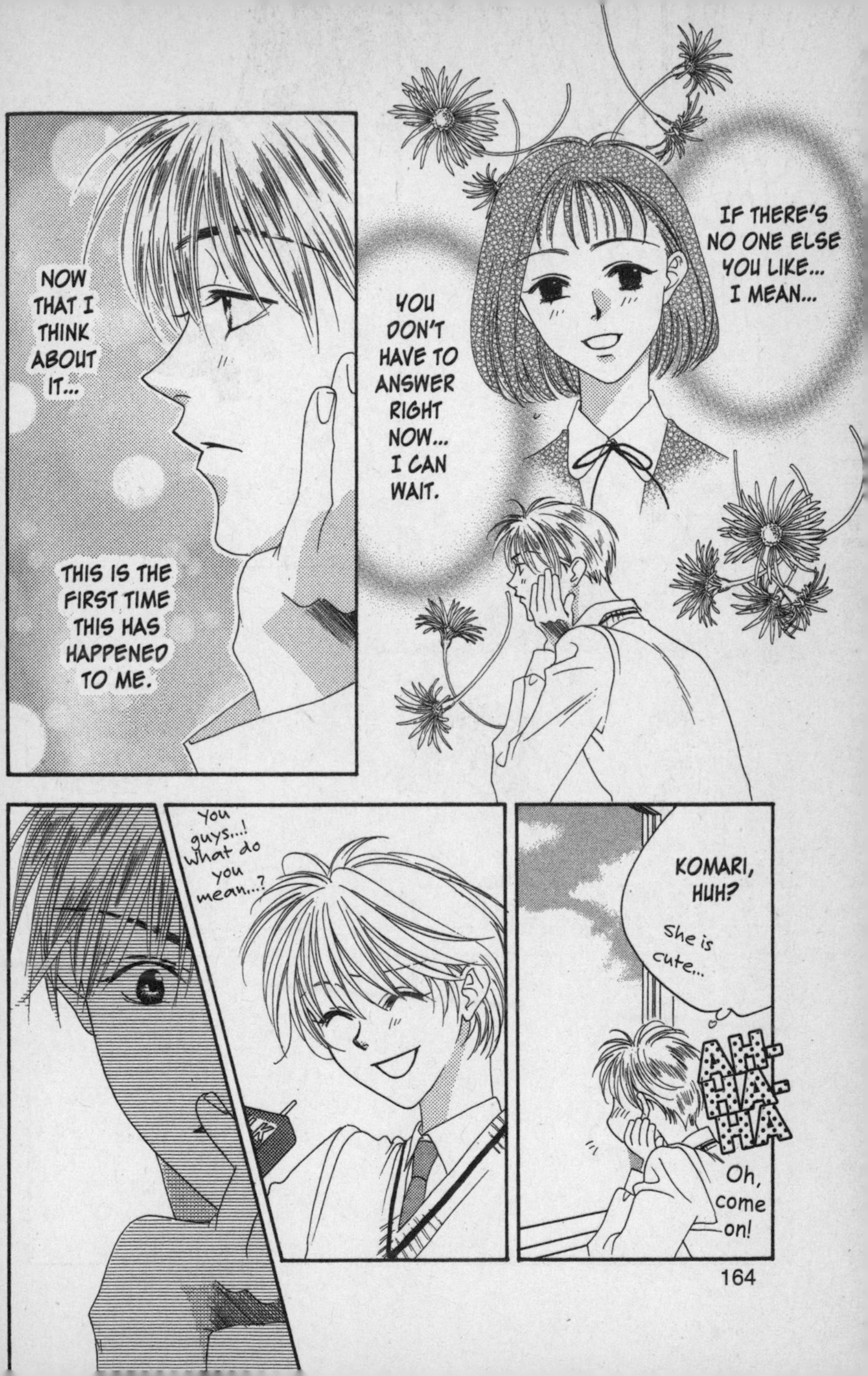
IF THERE'S NO ONE ELSE YOU LIKE... I MEAN...
YOU DON'T HAVE TO ANSWER RIGHT NOW... I CAN WAIT.
NOW THAT I THINK ABOUT IT...
THIS IS THE FIRST TIME THIS HAS HAPPENED TO ME.
KOMARI, HUH?
She is cute...
AH-HA-HA
Oh, come on!
You guys...! what do you mean...?

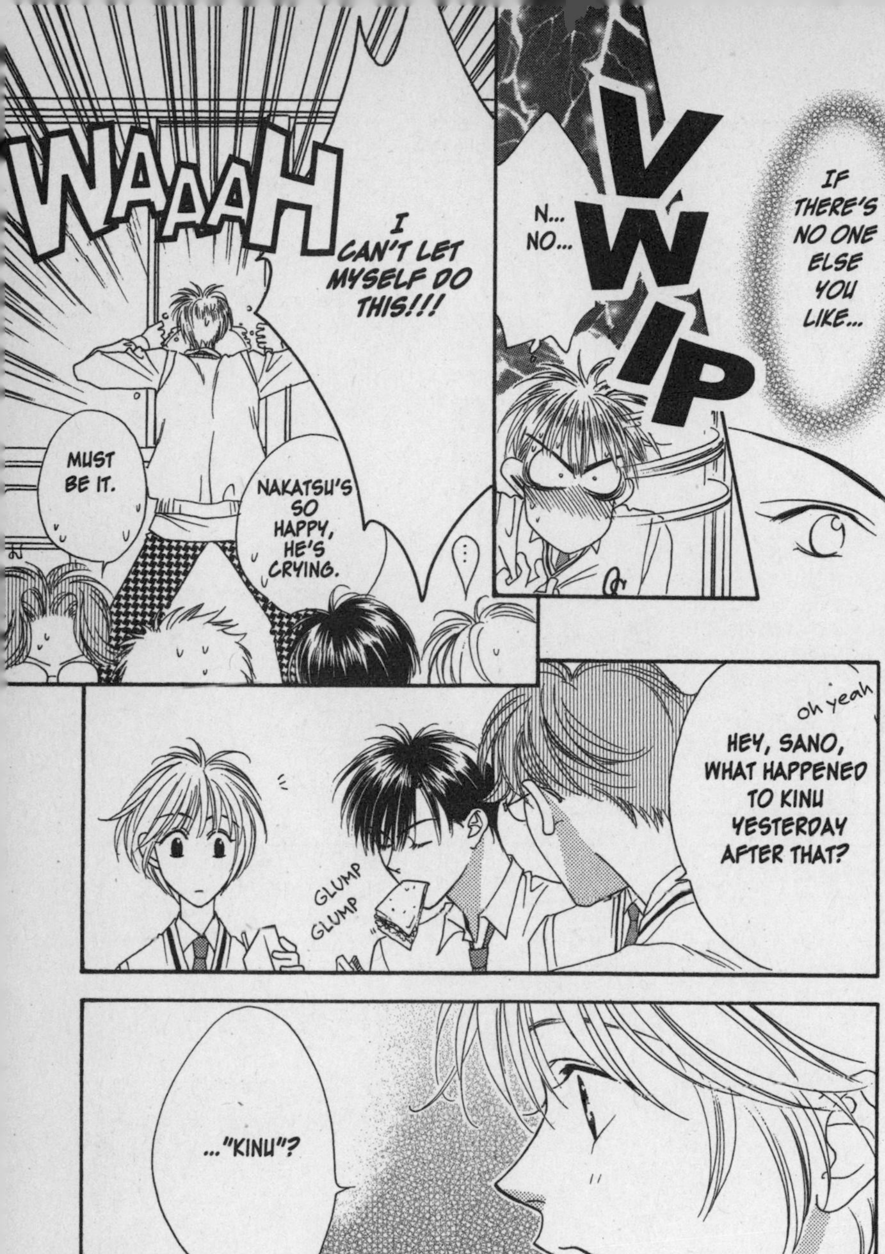
IF THERE'S NO ONE ELSE YOU LIKE...
N... NO...
VWIP
WAAAH
I CAN'T LET MYSELF DO THIS!!!
NAKATSU'S SO HAPPY, HE'S CRYING.
MUST BE IT.
...
oh yeah
HEY, SANO, WHAT HAPPENED TO KINU YESTERDAY AFTER THAT?
GLUMP GLUMP
..."KINU"?

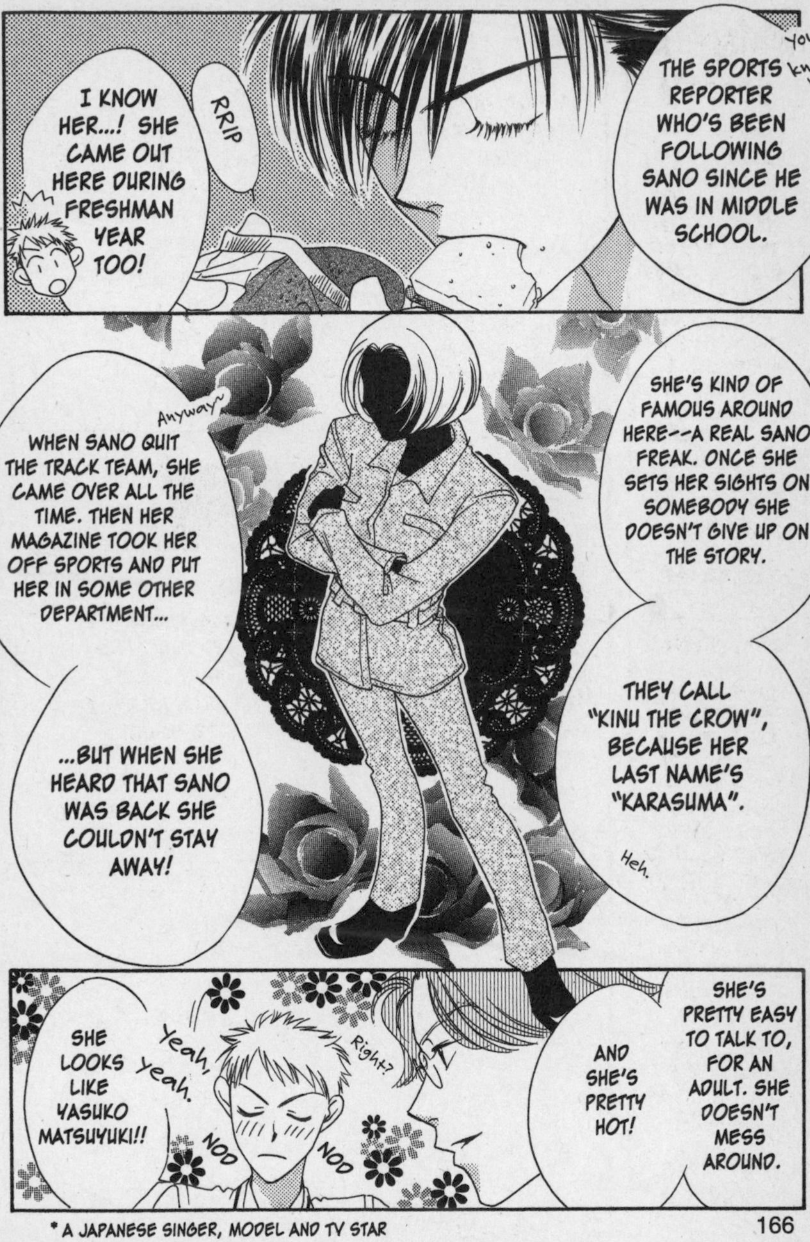
THE SPORTS REPORTER WHO'S BEEN FOLLOWING SANO SINCE HE WAS IN MIDDLE SCHOOL.
You know
RRIP
I KNOW HER...! SHE CAME OUT HERE DURING FRESHMAN YEAR TOO!
SHE'S KIND OF FAMOUS AROUND HERE--A REAL SANO FREAK. ONCE SHE SETS HER SIGHTS ON SOMEBODY SHE DOESN'T GIVE UP ON THE STORY.
THEY CALL "KINU THE CROW", BECAUSE HER LAST NAME'S "KARASUMA".
Heh.
Anyway~
WHEN SANO QUIT THE TRACK TEAM, SHE CAME OVER ALL THE TIME. THEN HER MAGAZINE TOOK HER OFF SPORTS AND PUT HER IN SOME OTHER DEPARTMENT...
...BUT WHEN SHE HEARD THAT SANO WAS BACK SHE COULDN'T STAY AWAY!
SHE'S PRETTY EASY TO TALK TO, FOR AN ADULT. SHE DOESN'T MESS AROUND.
AND SHE'S PRETTY HOT!
Right?
Yeah, yeah.
NOD
NOD
SHE LOOKS LIKE YASUKO MATSUYUKI!!

* A JAPANESE SINGER, MODEL AND TV STAR

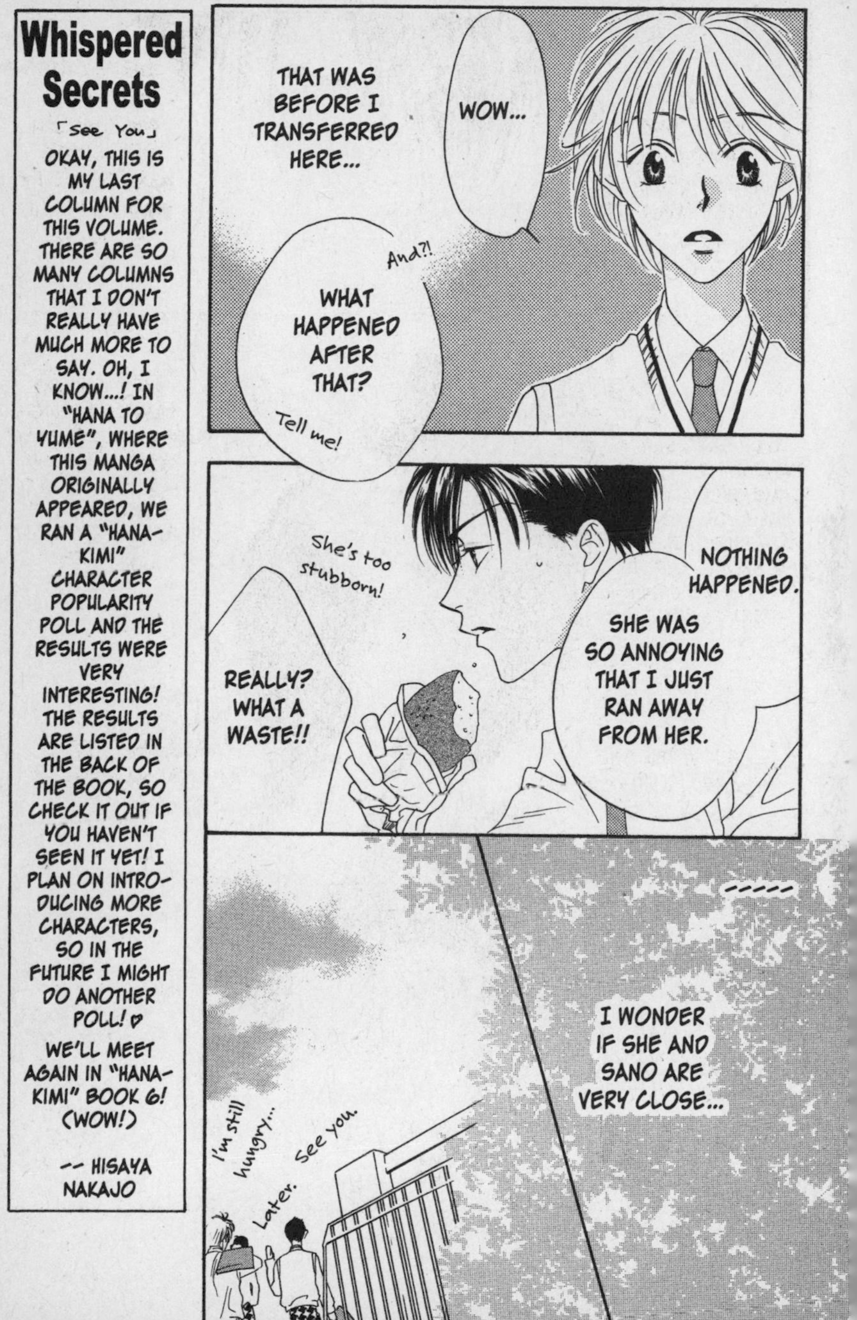
WOW...
THAT WAS BEFORE I TRANSFERRED HERE...
And?!
WHAT HAPPENED AFTER THAT?
Tell me!
NOTHING HAPPENED.
SHE WAS SO ANNOYING THAT I JUST RAN AWAY FROM HER.
She's too stubborn!
REALLY? WHAT A WASTE!!

I WONDER IF SHE AND SANO ARE VERY CLOSE...
See you.
Later.
I'm still hungry...

Whispered Secrets

「See You」

OKAY, THIS IS MY LAST COLUMN FOR THIS VOLUME. THERE ARE SO MANY COLUMNS THAT I DON'T REALLY HAVE MUCH MORE TO SAY. OH, I KNOW...! IN "HANA TO YUME", WHERE THIS MANGA ORIGINALLY APPEARED, WE RAN A "HANA-KIMI" CHARACTER POPULARITY POLL AND THE RESULTS WERE VERY INTERESTING! THE RESULTS ARE LISTED IN THE BACK OF THE BOOK, SO CHECK IT OUT IF YOU HAVEN'T SEEN IT YET! I PLAN ON INTRODUCING MORE CHARACTERS, SO IN THE FUTURE I MIGHT DO ANOTHER POLL! ♡

WE'LL MEET AGAIN IN "HANA-KIMI" BOOK 6! (WOW!)

-- HISAYA NAKAJO

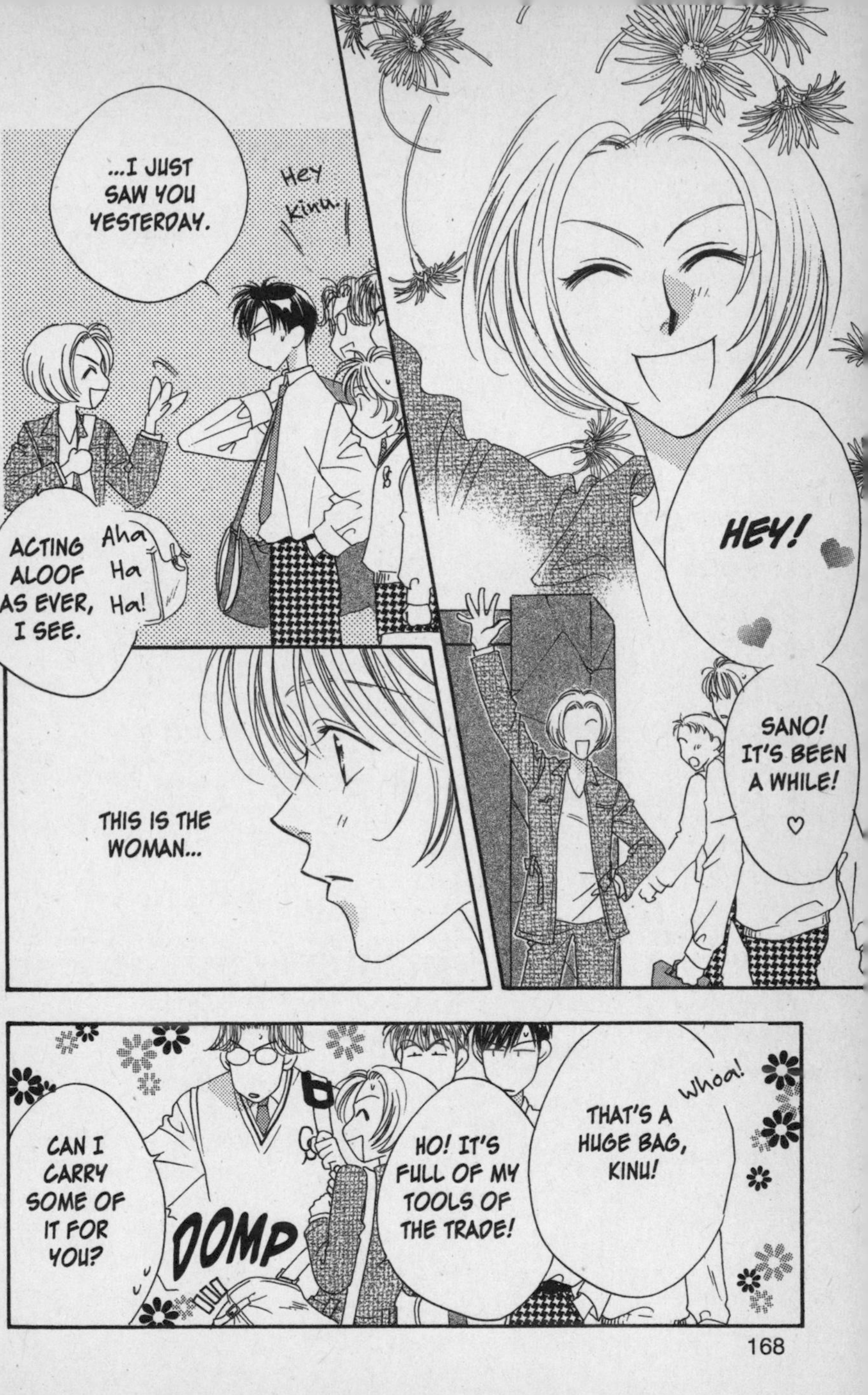
HEY!
SANO! IT'S BEEN A WHILE! ♡
...I JUST SAW YOU YESTERDAY.
Hey Kinu.
Aha Ha Ha!
ACTING ALOOF AS EVER, I SEE.
THIS IS THE WOMAN...
Whoa!
THAT'S A HUGE BAG, KINU!
HO! IT'S FULL OF MY TOOLS OF THE TRADE!
DOOMP
CAN I CARRY SOME OF IT FOR YOU?

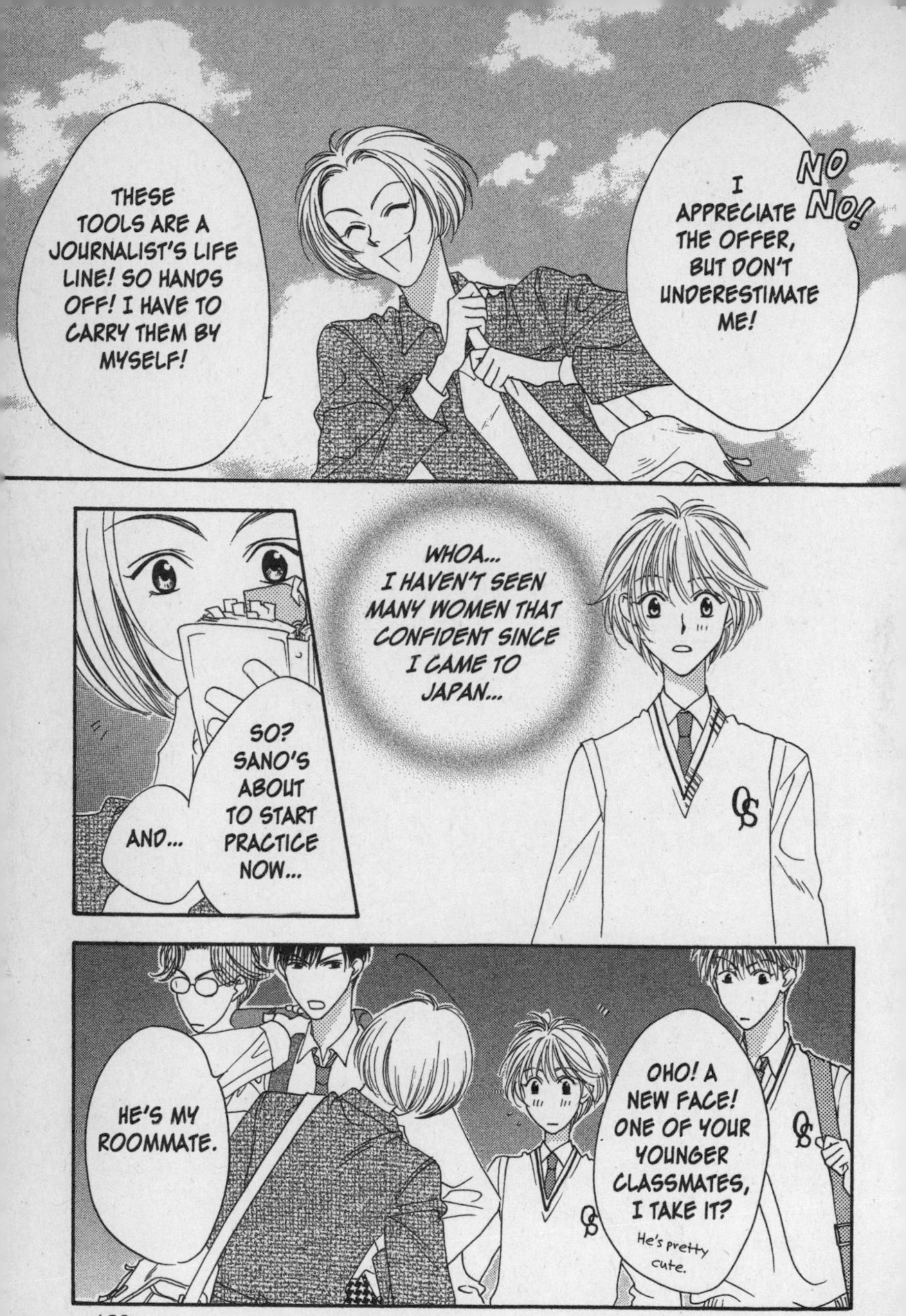
I APPRECIATE THE OFFER, BUT DON'T UNDERESTIMATE ME!
NO NO!
THESE TOOLS ARE A JOURNALIST'S LIFE LINE! SO HANDS OFF! I HAVE TO CARRY THEM BY MYSELF!
WHOA... I HAVEN'T SEEN MANY WOMEN THAT CONFIDENT SINCE I CAME TO JAPAN...
SO? SANO'S ABOUT TO START PRACTICE NOW...
AND...
OHO! A NEW FACE! ONE OF YOUR YOUNGER CLASSMATES, I TAKE IT?
He's pretty cute.
HE'S MY ROOMMATE.

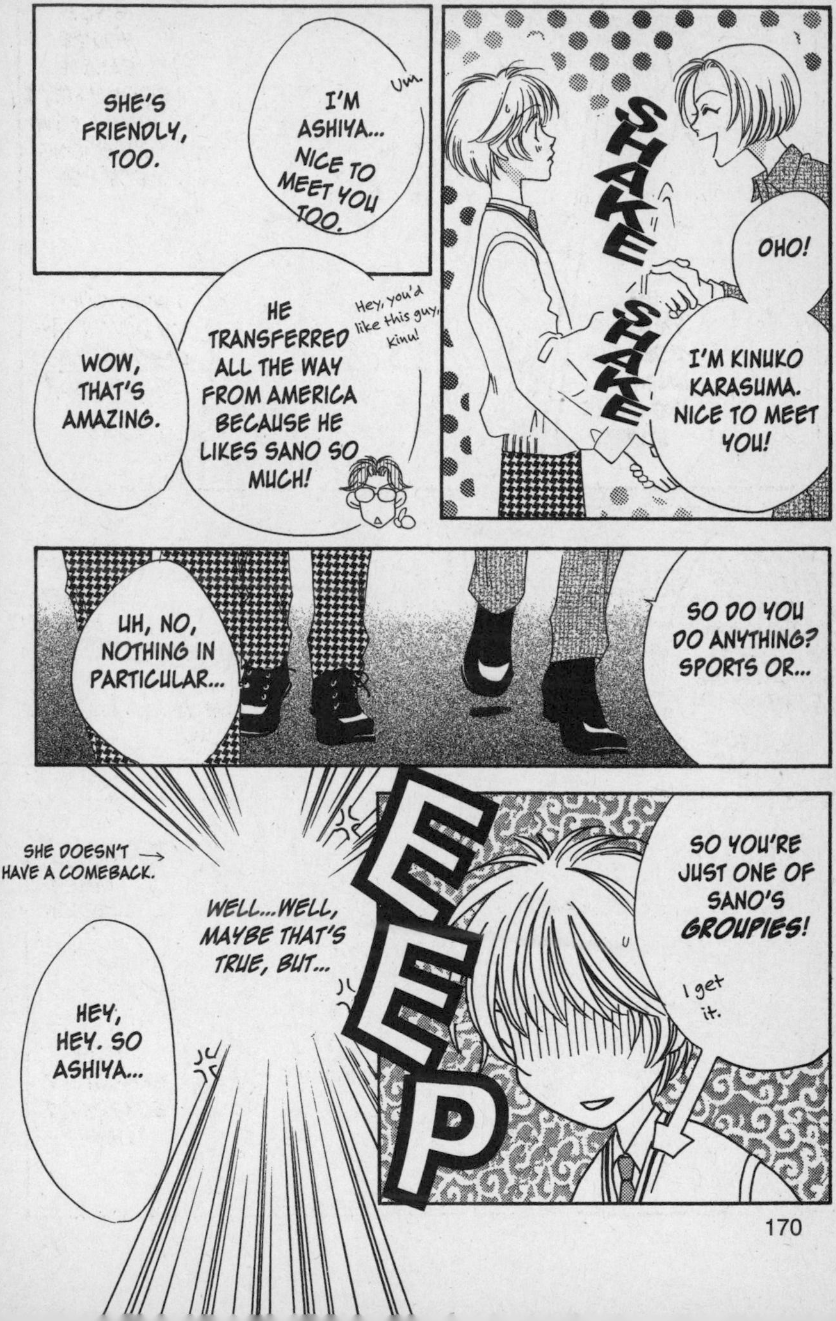

SHAKE SHAKE
OHO!
I'M KINUKO KARASUMA. NICE TO MEET YOU!
Um.
I'M ASHIYA... NICE TO MEET YOU TOO.
SHE'S FRIENDLY, TOO.
HE TRANSFERRED ALL THE WAY FROM AMERICA BECAUSE HE LIKES SANO SO MUCH!
Hey, you'd like this guy, Kinu!
WOW, THAT'S AMAZING.
SO DO YOU DO ANYTHING? SPORTS OR...
UH, NO, NOTHING IN PARTICULAR...
SO YOU'RE JUST ONE OF SANO'S GROUPIES!
I get it.
EEEP
WELL...WELL, MAYBE THAT'S TRUE, BUT...
SHE DOESN'T HAVE A COMEBACK.
HEY, HEY. SO ASHIYA...

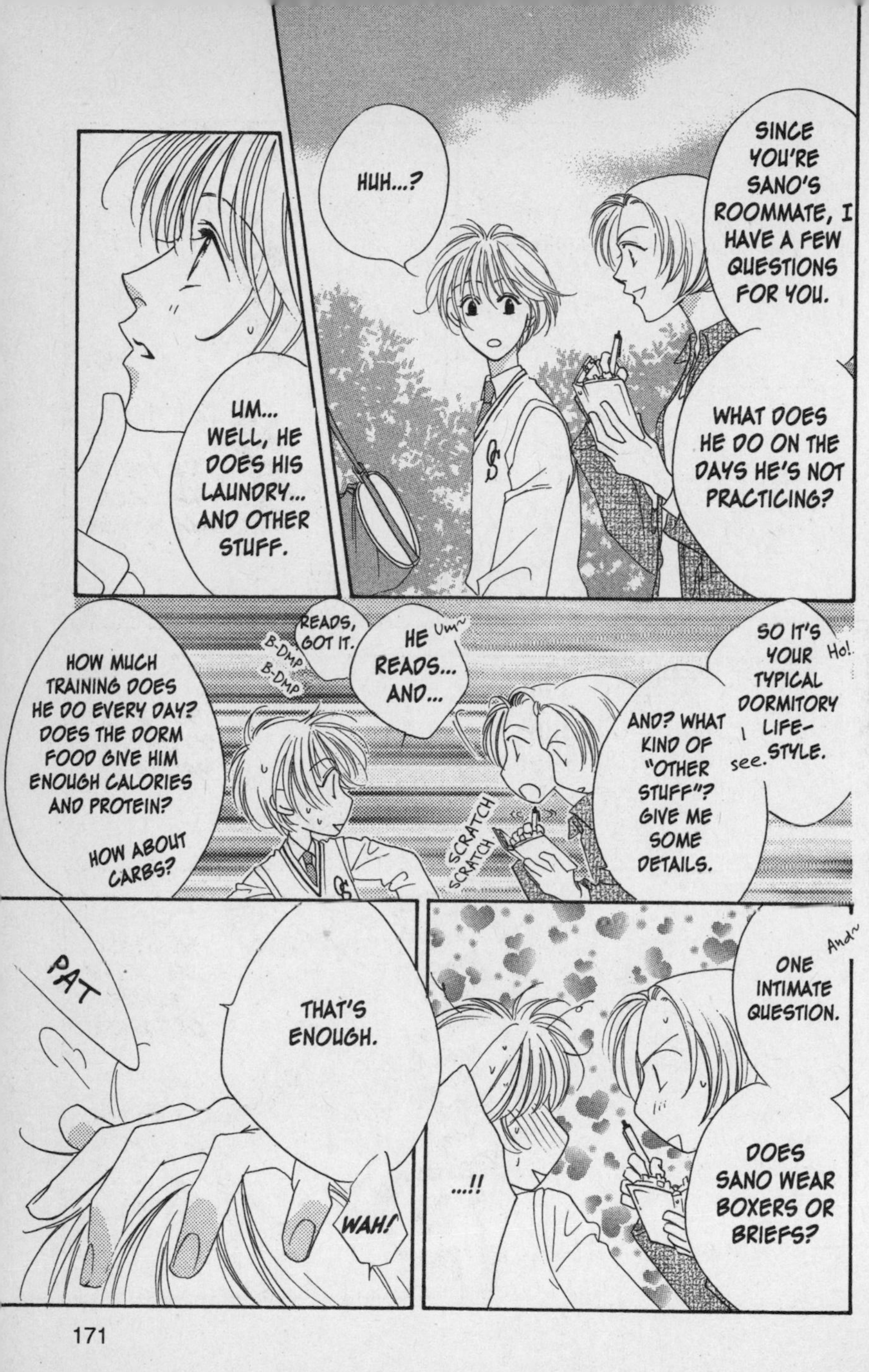
SINCE YOU'RE SANO'S ROOMMATE, I HAVE A FEW QUESTIONS FOR YOU.
HUH...?
WHAT DOES HE DO ON THE DAYS HE'S NOT PRACTICING?
UM... WELL, HE DOES HIS LAUNDRY... AND OTHER STUFF.
SO IT'S YOUR TYPICAL DORMITORY LIFE-STYLE.
Ho!
I see.
AND? WHAT KIND OF "OTHER STUFF"? GIVE ME SOME DETAILS.
SCRATCH SCRATCH
HE READS... AND...
Um~
READS, GOT IT.
B-Dmp B-Dmp
HOW MUCH TRAINING DOES HE DO EVERY DAY? DOES THE DORM FOOD GIVE HIM ENOUGH CALORIES AND PROTEIN?
HOW ABOUT CARBS?
And~
ONE INTIMATE QUESTION.
DOES SANO WEAR BOXERS OR BRIEFS?
...!!
THAT'S ENOUGH.
PAT
WAH!

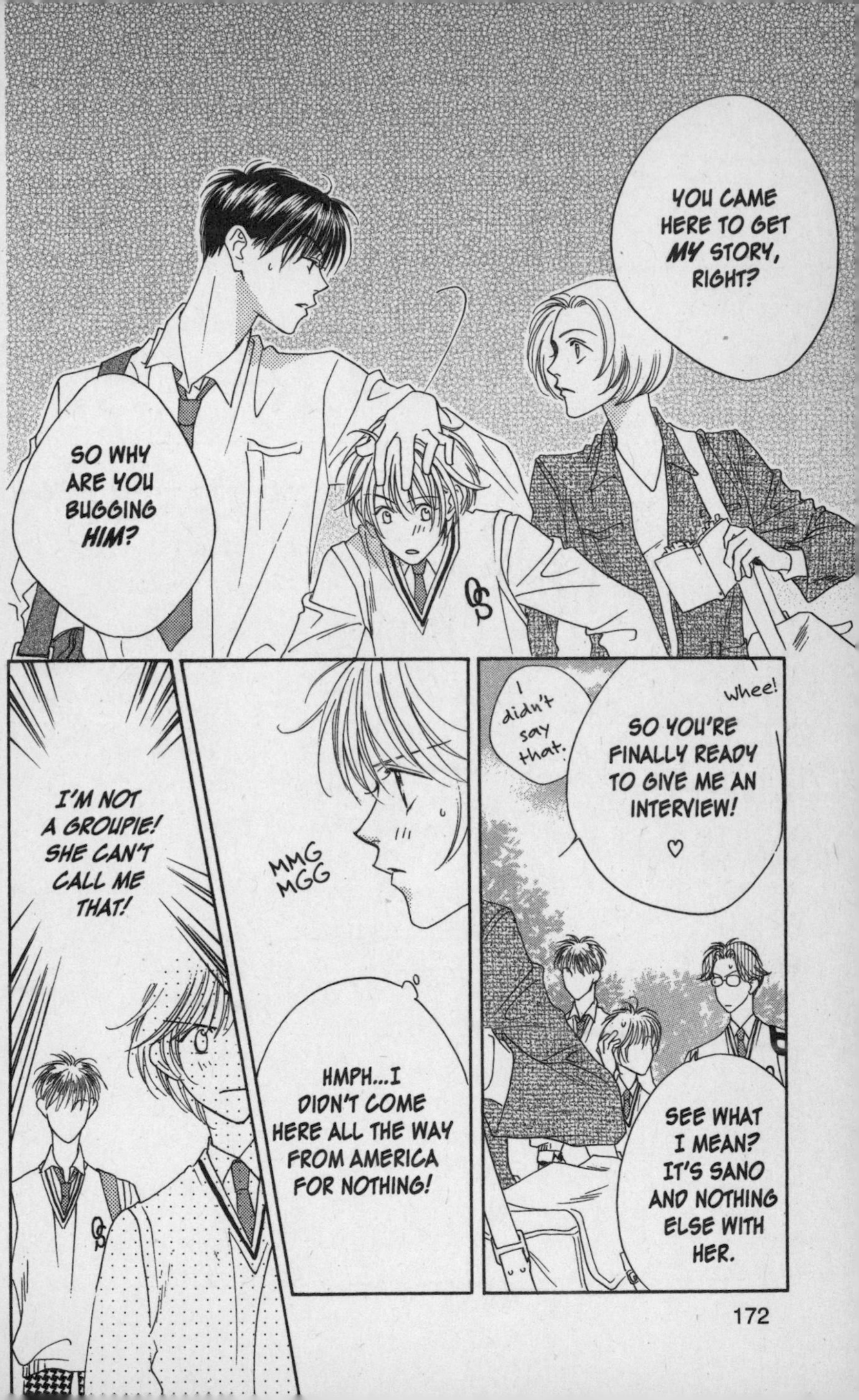
YOU CAME HERE TO GET *MY* STORY, RIGHT?
SO WHY ARE YOU BUGGING *HIM*?
Whee!
SO YOU'RE FINALLY READY TO GIVE ME AN INTERVIEW! ♡
I didn't say that.
SEE WHAT I MEAN? IT'S SANO AND NOTHING ELSE WITH HER.
MMG MGG
HMPH...I DIDN'T COME HERE ALL THE WAY FROM AMERICA FOR NOTHING!
I'M NOT A GROUPIE! SHE CAN'T CALL ME THAT!

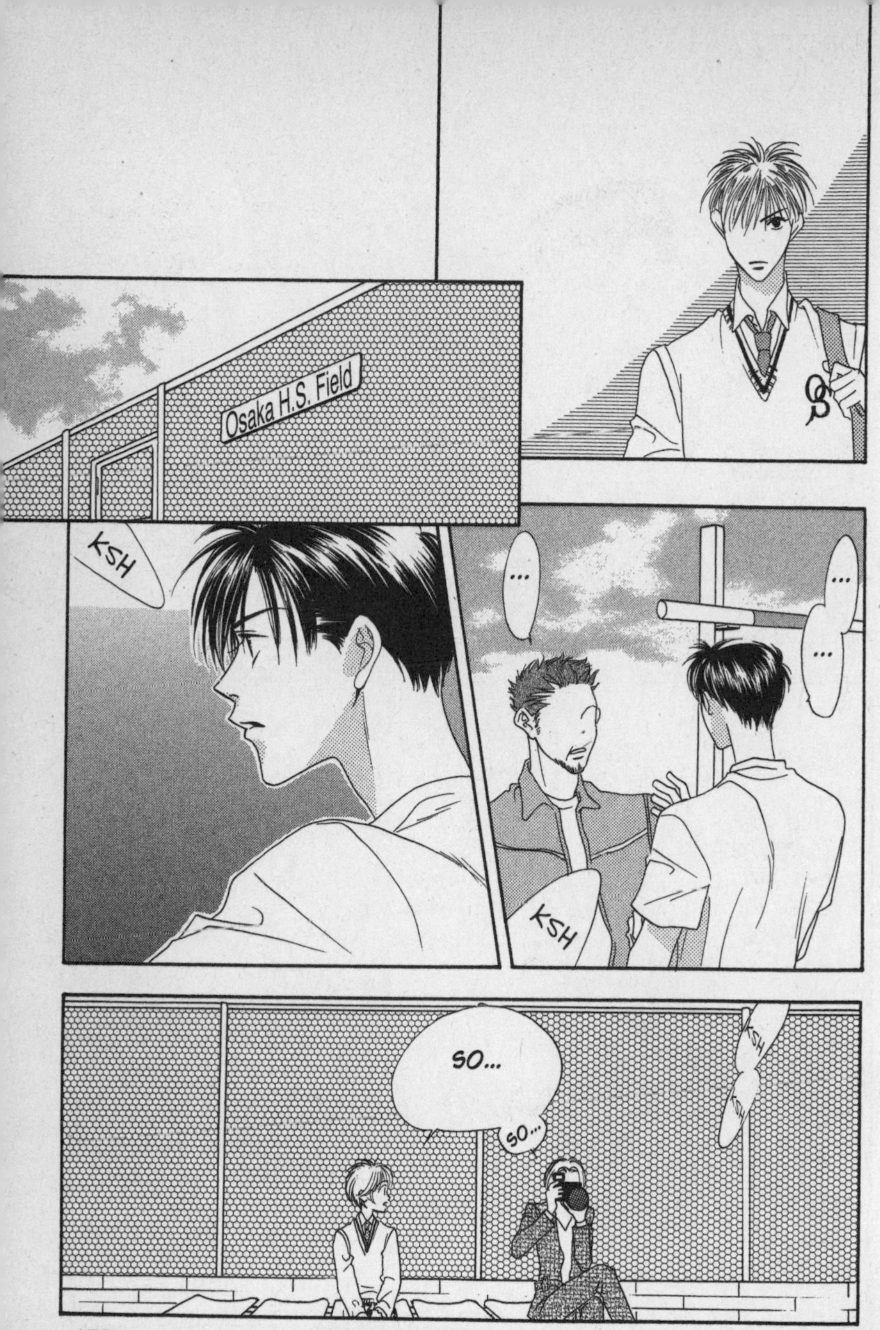
Osaka H.S. Field
...
...
...
KSH
KSH
KSH
KSH
SO...
SO...

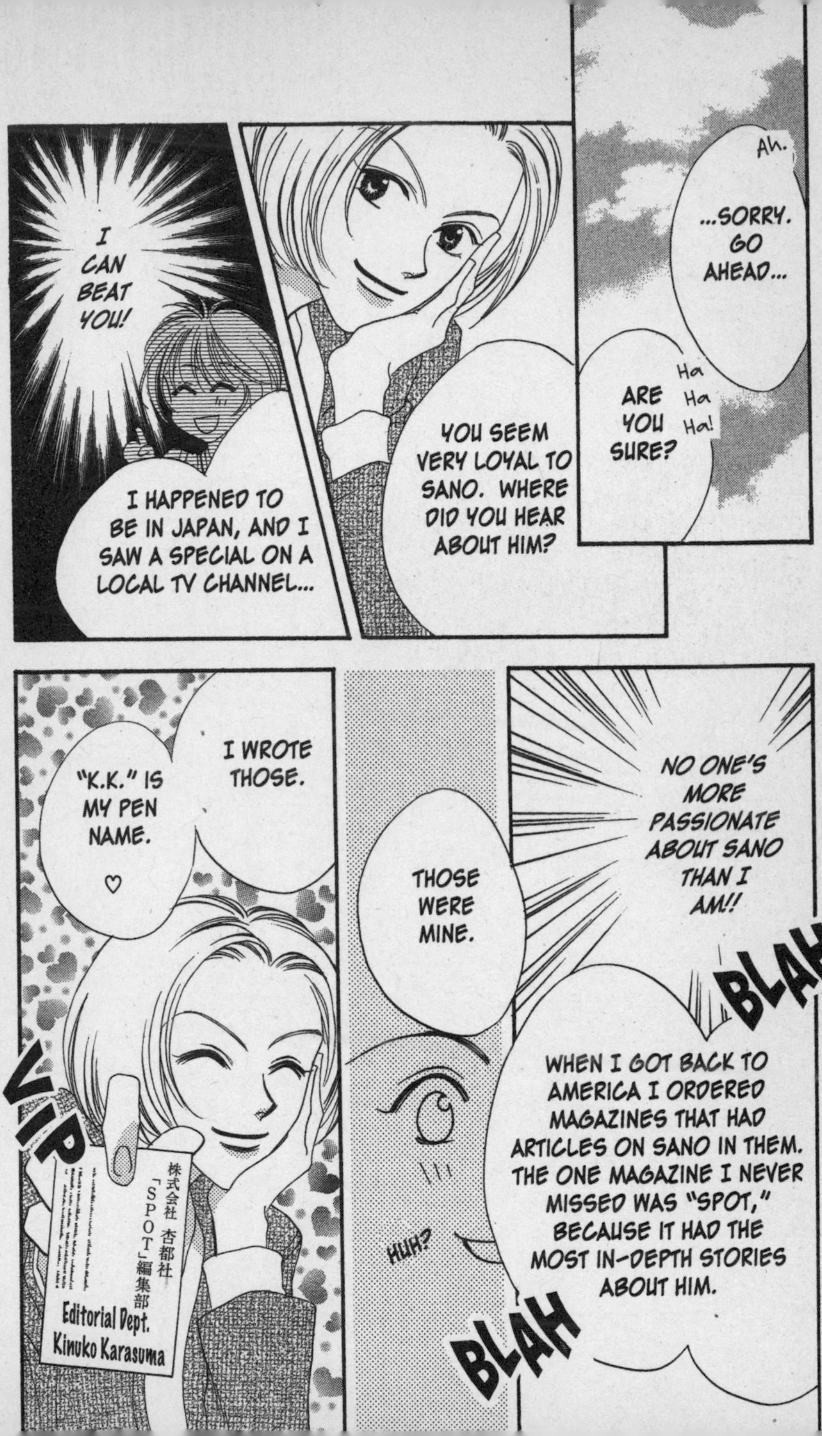
Ah.
...SORRY. GO AHEAD...
ARE YOU SURE?
Ha Ha Ha!
YOU SEEM VERY LOYAL TO SANO. WHERE DID YOU HEAR ABOUT HIM?
I CAN BEAT YOU!
I HAPPENED TO BE IN JAPAN, AND I SAW A SPECIAL ON A LOCAL TV CHANNEL...
NO ONE'S MORE PASSIONATE ABOUT SANO THAN I AM!!
BLAH
WHEN I GOT BACK TO AMERICA I ORDERED MAGAZINES THAT HAD ARTICLES ON SANO IN THEM. THE ONE MAGAZINE I NEVER MISSED WAS "SPOT," BECAUSE IT HAD THE MOST IN-DEPTH STORIES ABOUT HIM.
BLAH
THOSE WERE MINE.
HUH?
I WROTE THOSE.
"K.K." IS MY PEN NAME. ♡
VIP
株式会社 杏都社
「SPOT」編集部
Editorial Dept.
Kinuko Karasuma

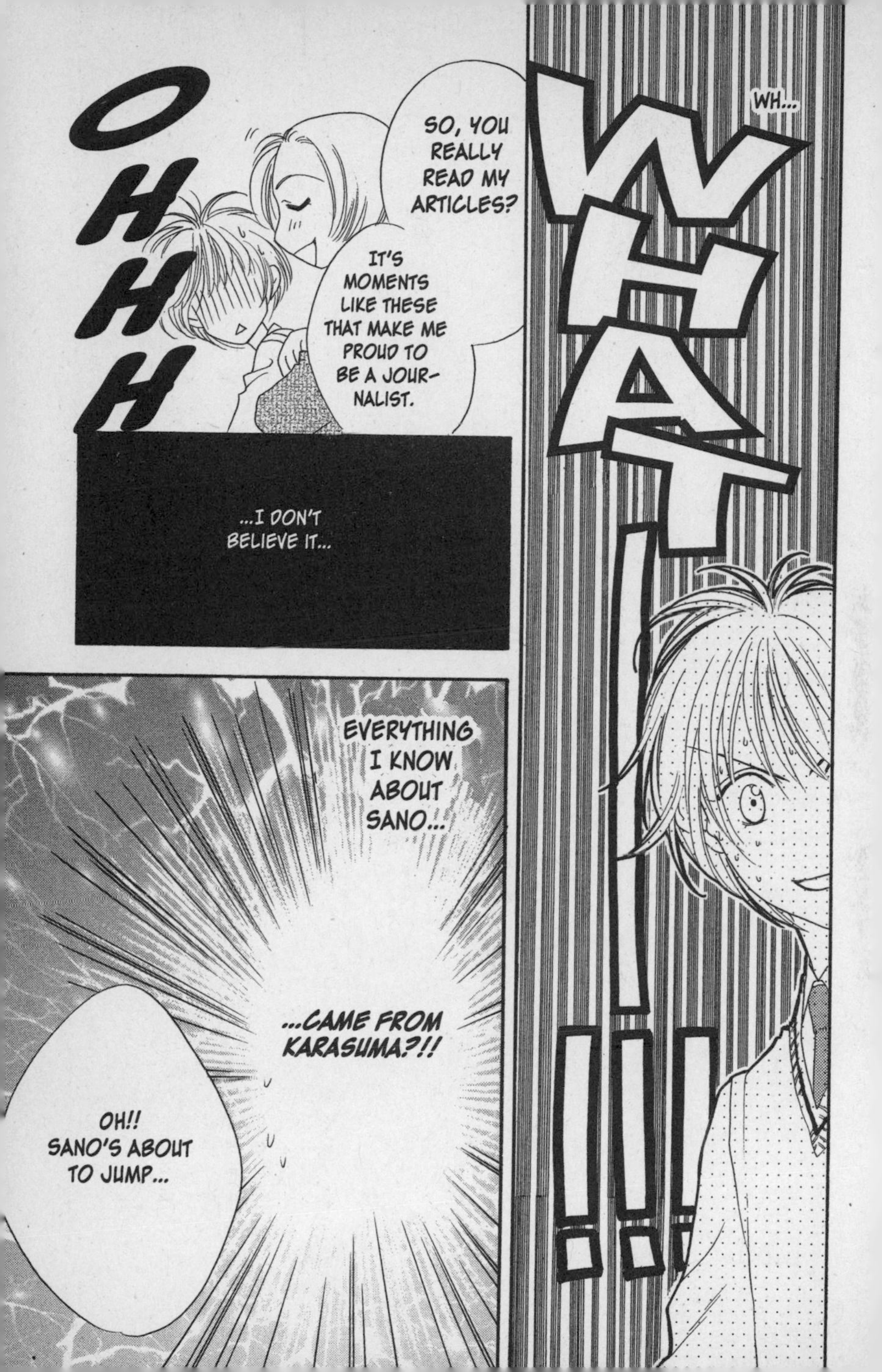
WH...
WHAT!!!!
SO, YOU REALLY READ MY ARTICLES?
IT'S MOMENTS LIKE THESE THAT MAKE ME PROUD TO BE A JOUR-NALIST.
OHHHH
...I DON'T BELIEVE IT...
EVERYTHING I KNOW ABOUT SANO...
...CAME FROM KARASUMA?!!
OH!! SANO'S ABOUT TO JUMP...

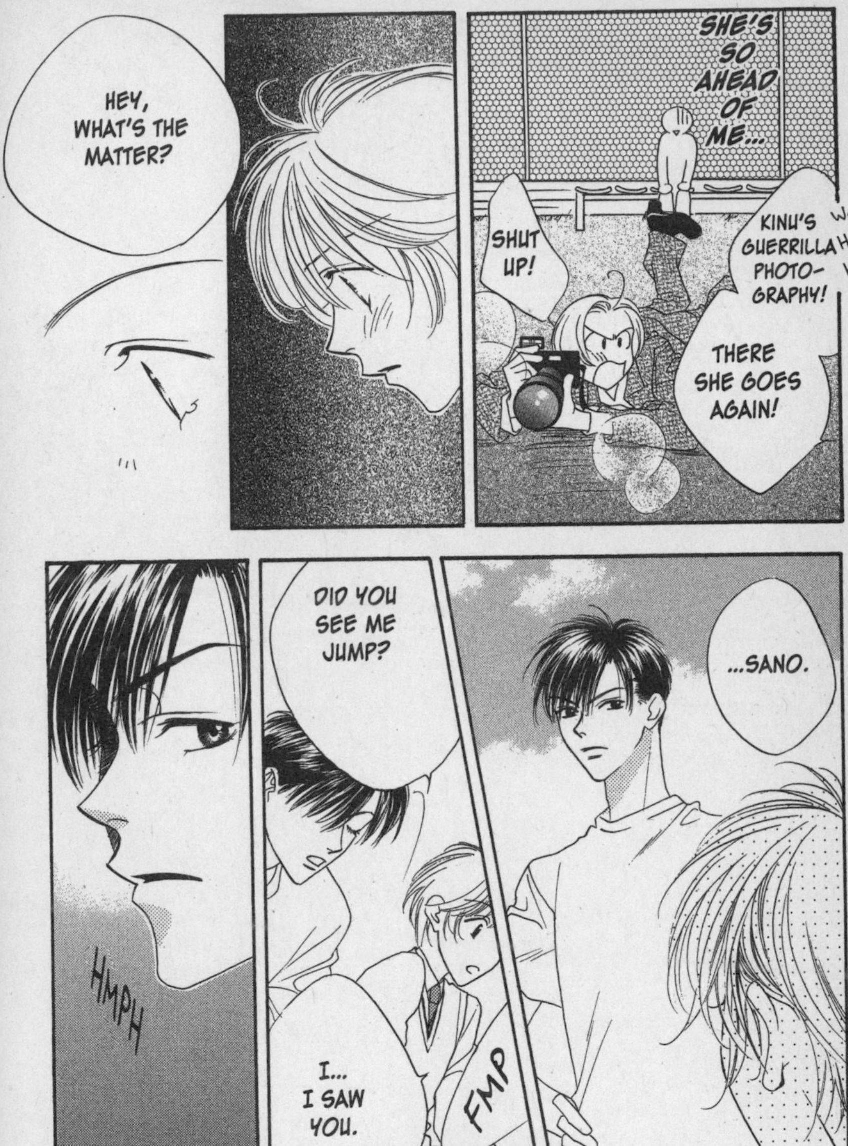
SHE'S SO AHEAD OF ME...
Wa Ha Ha!
KINU'S GUERRILLA PHOTOGRAPHY!
SHUT UP!
THERE SHE GOES AGAIN!
HEY, WHAT'S THE MATTER?
...SANO.
DID YOU SEE ME JUMP?
FMP
I... I SAW YOU.
HMPH

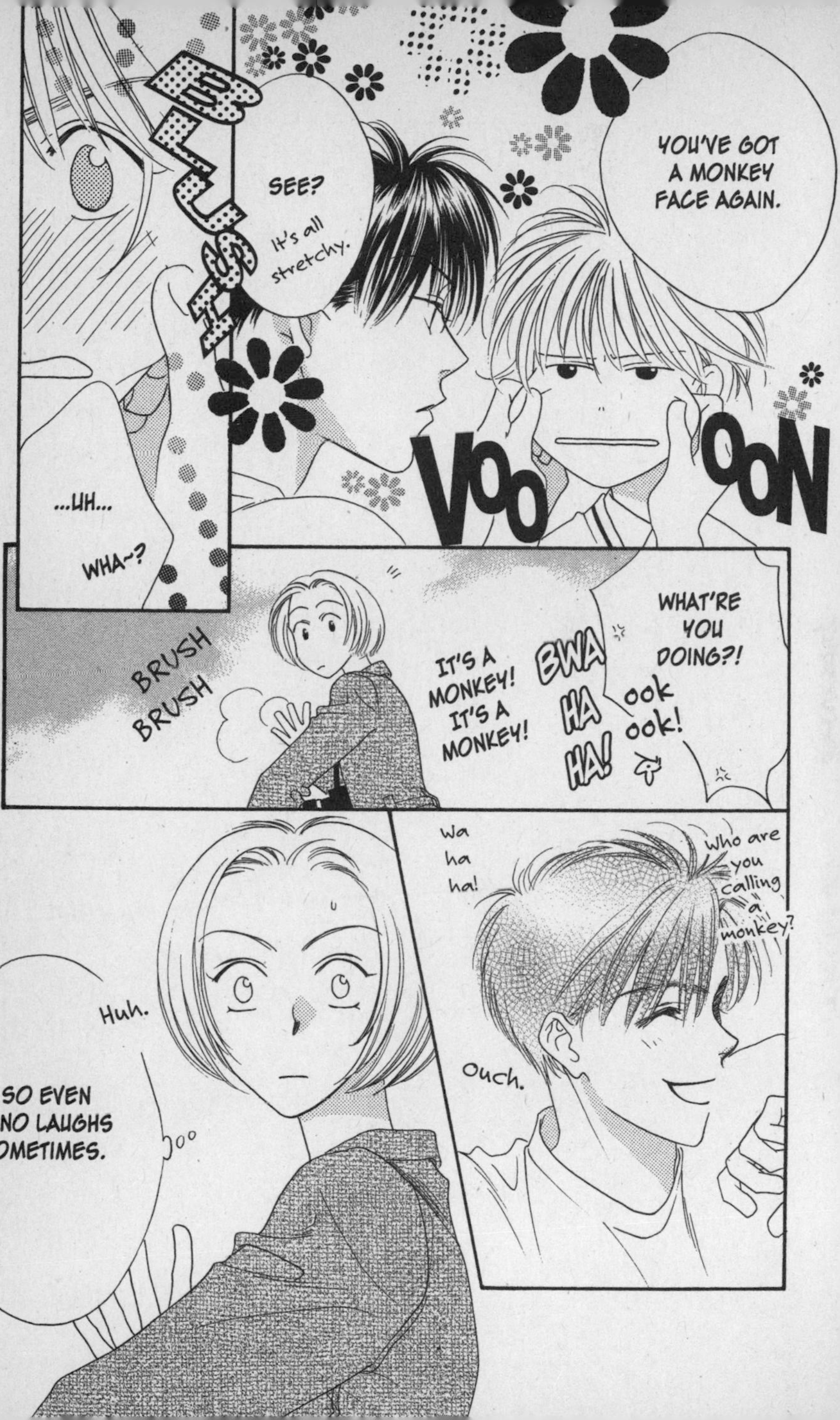
YOU'VE GOT A MONKEY FACE AGAIN.
SEE?
It's all stretchy.
VOO OON
BLUSH
...UH...
WHA~?
WHAT'RE YOU DOING?!
ook ook!
BWA HA HA!
IT'S A MONKEY! IT'S A MONKEY!
BRUSH BRUSH
Who are you calling a monkey?
Wa ha ha!
Ouch.
Huh.
SO EVEN SANO LAUGHS SOMETIMES.

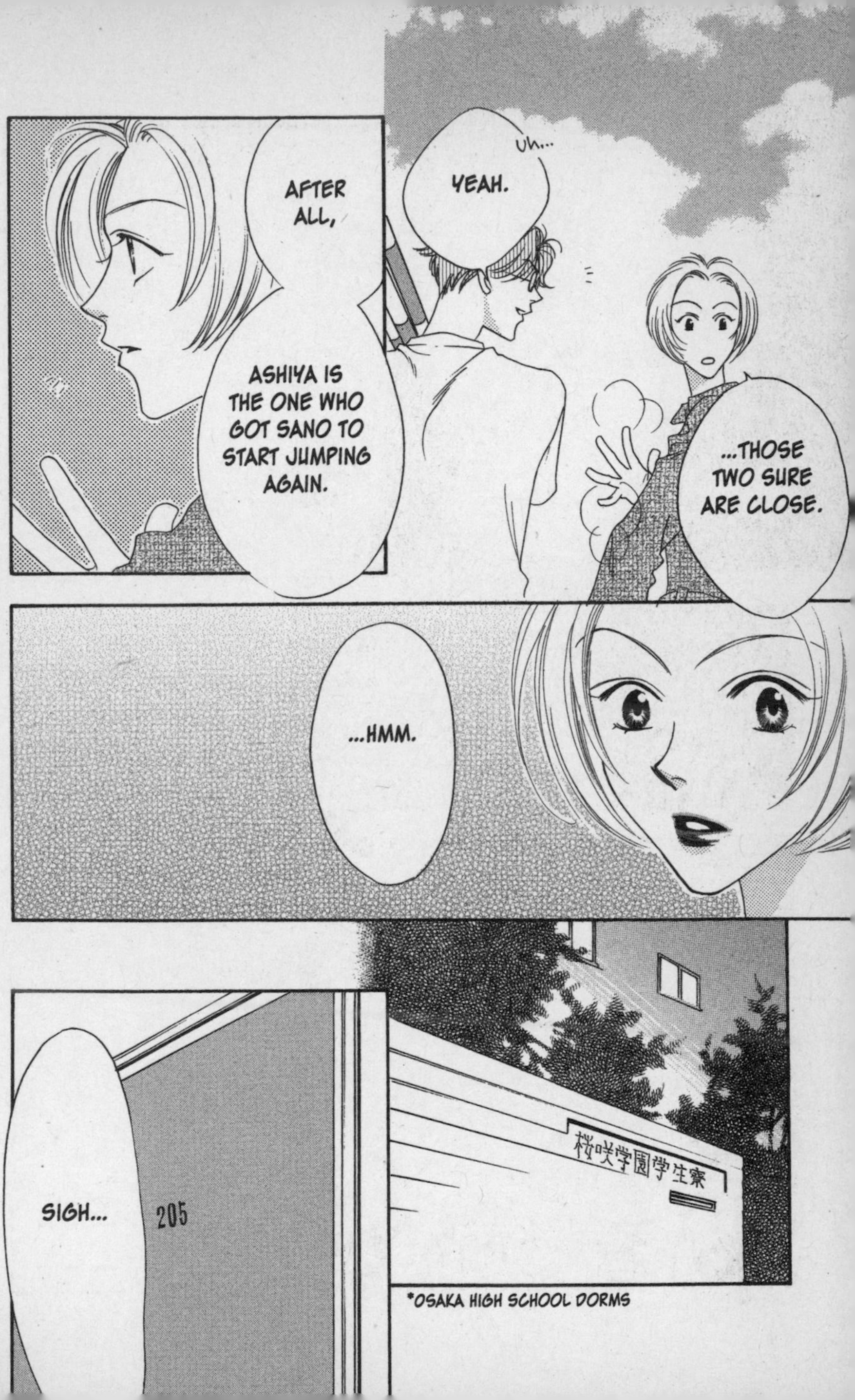
...THOSE TWO SURE ARE CLOSE.
Uh...
YEAH.
AFTER ALL,
ASHIYA IS THE ONE WHO GOT SANO TO START JUMPING AGAIN.
...HMM.
桜咲学園学生寮
*OSAKA HIGH SCHOOL DORMS
205
SIGH...

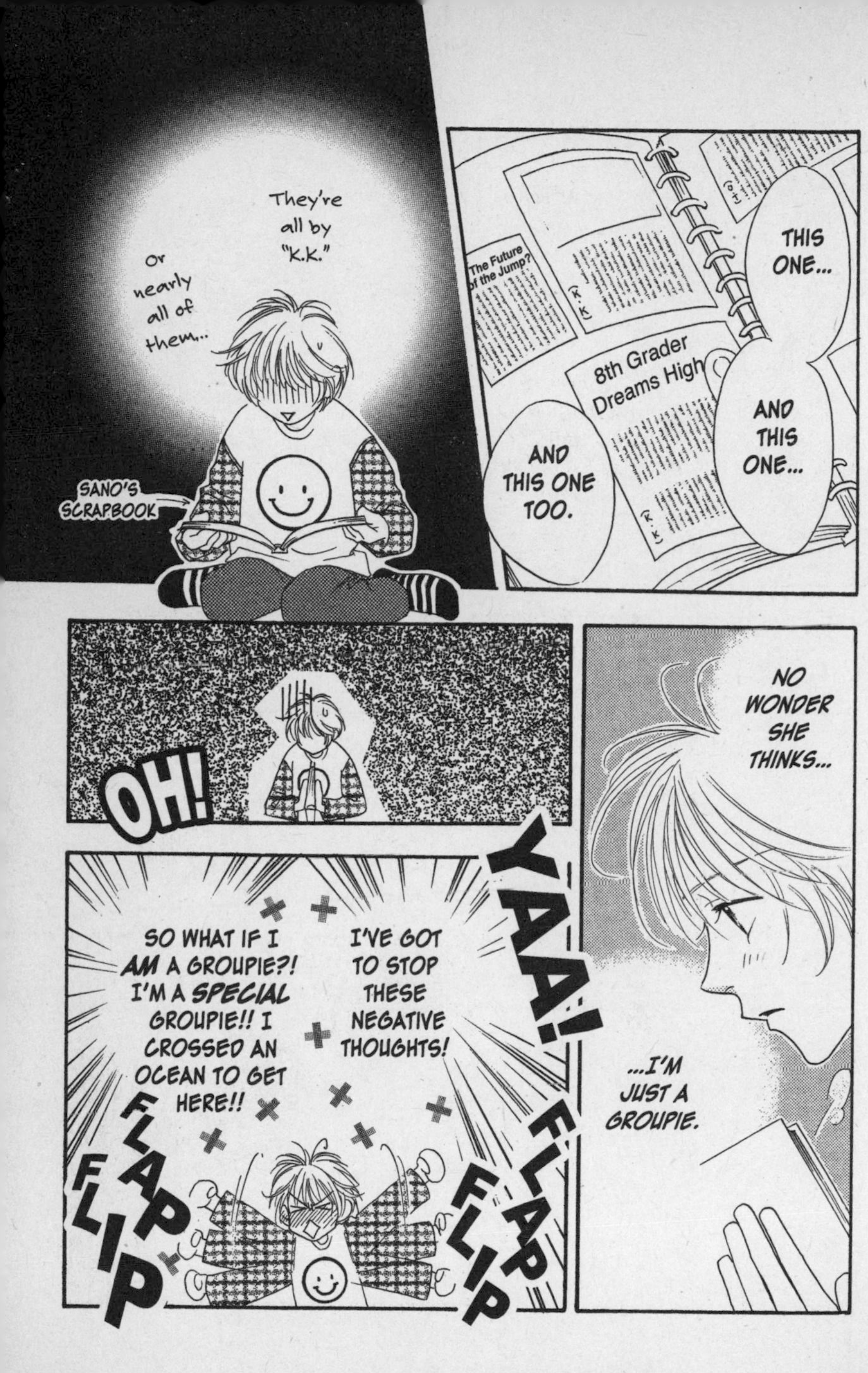
THIS ONE...
AND THIS ONE...
AND THIS ONE TOO.
The Future of the Jump?
8th Grader Dreams High
They're all by "K.K."
Or nearly all of them...
SANO'S SCRAPBOOK
NO WONDER SHE THINKS...
...I'M JUST A GROUPIE.
OH!
YAA!!
I'VE GOT TO STOP THESE NEGATIVE THOUGHTS!
SO WHAT IF I *AM* A GROUPIE?! I'M A *SPECIAL* GROUPIE!! I CROSSED AN OCEAN TO GET HERE!!
FLIP FLAP FLIP
FLAP FLIP

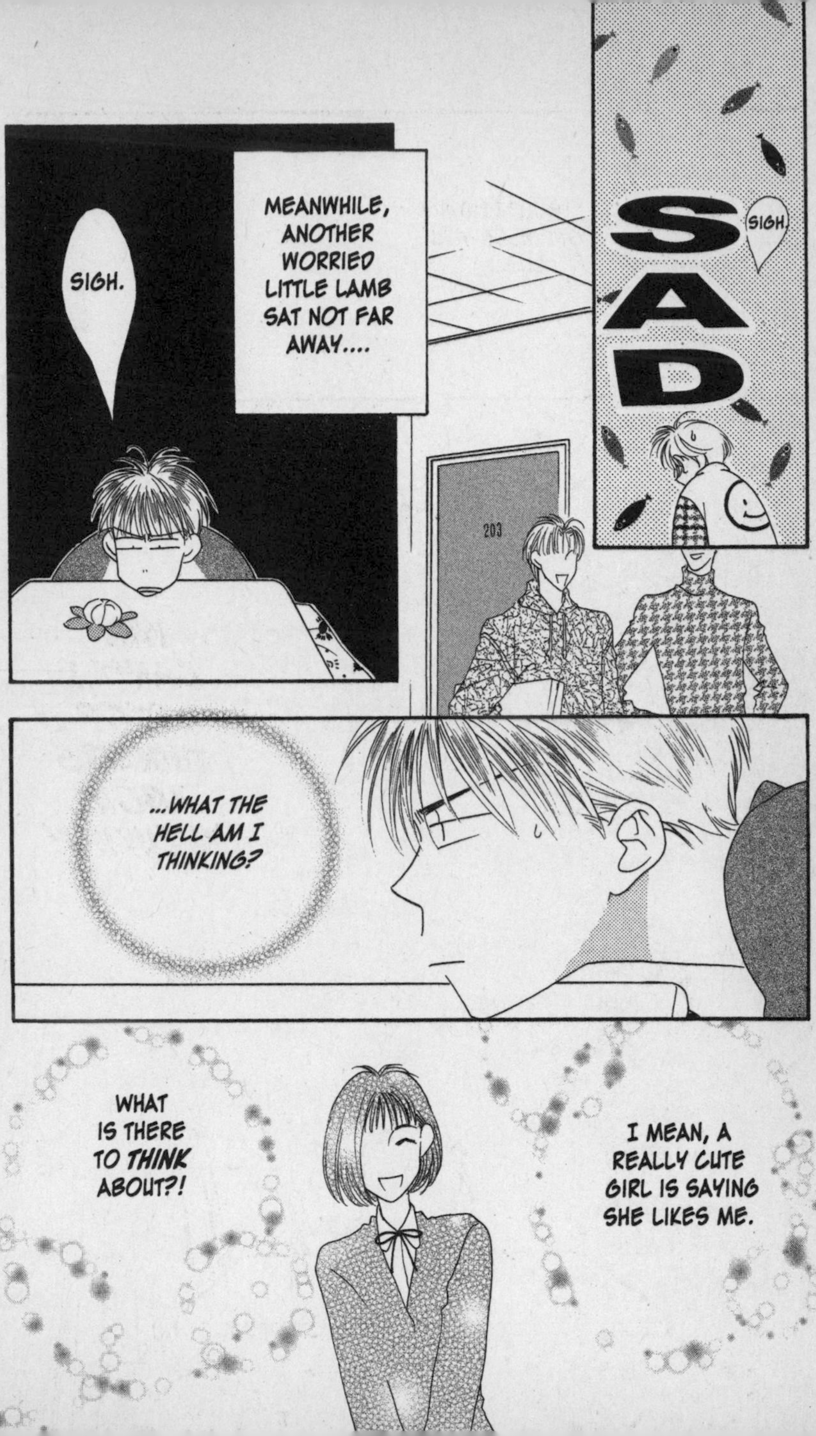
SAD
SIGH.
MEANWHILE, ANOTHER WORRIED LITTLE LAMB SAT NOT FAR AWAY....
SIGH.
203
...WHAT THE HELL AM I THINKING?
I MEAN, A REALLY CUTE GIRL IS SAYING SHE LIKES ME.
WHAT IS THERE TO THINK ABOUT?!

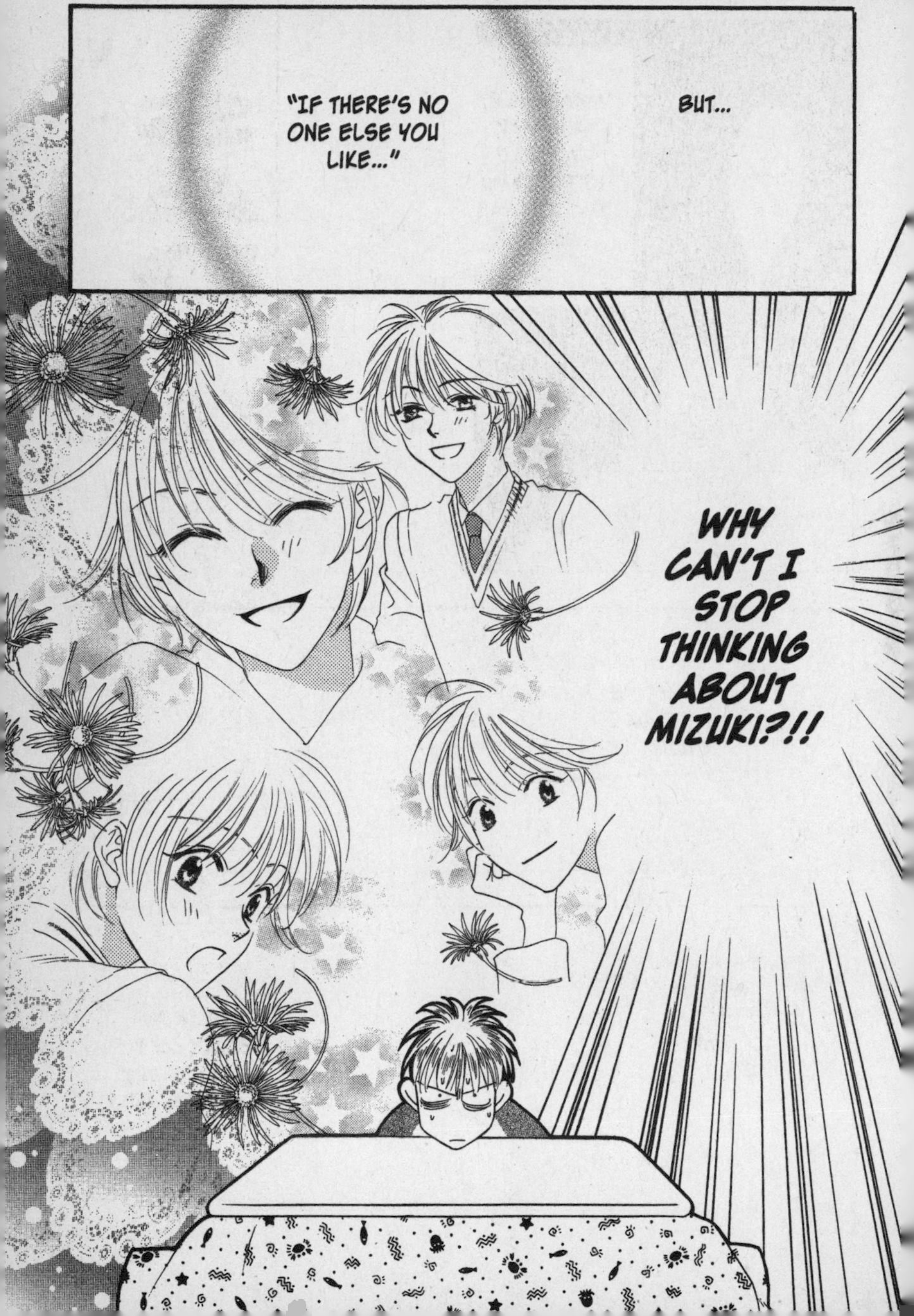
"IF THERE'S NO ONE ELSE YOU LIKE..."
BUT...
WHY CAN'T I STOP THINKING ABOUT MIZUKI?!!

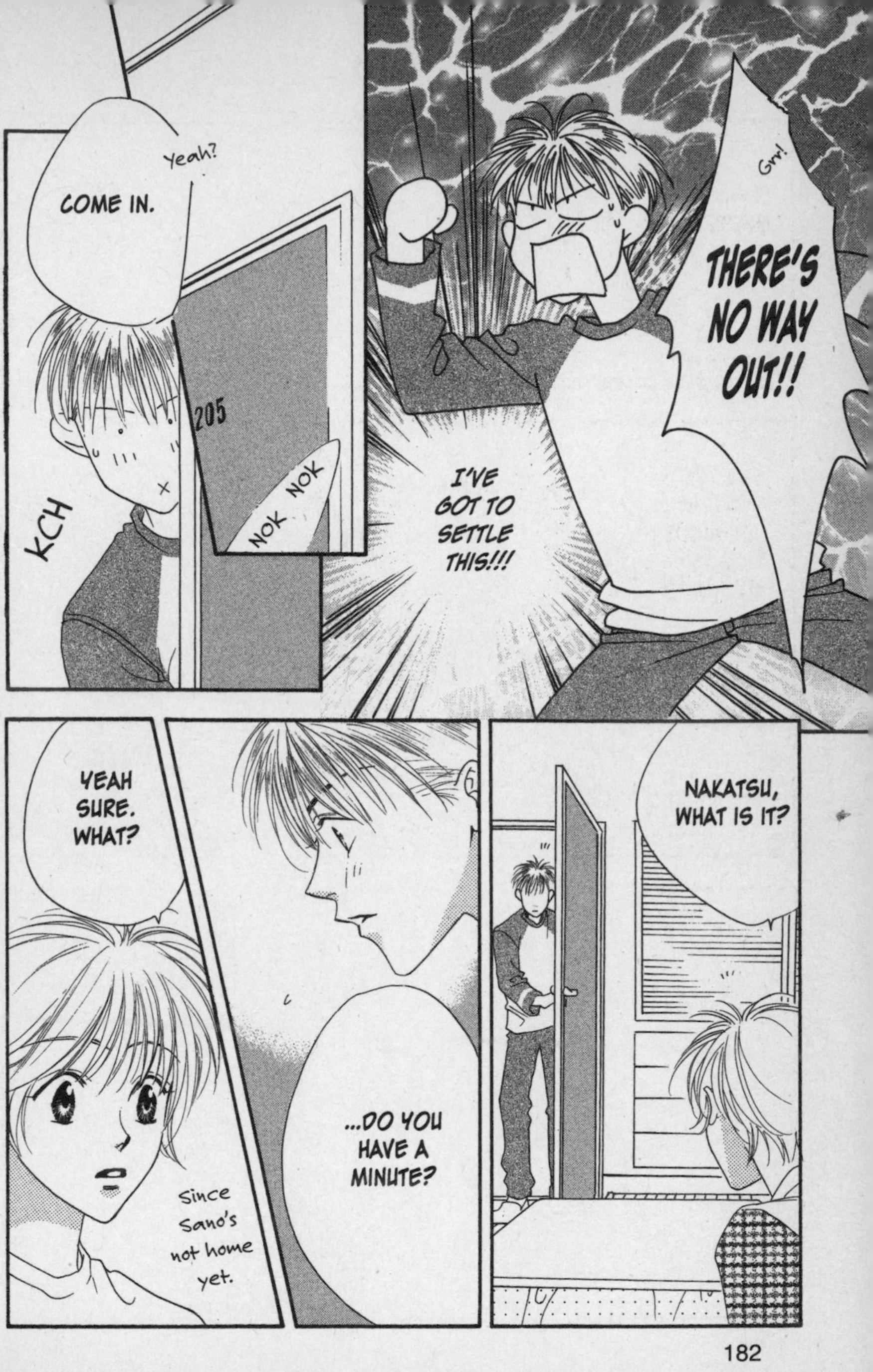
Grr!
THERE'S NO WAY OUT!!
I'VE GOT TO SETTLE THIS!!!
NOK NOK
205
Yeah?
COME IN.
KCH
NAKATSU, WHAT IS IT?
...DO YOU HAVE A MINUTE?
YEAH SURE. WHAT?
Since Sano's not home yet.

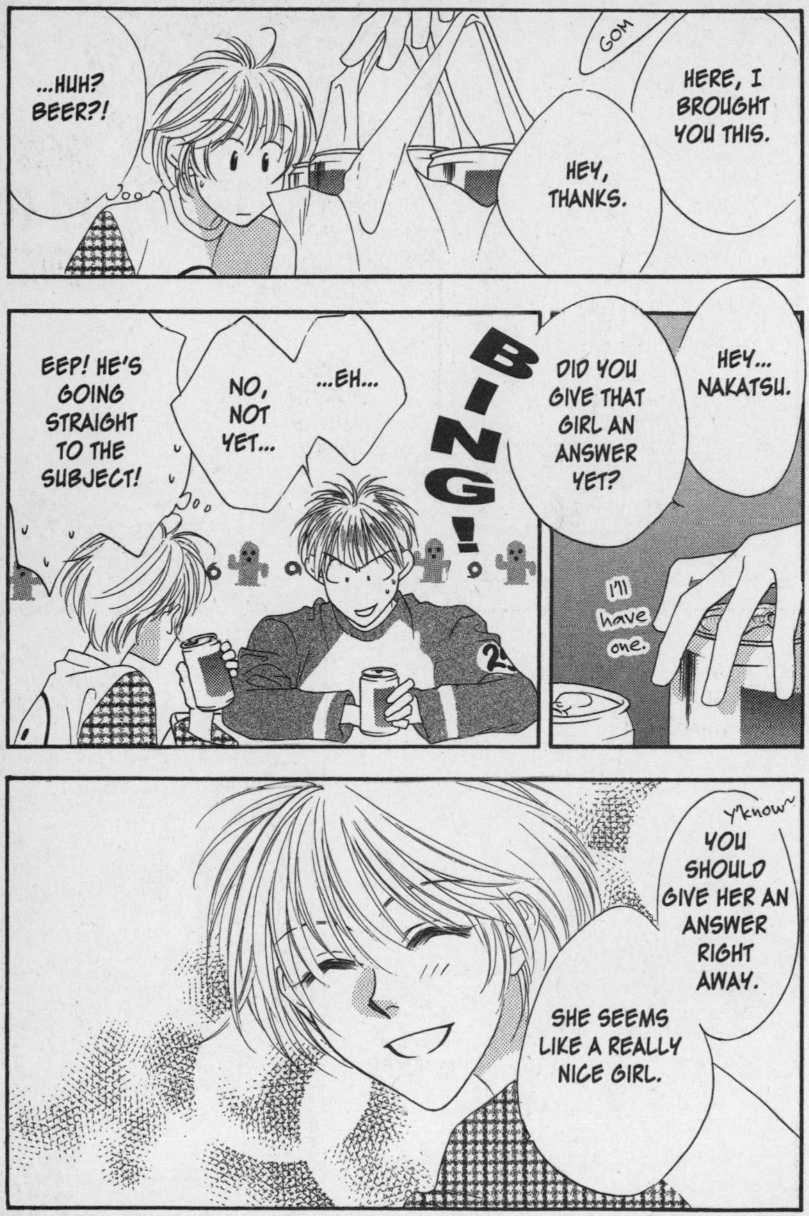
GOM
HERE, I BROUGHT YOU THIS.
HEY, THANKS.
...HUH? BEER?!
HEY... NAKATSU.
DID YOU GIVE THAT GIRL AN ANSWER YET?
I'll have one.
BING!
...EH...
NO, NOT YET...
EEP! HE'S GOING STRAIGHT TO THE SUBJECT!
Y'know~
YOU SHOULD GIVE HER AN ANSWER RIGHT AWAY.
SHE SEEMS LIKE A REALLY NICE GIRL.

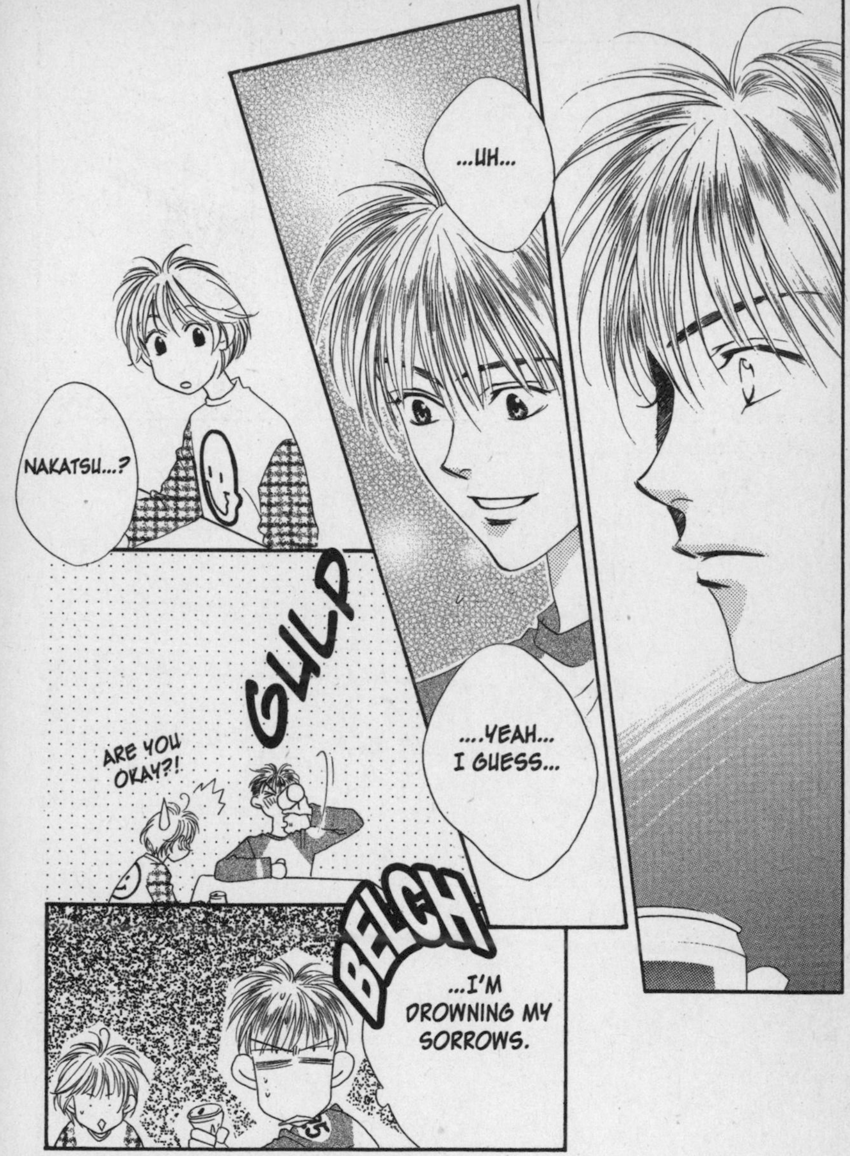
...UH...
....YEAH... I GUESS...
NAKATSU...?
GULP
ARE YOU OKAY?!
BELCH
...I'M DROWNING MY SORROWS.

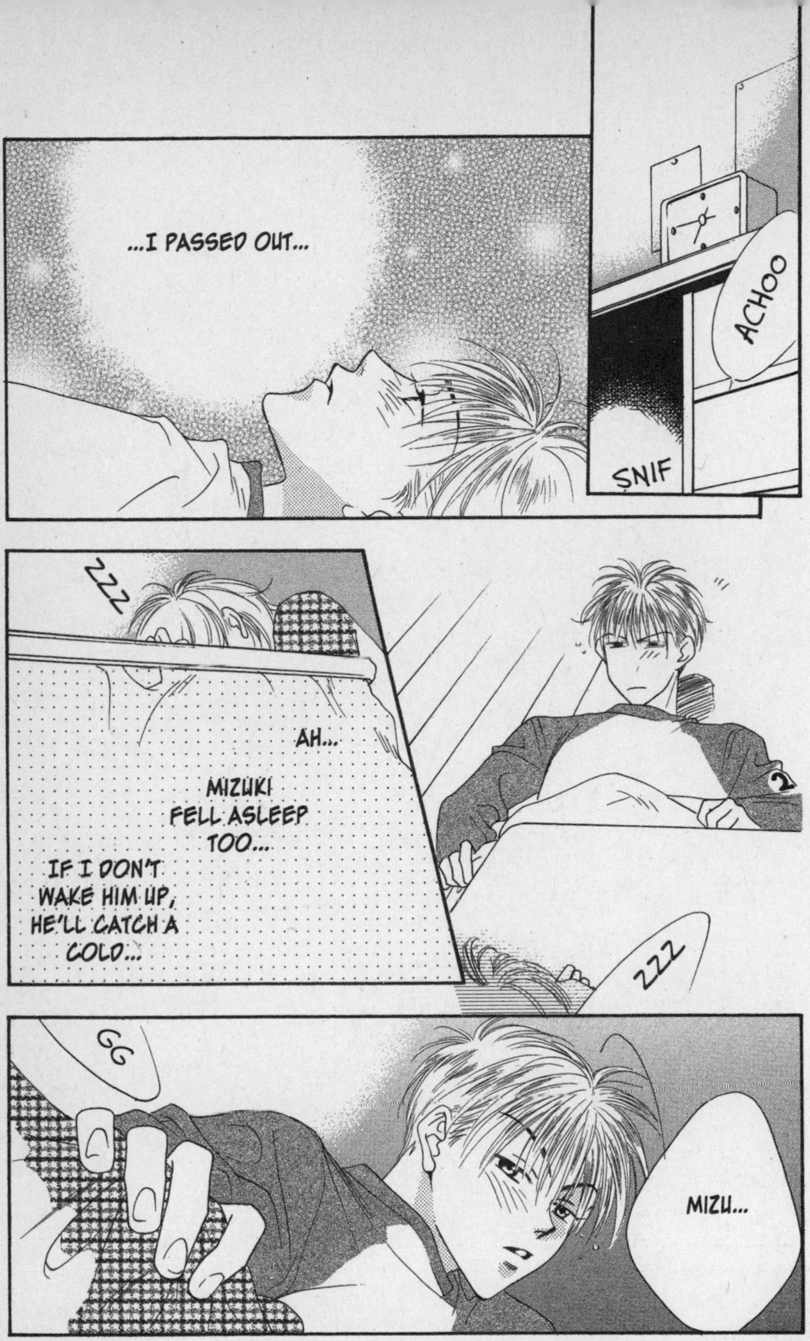

ACHOO
SNIF
...I PASSED OUT...
ZZZ
ZZZ
AH...
MIZUKI FELL ASLEEP TOO...
IF I DON'T WAKE HIM UP, HE'LL CATCH A COLD...
MIZU...
GG

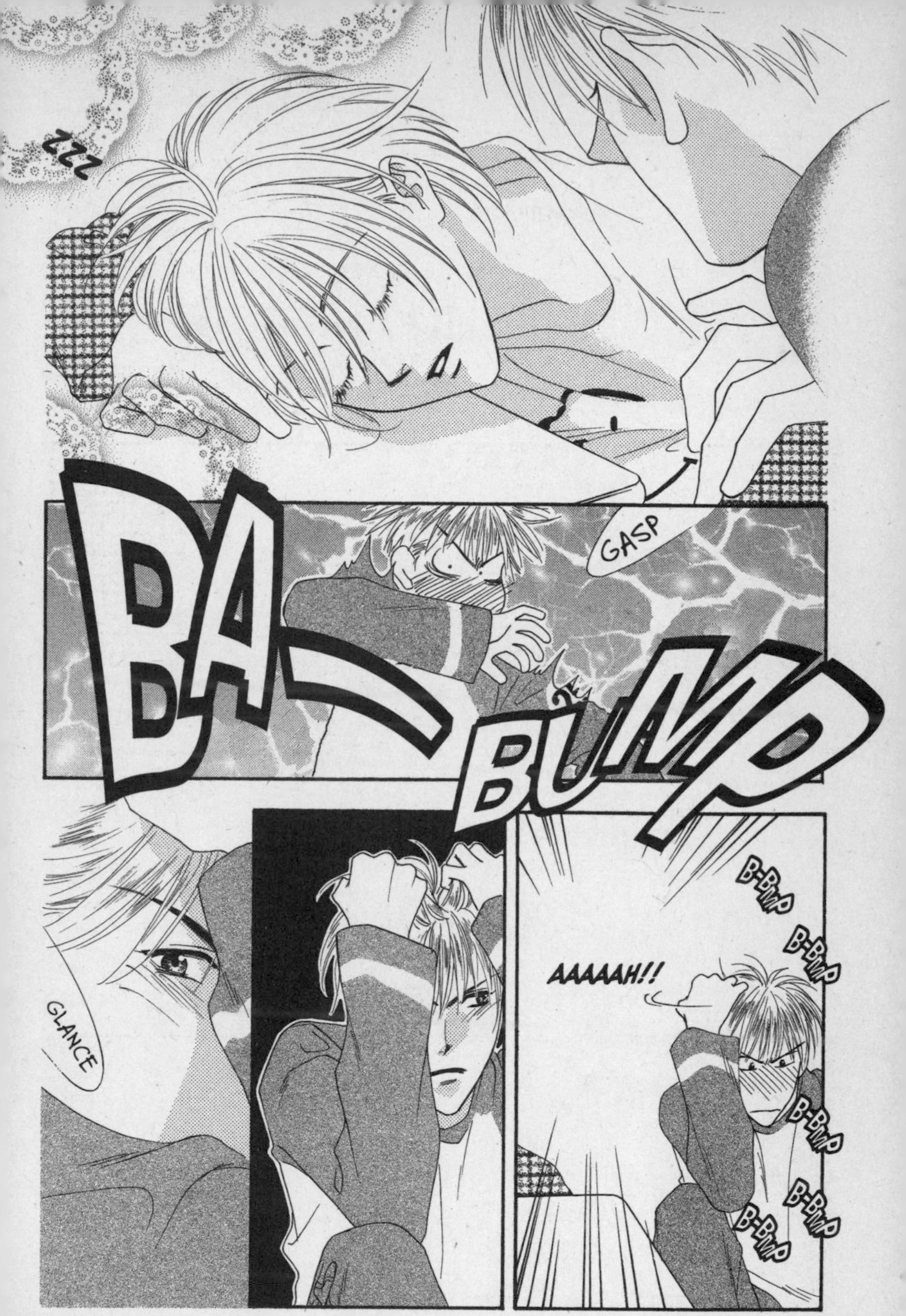
ZZZ
GASP
BA—BUMP
B-BMP
B-BMP
AAAAAH!!
B-BMP
B-BMP
B-BMP
GLANCE

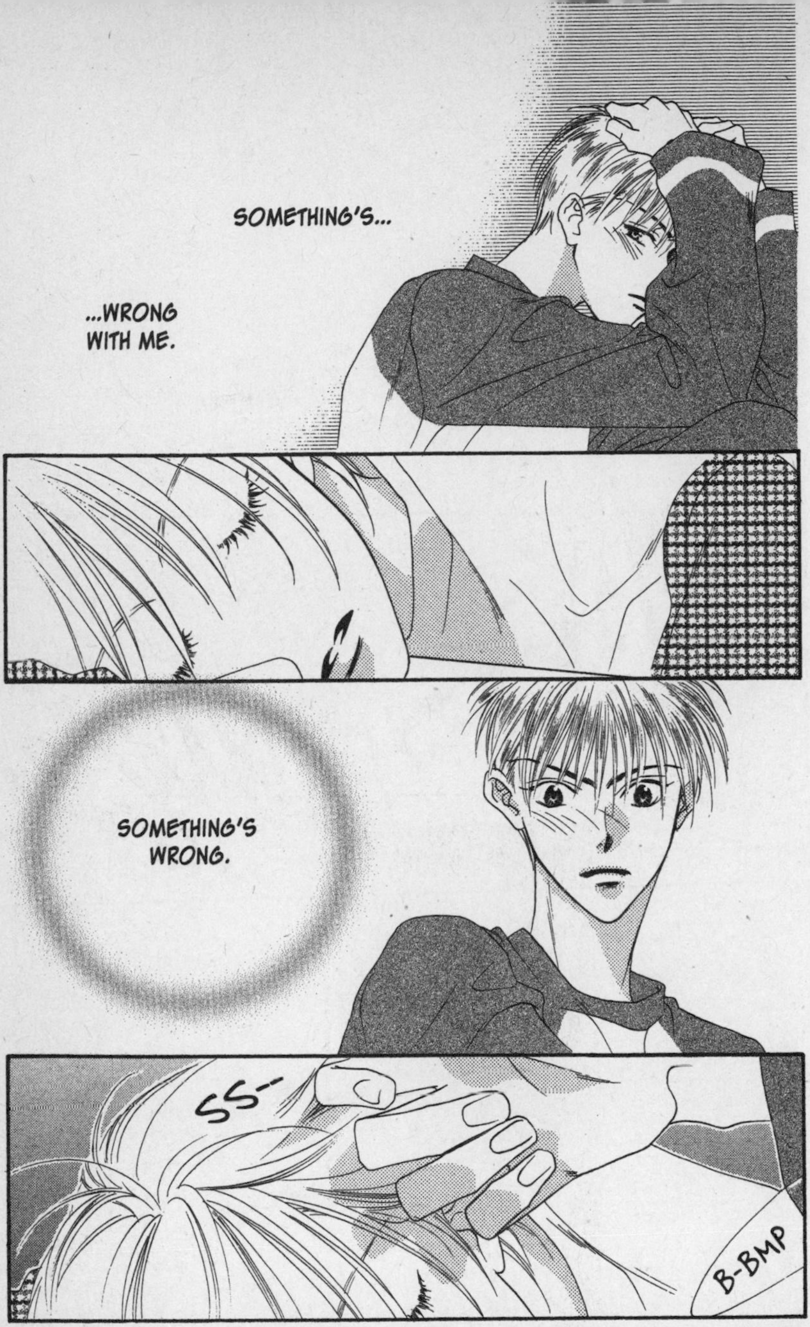
SOMETHING'S...
...WRONG WITH ME.
SOMETHING'S WRONG.
SS-
B-BMP

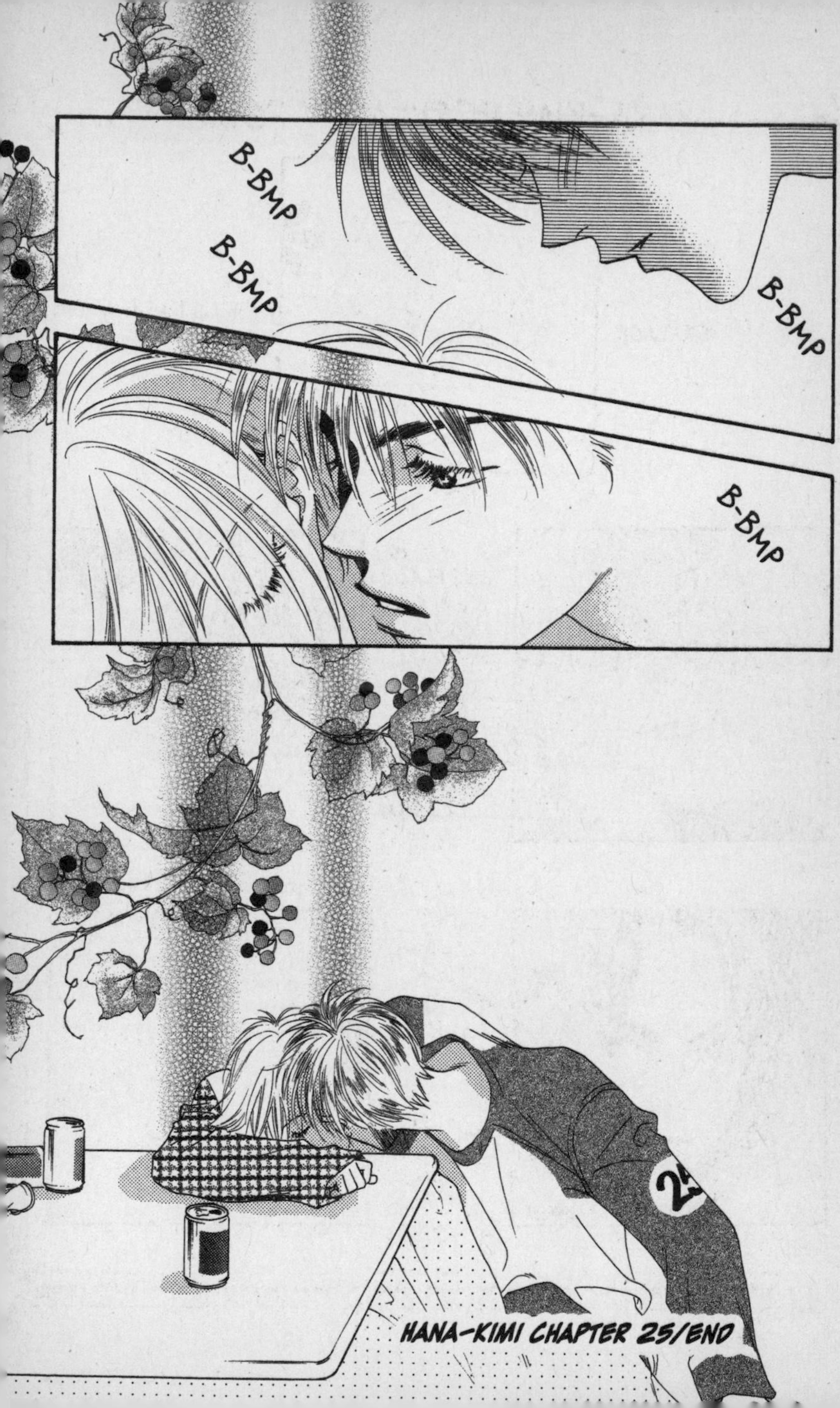
B-BMP
B-BMP
B-BMP
B-BMP
HANA-KIMI CHAPTER 25/END

HANA-KIMI POPULARITY POLL

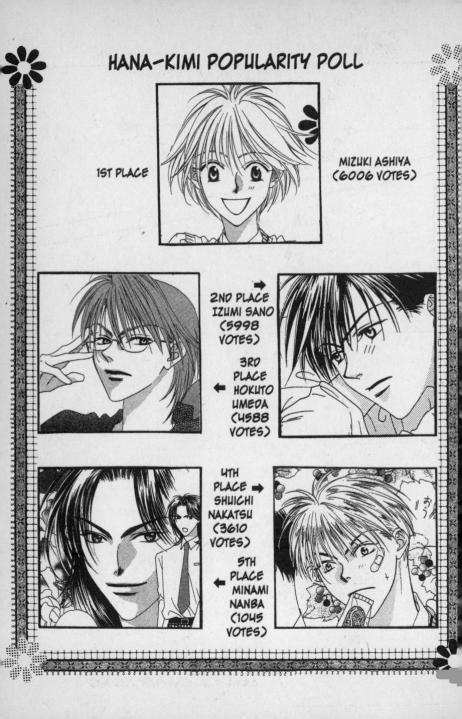

1ST PLACE

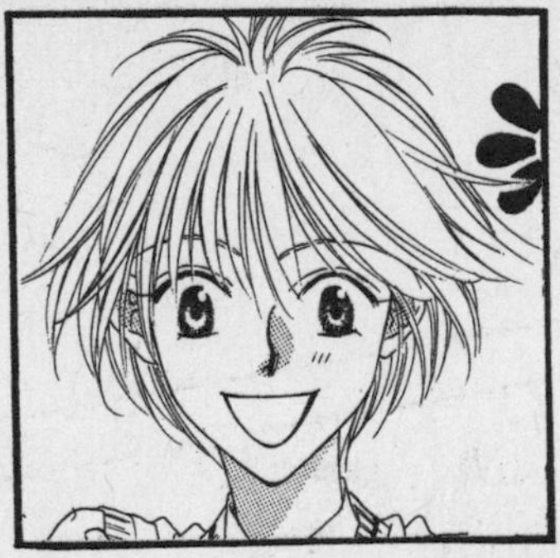

MIZUKI ASHIYA (6006 VOTES)

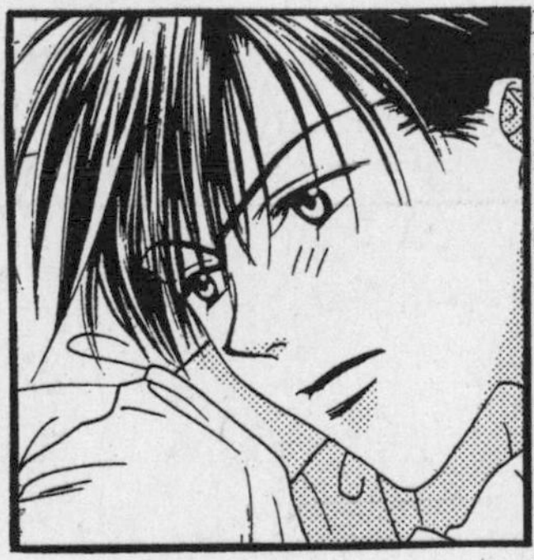

2ND PLACE IZUMI SANO (5998 VOTES)

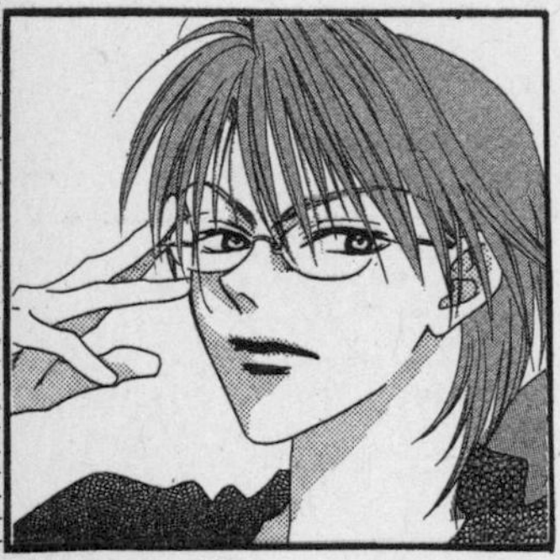

3RD PLACE HOKUTO UMEDA (4588 VOTES)

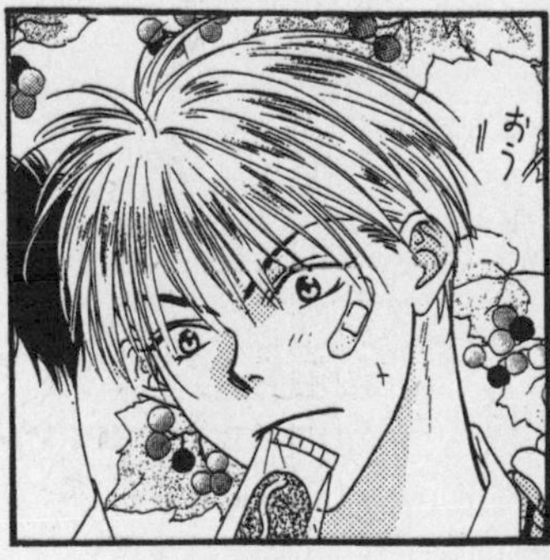
おう

4TH PLACE SHUICHI NAKATSU (3610 VOTES)

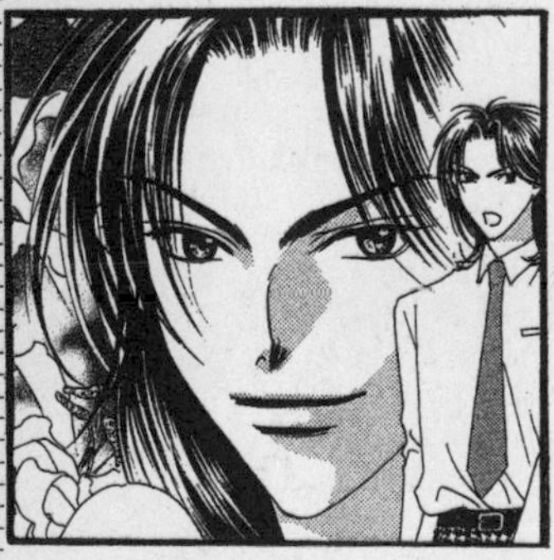

5TH PLACE MINAMI NANBA (1045 VOTES)

#6
YUJIRO
(440 VOTES)

#7
DAIKI
KAYASHIMA
(317 VOTES)

#8
ITSUKI KUJO
(248 VOTES)

#9
SENRI NAKAO
(223 VOTES)

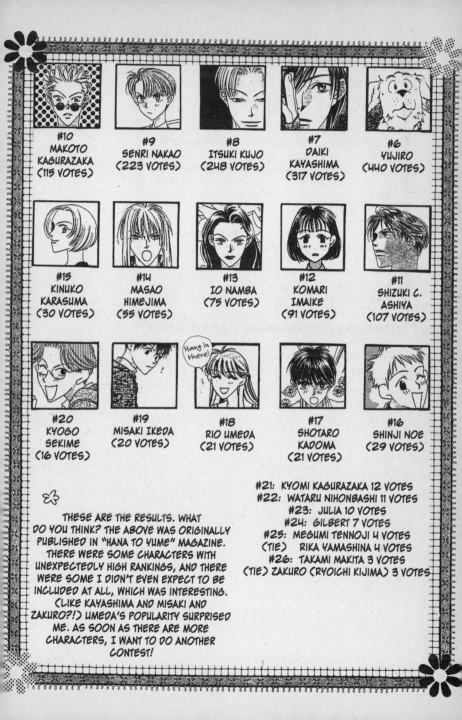

#10
MAKOTO
KAGURAZAKA
(115 VOTES)

#11
SHIZUKI C.
ASHIYA
(107 VOTES)

#12
KOMARI
IMAIKE
(91 VOTES)

#13
IO NAMBA
(75 VOTES)

#14
MASAO
HIMEJIMA
(55 VOTES)

#15
KINUKO
KARASUMA
(30 VOTES)

#16
SHINJI NOE
(29 VOTES)

#17
SHOTARO
KADOMA
(21 VOTES)

Hang in there!

#18
RIO UMEDA
(21 VOTES)

#19
MISAKI IKEDA
(20 VOTES)

#20
KYOGO
SEKIME
(16 VOTES)

#21: KYOMI KAGURAZAKA 12 VOTES
#22: WATARU NIHONBASHI 11 VOTES
#23: JULIA 10 VOTES
#24: GILBERT 7 VOTES
#25: MEGUMI TENNOJI 4 VOTES
(TIE) RIKA YAMASHINA 4 VOTES
#26: TAKAMI MAKITA 3 VOTES
(TIE) ZAKURO (RYOICHI KIJIMA) 3 VOTES

THESE ARE THE RESULTS. WHAT DO YOU THINK? THE ABOVE WAS ORIGINALLY PUBLISHED IN "HANA TO YUME" MAGAZINE. THERE WERE SOME CHARACTERS WITH UNEXPECTEDLY HIGH RANKINGS, AND THERE WERE SOME I DIDN'T EVEN EXPECT TO BE INCLUDED AT ALL, WHICH WAS INTERESTING. (LIKE KAYASHIMA AND MISAKI AND ZAKURO?!) UMEDA'S POPULARITY SURPRISED ME. AS SOON AS THERE ARE MORE CHARACTERS, I WANT TO DO ANOTHER CONTEST!

ABOUT THE AUTHOR

Hisaya Nakajo's manga series **Hanazakari no Kimitachi he** ("For You in Full Blossom," casually known as **Hana-Kimi**) has been a hit since it first appeared in 1997 in the shôjo manga magazine **Hana to Yume** ("Flowers and Dreams"). In Japan, a **Hana-Kimi** art book and several "drama CDs" have been released. Her other manga series include **Missing Piece** (2 volumes) and **Yumemiru Happa** ("The Dreaming Leaf," 1 volume).

Hisaya Nakajo's website:
www.wild-vanilla.com

IN THE NEXT VOLUME ...

As Kinu investigates every aspect of Izumi's private life, Mizuki's secret identity is endangered! Meanwhile Nakatsu, still unaware of Mizuki's female-ness, struggles to choose between his new girlfriend and his secret crush. It's times like this that you wish someone brash, forward and honest about their feelings would show up to clear up all the confusion...and that person is coming. Julia, Mizuki's best friend from America, is coming from Japan to go to school!

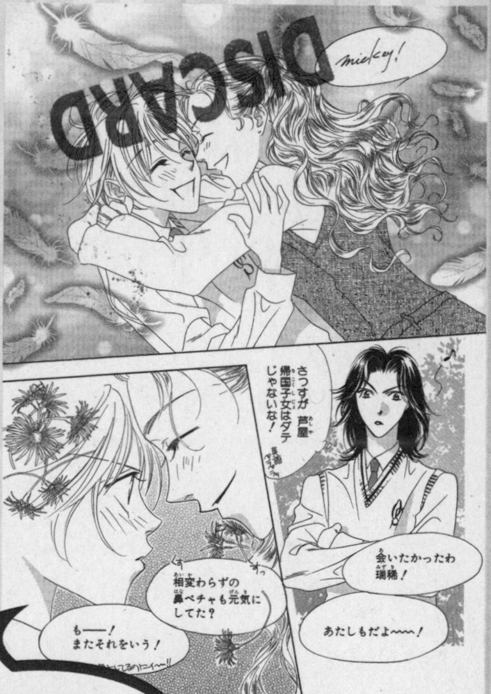
mickey!
さっすが 芦屋
帰国子女はダテじゃないな!
会いたかったわ
瑞稀!
あたしもだよ〜〜!
くす
すっ
相変わらずの
鼻ペチャも元気に
してた?
も——!
またそれをいう!

COMING APRIL 2005!